Greasers and Gringos

CRITICAL AMERICA

General Editors: Richard Delgado and Jean Stefancic

Greasers and Gringos,

Latinos, Law, and the American Imagination

Steven W. Bender

NEW YORK UNIVERSITY PRESS

New York and London

NEW YORK UNIVERSITY PRESS
New York and London
www.nyupress.org

The song "Techno Cumbia" appears on pages 173–74. Words and
music by A. B. Quintanilla III and Pete Astudillo © 1994 EMI
Blackwood Music Inc., A.Q.3 Music and Peace Rock Music. All
rights for A.Q.3 music controlled and administered by EMI
Blackwood Music Inc. All rights reserved. International copyright
secured. Used by permission.

The song "Speedy Gonazles" appears on page 65. Words and music
by Ethel Lee, Buddy Kaye, and David Hill © 1961 Budd Music Corp.
Copyright renewed and assigned to Bienstock Publishing Company,
Sony Music, and David Hess Music. All rights reserved. Used by
permission.

Library of Congress Cataloging-in-Publication Data
Bender, Steven
Greasers and gringos : Latinos, law, and the American imagination /
Steven W. Bender.
p.   cm. — (Critical America)
Includes bibliographical references and index.
ISBN 0-8147-9887-X (cloth : alk. paper)
1. Hispanic Americans—Legal status, laws, etc.—United States.
2. Hispanic Americans—Social conditions. 3. Hispanic Americans
and mass media—United States.   I. Title. II. Series.
KF4757.5.L38B46 2003
342.73'0873—dc22   2003014980

New York University Press books are printed on acid-free paper,
and their binding materials are chosen for strength and durability.

Manufactured in the United States of America

10 9 8 7 6 5 4 3 2 1

To my grandfather, Fernando Troncoso, who died shortly before my birth, and to my grandmother, Ramona Troncoso, whose grace led me to realize that he was blessed.

Contents

Acknowledgments

Many friends offered valuable comments on earlier drafts, such as Keith Aoki, Gil Carrasco, Heidi Kitrosser, and Pedro Malavet. I presented parts of the book to the faculty of the University of California at Davis School of Law, the faculty and students of Golden Gate University School of Law, participants in a critical race reading group at the University of Oregon School of Law, and as a panelist at the Western Law Professors of Color conference in Seattle, Washington, and the LatCrit VII conference in Portland, Oregon.

My research assistants were always enthusiastic, helpful, and supportive—Rosa Chávez, Denise Espinoza, and Gwen Thompson at the University of Oregon School of Law and Kirsten Andelman, Rosa M. Figueroa, and Carolyn Reyes at the University of California, Hastings College of the Law.

Angus Nesbit, a University of Oregon School of Law reference librarian, displayed his usual knack of finding obscure sources, and my secretary Debby Warren provided me with cheer when this undertaking seemed daunting.

Stephen Lothrop, word processing supervisor at Hastings, was particularly obliging during my visitorship there, even giving me access to his *I Love Lucy* tape collection with the admonishment that I not say anything bad about dear Lucy.

I am indebted to the NYU Critical America series editors Richard Delgado and Jean Stefancic for their steadfast encouragement of critical scholarship.

My *familia* provided much of the inspiration for the personal narratives I occasionally share, and I hope I do not embarrass anyone.

Preface

Originating in the mid-1800s, the term *greaser* first came to be used against those of Mexican appearance in California and the Southwest. Although some suggest the derogatory description came from the practice of Mexican laborers in the Southwest greasing their backs to facilitate the unloading of hides and cargo,[1] others suppose it stemmed from a similarity between Mexican skin color and grease.[2] Its origin may be more disparaging still—the "greasers" label may derive from long-standing conceptions of Mexicans as unkempt and unclean, with unwashed, greasy black hair. "Greasers" was a popular reference by U.S. troops in the U.S.-Mexico war of 1846–1848, as well as by settlers in gold rush California.[3] Its original usage appears to have been sexualized, a way to describe a "treacherous Mexican male who was sexually threatening to and desirous of white women."[4] Although the term continued to be associated with Mexican men in its Hollywood usage, "greasers" came to refer to Mexicans generally, encompassing both sexes as well as both Mexicans and Mexican Americans.[5] Further, the term originated as a derogatory reference toward those of Mexican origin, but its use expanded over time to encompass Peruvian and Chilean miners during the California gold rush and, more broadly, to describe anyone of Spanish origin.

The term *greasers* and the negative sentiments behind it had legal bite too. In 1855, California adopted the Vagrancy Act, known popularly as the Greaser Act, addressing "all persons who are commonly known as 'Greasers' or the issue of Spanish and Indian blood . . . and who go armed and are not peaceable and quiet persons." Targeting the supposed "idle Mexican," this antiloitering law was the precursor to modern laws directed at loitering, gang activity, and other apparently race-neutral offenses that in practice are often used to justify interrogatory stops of persons of color.[6]

Hollywood embraced the "greasers" label to describe its unflattering creation of despicable Mexicans who robbed, raped, and murdered their way through the Southwest. Familiar enough to reach the marquee, the Hollywood greaser image of the 1900s was the villain of such films as *The Greaser's Gauntlet* (1908), *Tony the Greaser* (1911), *The Girl and the Greaser* (1913), *The Greaser's Revenge* (1914), *Bronco Billy and the Greaser* (1914), and, simply, *The Greaser* (1915).[7] Although almost uniformly villainous, the Hollywood greaser occasionally had a good heart, as reflected in the movie advertisement for the 1911 silent *Tony the Greaser*: "From force of habit, some might call him a 'Greaser'; true, he is a Mexicano, but a man of noble instincts and chivalrous nature."[8]

Prompted in the 1930s by the threat of losing distribution of Hollywood films to crucial Mexican and Latin American markets, Hollywood's self-policing body at the time, the Production Code Administration, helped eliminate the most virulent anti-Latina/o references from Hollywood films, including references to greasers. By the time these economic pressures had relaxed in the 1950s and this self-censorship board's influence had waned, the term *greaser* and its close cousin *greaseball* had gradually given way in Hollywood and American society to other derogatory references to Latinas/os—although Hollywood resurrected the greaser from time to time, beginning with the 1961 western *One Eyed Jacks*. Particularly in the 1940s, Mexicans and Mexican Americans in Los Angeles, especially young boys, were labeled "pachucos" or "zoot suiters." Later, Mexicans and Mexican Americans became "wetbacks," "aliens," and "illegals" as the U.S.-Mexico border was fortified against entry by undocumented Mexican immigrants. Border Patrol officials have referred to undocumented immigrants from Mexico as *pollos*. Mexicans in particular also came to be known disparagingly as "beaners," presumably for their staple diet; the demeaning reference to Mexicans as "chilies" likely has similar origins. In the 1999 premiere episode of the popular sitcom *Will and Grace*, one of the regulars belittled her Salvadoran maid as a "tamale" [*sic*]. Even the term *Mexican* is used debasingly, especially when accompanied with expletives, as in late 2001 when then professional basketball coach Dan Issel yelled to a heckling fan, "Go drink another beer, you fucking Mexican piece of shit," while captured on videotape.

Puerto Ricans, especially those living in New York City, garnered their own degrading moniker—*spic*, the term of choice in films such as *West Side Story* (1961) and *Saturday Night Fever* (1977). "Spic," like "greaser," has disputed origins. Some say it derives from the term *His-*

panic; others suggest it refers to the accent-thick response of those Latinas/os who "don't speak English"; and still others claim the term is an acronym for those of Spanish, Indian, and colored origin. Regardless of its exact origin, this term, like "greasers," eventually came to represent Latinas/os of all backgrounds.

1

The Confluence of Stereotype and Law

Evident in this study of Latina/o stereotypes is the role of American[1] media in sustaining derogatory stereotypes that have plagued Latinas/os for decades. Although others have identified and explored the undeniable linkage between media and Latina/o stereotypes,[2] particularly the influence of motion pictures, less attention has been paid to stereotypes as contributing to the maltreatment of Latinas/os under American law and legal systems. This book contends that most of the long-standing demeaning social constructions of Latinas/os have helped ensure their legal detriment.[3] In turn, the legal rules that disadvantage Latinas/os, as well as the underlying images, often spur private citizens to enforce their dictates through injurious vigilantism. Thus, the consequences of stereotypes in American society go beyond displays of prejudice such as name-calling and the hurt feelings that result. For Latinas/os and certain other groups,[4] stereotypes actually drive their distressing legal and societal treatment.

Some readers might contend that blame is placed unfairly on media as creating and perpetuating negative attitudes toward Latinas/os. Rather, media might be exculpated as merely reflecting the attitudes of producers, writers, reporters, and artists, as well as those of the audience. Establishing either side of this debate is challenging, especially given the relative absence of studies interrogating the media's role in creating and perpetuating negative stereotypes, at least those directed at Latinas/os. The few studies linking media to societal impressions of persons of color tend to focus on African Americans[5] and on the analogous effects of media representations on the self-esteem of children and adults of color. In the arguably related context of whether television and other media promote violence, more studies exist but experts disagree on the causal link, if any, between mass media and violence. Although a number of empirical studies suggest a causal connection, particularly when violent images are viewed by children or young adults,[6] some critique this social science research.[7] Nevertheless, according to a 1993 public opinion poll, nearly four in five Americans surveyed believed that television violence directly contributed to violence in society.[8]

Similarly, the causation issue is complex and disputed on the question of whether pornographic representations fuel sexual violence against women. This context is closely analogous to stereotypes based on race and ethnicity because, the argument goes, pornography helps construct a social image of women as subordinate, justifying sexual violence against them. Although a number of social scientists contend that viewers of pornography are more likely than nonviewers to rape and sexually abuse women, others deny any such causal link, even suggesting that pornography defuses sexual violence.[9]

The likelihood is that media and social attitudes feed each other—media play some role in creating and perpetuating Latina/o and other racial/ethnic/gender/sexual orientation stereotypes, and preexisting biases and prejudices in society also spread through private means such as schools, families, and friends, thus shaping the consumptive expectations of media audiences and the prejudices of those in media. Larger societal forces can be blamed for creating some negative images. For example, the need to justify colonization of Puerto Rico for military and other objectives demanded the construction of Puerto Ricans as inferior to Anglos.[10] Similarly, the need to legitimize expansionist designs of the United States leading to the U.S.-Mexico War fueled the conception of Mexicans as subhuman. Indeed, these examples raise the broader question of whether media images and societal stereotypes shape legal treatment of Latinas/os or whether the need for certain defined legal and subordinating relationships drives impressions of and attitudes toward Latinas/os. The forces influencing these persistent negative images, here of subhuman Mexicans and Puerto Ricans, came from outside the media, yet media played a crucial role in disseminating this propaganda in newspapers and, later, film and other media. At the same time, history is replete with examples of media serving more than a mere communicative role in the development of negative attitudes toward Latinas/os. Disparaging newspaper articles and captions in Los Angeles helped incite the so-called Zoot Suit Riots in the summer of 1943, in which off-duty Anglo servicemen and civilians stormed barrio neighborhoods to assault Latino youth, particularly those dressed in zoot suits. Media headlines referred to "marauding Latin gangs," "Mexican goon squads," "pachuco killers," and to Mexicans as "roving wolf-packs." During the violence, the Los Angeles Times headline one day read "Zoot Suiters Learn Lesson in Fight with Servicemen." One journalist at the time blamed the local press for inciting the riots:

> Immediate responsibility for the outbreak of the riots must be placed upon the Los Angeles press and the Los Angeles police. For more than a year now the press (and particularly the Hearst press) has been building up anti-Mexican sentiment in Los Angeles. Using the familiar Harlem "crime-wave" technique, the press headlined every case in which a Mexican had been arrested, featured photographs of Mexicans dressed in "zoot suits," checked back over criminal records to "prove" that there had been an increase in Mexican "crime" and constantly needled the police to make more arrests.[11]

Although not all the blame for negative attitudes toward Latinas/os can be placed on media, pending further study media must share some of the responsibility. Further, apart from their influence in shaping derogatory social conceptions of Latinas/os, disparaging portrayals in the media help establish negative self-images among Latina/o viewers, particularly youth. Much of the existing research has concerned Black children, with social scientists concluding that television in particular fosters and reinforces unflattering beliefs that Black children hold of themselves.[12] Research sponsored by the organization Children Now concluded that children learn about the legitimacy or illegitimacy of their race in society by seeing how and how often the media represent the particular group.[13] Demeaning media portrayals help shape children's opinions about their societal and self-worth, causing humiliation, isolation, and despair as well as cultural and self-hatred. As Richard Delgado has suggested, when compared with other grounds for stigmatization such as class, racial stigmatization through negative stereotyping is particularly deleterious because of the immutable, inescapable characteristics of race.[14] Moreover, Ediberto Román has hypothesized that stigma and stereotyping may be more insidious and dangerous than classical forms of overt discrimination in preserving the social irrelevance of Latinas/os because:

> [i]nstead of inciting or provoking opposition [they] cause[] both the dominant and the dominated to become convinced "that the existing order is satisfactory." In light of the fact that Latinas and Latinos are

inundated with negative reinforcement from film, television and print media, there is good reason to believe that this group will become complicit in embodying the characterizations the dominant culture has assigned. In effect Latinas and Latinos will become experts in their discrediting attributions, believing that the dominant gaze accurately depicts them.[15]

A staggering variety of media sources have helped to create and perpetuate damaging views of Latinas/os. Motion pictures have long portrayed Mexicans as ruthless *bandidos,* evolving in recent years to depict Mexicans and other Latinas/os as urban gang members and soulless drug dealers. Television reality shows such as *Cops* and the 1980s crime drama *Miami Vice* have showcased Latinas/os as television's designated criminals. This association of Latinas/os and crime is particularly apparent against the backdrop of a relative absence of Latinas/os in other prominent roles on television. Media's shabby treatment of Latinas/os transcends television and motion pictures. Popular songs sometimes reflect negative social conceptions of Latinas/os, such as the 1948 number-one hit of Peggy Lee and Dave Barbour, "Mañana (Is Soon Enough for Me)," depicting Latinas/os as lazy and unmotivated, and Pat Boone's top ten novelty hit in 1962, "Speedy Gonzales," suggesting that Latinas/os (even the seemingly enterprising Speedy) are lazy, unfaithful drunkards. American literature contributes to the negative social construction of Latinas/os. John Steinbeck's classic novel *Tortilla Flat* portrays Latinos as lazy, shiftless, drunken, and thieving, and Latinas as sexually irresponsible and fertile. Media advertising campaigns have featured caricatures of the Mexican *bandido* image, the most prominent being the late 1960s campaign with the pistol-packing "Frito Bandito" hawking Fritos Corn Chips. The Mexican *bandido* even appeared in Walt Disney's *Toy Story 2* video game as a human target for players to destroy. Latina/o stereotypes comprised the act of comedian Bill Dana, whose dim-witted fictional persona José Jiménez appeared on stage as well as on television shows and record albums in the late 1950s and the 1960s.

Television news and other news media share blame for fostering demeaning views of Latinas/os. A 1998 study of children of all backgrounds revealed that although 42 percent thought that television news showed "White People" doing "good things," only 14 percent saw "Latino People" doing good things.[16] Another study of television news concluded that Blacks and Latinas/os were twice as likely to be shown in crime stories as in human-interest features.[17] News media's focus on uncontrolled immigration of "illegal aliens" from Mexico contributes to the image of Latinas/os as a subordinate people who flout the law while seeking government handouts. Press coverage in 1940s Los Angeles of the so-called Sleepy Lagoon incident and the subsequent Zoot Suit Riots transformed the image of Mexicans as rural *bandidos* to that of urban gangsters. Similarly, sensationalized press coverage in 1959 of a murder in New York City by Puerto Rican gang members, one of them Salvador "Capeman" Agron, led the public to regard Puerto Rican youth on similar threatening terms.

The extent to which derogatory stereotypes influence the legal treatment of Latinas/os parallels the depth to which Latina/o stereotypes penetrate the media. Some of the more apparent links between stereotype and law are evident in citizen initiatives that target immigrants and Latinas/os. For example, California's Proposition 187 was an assault on the conception of Latina/o immigrants as overly fertile and as lazy charges of the state. Earlier, California's initiative declaring English as the state's official language was prompted by the perception that Latinas/os and certain other immigrant groups are reluctant or unable to assimilate by learning English. Less obvious connections between stereotype and law include assaults on affirmative action, carried out in California by the voters' adoption in 1996 of Proposition 209. Affirmative action programs in higher education are seen as marginalizing the educational experience of students and as treating Anglo applicants unfairly by giving preference in the admissions process to the stereotypical unintelligent Latina/o (and African American). Other invidious examples of the role that stereotypes play in shaping the interface of Latinas/os and American law include the influence of stereotypes on exercises of police discretion (so-called racial profiling) as well as prosecutorial and even juror discretion in criminal proceedings. This book details these and further examples of the unceasing and long-standing dynamic between stereotype and law.

Emerging from the study of stereotype and law is the relationship between government and citizen enforcement of legal standards against Latinas/os. Latinas/os face often injurious vigilante encounters that take their cue from legal doctrines meant only for public enforcement. In the southwestern United States, rancher patrols on horseback with tracking dogs and automatic rifles joined federal immigration officials in the effort to intercept "illegal aliens." Throughout the United States, businesses and private citizens assumed a duty to enforce state language laws that declare English as the state's official language. Employers who adopt English-only rules to govern the language of their employees at the workplace, as well as restaurant and tavern owners who impose similar rules on customers in their establishments, may believe they are carrying out the mandates of these laws to encourage the speaking of English and to outlaw the speaking of Spanish as unpatriotic and un-American. In California, citizens voting for Proposition 187—the initiative purporting to withhold government services from "illegal aliens"—sought to enforce the new law in private settings by demanding that Latinas/os produce evidence of their citizenship or legal immigration status. Nationally, law enforcement officials frequently engage in racial profiling, singling out Blacks and Latinas/os for traffic and other interrogatory stops in the hopes of discovering criminal activity. Racial profiling by citizens is evident in the criminal justice system and beyond. No doubt juries, armed with stereotypical images of Latinas/os as violent and criminally minded, often make decisions consistent with their beliefs. Racial profiling extends to settings such as the classroom, where teachers may act on their assumptions about the intelligence of Latina/o children in relation to Anglos and other groups in evaluating and encouraging student performance.

In prompting vigilantism against Latinas/os and other subordinated groups, American law has taken the shape of a communicative channel, complementing the media, for conveying the subordinate role of Latinas/os in American society.[18] Each feeds the other—media shape attitudes of voters that dictate the enactment of formal legal standards through legislation or citizen initiative. Concurrently, laws aimed at people of color or laws enforced in a discriminatory manner through racial profiling dominate media coverage and influence public perception of the supposed criminal character of Latinas/os.[19]

The government's response to the terrorist events of September 11 will only aggravate the public's inclination to assume its role as vigilantes, enforcing media-fueled conceptions of legal obligations and the public good. Unfortunately, this vigilante climate will ensnare many innocent parties, including Latinas/os. President George W. Bush's 2002 State of the Union address called upon the "eyes and ears of alert citizens" to help defend against terrorism. Because undocumented immigrants are portrayed as a national security threat, as would-be terrorists, it is likely the public will see its role as extending to the enforcement of open-ended anti-immigrant agendas. During the military campaign against Iraq in

2003, the leader of an Arizona armed militia warned Mexican immigrants "Do not attempt to cross the border illegally; you will be considered an enemy of the state." Even if not viewed as terrorists themselves, Latina/o immigrants have been called into question for their supposed willingness to aid terrorists in anti-American plots.[20] In this frenzied public and private hunt for terrorists and those who might aid them, vigilante ranchers in the Southwest, rather than being criticized for abusing the human rights of vulnerable immigrants, might be valorized as heroes helping to control border "security breaches." Citizens employing profiling to harass Latina/o-looking people by seeking to confirm their citizenship might be regarded as carrying out the vital function of ensuring that those present in the United States who appear to be foreigners are not interlopers with terrorist agendas. Just a few years ago, in the mid-1990s, vigilante groups in California policed the San Diego airport as the "Airport Posse," to search for and intimidate arriving undocumented immigrants. Will the events of September 11 revive these posse patrols, with Latinas/os among their primary targets?

One of the issues to be confronted in any study of the deleterious consequences of stereotypes and prejudice on Latinas/os through law and vigilante action is whether attention on stereotypes rather than on institutional causes of subordination is misplaced. This tension derives from the assumption that if attitudinal racism were to disappear, Latinas/os would remain encumbered by disparities in wealth and in political and other forms of power. As the argument goes, solutions to the subordination of Latinas/os that focus on individual intolerance are misdirected, as the crucial roots of subordination lie in institutional and structural inequities, such as school funding systems, rather than in individual conceptions of group worth. Thus, the question might be posed as whether eradicating derogatory stereotypes would aid in the acquisition of wealth, for instance, by property ownership, or the acquisition of power, for instance, by political representation and corporate ownership. My study of stereotypes is based on the belief that the distinction between individual attitudes and institutional subordinating structures is overstated and sometimes overlooks the degree to which individual attitudes influence the perpetuation of wealth and power structures.

The links between individual attitudes and institutional inequities of wealth and power are substantial, particularly when those attitudes are created and reinforced on a pervasive, societal basis by the influence of mass media. For example, inequities in political redistricting, campaign finance structure, and lobbyist influence impede the ability of Latinas/os to gain election to political office and to compel legislators to address effectively issues of concern to Latinas/os. But individual attitudes are far from irrelevant in politics. In the 2001 mayoral election in Los Angeles, for example, media advertisements for James Hahn tapped into stereotypes to portray Latino challenger Antonio Villaraigosa as a friend of drug dealers and drug addicts. Villaraigosa ultimately lost the election to the Anglo Hahn, who stormed from behind in the polls largely on the strength of these soft-on-crime images. Moreover, even if Latinas/os can gain legislative clout through increases in their population, they still face, in Latina/o-populous states such as California and Arizona, the prospect of backlash action through citizen initiatives to adopt retaliatory laws that the legislature is politically unwilling to enact. For example, California has adopted laws by initiative that eradicate bilingual education, deny education and other public benefits to undocumented immigrants, declare English as the official state language, and abolish affirmative action programs in public education, employment, and contracting.

A relationship also exists between attitudes and temporary solutions to institutional inequities. For example, school funding systems based on local property tax revenues cripple the ability of inner-city and poor rural schools to compete with the educational resources and programs of suburban and private schools. Affirmative action in higher education admissions programs in large part aims to address these structural inequalities as a stopgap measure. Yet stereotypes that construct Latinas/os and other beneficiaries of affirmative action programs as fundamentally inferior in intelligence and in educational ability have fueled the movement to dismantle affirmative action programs through lawsuits and citizen initiatives. Moreover, overcoming unsupportive attitudes and prejudices of individual teachers toward Latina/o children is instrumental in reversing spiraling dropout rates of Latina/o students.

Surely structural inequities exist in the American criminal justice system, where most Black and Latina/o defendants cannot afford a "Dream Team" in their defense, and where laws are enforced that deem possession of ghetto crack a more serious offense than possession of an equal amount of suburban cocaine or rural methamphetamine. Yet attitudes contribute to the mistreatment of Latinas/os in the criminal justice system. Racial profiling by law enforcement authorities is based on their perceptions of the criminality of racial and ethnic groups. Juries and judges sometimes engage in similar attitudinal profiling in their conviction and sentencing of Latina/o defendants.

At the same time, institutional discrepancies sometimes drive societal attitudes toward Latinas/os and other subordinated groups. For example, substandard schools in urban barrio neighborhoods and poor rural agricultural communities deprive Latinas/os of opportunities in higher education and contribute to Latinas/os having the highest dropout rate of any group. The resultant lack or inferiority of Latina/o education contributes to the perception of Latinas/os as unintelligent. As well, the absence of educational opportunity that leads some to gangs, drugs, or crime adds to the societal perception of Latinas/os as biologically criminal-minded.

Before undertaking to review the range of derogatory stereotypes and concomitant negative treatment of Latinas/os in the legal system, I offer as a guidepost that the relationships among social attitudes, mass media, and social institutions, including the legal system, are intertwined and not easily untangled. There probably is substantial truth to the notions that media influence attitudes; attitudes influence media content; attitudes help shape political, legal, and economic institutions and contribute to institutional inequities; and institutional inequities in turn influence individual and societal attitudes. Whatever the exact recipe, no doubt the resulting concoction is a manifestly potent and sometimes deadly brew for Latinas/os, as it is for other subordinated groups.

Chapters 2 and 3 provide an overview of the derogatory images of Latinas/os in American media and society, as well as images of other subordinated groups. My primary focus in constructing Latinas/os in the American imagination is on Anglo attitudes, which I define as those of non-Latina/o Whites in the United States. At the same time, as I examine in Chapter 10, I am mindful that non-Anglos sometimes share the same unfavorable conceptions of Latinas/os.

Chapters 4 through 8 examine the principal demeaning constructions of Latinas/os that influence their legal and societal treatment at the hands of such government and citizen operatives as police, prosecutors, juries, teachers, voters, and vigilantes. After providing extensive examples of injurious imagery from American media, I attempt to debunk the derogatory constructions where contrary evidence exists. Where stereotypes and law intersect, I endeavor to provide a thorough background of the relevant legal doctrines to make them accessible for nonlawyers.

In Chapter 9, I reverse the dominant gaze and interrogate how Latinas/os and Latina/o media construct Anglos (*gringos*). In Chapter 10, I examine how, by internalizing their negative social images, Latinas/os and other subordinated groups come to see themselves and each other as inferior, as well as the inter- and intraethnic conflict this internalized racism may spark.

Chapters 11 through 14 begin the daunting task of imagining a new societal vision for Latinas/os through community-based efforts of protest and counterspeech aimed at media and society and by transformative political and social movements directed at discriminatory social institutions. Realizing that most litigation and lawyer-based strategies against stereotype are derailed by constitutional free-speech guarantees, I articulate an agenda toward dignity that relies on such diverse nonlegal sources as voluntary media industry reform and interracial coalition building to aid in reimagining Latinas/os as legal and societal equals.

2

Latinas/os in the American Imagination

In the aggregate, stereotypes of Latinas/os paint a staggeringly negative view of America's most populous minority group. Most years, I teach a course to undergraduate college students on the intersection of law and Latina/o identity and culture. When I ask my students, a mix of Latinas/os, Anglos, and others, how American society imagines Latinas/os, I expect a familiar response. Perhaps the first trait they mention will address criminal tendencies—involvement with gangs, drugs, or some other criminal livelihood or inclination ("they carry knives"). Following this prompt, the social construction of Latinas/os unfolds as the students suggest, sometimes drawing laughter, other times revulsion, that Latinas/os are also marked by their tendencies to be lazy (they "siesta" all day) and to party (they "fiesta" all night), as well as their preoccupation with sex and seduction (the "Latin lover"). Latinas are promiscuous and fertile ("they have lots of babies"). Latinas/os possess hot Latin blood (both sexually and criminally) and quick tempers. Other stereotypes emerge—Latinas/os are wards of the state ("they're all on welfare"), and they refuse to learn English or otherwise to assimilate. Someone will suggest they are seen as unintelligent—or as less intelligent than Anglos—another that they are dirty, unclean and unsanitary.

Listening to my students validates my conception of the established nature of these stereotypes. They don't need my lecture or any written materials to inform their response. Their answers flow from shared understandings and imaginations. Compelling proof of the settled nature of the stereotypes examined herein comes from ethnic jokes, now warehoused on Internet joke sites. As they relate to Latinas/os, particularly to Mexicans and to a lesser extent to Puerto Ricans, these jokes have anchored America's inventory of humor for years. The same themes were rendered and punch lines delivered in my own schoolyard. Consider:

Do you know why Mexicans have those little steering wheels in their cars?
So it's easier to drive with handcuffs on.

What do you call a Mexican in a three-piece suit?
The defendant.

How do you fit one hundred Mexicans (or Puerto Ricans) in a phone booth?
Throw in a food stamp.

Media portrayals of Latinas/os further validate these demeaning views, as this book will illustrate exhaustively. Popular songs, movies, television shows, news media, and advertising campaigns, when they portray Latinas/os, invariably draw on this store of stereotypical conceptions.

A striking aspect of Latina/o stereotypes is their longevity. Most of the stereotypes addressed here date back to the nineteenth-century Southwest. Some scholars believe that negative conceptions of Latinas/os in the United States originated at least as early as needed to justify this country's territorial designs on the Southwest, culminating in the U.S.-Mexico War. Examples illustrating the longevity of negative constructions of Latinas/os include the Texas newspaper that editorialized in 1871 about the lack of sanitation among Mexicans, suggesting that "the hogs lived as much in the [Mexicans'] houses [as the Mexicans did] . . . and from the similarity it was hard to tell where the hogs left off and inhabitants began."[1] A 1932 letter by a Rockefeller Institute researcher published in Puerto Rico suggested that Puerto Ricans were "the dirtiest, laziest, most degenerate and thievish race of men ever inhabiting this sphere."[2] A 1940 public opinion poll in the United States gave respondents a choice of nineteen adjectives to describe Central and South Americans. Almost half the respondents selected the descriptions of "quick-tempered," "emotional," "superstitious," "backward," "lazy," "ignorant," and "suspicious." The least-selected adjective was "efficient." Near the bottom, with none selected by more than 16 percent of respondents, were "progressive," "generous," "brave," "honest," "intelligent," and "shrewd."[3] Before the advent of sound, Hollywood depicted Mexicans routinely as treacherous *bandidos* who would rob and kill indiscriminately. Both Hollywood and popular music have long depicted Latinas/os as lazy and lacking industry. One silent film from 1923 described a south-of-the-border location as a lazy place where "Rip Van Winkle's twenty-year sleep would be considered a nap."[4] The 1948 hit song by Peggy Lee and Dave Barbour, "Mañana (Is Soon Enough for Me)," featured the lyrics:

> My mother thinks I'm lazy and maybe she is right.
> I'll go to work mañana, but I gotta sleep tonight.
> Mañana . . . is soon enough for me.[5]

Hollywood has even projected derogatory stereotypes of Latinas/os into the future—in the twenty-third-century setting of the film *The Fifth Element* (1997), Bruce Willis confronts a Latino-appearing hoodlum with a Spanish accent and a futuristic assault weapon, bent on a home invasion, until he is trumped by the more menacing weapon that hero Willis keeps handy.

Some might contend that the longevity of Latina/o stereotypes lends proof to the soundness of these unflattering conceptions. A contrary explanation is that due to geographical proximity of the Americas as well as continued immigration, Latinas/os have posed the same threat to Anglos over the last 150 years and beyond. Thus, the unceasing fear and the territorial aggression that fuel these stereotypes have sustained them through the years, valid or not.

Of course, the perception of Latinas/os in the American imagination has shown some fluidity over the years. As socioeconomic and related forces have demanded, such as when American industries needed cheap labor to replace workers departing to fight World War II, immigration laws (in the form of the Bracero Program) were eased and media images softened,[6] evidenced most pointedly by the wartime efforts of Hollywood's Production Code Administration to remove derogatory references to Mexicans, such as "greaser," from film. Yet, when labor pressures eased, federal authorities launched the oppressive, military-minded Operation Wetback to deport undocumented immigrant workers, and thus arose the subhuman image of the Latina/o "wetback" or "illegal alien" that still dominates hate radio, other media, and the American imagination.

Historically, while negative Latina/o stereotypes have remained centered on Mexicans and Mexican Americans, over time these same stereotypes have encompassed other Latina/o groups, particularly Puerto Ricans and Cuban Americans. A 1949 study of American attitudes found Puerto Ricans were viewed as excessively promiscuous, that "the men carry knives and use them unrestrainedly, that all Puerto Ricans are ignorant, unintelligent and stupid because they do not speak English . . . [and] that they are very temperamental and hot-headed."[7] Not surprisingly, this spread of negative perceptions across the Latina/o landscape coincided with the migration of Puerto Ricans and Cubans to the mainland United States, where Puerto Ricans established a substantial presence in New York City and Cubans in Florida. Thus, when Latinas/os other than Mexicans began to enter the mainland United States, the threats these migrations posed led to the construction by Anglos of Cuban, Puerto Rican, Dominican, and other Latina/o identities on terms established previously for Mexicans. Despite the expanding diversity of Latina/o groups in the mainland United States, media stereotypes and the public's critical eye continue to focus on Mexican Americans, which reflects that Mexican Americans constitute the majority of Latinas/os in the United States. As reported by the 2000 U.S. Census, two-thirds of the Latina/o population in the United States is of Mexican origin (66.1 percent). Puerto Ricans are the next largest single group of Latinas/os (9 percent), followed by those of Cuban origin (4 percent), with 14.5 percent of Latinas/os identifying as Central or South American and 6.4 percent as "other Hispanic origin."[8]

Critical race scholars, particularly the Latina/o Critical Legal Theory (LatCrit)[9] community, which focuses on the intersection of Latinas/os with law and society, have struggled to articulate a unifying basis of identity for the diverse racial and ethnic groups that compose Latinas/os. Language, for example, fails as a unifying identity, since many Americanized Latinas/os may be one or two generations removed from their ancestors' fluency in Spanish. Moreover, the primary language of many Latinas/os in the United States is an indigenous language, such as the Mixtec language of some Mexican Indian immigrants from Oaxaca, Mexico. In Mexico and Guatemala alone, residents speak approximately 260 different indigenous languages;[10] in Mexico, over 5 million people speak an indigenous language.[11] Moreover, Brazilians speak Portuguese, rather than Spanish, as their colonized language. The Spanish spoken by Mexican Americans differs somewhat from that of many other Latinas/os, particularly those from Spain. The diversity of languages among Latinas/os has sometimes led to tragic outcomes when Anglos essentialize them. In Oregon, or example, a migrant worker from Oaxaca, Adolfo Gonzales, was actually institutionalized in the state's mental hospital for two years in the early 1990s after officials assumed he was able to speak Spanish and mistook his efforts to communicate in Trique, his only tongue, as paranoid schizophrenia.[12]

As a construction of identity, race fails to capture the diversity of Latinas/os, who may be Black, White, indigenous, or of other racial background.[13] Due to this racial diversity, physical appearance carries the same limitations. National origin is similarly deficient—the 2000 Census estimated that more than one hundred thousand foreign-born Latinas/os came from myriad countries: Mexico, Cuba, the Dominican Republic, El Salvador, Guatemala, Honduras, Nicaragua, Brazil, Colombia, Ecuador, Guyana, Peru, and Venezuela.

Religion likewise cannot serve as a universal marker for Latinas/os. Although Mexican Americans are predominantly Catholic (65 percent, as reported in 1993),[14] many Latinas/os are Protestant, some are Mormon, and one of my favorite former law students, a Puerto Rican woman, was a practicing Jehovah's Witness. An estimated twenty-five thousand Latinas/os are Muslims.[15] As of the late 1980s, in South Florida alone there were estimated to be at least fifty thousand practitioners of Santeria, most of them Cuban Americans.[16]

Latinas/os are also divided along the political spectrum, with prominent Latina/o conservatives such as Richard Rodriguez and Linda Chávez (apparently now joined by Florida governor Jeb Bush's Latino son George), as well as most Cuban Americans, at one end of the political spectrum, while most Mexican Americans and Puerto Ricans tend to vote Democratic. A 1999 national survey of Latinas/os by the *Washington Post* found that 44 percent of Latinas/os identified themselves as Democrats, compared with 16 percent Republican and 40 percent labeling themselves as Independent, members of other parties, or giving no opinion. In the same survey, Blacks identified themselves more decidedly as Democrats, with respective percentages of 61 (D), 4 (R), and 35 (others).[17] Economic class, too, does not fully capture the growing economic diversity of Latinas/os as they continue to enter the middle class.

Ironically, at the same time that critical race scholars have struggled to articulate a unifying basis for Latina/o group identity, stereotypes have not been so constrained. Most of the stereotypes described in this book apply with equal vigor to Latinas/os of all origins. For example, in the media's portrayal and in the American imagination, Latinas/os of all backgrounds anchor America's illicit drug trade. In movies and in television series such as *Miami Vice,* Mexicans, Colombians, Cubans, Nicaraguans, Bolivians, Peruvians, Dominicans, and other Latinas/os have outpaced Anglos, Asians, and all other groups as the designated drug run-ners in American media. Similarly, Latinas/os of all backgrounds are re-garded by Anglos as gang members. Mexican Americans have long been associated with gang activity, dating at least to the news media's over-blown and misleading coverage of the 1943 Zoot Suit Riots in Los An-geles. But the American public also views Puerto Ricans as gang mem-bers, dating from the sensationalized attack on White teenagers in 1959 by gang member Salvador "Capeman" Agron, which launched Holly-wood's conception of Puerto Rican gang members in the films *Young Sav-ages* (1961) and *West Side Story* (1961), through the arrest in 2002 of Puerto Rican former gang member José Padilla for his alleged soliciting of a "dirty bomb" terrorist attack. Cubans, as well, took on the related construction of an unruly mob in the media's portrayal of the Elian Gon-zalez custody battle, and Cuban gang members were portrayed as ruth-less drug dealers in the film *The Substitute* (1996), with Miami locations.

American media have contributed to the blurring of stereotypical dis-tinctions among Latina/o groups by their interchangeable casting of Lati-nas/os from one group to portray another. In film, Puerto Rican Jennifer Lopez was cast as the slain Mexican American singer Selena. Lou Dia-mond Phillips, of Spanish, Native American, and Filipino heritage, played Mexican American guitarist Ritchie Valens in *La Bamba* (1987). Puerto Rican Benicio Del Toro won an Academy Award as Best Supporting Actor for his role as a Mexican law enforcement officer in *Traffic* (2000). Puerto Rican–Hungarian Freddie Prinze played a Chicano in the 1970s television sitcom *Chico and the Man*.

This media conflation of Latina/o identity erases cultural differences and essentializes the Latina/o experience into a single stereotypical image, leading to such portrayals as the spring 2002 episode of the animated television series *The Simpsons* that depicted Brazilians in Rio de Janeiro as having Spanish accents, wearing mustaches, and dancing the conga. Recently, in the rush to conflate and commodify the Latina/o culture for the American record-buying public, Ricky Martin was termed a "hot tamale," although the *tamal* is not part of Puerto Rican cuisine, and singer Marc Anthony was celebrated as a "hot jalapeño," although as a Puerto Rican he had never tasted one.[18] Ironically, as Hollywood casts Puerto Ricans to play Mexicans, the recording industry and news media employ a Mexican diet to describe Puerto Rican singers.

In mapping the various stereotypes of Latinas and Latinos, it becomes evident that if not on the basis of national origin, some of these stereotypes may nonetheless break down along the lines of gender, skin color, immigrant/native status, language, and other grounds. The Latin lover stereotype, for example, often has a romanticized and desirable edge when applied to Latino men. Notable "Latin lovers" include former big screen stars Gilbert Roland, Ricardo Montalban, and Fernando Lamas, as well as singers Julio Iglesias and current pop icons Enrique Iglesias and Ricky Martin. Yet, while portrayed by American media as equally singularly inclined toward sex, Latinas are presented in less flattering terms, as easy, as whores, and even as willing to engage in unnatural sex such as bestiality.

Latinas/os speaking Spanish can trigger certain stereotypes. Spanish prompts Anglos to view the speaker as reluctant or unable to assimilate by adopting English. Spanish is even associated with lesser intelligence. Recently, a candidate for Washington State's top education post declared that "Spanish is the language of doormen, dishwashers, and fruit pickers." He went on to suggest that instead of learning Spanish, children should learn English, "the language of doctors, dentists, and lawyers."[19]

Color lines may also be relevant in confronting stereotypes. Negative Latina/o perceptions, such as the inability or unwillingness to assimilate, absence of initiative, and lack of intelligence, are heightened as the color of the Latina/o's skin darkens. Arguably the most prominent media Latina/o of the last century, Cuban American Desi Arnaz (Desiderio Alberto Arnaz y de Acha, *I Love Lucy*'s Ricky Ricardo), was light-skinned. Although he spoke with an accent and often mispronounced words ("Lucy, you got some 'splainin' to do"), he spoke English instead of Spanish (except when his hot Latin temper erupted). Television's Ricky Ricardo came across as entrepreneurial and upwardly mobile and as possessing an urban and urbane intelligence and character. Aside from his temper, he would never be taken by viewers for a criminal or an urban gang leader (an upscale nightclub band leader, yes). By contrast, Freddie Prinze, television's Chico in the 1970s *Chico and the Man* series, was a darker-skinned Latino befriended by the Anglo "Man." One of Chico's signature lines, "It's not my job," reflected his less-than-stellar work ethic. His origins on the show as a petty thief[20] seem more consistent with the media's usual conception of Latinas/os than Ricky Ricardo's class-climbing, honest work ethic.

Conceptions of Latinas/os who are recent immigrants may differ from those of native-born and later-generation Latinas/os. Given the media focus in the 1990s on immigrants coming to the United States ostensibly to collect welfare benefits and other free government services for them-selves or their children, it is possible that recent immigrants are seen as more inclined than native Latinas/os to seek out public assistance. Gen-erally, though, Latinas/os will be imagined in similar terms, whether na-tive or immigrant. In his study of frontier California history, Leonard Pitt observed that from the perspective of Anglos, "whether from California, Chile, Peru, or Mexico, whether residents of 20 years' standing or immi-grants of one week, all Spanish-speakers were lumped together as 'inter-lopers' and 'greasers.'"[21]

Stereotypes of some subordinated groups vary along geographic lines. For example, the view of Native Americans in the eastern United States might be described as more flattering (the "noble" Indian)[22] than the stereotype in some Western states, where Native Americans are regarded as drunken, lazy Indians. For African Americans, studies have confirmed that negative perceptions are more prevalent in the southern United States.[23] Latinas/os are spread geographically throughout the United States, although significant regional concentration exists within different Latina/o groups. More than half of Latinas/os of Mexican origin live in the West (56.8 percent). Puerto Ricans tend to live in the Northeast (63.9 percent), and eight of ten Cuban Americans live in the South.[24] For Latinas/os, a clear geographic fault line does not emerge in their stereo-typical identity. For example, views of Puerto Ricans in the Northeast differ little from those of Mexican Americans in the Southwest. And whether they are laboring in the agricultural fields of California or the Pacific Northwest, working in the Midwest meatpacking industry, or picking tobacco in the Southeast, Mexicans are imagined by Anglos in similar unflattering terms.

The prevalence of Latinas/os of mixed ethnicity complicates any analy-sis of social construction. Those Latinas/os of mixed ethnicity, such as Anglo-Latinas/os, should not assume they fall outside the long shadow of negative perceptions of Latinas/os. At the end of the nineteenth century, for example, scientists regarded the dual-race children of Black and White parents as inferior.[25] I am uncertain as to which stereotypes comprise the identity of mixed Anglo-Latinas/os such as myself. I imagine what people think when they learn I am half Mexican and that I was born and raised in East Los Angeles by my Mexican American mother and my late Mex-ican American stepfather. Given my profession as a law professor, I doubt they assume I yearn for public assistance. Similarly, I doubt they view me as inclined toward thievery. Yet, although it is sometimes barely perceptible, I get the sense from some colleagues and peers that they regard me as less intelligent than Anglos in my position. This impression has dogged me for years and is consistent with the opinion of others of color in academia that they need to outperform their colleagues in teaching and in their scholarship in order to be considered intellectual equals.

Not all stereotypical constructions of Latinas/os endanger them. Yet even many seemingly innocuous conceptions have contributed to the subordinate treatment of Latinas/os. In particular, the image of Latinas/os as festive and party-going seems innocent enough. But the image of the fiesta-loving Latina/o is closely associated with that of the drunken Latina/o, particularly the drunken Mexican. As will be shown, the construction of Latinas/os as drunk and lazy is linked to the perception of them as being unduly reliant on government aid and thus a burden to a civilized society. The societal image of the Latin lover, too, suggests desirable traits of romance, passion, and allure) Singer Ricky Martin invoked this conception when he implored, "I wanna be your . . . only Latin lover."[26] But Latin lovers are not separated easily from constructions of the hot-blooded and hot-tempered Latina/o, nor from images of Latinas as excessively fertile and sexually available. Apart from the relationship of these views to laws attacking the reproduction of Latinas/os, such as California's Proposition 187,[27] the conception of sexuality without bounds underlies legal treatment of Latinas/os with regard to unwanted sex. Following the arrest of a fifteen-year-old Latino on charges he sexually abused a girl on the school campus, a Salem, Oregon, high school rounded up Latino-appearing boys for a Latinos-only sexual harassment training assembly. Parents complained that their sons were told their culture treats women improperly and that the boys needed to change their ways.[28] A lawsuit filed against the school district claimed further that the Latino boys were instructed that American girls would not welcome their Hispanic culture.[29] Media contribute to the conception of Latinos as overly desirous of Anglo women, indeed, as willing to rape them if necessary. For example, in the film *The Substitute* (1996), a Cuban gang member terrorized his Anglo high school teacher by climbing onto her car windshield wagging his tongue and threatening, "I'm gonna lick your pussy like this," implying rape. In the blockbuster film *Training Day* (2001), narcotics officer Denzel Washington frightened an Anglo drug purchaser by warning that if she returned to the neighborhood, he'd let the Latino homeboys up the hill "run a train on" (rape) her.

For Latinas, the sexually promiscuous suggestion of the Latin lover image has been equally, if not more, injurious. Scholars have demonstrated that this view creates credibility problems for Latinas in sexual violence trials, leading juries more readily to find consent as a defense to the charges when the victim is perceived as easy and willing.[30]

3

Centering Latina/o Stereotypes in Those of Other Groups

Stereotypical constructions abound in American society; some intersect with Latinas/os and others do not. Stereotypical "fault lines" are evident on such diverse grounds as gender, sexual orientation, hair color, and religious beliefs, as well as race, geographical region of residence, economic class, skin color, and national origin. For example, Americans construct those of Irish origin as drunkards and violent. Those of Polish origin have been subjected to an onslaught of "Polish jokes" ridiculing them as unintelligent and sexually desperate. The French are rude, Italians are mobsters, Gypsies are thieves and cheats ("I was gypped"), Russians are heavy drinkers, and Greeks are sexually deviant. Long stereotyped on religious grounds as smart but stingy, and even as subhuman, Jews were likened to rats and insects by Nazis and others, leading to genocide in Europe and to hate crimes and discriminatory treatment in the United States.

In American society, some of these stereotypical fault lines have driven the legal treatment of groups, while others are less connected to law and social policy. For example, a compelling relationship exists between stereotype and legal treatment of gays and lesbians, who are constructed in American society as promiscuous and subhuman. Among other effects of their construction, they generally are excluded from the institution of marriage[1] and lack the legal status and benefits of married couples (or heterosexual partners) in settings ranging from workplace benefits to income taxation. Their sexual expression is criminalized in several states.[2] The FDA prohibits most gay men from donating blood. Gay and lesbian single parents are often denied custody of their children on assumptions the children will be raised in an immoral environment.[3] Florida state law prohibits gays and lesbians from adopting children.[4] They are discriminated against in public employment and military service—only a handful of states protect gays and lesbians from employment discrimination.[5] On the basis of their social construction, gays and lesbians are routinely subjected to subordinate private treatment that ranges from housing and employment discrimination to vigilante savagery. Just one of the horrific examples of sexuality-based hate crimes, apart from the murder in Wyoming of Matthew Shepard, left beaten and tied to a fence, was the 1993 attack in Laguna Beach, California, on a gay Vietnamese American, Loc Minh Truong, who was stomped into the rocky ground and left bleeding and disfigured, with a rock impaled in his head, by Anglo youths who went looking to terrorize gays.[6]

Throughout American social and legal history, the construction of women as subordinate to men and as incompetents incapable of managing their affairs or of conducting business has had grave consequences. Married women were unable to own property or to enter into valid contracts until the passage of Married Women's Property Acts in the nineteenth century.[7] Women were denied political expression until they secured the right to vote in 1920. Like gays and lesbians, women have faced private discrimination in housing and employment. Media continue to depict women in subordinate roles, most blatantly in pornography, which objectifies women and depicts them often as enjoying rape.[8] In American society, women have been brutalized by vigilantes reminding women of their subordinate societal and legal role through rape, domestic abuse, sexual harassment, and stalking.[9]

By contrast, other stereotype fault lines are less connected to formal legal treatment. For example, although blonde women are the subject of humor, song,[10] and film ("If I'm going to be a senator, I need to marry a Jackie, not a Marilyn")[11] suggesting their lesser intelligence while touting their enhanced enjoyment of life ("Blondes have more fun"), these stereotypical views have not prompted significant legal treatment unique to hair color.

Complicating any analysis of stereotypes is the reality of the growing number of mixed-race and mixed-ethnicity Latinas/os. The potent conflation of stereotypes that results is perhaps reflected best by long-standing ethnic jokes such as:

What do you get when you cross a Mexican with a Chinaman?
A car thief who can't drive.

Why didn't the Black man want to marry a Mexican?
He didn't want his kids to grow up too lazy to mug.

Latina/o intersections with African, Asian, and Native Americans, both in terms of mixed race and ethnicity, as well as in similarities of stereotypical construction and in their legal and societal treatment, compel examination of stereotypes targeting these identities.

Black men and women are the subject of numerous derogatory stereotypes, several of which mirror Latina/o constructions. One legal commentator has suggested that White Americans view Black males as "overly aggressive, violent, involved in drugs, dishonest, shiftless and lazy, desirous of white women, lacking in work ethics, and . . . often [as] rapists and criminals."[12] A 1990 poll of all ethnic backgrounds revealed that although only 18.8 percent of respondents believed violence was a trait attributable to Whites, 52.8 percent saw violence as characteristic of Blacks (and 42.8 percent felt violence was a trait of Latinas/os).[13] Black women are imagined as preoccupied with sex (the controversial Rolling Stones song "Some Girls" suggested matter-of-factly that "Black girls just wanna get fucked all night"). Black men and women are considered unintelligent and as inclined toward welfare. As determined in a 1990 poll by the National Opinion Center, over half of Whites (53.2 percent) regarded Blacks as less intelligent than Whites, and even greater numbers viewed Blacks as less hard working (62.2 percent) and as preferring welfare to employment (77.7 percent).[14] CBS *60 Minutes* humorist Andy Rooney allegedly echoed these views when a newspaper attributed these remarks to him in 1990: "I've believed all along that most people are born with equal intelligence, but blacks have watered down their genes because the less intelligent ones are the ones that have the most children. They drop out of school early, do drugs, and get pregnant."[15] Concurrent with their profoundly negative, indeed subhuman, perception is the image of Blacks as in some ways superhuman, in their "supersexuality, inborn athletic and musical power, [and] natural rhythm."[16] Reflecting this dichotomy, a study of media coverage of college basketball and professional football games revealed that 77 percent of the adjectives used to describe White football players and 63 percent of those for White basketball players referred to their brains, whereas for Blacks, 65 percent of the references to football players and 77 percent for basketball players referred to their brawn.[17]

Media images fuel these negative perceptions, particularly the view of African Americans as criminals and Black men as savage "brutes." The most defining media representation of Blacks, *The Birth of a Nation* (1915), depicted two White men in blackface makeup menacing a White virgin until she leapt to her death.[18] Black men routinely have been portrayed in film as gang members (*Colors,* 1988), drug dealers (*Traffic,* 2000), and criminals (*Dirty Harry,* 1971)—one of cinema's greatest lines came at Black men's expense, as Clint Eastwood (policeman "Dirty Harry") asked the Black gunman lying bleeding on the sidewalk, who pondered whether to grab his shotgun, "I know what you're thinking, did he fire six shots or only five? You've got to ask yourself one question— Do I feel lucky? Well, do you punk?" As recounted by one observer, the dominant media images of Blacks include the

> Savage African, Happy slave, Devoted servant, Corrupt politician, Irresponsible citizen, Petty thief, Social delinquent, Vicious criminal, Sexual superman, Unhappy non-white, Natural-born cook, Perfect entertainer, Superstitious churchgoer, Chicken and watermelon eater, Razor and knife "toter," Uninhibited expressionist, Mentally inferior, [and] Natural-Born musician.[19]

Media's and society's criminalization of the Black body holds consequences for African Americans in all reaches of the criminal justice system, from initial police stops based on skin color ("Driving While Black") to disproportionate imposition of the death penalty. The subordinate social construction of African Americans, employed first to justify slavery of and later government and private discrimination toward Blacks, has prompted unrelenting vigilante violence against them throughout Anglo-American history.

Native Americans are viewed as warlike, savage, and treacherous, as well as prone to alcoholism and to rely on government aid.[20] These stereotypes emerged from countless film and television westerns. In its reflection and creation of societal images of subordinated groups, Hollywood has been no less cruel to Native Americans. Using the same devices that it employs in portraying most other marginalized people, cinema casts Anglo actors in Native roles, essentializes the Native American experience by giving all tribes the customs of the Apaches or a few other tribes, centers on a particular period of conflict between Native Americans and White settlers without providing historical reference, depicts Native Americans as murderous savages ambushing and attacking settler wagon trains, constructs Native American men as a threat to White women through rape and murder, and, in the rare instances where cinema aims to portray Natives sympathetically, calls on a prominent Anglo to serve as an ethnic tour guide and narrator.[21] According to Richard Delgado and Jean Stefancic, "Cowboy and Indian" films have showcased "war dances, exotic dress, drunkenness, surprise attacks, scalping, raiding, raping, tomahawks, tomtoms, and torture."[22] Masking the precision of Native languages, one of which contains five times as many words as English, cinema relegates Native dialogue to "ughs," war whoops, grunts, and broken English ("me gettum").[23] As with Latinas/os and others, this cinematic choice to use broken English to replicate experiences of a non-English tongue conveys a lack of intelligence. For Native Americans, their subhuman media and social construction has legitimized their genocide—legal (as by the Indian Removal Act), cultural, and actual (by enslavement and the mass murder of several million Indians)—in the American experience of the last several centuries.[24]

Asian stereotypes are complex, fluid, and sometimes contradictory. At the same time that Anglos have constructed Asian Americans as subhuman (as through product advertisements in the early 1900s that depicted the Chinese as willing to consume rats),[25] Anglos have also viewed Asians as superhuman in their treachery, deviousness, resistance to pain, and capability to work long hours as unfair business competitors.[26] Such diverse media as film, television, product advertisements, and newspapers have conveyed these contradictory sub/superhuman images. Keith Aoki recounts that:

> William Randolph Hearst's papers generated and widely promoted negative stereotypes of immigrants in general and Chinese in particular, portraying west coast Chinatowns as teeming containment zones of unbridled lawlessness, licentiousness, and unchecked evil. Opium smoking, gambling, prostitution, rats, and honeycombs of secret underground tunnels characterized Hearst's Chinatowns, filthy breeding grounds of depravity, degradation, and disease—in short, a serious and imminent moral and physical threat to public health and welfare. This form of "yellow journalism" convinced many white readers that "Chinatowns" were dangerous and imminent menaces.[27]

These images engendered discriminatory laws in residential, educational, employment, and other settings, such as an 1890 resolution passed by the San Francisco Board of Supervisors that made it "unlawful for any Chinese person to locate, reside or carry on a business anywhere in San Francisco except . . . in an area set aside for slaughterhouses, tallow factories, hog factories and other businesses thought to be prejudicial to the public health or comfort."[28] Fears of Asians as menaces led to discriminatory federal immigration laws such as the 1882 Chinese Exclusion Act, the first American law to restrict immigration on the basis of race, and later the Immigration Act of 1924 (targeting Japanese), preventing all "aliens ineligible for citizenship" from entering the United States. The latter law (not repealed until 1952) effectively barred all Asians from entry, as they were not among those groups eligible for citizenship.[29] These fears also fueled laws and ballot initiatives, known as Alien Land Laws, in several western states in the early 1900s. The Alien Land Laws restricted or prohibited ownership of land by aliens ineligible for citizenship (targeting the Chinese and Japanese).[30]

World War II media propaganda attempted to construct Japanese on two levels—as subhuman ("likened to monkeys, baboons, gorillas, dogs, rodents, rattlesnakes, vipers, cockroaches, bees, [and] ants") and as superhuman ("monstrously large or strong, preternaturally cunning and devious; resistant to pain").[31] Japanese and Chinese immigrants were portrayed and perceived as foreigners, incapable of assimilation and, most important, as unable to abandon their loyalty to their Asian nations.[32] These suspicions of disloyalty and fears of a subhuman Asian peril helped justify the abominable, forcible relocation and internment in remote camps in the California desert and elsewhere of over 110,000 Japanese Americans during World War II.[33] Anti-Asian constructions and attitudes have prompted vigilante violence too, from the White supremacists who doused four Chinese in kerosene and set them ablaze in 1877 California, to the 1982 killing in Detroit of Vincent Chin by autoworkers who regarded Asians as an unfair competitive threat.[34]

These attitudes toward Asian Americans persist. In the Civic Center of San Francisco, where construction has been underway in 2002 for the Asian Art Museum, vandals defaced a mural painted by Chinese American youth that surrounds the construction perimeter. At the base of the mural, which credits the Chinese American student artists, someone wrote the words "Traitors to USA," "Shit," "Evil Aliens," "Animals," "Espyanage [sic]," "Spys [sic]," and "Garbage." Over six months after I first noticed them, these words remained. Reflecting this societal image of disloyalty, particularly of Chinese Americans, was the recent imprisonment and criminal investigation of Los Alamos scientist Wen Ho Lee on overblown suspicions of espionage with China.[35]

Even before September 11, 2001, these perceptions of Asian disloyalty and subhumanity were directed toward such Arabs and Arab Americans as Iranians and Iraqis, described by Hollywood variously as "devil-worshipers," "jackals," "towel-heads," "sons-of-dogs," "scum-buckets," "sons of unnamed goats," and "camel-dicks."[36] The dominant view of Arab Americans and of Muslims is that they are violent terrorists who are disloyal to the United States and waging a holy war. Images of the terrorist Arab, popular in cinema (such as the films *Delta Force* [1986] and *True Lies* [1994]), were aggravated by the September 11 attacks. For Arab Americans, their media and social construction as terrorists has led to racial profiling, particularly in the transportation industry. A nationwide poll taken shortly after September 11 confirmed that 35 percent of respondents had less trust of Arab Americans after the attacks. Translating to legal policy, over half surveyed favored subjecting Arabs, including Arab Americans, to "special, more intensive security checks before boarding airplanes in the US."[37] Even before September 11, early terrorist attacks had galvanized public opinion against Arabs and Arab Americans as a whole—in a 1991 poll conducted during the Gulf War, 59 percent of Americans associated Arabs with terrorists, 58 percent with violence, and two-thirds felt there were too many Arab immigrants.[38]

Although some Latina/o scholars have suggested that Filipinas/os ought to be categorized as Latinas/os because they share the legacy of Spanish colonization, most observers regard Filipinas/os as Asian.[39] American stereotypes of Filipinas/os to some extent mirror those of Latinas/os—Filipinas/os have been described as inassimilable,[40] as savages, and as "the most worthless, unscrupulous, shiftless, diseased semi-barbarian[s] that ha[ve] ever come to our shores."[41] Violence in California against Filipinos, reaching its peak in the late 1920s and early 1930s, included the stoning and clubbing of Filipinos and the dynamiting of Filipino labor camps.

For Asians, their construction as superhuman (while simultaneously subhuman) evolved into one that regarded most Asian Americans more favorably as the "model minority" for their work ethic and for their intelligence, at least as compared with perceptions of other minority groups.[42] Progressive Asian American scholars have deconstructed the Asian model-minority image as a myth used against impoverished Asian immigrant groups needing economic assistance, and as a means of placing blame on other minority groups, particularly Blacks and Latinas/os, for supposedly lagging behind and lacking this initiative and intelligence.

Latinas/os were compared unfavorably with Chinese and Japanese residents in California as early as a 1942 Los Angeles police captain report submitted to a grand jury in connection with the Sleepy Lagoon murder case:

> Representatives of the Mexican colony . . . may be loathe to admit that [this crime wave] is in any way biological—for reasons one can quite understand, pride of race, nationality, etc., but the fact remains that the same factors, discrimination, lack of recreation facilities, economies, etc., have also always applied to the Chinese and Japanese in California, yet they have always been law abiding and have never given our authorities trouble except in that of opium among the Chinese and that of gambling among both the Japanese and Chinese, but such acts of violence as now are in evidence among the Mexicans has [*sic*] been entirely unknown among these two Oriental peoples.[43]

In fact, the Asian model-minority myth may have been shaped by immigration policies and geopolitical influences in the mid-1960s and thereafter that led to many Asian immigrants being those more highly educated than Asians generally and coming from the middle or upper class.[44]

Latinas/os have encountered their own model-minority construction, similar to the Asian conception. In the late 1950s, the first major exodus from Cuba precipitated by the 1959 revolution was viewed as a model-minority group for its education and enterprise. Of course, those Cuban immigrants were predominantly light-skinned (White) middle- and upper-class, educated professionals.[45] They were represented in the media mainstream by Desi Arnaz's Ricky Ricardo in the television comedy *I Love Lucy,* as the enterprising, upwardly mobile Latin bandleader married to a White woman. Favorable legal status accompanied this privileged construction, with Cuban immigrants classified as "political refugees" entitled to special immigration treatment.[46] Societal perceptions changed with the shift in Cuban migrants in 1980 (the so-called Mariel boat lift) to those with darker skin (Afro-Cubans) and those who were impoverished. Movies such as *Scarface* (1983) began to depict Cuban immigrants as ruthless criminals anchoring the drug trade, now in stereotypical brotherhood with other Latinas/os. That film opened with a photojournal description of the Mariel boat lift, warning, "It soon became evident that Castro was forcing the boat owners to carry back with them [to Miami] not only their relatives, but the dregs of his jails." Immigration policies toughened along with the media portrayals, allowing the United States to intercept Cuban migrants on the high seas and return them to Cuba.[47]

In Florida, fears that these Cuban migrants were failing to assimilate led in the 1980s to the formation of the modern English-language movement to seek enactment of laws and citizen initiatives declaring English the official language of state and federal government, as well as to eradicate bilingual education and other government programs recognizing languages other than English.[48]

As some advocates have argued that a particular subordinated group is more oppressed and therefore most deserving of redress,[49] so too have some argued that a particular group's social construction is more negative than others. When directed at Latina/o stereotypes and oppression of Latinas/os, these arguments by Anglos and others often proceed along the lines that Latinas/os generally can be viewed as White, or at least as non-Black, and therefore Latinas/os are less likely than Blacks to be negatively stereotyped or to face discrimination or other oppression. Calling this impression into question is a 1989 survey that determined that of fifty-eight ethnic groups in America, all Latina/o groups listed were ranked forty-ninth or lower in "perceived social standing," with only Gypsies ranking below Mexicans and Puerto Ricans and the fictitious ethnic group "Wysians" outranking all the Latina/o groups.[50] Although this book depicts a decidedly negative social conception of Latinas/os, as well as the abusive gauntlet of legal and private mistreatment they face, it does not engage in any assessment of which group fares worst in American society. Rather, it often points out similarities in both social conceptions and legal and private mistreatment of Latinas/os with other groups, mindful that solutions may stem from interethnic coalition rather than from individual or intraethnic efforts.

4

Greasers and Gangsters
Latinas/os and Crime

How do you make a Mexican omelet?
Well, first you steal three eggs.
—"Joke" told by a Texas judge in court[1]

What are the three times that a Mexican sees a priest?
When he's baptized, when he gets married, and at his execution.

Why don't Mexicans have checking accounts?
Because checks are too small to spray paint their name on.

How did break dancing get its start?
From Puerto Ricans trying to steal hubcaps from cars that were still
    moving.

A Mexican in a bar is discussing fighting styles with Chuck Norris.
He tells Norris that he is an expert in Mexican judo.
    Norris asked, "What the hell is Mexican judo?"
    The Mexican replied, "Judo know if I have a gun, or judo know
if I have a knife!"

Latinas/os are seen as criminally inclined. Their trademark is
thievery, often by force rather than by stealth. Latinas/os are also constructed as predisposed toward violent, vicious behavior, so that their
crimes may be cold-blooded. Latina/o youth are assumed to be gang
members who will eventually graduate from wielding spray-paint canis-
ters to carrying knives and guns. Latinas/os young and old are viewed as
suppliers and users of illicit drugs.

Roots of these conceptions predate reality television shows such as
Cops. In 1942, a Los Angeles sheriff's captain presented to a grand jury

a report arguing for the indictment of twenty-two Mexican gang members in a murder known as the Sleepy Lagoon incident. His report alleged a desire to kill that he attributed to Mexican ethnicity:

> When the Spaniards conquered Mexico they found an organized society composed of many tribes of Indians ruled over by the Aztecs who were given over to human sacrifice. . . . Historians record that as many as 30,000 Indians were sacrificed on their heathen altars in one day, their bodies being opened by stone knifes and their hearts torn out while still beating. This total disregard for human life has always been universal throughout the Americas among the Indian population, which of course is well known to everyone.
>
> The Caucasian, especially the Anglo-Saxon, when engaged in fighting, particularly among youths, resort to fisticuffs and may at times kick each other, which is considered unsportive, but this Mexican element considers all that to be a sign of weakness, and all he knows and feels is a desire to use a knife . . . to kill, or at least to let blood.[2]

The construction of Mexicans as thieves or as budding thieves was reflected in a 1929 school guidebook for Americanization curriculum that suggested:

> The noon lunch of the Mexican child quite often consists of a folded tortilla with no filling. There is no milk or fruit to whet the appetite. Such a lunch is not conducive to learning. The child becomes lazy. His hunger unappeased, he watches for an opportunity to take food from the lunch boxes of more fortunate children. Thus the initial step in a life of thieving is taken.[3]

Perceptions of criminal-mindedness are not limited to Mexicans. Puerto Ricans and other Latinas/os share the same unsavory reputation. For example, in 1940, *Scribner's Commentator* published an article titled "Welcome Paupers and Crime: Puerto Rico's Shocking Gift to the U.S.," claiming that all Puerto Ricans wallow "in the most abject moral degradation."[4]

Media depictions have done much to instill the view of Latinas/os as *bandidos,* gang members, drug dealers, and drug users. Television shows in particular have consistently portrayed Latinas/os as criminally minded. A Center for Media and Public Affairs study of television programming from 1955 to 1986 determined that Hispanic characters were twice as likely as Whites, and even three times more likely than Blacks, to commit a crime in their roles—22 percent of Hispanic television characters were criminals, compared with only 11 percent of Whites and 7 percent of Blacks.[5] Another study of twenty years of television programming found that for every one hundred White characters with positive values, thirty-nine evil/bad White characters appeared. With Hispanics, however, for every one hundred "good" Hispanic characters there were seventy-five "villains."[6] A study of reality-based television shows such as *Cops* concluded that in the 1992–93 season, a stunning 45 percent of the Latinas/os depicted were criminals or suspected criminals, as opposed to only 10 percent of White appearances.[7] A later study did reveal that the percentage of Latina/o characters appearing on television as criminals had declined by the 1994–95 season, particularly in reality television shows, although Latinas/os still outpaced White or Black criminal characters and had retained their status as television's designated criminals.[8]

News media also portray Latinas/os as criminals or otherwise cast them in a negative light. Los Angeles newspapers helped incite the 1943 Zoot Suit Riots, in which off-duty servicemen and other Anglos stormed into barrio neighborhoods looking to strip and beat Latino "pachucos," whom they perceived as troublemakers and as needing a reminder of their subordinate societal status. More recently, a National Association of Hispanic Journalists report determined that more than 85 percent of network news stories about Latinas/os addressed crime, affirmative action, immigration, or welfare,[9] all issues with negative connotations among Anglos.

The motion picture industry may have left the deepest media impression of Latina/o criminal-mindedness. The history of motion pictures reflects a gradual shift in the designated film villain from the rural Mexican bandit to the urban Latina/o gang member or Latina/o drug dealer. The cinematic Mexican *bandido* originated in silent films depicting the Mexican "greaser." He was dirty, with missing teeth and oily hair, as well as treacherous, violent, and dishonest.[10] In the 1923 film *The Bad Man*, the antagonist *bandido* bragged, while tweaking his mustache, that he had killed a gringo for breakfast because "[h]eem call me dirty crook." For lunch, he suggested, "I keel some more and steal ees pocketbook."[11] The Mexican *bandido* did his most famous turn in the film classic *The Treasure of Sierra Madre* (1948). While gold mining in the Mexican mountains, Humphrey Bogart and his Anglo partners encountered the Mexican *bandido* they called Gold Hat and his gang. Gold Hat announced, "We are *federales,* you know, the mounted police." Bogart questioned suspiciously, "If you're the police, where are your badges?" Gold Hat responded angrily, "Badges? . . . We don't need no badges! I don't have to show you any stinking badges!" The rural greaser-*bandido* image persevered despite his eventual transformation to a vicious urban gang member or a ruthless drug dealer. In the 1960s, spaghetti western films restored the *bandido* to moviegoer consciousness in such films as *A Fistful of Dollars* (1966) and *The Good, the Bad, and the Ugly* (1967) (featuring the fictional Mexican *bandido* Tuco the Terrible).[12] The Mexican *bandido* also appeared, with his tequila-swilling, gun-slinging tendencies intact, in the film comedy *Three Amigos* (1986). More recently, actor Brad Pitt braved a countryside rife with stereotypical *bandidos* in *The Mexican* (2001). When traveling in present-day Mexico to retrieve a legendary pistol, Pitt was warned by the local bartender that his Mexican town had only "farmers and *bandidos*." As Pitt left the bar, he encountered drunk Mexicans urinating and stumbling down the street while shooting their pistols into the air. As the aghast Pitt complained from a nearby pay phone, "There's all these maniacs shooting goddamn guns up into the sky." Failing to defy the laws of gravity, one of the reckless bullets killed a Mexican youth next to Pitt, hitting him "right in the fucking head."

The Mexican *bandido* made television appearances too. A Bob Hope television comedy skit once featured Hope in a disheveled black wig as the fictional Mexican bandit "El Crummo," carrying a gun in one hand with an ammunition belt around his chest. Appearing in television commercials as well as in print ads and on supermarket shelves, the gun-wielding Frito Bandito (misspelled from *bandido*) menaced buyers of Fritos Corn Chips from 1967 until protest led to his demise in 1971. One ad warned, "He loves cronchy Fritos Corn Chips so much he'll stop at nothing to get yours. What's more, he's cunning, clever [admittedly, this was saying something positive for media's Mexican *bandido*]—and sneaky!" Print advertisements were styled as bullet-ridden "Wanted" posters. Further, the Frito Bandito's trademark sombrero had been pierced by a bullet. Around this time, the Mexican *bandido* image was the front man for several other product lines. Bristol-Myers introduced a gang of *bandidos,* whose leader sprayed on underarm deodorant while the announcer suggested, "If it works for him, it'll work for you." In 1970, the Elgin watch company ran a newspaper ad suggesting that it was a good thing that Emiliano Zapata, a Mexican Revolution hero, was dead, as "[h]e'd be stealing Elgins as fast as we could make them."[13]

Although the media often depicted their conception of the Mexican *bandido* as a comical buffoon, the *bandido* image was not always harmless. He could be cold-blooded and savage, as in the silent film *Cowboy's Baby* (1910), in which a Mexican villain threw a child into a river to drown; or in the silent *Bronco Billy's Redemption* (1910), which featured a Mexican who resorted to stealing the money meant to purchase medicine for a dying child. In modern cinema, the *bandido*, although often urbanized, retains his depraved heart. In *Hard to Kill* (1989), for example, Steven Seagal manhandled a group of urban Latino desperadoes he encountered as they robbed a convenience store. One of the Latinos killed the outnumbered store clerk with a blast to the chest from his shotgun while laughing hysterically and joking. Seagal dispatched the gangsters, including one who approached with a trademark knife, threatening, "I'm gonna cut your fucking heart out."

Media's Mexican *bandido* is skilled with a knife, a proficiency the media attribute to Latinos generally, whether they are Puerto Rican youth in *West Side Story* (1961) or the Mexican bar patron in the hit country song "Colorado Cool-Aid," who deftly handled his switchblade to teach a drunk Anglo an ear-severing lesson. Singer Johnny Paycheck narrated this story of a "big mean drunk" who spit beer into his Mexican drinking buddy's ear:

> Sure enough that made my buddy real mad. . . .
> Well sir, he pulled out a big long switchblade knife.
> Quick as a whistle he begin [*sic*] to slice.
> That big mean drunk stood back, a face full of tears.
> Looking down at the floor, at one of his ears.
> He cut that thing off even with the sideburn. . . .
> [The Mexican courteously handed the drunk his ear from the barroom
>   floor, suggesting:]
> Now big man, you get the urge to spit a little beer,
> Just open up your hand there and spit it in your own ear.

Despite his skill with guns and knives, the media's Mexican *bandido* is a cowardly sort who will cross the border into the United States to conduct his nefarious business and then dash for the border to his criminal den in Mexico with bloody hands or blood money. The long-standing Taco Bell restaurant advertising slogan "Run for the Border" tapped into this impression that border crossings are in pursuit of some criminal enterprise, rather than for job opportunities north.

Bandido imagery primarily emphasized Mexicans and Mexican Americans, probably because Hollywood's conception of Mexicans as lawless *bandidos* grew out of the experience of a few real-life bandits who emerged from the physical, cultural, political, and economic displacement of Mexicans in the U.S.-Mexico War and thereafter. As Alfredo Mirandé has suggested, Anglos viewed these Mexican Robin Hoods in unglamorous terms—"[I]f an Anglo took the law into his own hands, he was generally labeled a hero or a revolutionary, but a Chicano who engaged in lawlessness was somehow a bandit."[14]

The eventual shift in media focus from the rural *bandido* of the early 1900s to the urban Latina/o gang member and gangster occurred largely through two widely publicized incidents in Los Angeles that triggered sensationalist press coverage. The first event, known as the Sleepy Lagoon incident, concerned a young Mexican boy found dead in August 1942 near the Sleepy Lagoon swimming hole. Police supposed that the boy was killed in a clash of two rival Mexican gangs, and they arrested twenty-two members of the so-called 38th Street Club. For months before their trial, the defendants were not permitted a haircut; during trial, the prosecutor arranged to have clean clothing meant for the defendants intercepted by jail staff.[15] Throughout the trial, the prosecution described the boys as gang members. In 1943, an all-Anglo jury convicted seventeen of the defendants on charges that ranged from assault to murder.[16] Five of those convicted were acquitted of murder, but the remaining twelve were adjudged guilty of murder—three for first-degree murder and nine for second-degree murder. On appeal by those convicted, a California appellate court found a "total lack of evidence" establishing that the defendants murdered the victim and reversed their convictions. The court did reject the defendants' contention that their prosecution stemmed from racial prejudice, finding "there is no ground revealed by the record upon which it can be said that this prosecution was conceived in, born, or nurtured by the seeds of racial prejudice."[17]

Racial turmoil in Los Angeles exploded in the second incident, the so-called Zoot Suit Riots, occurring during about ten days in the summer of 1943. These "riots" were precipitated by off-duty Anglo servicemen, with the aid of Anglo civilians, who raided barrio neighborhoods to assault Latino youth, particularly those dressed in zoot suits. Although no Mexican Americans were killed, scores were stripped and beaten with fists and chains, and their heads were shaved. Even young Mexican American boys aged twelve and thirteen were battered. Like crosses lit on lawns of African Americans, piles of clothing stripped off the victims were torched by the servicemen. Despite the source of the aggression, local and national press heaped blame on the Mexican targets of the violence. Media headlines referred to "marauding Latin gangs," "Mexican goon squads," "pachuco killers," and to Mexicans as "roving wolf-packs."[18] The Los Angeles Times headline one day read "Zoot Suiters Learn Lesson in Fight with Servicemen."[19] During the "riots," the Los Angeles City Council even outlawed zoot suits by resolution as a public nuisance:

> NOW, THEREFORE BE IT RESOLVED, that the City Council by Resolution find that the wearing of Zoot Suits constitutes a public nuisance and does hereby instruct the City Attorney to prepare an ordinance declaring the same a nuisance and prohibit[ing] the wearing of Zoot Suits with reet pleats within the city limits of Los Angeles.[20]

A few years later, early Christmas morning 1951, another group beating occurred, this time in a Los Angeles jail, where drunk police officers beat seven Mexican American prisoners in what is known as Bloody Christmas. Los Angeles police also played a role in facilitating the Zoot Suit Riots, implementing a policy of following the Anglo mob of servicemen and civilians at a "conveniently spaced interval," allowing the mob to have its way with the Mexican American youth, and then mopping up by arresting the attack victims, many of them severely injured, on charges that these Mexican American boys had disturbed the peace.[21]

Today, zoot suits have been replaced as the media markers of Mexican gang affiliation by gang colors and low-riders. Several modern films depict their lowly vision of Mexican gang life—*American Me* (1992), *Blood In, Blood Out (Bound by Honor)* (1993), *Boulevard Nights* (1979), *Colors* (1988), *Mi Vida Loca* (1994, showcasing Latina gang members and drug dealers), *187* (1997), and *Walk Proud* (1979). These films tend to regard East Los Angeles as the urban territory for Mexican American gang violence. In a 1986 airing of the television game show *The $25,000 Pyramid,* in which contestants gave word clues to their partners, the word *gangs* appeared. As one commentator relates, the contestant shouted his clue, without hesitation, "They have lots of these in East L.A." His partner immediately identified the word as *gangs*.[22] I wonder how I might have responded to this clue. Having lived in or next to East Los Angeles for many years, I probably would have answered Mexicans (Mexican

Americans), or perhaps immigrants, or Mexican restaurants. When I mentioned to a law school employee once that I had been born and raised in the East Los Angeles area, his reaction was closer to that of the game-show contestants, as he retorted mockingly that he had better watch his back around me because I must be treacherous to have survived there.

A mock school examination that has circulated for years, now as e-mail humor, is styled as "The East Los Angeles High School Math Proficiency Exam." Among the "questions" in this knock off of what has been circulated as the "South Central High School Exam," targeting Blacks, are:

1. Little Johnny has an AK 47 with a 30 round clip. He usually misses 6 out of every 10 shots and he uses 13 rounds per drive-by shooting. How many drive-by shootings can Little Johnny attempt before he has to reload?
2. Jose has 2 ounces of cocaine. If he sells an 8 ball to Antonio for $320 and 2 grams to Juan for $85 per gram, what is the street value of the rest of his hold? . . .
7. If an average can of spray paint covers 22 square feet and the average letter is 3 square feet, how many letters can be sprayed with 3 eight ounce cans of spray paint with 20% paint free?
8. Hector knocked up 3 girls in the gang. There are 27 girls in his gang. What is the exact percentage of girls Hector knocked up?

Gang portrayals in media extend beyond Mexican Americans in East Los Angeles. Set in Miami, the film *The Substitute* (1996) depicted a Cuban high school gang, the "Kings of Destruction," whose leader, Juan, was handy with a switchblade. Cinematic portrayals of Puerto Ricans are rife with depictions of junkies (*Piñero* [2001] and *Fort Apache, The Bronx* [1981]), criminals (*Badge 373* [1973]), and drug dealers (*Carlito's Way* [1993]), but the most defining image is of Puerto Rican gangs.[23] In *Young Savages* (1961), a fifteen-year-old blind Puerto Rican, killed by members of the Italian American gang the Thunderbirds, is revealed in the murder investigation to have been the "top warlord" for the rival Puerto Rican gang the Horsemen, as well as a "pickup man" for his sixteen-year-old sister, a prostitute since age fourteen. The classic film *West Side Story* (1961) pitted the Italian-Irish-Polish Jets against the Puerto Rican Sharks, a gang whose members "keep coming like cockroaches." Both gangs were ready to rumble for their Manhattan turf with "skin" (fists), "zip guns," or "blades."[24] Both these Puerto Rican gang films had been preceded by a sensationalized killing that prompted New York City tabloids to spotlight Puerto Rican gangs. In 1959, Salvador Agron, while wearing a cape, together with several other gang members, stabbed to death two White teens in a New York City playground, mistaking them for rival Irish gang members. Although sentenced to death by electric chair, Agron's death sentence was commuted by then-governor Nelson Rockefeller, and ultimately he was paroled from prison twenty years later. Agron's life story was dramatized in Paul Simon's Broadway musical flop *The Capeman,* which included Marc Anthony and Ruben Blades as performers.[25]

As compared with Anglos, Latinas/os are disproportionately members of gangs. A 1995 study concluded that Latina/o children were almost three times as likely as Anglos to report the presence of "many gangs" at their schools.[26] Gang membership is not limited to Latino males—about 3 percent of Latinas are also involved with gangs.[27] A 1997 study found that five out of one hundred Latinos aged twelve to sixteen (compared with 2 percent of Whites) and two out of one hundred Latinas aged twelve to sixteen had belonged to a gang in the last year.[28] Although a matter of concern among Latinas/os, the number of Latinas/os participating in gangs is neither overwhelming nor defining of a people. Yet some Anglo sociologists have contended that Latina/o gang behavior stems from Latina/o culture, particularly the influences of machismo on Latino youth.[29] Other experts have correctly identified as determining factors the poverty and un-/underemployment facing many Latinas/os in the inner cities, as well as the cultural ostracization and discrimination Latina/o youth experience.

Media tend to spotlight gangs and their supposed resurgence during any economic recession. Perhaps gangs serve as a handy clarion call to arms against the Latina/o community in times of economic strife, generating public hysteria and justifying enhanced border security and local policing measures. Taking its cue from the latest economic recession, in fall 2001, an MTV special, *Breaking It Down with Serena,* trailed Latina/o gangs in Los Angeles. *Time* magazine declared in September 2001 that "L.A. Gangs Are Back."[30] Focusing on Latina/o gangs too, the *Time* article explained that although gang-related property crimes have declined in recent years, certain violent crimes attributed to gang members, such as gang murders, felonious assaults, and attacks on police officers, have increased—statistics the new mayor of Los Angeles, James Hahn, called a "disturbing trend" that would be his top priority. Given the link between poverty and gang membership, a strong likelihood exists that recession increases hopelessness and aggravates the root causes of gang association.

Gangs, though, have long been active in East Los Angeles. They are not "back"—they never left. I remember well the specter of gangs while growing up in East Los Angeles. But since these gangs tended to leave non–gang members alone, I never had an actual encounter with gangs in my neighborhood, despite having lived for several years in what I refer to now as project housing. When my Mexican American stepfather suffered a fatal heart attack, I moved with my mother, also Mexican American, to eastern Oregon at age fourteen to join her brother's family in an otherwise Anglo town. There I experienced my first violent attacks by schoolyard bullies "welcoming" me as a Californian and as a member of one of only three or four Latina/o families in the area. Further, one afternoon in my high school freshman wood-shop class, the Anglo students all prepared weapons—bats, sticks, and other wooden implements—in anticipation of a "rumble" at a parking lot that evening. I chose not to attend what would have been my first witnessed gang warfare—in the streets of an Anglo "feed and seed" town far from the supposed "mean streets" of my barrio youth.

Although some observers view membership in Latina/o gangs as stemming from Latina/o biology or culture, Anglos are not regarded in such terms; they tend to be judged on their individual merits. This mind-set encompasses such notorious Anglo gangs in modern history as the motorcycle gangs of northern California. In spring 2002, Hell's Angels bikers clashed with rival bikers in a melee at Harrah's casino in Laughlin, Nevada, leaving three bikers dead and a dozen shot or stabbed. Few observers regard the Hell's Angels as signaling some character flaw of Anglos generally, or as being representative of Anglos. Instead, the biker-gangsters are dismissed as wayward youth, as disturbed adults, or perhaps as under the influence of dangerous drugs.

Related to the perception of Latinas/os as gang members is the media-fueled image of a mob mentality among Latina/o groups. For Mexicans, the print media portrayed the Zoot Suit Riots as violent group chaos. Puerto Ricans, too, have been depicted in this manner. A 1998 episode of the hit television comedy *Seinfeld* found the mercurial Kramer accidentally setting fire to the Puerto Rican flag during the annual Puerto Rican Day parade and stomping on it to extinguish the flames. When a group of incensed Puerto Ricans retaliated by vandalizing his friend Jerry's car, Kramer remarked, "It's like this every day in Puerto Rico."[31] Cuban Americans in Miami came to the fore of the mob-mentality image in the news and television coverage of the Elian Gonzalez custody battle. Media described the Miami demonstrators as a "deranged mob," "the Miami mob scene," or as "anti-Castro fanatics."[32] Earlier, in the 1980s, mass rioting by Cuban Mariel boat-lift detainees in federal prisons and detention centers contributed to this perception.[33] Films such as *Havana* (1990) and *Godfather II* (1974) depicted pro-Castro revolutionaries similarly, as an unruly mob looting in the streets of Cuba.[34]

Latinas/os are seen, too, as hot-blooded and foul-tempered. Thus, in society's perception, their criminal behavior may stem not merely from their supposed livelihoods of thievery but from their violent responses to everyday situations. In the film *Bordertown* (1935), Anglo actor Paul Muni played the fictional Johnny Ramírez, a Latino who struggled against poverty in Los Angeles toward his dream of becoming a Supreme Court justice. In his first trial following his graduation from night law school, Ramírez's hot Latin temper surfaced and he physically attacked his opposing and more skilled Anglo counsel. Stripped of his license to practice law, Ramírez drifted south of the border, where he was to encounter Bette Davis for the film's main events. *I Love Lucy*'s Ricky Ricardo also was foul-tempered—in one series episode, he lost his cool and broke everything in the room.[35] In another, wife Lucy remarked to friend Ethel about Ricky, "You know how wild those Cubans get when they get mad!"[36]

Latinas/os are portrayed routinely in film and other media as quick to kill any romantic challenger. In the film *The Mexican* (2001), Brad Pitt went to Mexico to retrieve a pistol known as the "Mexican." This legendary pistol had been crafted for a nobleman's son as a wedding present. When the son realized that his bride-to-be loved the gunsmith's poor, simple assistant, a man "far less than he," the enraged son shot the assistant. Similarly, a tequila-swilling Latino *vato loco* told Pauly Shore in the comedy *Encino Man* (1992), "If I see any man looking at my *muchacha* [girlfriend], that man will no longer be recognizable as a man!"[37] In the opening scene of *The Mambo Kings* (1992), a Cuban nightclub owner cuts a man's throat after the man defended his brother's still-smoldering torch for the owner's new wife. Hot-blooded Latinas/os populated Barry Manilow's disco anthem "Copacabana," a famous Latin nightclub where music and passion are always in fashion. Here, showgirl and Spanish dancer Lola and her lover, bartender Tony, both worked until diamond-tinted Rico entered their lives. Rico's overtures toward Lola prompted a fistfight with Tony that Rico ended with a single gunshot, leaving Lola alone to drink herself half-blind. Whether in New York's Copacabana, the urban barrio of East Los Angeles, or the rural farm labor camp, the typical night of Latina/o passion in the American imagination invariably leaves someone fallen by gun or switchblade.

The social construction of Latinas/os as hot-tempered is evident. A 1990 national poll revealed that half of Whites regarded Hispanics as more likely than Whites to be violence prone.[38] In 1986, Senator Jesse Helms remarked, "All Latins are volatile people." Explaining the actions of his pitcher Armando Benitez in hitting a batter, Baltimore Orioles general manager Pat Gillick suggested in 1998 that Benitez comes from a different culture—"Latin American people can be quite emotional and become quickly frustrated. I think Latin American people have a different temperament than people in North America."[39]

The most unifying stereotype among Latina/o groups today might be their construction as drug dealers or drug users. The television series *Miami Vice* showcased a parade of Central and South American drug lord characters, whether Colombian, Nicaraguan, Cuban, Bolivian, or Peruvian.[40] Motion pictures have tapped into this ethnically diverse pool of Latino drug lord images as well. *Traffic* (2000) and *Tequila Sunrise* (1988) centered on Mexico, Cheech and Chong's *Up in Smoke* (1979) and *Nice Dreams* (1981) on Mexican Americans, while *Scarface* (1983) featured a Cuban cocaine dealer, as did *The Substitute* (1996), which depicted a violent gang of BMW-driving Cuban American high school students supplying their classmates with cocaine. *Carlito's Way* (1993) cast Anglo Al Pacino as the fictional Puerto Rican Carlito Brigante, a former murderous heroin dealer. In *Empire* (2002), John Leguizamo was a Puerto Rican drug dealer trying to parlay his blood money from the Bronx into a Wall Street fortune. *Above the Law* (1988) featured a Salvadoran dealer, the "biggest" in the city, while the remake of *Shaft* (2000) included a Dominican dealer (played by an African American actor) who declares, "In this neighborhood, I am the motherfucking king snake. I go like this [points] . . . three people die." Colombian cocaine dealers took the spotlight in *Blow* (2001), *Crocodile Dundee II* (1988), *Delta Force 2: The Columbian Connection* (1990), and *Let's Get Harry* (1987), as well as the comedy *Bedazzled* (2000). In this last remake, actor Brendan Fraser receives seven wishes from the devil, Elizabeth Hurley, in exchange for his soul. His initial ill-fated wish is to be "very rich and very powerful." All seems well at first when the Anglo Brendan is transplanted as the lord of an immense South American estate who speaks fluent Spanish. Soon enough, though, he realizes, to his horror, "I'm a Colombian drug lord. A rich and powerful Colombian drug lord." The film's DVD packaging captions this sequence as "Rich, Powerful & . . . Spanish?" suggesting that the only means for Latinas/os to acquire wealth and power are illicit ones. Indeed, the overwhelming media portrayal of Colombia is as a haven for drug lords and drug production. Illustrating the association of drugs with all things Colombian: in 2001, White rapper/singer Kid Rock introduced singing sensation Shakira on MTV as "Colombia's other mood-altering export."[41] That same year, *Late Show* television host David Letterman joked about beauty pageant talent competitions becoming more impressive: "For example, Miss Colombia, she swallowed 50 balloons full of heroin."[42] Media's Latina/o drug dealers also find their identity and haven in fictional countries—in *License to Kill* (1989), for example, James Bond brought down a Latino drug cartel that had built a cocaine empire from "Chile to Alaska"; the nationality of these Latinos was never established, since the film was set in the fictional south-of-the-border location of Isthmus City.

Media have long centered their portrayals of drug dealers and smugglers in south-of-the-border locations in Mexico (most recently, NBC's 2003 miniseries *Kingpin*) as well as in Latina/o communities in the United States. Media's Latina/o drug dealers have operated from Miami (*Scarface*, 1983); Los Angeles (*8 Million Ways to Die*, 1985; *Mi Vida Loca*, 1994, including Latina dealers); New York City (*Empire*, 2002; *Carlito's Way*, 1993; *Fort Apache, The Bronx*, 1981); and Chicago (*Running Scared*, 1986, with "the first Spanish Godfather of Chicago" dealing cocaine), as well as from within penitentiaries (*American Me*, 1992). As early as 1923's *Quicksand*, Hollywood depicted the smuggling of narcotics across the Mexican border into the United States. The 1950 film *Borderline* sent Fred MacMurray as a federal agent to Mexico to confront peddlers of hashish and heroin there.

Not limited to motion pictures, the connection between Latinas/os and the dealing of drugs was made in the music video and lyrics of the 1989 hit song "Dr. Feelgood" (here the "Mexican mob" trafficking "candy-caine") by the notorious Anglo rockers Mötley Crüe, who allegedly knew their own way around the wide world of drugs.

The media's Latino drug dealer occasionally has a good heart. In *Romancing the Stone* (1984), a *simpático* Colombian dealer helped Michael Douglas and Kathleen Turner escape the military police in his little "mule" (a bulletproof truck) once he realized that Turner was an American romance novelist he and his men treasured. "Cheech" Marin played a drug dealer for laughs. In *Nice Dreams* (1981), for example, Cheech and his comic partner Tommy "Chong" dispensed marijuana "push-ups" from their California ice-cream truck, with Cheech lecturing the hapless Chong on the mores of drug dealing—"don't take a check!" On the Fox television sitcom *That 70's Show*, Fez, a Latino cast member, appeared in a dream sequence as a drug dealer smuggling marijuana "fresh from whatever the hell country I am from."[43]

Yet media's characteristic Latino drug dealer shares the ruthless heart of the Hollywood *bandido*. The film *Blow* (2001) typifies the subhuman depictions of Latino drug dealers. Based loosely on a true story, *Blow* focuses on the Anglo who fronted the U.S. cocaine distribution network for Colombian "drug lord" Pablo Escobar. Played by Johnny Depp, this Anglo character is portrayed from his youth through his eventual imprisonment as an intensely loving family man in his relationships with his father and daughter. By contrast, Pablo Escobar is introduced in a scene in which he shakes a man's hand as last rites before one of Escobar's cohorts shoots him in the head, presumably for some violation of the code among drug dealers. All the Colombian characters in the film, including Depp's wife, are portrayed as treacherous and double-crossers. Similar to *Blow*, in *Crocodile Dundee II* (1988), the Colombian drug dealer Louis Rico is introduced when he kills a bound man placed before him on his knees. In the next scene, Rico's men kill the Anglo photographer who witnessed the murder. Later, Rico kidnaps Crocodile Dundee's girlfriend, the ex-wife of the slain photographer. Rejecting Rico's efforts to impress her with his wealth, she tells her kidnapper, "You're a drug dealer—a grubby little parasite," prompting his cruel response that it is "not wise to annoy me. [Your ex-husband did] and I had his head blown off like that." In *Tequila Sunrise* (1988), the late Raul Julia played a murderous Mexican cocaine dealer who tried to rekindle his friendship with his former cohort, played by Mel Gibson, by plying Gibson with marijuana, cocaine, and tequila while Julia watched televised bullfighting from his yacht. Believing Gibson's lover (Michelle Pfeiffer) to be an informant, Julia showed his tender side: "Don't worry buddy, I won't kill her unless you approve." Yet another example of the ruthless Latino drug dealer comes from the Chuck Norris revenge vehicle *Delta Force 2* (1990), where the murderous Ramon Cota, the "world's wealthiest drug dealer," stabs one of his cocaine harvesters, then rapes the worker's wife, orders her baby killed, and uses the baby's body to smuggle cocaine. Cota murders by gun, switchblade, poisonous gas, and, finally, a machete to the heart of the widow he had raped earlier, pulling her to him and kissing her on the lips while she dies. In the most recent example of heinous media drug dealers, one of the Latino characters from NBC's 2003 miniseries *Kingpin* tortured a captive law enforcement official with a blowtorch to the face.

Print media's account of the "real" Latino drug dealer has introduced such terminology as the "Colombian necktie," in which Latino drug dealers cut an informant's throat below his chin, then pull his tongue through the bloody wound as he dies. A 2001 *Time* magazine account of United States–Mexico border life and relations included an extensive discussion of a "bloodthirsty" cartel led by two Mexican brothers it described as the "border's worst bad guys." The account suggested that one of the brothers often rises in the morning and announces, "I feel like killing somebody today." The cartel's ruthless trademarks reportedly go beyond the Colombian necktie to include suffocating rivals with a clear plastic bag placed over their heads while "El Gordo" (the fat man) bounces on their chests. According to *Time*'s account, one brother's favorite ritual is that of *carne asada* (roasted meat), in which he slaughters whole families and then tosses their bodies on a bed of flaming tires as he and his henchmen celebrate with tequila and cocaine.[44]

U.S. drug enforcement efforts have mirrored the media in their focus on Latino (and Black) dealers and on inner-city users, largely to the exclusion of suburban Anglo users. The emphasis on Latino dealers both within and outside the United States overlooks the fact that the largest cash crop from California and Hawai'i is marijuana, which is produced there primarily by Anglos in amounts that surpass that exported from Mexico. Heroin typically comes from Afghanistan, Burma, Thailand, Laos, and other non-Latino countries. Methamphetamine is a predominantly North American product; the designer drug Ecstasy originates in the Netherlands and the United States. (Ironically, a Mexico City youth in the teen sex comedy *Y Tu Mamá También* [2002] boasts of acquiring Ecstasy imported from San Francisco.) At a Washington State methamphetamine conference in August 2001, Asa Hutchinson, head of the federal Drug Enforcement Administration, remarked, "We can't blame methamphetamine on our neighbors across the border," implying that the U.S. drug problem, aside from "meth," can be attributed to Latinas/os.[45] Mexico's president Vincente Fox has criticized U.S. authorities' and commentators' view of Mexico as a corrupt haven for drug smugglers, demanding that the United States take responsibility for its drug use as a nation.[46] One commentator decried the placing of blame on Mexico, concluding:

> The characters change from time to time, but the coca leaf still only grows in Colombia, Peru, and Bolivia; the heroin still comes from Asia and the Middle East and the best marijuana still comes from Northern California and Hawaii. And, the dollars that pay for them still come from suburban, White middle-class America.[47]

The enforcement emphasis on inner-city users targets Latinas/os and Blacks but ignores the suburban Anglo drug problem. Indeed, overall drug use among Anglo, Black, and Latina/o groups differs little. A 1992 U.S. Public Health Service study estimated that 76 percent of illicit drug users were White, 14 percent were Black, and 8 percent Hispanic, figures that roughly corresponded to population percentages at the time.[48] In 1995, a U.S. Department of Health and Human Services survey concluded that rates of drug use among White, Black, and Hispanic youth were about the same.[49] Researchers at the Harvard School of Public Health, studying marijuana use among college students, concluded use had risen 22 percent from 1993 to 1999. Yet, although marijuana usage had increased for nearly all student demographic subgroups, it had not increased for Hispanic students.[50] Moreover, the study confirmed that marijuana users tend to be single and White, which would reflect the dominant composition of college campuses. A 1997 study of American youth aged twelve to sixteen found that marijuana use of Latinos (9 percent) and Latinas (9 percent) in a thirty-day period was roughly the same as rates for White boys (10 percent) and girls (9 percent).[51] In Mexico, overall drug use, although increasing, is much lower than the rate among Americans in the United States. According to United Nations estimates, fewer than five out of one thousand Mexican citizens use illicit drugs, as compared with sixty out of one thousand Americans.[52] Yet drug enforcement policies view Mexican and Mexican American users and dealers, as well as Blacks and other Latinas/os, as their target. Black users are faced with enforcement policies that prioritize crack cocaine usage in the inner city over powder cocaine usage by Anglo addicts in the suburbs and Ecstasy usage by Anglo youth. Latinas/os are targeted by policies that focus on Latina/o dealers of marijuana and cocaine over the typical Anglo user.

A shift in enforcement emphasis from users to dealers paralleled the spread of marijuana use among the Anglo middle and upper class in the 1960s and 1970s. Rather than imprison these Anglos, states reduced penalties for marijuana consumption, at the same time that drug policing efforts began to target dealers and to leave users alone, at least in the suburbs and on college campuses.[53]

The most prominent movie to confront America's drug problem, *Traffic* (2000), predictably lays blame on dealers rather than on users. Although *Traffic* acknowledged drug use by White upper-class suburban youth, a pivotal scene made clear that White users deserve our sympathy and treatment-oriented options, while dealers of color deserve our scorn. In that scene, an upper-class yet addicted White girl lay underneath her dealer, a Black man, as he had sex with her in his decrepit room. This Black/White dichotomy had the effect of vilifying dealers, by portraying them as savaging White girls, and of garnering sympathy for the tragic illness of addiction that would cause a White girl to sell her body to a Black man for poison. I have wondered whether audiences would react the same way if the woman addict were a Latina. Would the audience remain shocked at how someone could sink so low as to offer her body in exchange for drugs? Or would the message lose its force because Latinas might be seen as naturally inclined toward drug use[54] or toward engaging in casual sex or even sex for trade? How do Americans regard Noelle Bush's addiction to prescription drugs? Do they implicate her ethnicity (assuming they are aware that Governor Jeb Bush's daughter is Latina)?

As a presidential candidate, Richard Nixon announced that he would wage a "war" on drugs; later he deployed customs agents at the Mexican border as part of "Operation Intercept" to curtail drug smuggling. In 1986, President Ronald Reagan issued a security directive classifying drugs, for the first time, as a national security threat.[55] Following the September 11, 2001, terrorist attacks, drug-producing and drug-smuggling operations have come to be viewed as terrorist enterprises. In February 2002, the Office of National Drug Control Policy announced its initiative to educate Americans on the link between illicit drugs and international terrorism. Pursuant to this campaign, two commercials debuted during the 2002 Super Bowl, warning drug users that they were financing terrorists. According to Congressman Mark Souder (R–IL), "Americans who buy and sell illegal narcotics are lending a helping hand to people like those who attacked America on September 11."[56]

To justify military intervention and policing measures in the national and international war on drugs, government officials now need only point to the funding of al-Qaeda terrorist campaigns with proceeds from heroin produced in Afghanistan, a world leader in opium production. But Latinas/os in Texas remember the tragic consequences of militarizing anti-drug efforts, especially when they entail placing military troops along the U.S.-Mexico border. In May 1997, a camouflaged squad of U.S. Marines patrolling near the Rio Grande on an anti-drug assignment shot and killed teenager Ezequiel Hernandez, who was tending goats on horseback as part of a church project. Hernandez, who hoped to become a park ranger, carried an old pump-action .22 rifle to fend off rattlesnakes and predators. Although the marines claimed that Hernandez fired at them and they acted in self-defense, he was shot in the side, an angle inconsistent with this account. More chilling still, while the marines waited twenty-two minutes before rendering first aid or calling for emergency help, young Hernandez bled to death.[57] The marine who fired the fatal shot was investigated by a local grand jury and by the Justice Department but not charged; a lawsuit by Hernandez's family resulted in a substantial settlement from the federal government. As a consequence of the shooting, then–defense secretary William Cohen ordered the disarming of all federal troops engaged in anti-drug missions at the border. Though it may be forgotten in the haste to fight terrorism, Hernandez's death provides "smoking gun" evidence of the folly of militarizing the Mexican border.

Just as many Arab Americans have come to be regarded as terrorists because of their ethnicity and national origin, the association of Latinas/os with drugs may produce a similar conception of Latinas/os as a security and terrorist threat. Apart from the media's and the public's association of Latinas/os with drugs, the history of struggle for Puerto Rican self-determination presents the possibility for constructing Puerto Ricans as terrorists. Particularly in the 1950s, and again in the 1970s and early 1980s, media coverage of violence in the United States by pro-independence supporters prompted stereotypes of Puerto Ricans as revolutionary-minded and terroristic. Among the notorious incidents was the attempted assassination of President Harry Truman in 1950 by Oscar Collazo and Griselio Torresola, two activists in the Puerto Rican Nationalist Party, which was seeking independence from U.S. colonialism. While attempting to enter Blair House in Washington, D.C., where President Truman was staying, Collazo and Torresola killed one White House guard and wounded two others. Guards killed Torresola and injured Collazo. Truman ultimately commuted Collazo's death sentence to one of life imprisonment, and President Jimmy Carter freed him in 1979.

In 1954, four Puerto Rican nationalists entered the public gallery overlooking the floor of the U.S. House of Representatives. One of them, Dolores "Lolita" Lebrón, shouted "Free Puerto Rico" and, with her companions, began shooting onto the House floor. Together, they wounded five congressmen before being overpowered. They were sentenced to fifty years imprisonment. Also charged and convicted were several Puerto Ricans alleged to have engaged in seditious conspiracy in planning the attack.[58]

In the 1970s, the Puerto Rican nationalist group FALN (Fuerzas Armadas de Liberación Nacional, or Armed Forces of National Liberation) claimed credit for several bombings in Chicago, New York, and Puerto Rico, including the so-called Fraunces Tavern bombing, which killed four people and injured over fifty in a historic New York tavern.[59] Those convicted for the bombing campaign ultimately were given clemency by President Bill Clinton in 1999. The film *Badge 373* (1973) offered Hollywood's fictional conception of Puerto Rican revolutionaries as murderous gangsters purchasing $3 million in stolen machine guns as part of a "Million Guns for Puerto Rico" plot toward independence. At an activist rally detailing this fictional stockpiling, one pro-independence speaker declared, "We'll do whatever is necessary to free our island from the shackles of American imperialism," including "shooting our way" to freedom.

While acknowledging the gravity of the real-life violence from the 1950s through the 1970s, what went unpublicized was the counterrecord of political violence and persecution carried out against pro-independence activists in Puerto Rico by Puerto Rican authorities and U.S. intelligence agencies such as the FBI. Indeed, from 1948 until 1957, Puerto Rican law criminalized the mere advocacy of independence.[60] These long-running government efforts to sabotage the nationalist movement, highlighted by the bloody Ponce Massacre in 1937, have been well documented by Pedro Malavet.[61]

In addition to their societal association with drug trafficking, Mexican Americans have been linked to terrorism by at least two other avenues—a revision of their long-standing *bandido* construction and their supposed affinity with the villainized image of suicide bombers that has come to define America's view of Palestinians. Within days after September 11, some media began to suggest the parallels between the hunt launched in Afghanistan for Osama bin Laden and the major military mission initiated in 1916 to hunt Mexican general Francisco "Pancho" Villa in northern Mexico. A former ally of the United States, as was bin Laden, Villa attacked a New Mexico town in early 1916, killing seventeen Americans[62] while stealing horses and guns. (The Mexican government later compensated the families of the victims.) Villa's motivation for the raid remains unclear. Most suggest that a change in U.S. policy, which once supported Villa's endeavors in Mexico with guns and arms, led him to attack the town that had formerly supplied him with weapons. A few even suggest that the U.S. government orchestrated the raid by payment to Villa, hoping to spark a patriotic reaction and military enlistment toward American participation in World War I. Whatever the raid's motivation, President Woodrow Wilson responded by mobilizing as many as 150,000 troops and sending battalions into Mexico with horses, tanks, trucks, and open-cockpit planes, in a failed effort to find Villa in the hill country of Chihuahua, Mexico.

Post–September 11 comparisons between Villa and bin Laden were drawn not merely for the similarities between unfruitful searches by American military but also for the "terrorist" identity of both men. For example, a relative of one of the dead in New Mexico suggested that although Villa was once considered a bandit, "[b]y today's terms, he was a terrorist."[63] Hollywood and other media have already succeeded in transforming the *bandido* image to that of the urban gangbanger. Now, after September 11, the *bandido* is being reenvisioned as a terrorist. Indeed, even the image of the urban Latina/o gangbanger has taken on terroristic dimensions in the media, following the arrest in 2002 of Puerto Rican Abdullah al Muhajir, formerly José Padilla, once a gang member in Chicago, who has been held in military prison without charges and deprived of counsel as an "enemy combatant" while being interrogated for his role in planning a potential "dirty bomb" attack.[64] A former FBI deputy director of counterterrorism made the leaps from Latina/o ethnicity to Latina/o gang membership to terrorism seem like baby steps in contending, "If you look at Padilla's background—Puerto Rican, gang member, time in prison, a convert to Islam—what you see is a potential resource for al-Qaeda."[65]

In the 1970s, the Brown Berets, a paramilitary group of Chicanas and Chicanos dressed in army fatigues and brown berets, modeled after the Black Panthers, helped create a stereotype of Chicanas/os as violent activists.[66] Today, some American vigilantes frustrated with the government's inability to bring bin Laden to justice have resurrected this image of the violent Chicana/o to construct Mexican Americans and other Latinas/os as a more accessible terrorist enemy on American soil. College campus MEChA (Movimiento Estudiantil Chicano de Aztlán) organizations, comprised mostly of Chicana/o students but also of other Latinas/os, have been targeted by hate speech that compares their organizations to al-Qaeda. Ostensibly, these vigilantes point to the supposed campaign by MEChA organizations to liberate the Southwest from the United States and return it to Mexico, as reflected in "El Plan Espiritual de Aztlán" from 1969, an activist Chicana/o manifesto that provides in part:

> In the spirit of a new people that is conscious not only of the proud historical heritage but also of the brutal "gringo" invasion of our territories, we, the Chicano inhabitants and civilizers of the northern land of Aztlán from whence came our forefathers, reclaiming the land of their birth and consecrating the determination of our people of the sun, declare that the call of our blood is our power, our responsibility, and our inevitable destiny. . . . Brotherhood unites us, and love for our brothers makes us a people whose time has come and who struggles against the foreigner "gabacho" who exploits our riches and destroys our culture.[67]

A hate e-mail sent to a West Coast campus MEChA organization quoted part of this "Plan de Aztlán" in contending that MEChA is a "terrorist organization" of "evil terrorists . . . no better than Osama Bin Laden" seeking to "destroy the country." In April 2002, I was interviewed by a conservative radio talk-show host in Portland, Oregon, who strove to construct Chicana/o college students as terrorist operatives. He drew a connection between struggles of Palestinians for land and nationhood in the West Bank and a supposed Chicana/o mission to reclaim Aztlán, enabling him to transfer his construction of all Palestinians as suicide bombers to Chicanas/os and other Latinas/os by asking me the absurd question: "When will the suicide bombings start in Aztlán?"

Latinas/os are arrested and convicted for crimes at rates disproportionate to their percentage of the population and to the arrest/conviction rate for Anglos. Nationally, about 16 percent of the state prison population is Latina/o, and about half the inmates, a far greater disproportion, are African American.[68] A comprehensive national report released by Human

Rights Watch in 2002 found ten states in which Latino men are incarcerated at rates between five and nine times greater than White men, and eight states in which Latinas are imprisoned at rates between four and seven times greater than White women. In only two states, Delaware and Maryland, are Latinas/os imprisoned at rates below those for Whites.[69] In California, Latinas/os comprise 32.4 percent of the state's residents and 36.1 percent of its incarcerated population. In New York, Latinas/os represent 15.1 percent of the state's residents and 26.7 percent of the state's prison population.[70] Federal prison statistics from 1991 counted 28 percent of federal inmates as Hispanic, compared with 17 percent of state prisoners at the time. The difference is due largely to the federal enforcement emphasis on drugs—58 percent of all federal inmates were imprisoned for drug offenses, compared with only 21 percent of state inmates.[71]

Although some may point to these statistics as evidence of an inherent criminal character of Latinas/os, the statistics are misleading. First, much crime stems from poverty, and Latinas/os are overrepresented in the ranks of the poor. A Massachusetts study determined that poverty, rather than race, is the most important factor behind crime.[72] Latinas/os, as well as Blacks, suffer a poverty rate far exceeding that for Anglos—in 1999, the Latina/o poverty rate was 22.8 percent and the Black rate 23.6 percent, while the rate for non-Hispanic Whites was only 7.7 percent. Second, Latinas/os are disproportionately young and are overrepresented in the age group of twenty- to twenty-nine-year-olds that tends to commit the majority of all crimes. Moreover, discretion exercised at every stage of the criminal justice system has worked against Latinas/os. Police officers target Latinas/os for traffic and other stops, leading to questioning and the search for criminal activity. Prosecutorial discretion can work against Latinas/os in the decision whether to prosecute following an arrest and in the nature of the plea bargain offered the defendant. Prejudice can sway juries and also influence the sentencing of defendants. More comprehensive exercises of discretion can also imperil Latinas/os. For example, a local police force can choose to deploy more resources in areas with substantial Latina/o populations or to target a criminal offense that will result in a higher percentage of Latinas/os being arrested (such as emphasizing tagging and other gang-related crimes). Legislative discretion may even come into play in the decision to criminalize certain activity, such as gang association or loitering, that disproportionately affects impoverished Latinas/os.

Latinas/os fare worse than Anglos in every stage of the American criminal justice system—from their initial encounter with law enforcement officials to their sentencing. Perceptions of Latinas/os as criminals help explain the practice of racial profiling, in which law enforcement officers target Latinas/os (and Blacks) for traffic stops and other interrogatory encounters. This phenomenon, known in the Black community as DWB, "Driving While Black," is referred to by Latinas/os as DWH or DWL, "Driving While Hispanic/Latina/o." Asian Americans have also confronted racial profiling, most dramatically when Japanese were interned during World War II, as have Arab Americans, profiled as terrorists. In the case of Latinas/os, racial profiling for traffic stops tends to be based on such physical appearance markers as the skin color of the vehicle's occupants. Thus, while I can often pass for White as a White/Brown man, my Latina/o friends who are darker in appearance confront profiling on a regular basis, ranging from recurrent "once-over" stares from officers to intrusive traffic stops. Indeed, some police officers have been trained overtly by their superiors to racially profile Latinas/os. For example, the Louisiana State Police Department once used a training film that exhorted officers enforcing drug laws to make traffic stops on the basis of skin color. It instructed officers attempting to interdict drug couriers to seek out "males of foreign nationalities, mainly Cubans, Colombians, Puerto Ricans or other swarthy outlanders."[73] Additionally, the film suggested the officers ask themselves whether the person "fits the car," implying that a person of color in an expensive car is suspicious.

Latinas/os have been profiled in the "war on drugs" (along with African Americans) on the assumption that they are more likely than Anglos to be engaged in illicit drug-related activity. Statistics point to drug enforcement's reliance on profiling based on race and ethnicity. The U.S. Customs Service, which searches airport travelers suspected of drug possession or trafficking, disproportionately targets Black and Latina/o travelers—they comprised 43 percent of those travelers searched in 1998. Yet the actual "hit rates" for finding contraband were much lower for Latinas/os searched than for travelers of another race or ethnicity—in 1998, 6.7 percent of Whites, 6.3 percent of Blacks, and 2.8 percent of Latinas/os searched had contraband.[74]

Subsequent to initial interrogatory traffic stops, Latinas/os are subjected to more frequent searches for criminal activity than are Anglos. A study by the Texas Department of Public Safety concluded that Hispanic motorists (as well as Blacks), once stopped, were twice as likely to be searched by state troopers than were White motorists. The findings revealed that one in thirty-eight White drivers stopped were searched; by comparison, one in eighteen Hispanics and one in nineteen Blacks were searched.[75] These practices are part of the vicious cycle affecting Latinas/os—as the subjects of more frequent stops, they are more likely to be searched; when subject to more frequent searches, more criminal activity is likely to be discovered. Thus, more Latinas/os tend to be arrested and processed through all stages of the criminal justice system, not because they are more prone than Anglos to engage in criminal conduct but because they undergo heightened scrutiny of their behavior. These escalated encounters with the criminal justice system contribute to the reputation of Latinas/os as criminally inclined and thus increase the likelihood of initial interrogatory stops by officers hoping to uncover criminal activity.

Racial profiling by law enforcement officials has even spread to the private sector, with private security officers in some stores employing racial profiling aimed at Blacks and Latinas/os to detect shoplifters and gang members, and with amusement-park security forces, most prominently in California, using racially constructed gang membership profiles to exclude Blacks and Latinas/os. Lawsuits stemming from alleged racial profiling have been brought against the Great America amusement park in Santa Clara and Six Flags Magic Mountain park in Valencia, California. One such lawsuit, filed in 1988 by a Latino against Magic Mountain, contended that the park had a policy

> refusing admission to their business establishment to anyone purportedly suspected of being a gang member, and that these suspicions are based solely upon improper racial and ethnic stereotyping, and upon the clothing, physical appearance, race and/or national origin of individuals seeking entrance to the business establishment and that this policy is not based on any reasonable criteria, including unlawful conduct or acts inconsistent with the proper use and enjoyment of an amusement park.[76]

The current legal standards applicable to racial profiling by government do not sufficiently discourage these law enforcement practices—enough leeway resides in present law to disguise profiling or, in some circumstances, to rely explicitly on racial and ethnic profiles to justify interrogatory stops. Consider the scenario in which it is assumed (for sake of argument) that a law enforcement officer regards Latinas/os as more likely than another ethnic group to embrace criminal activity. Given the variety and indeterminacy of vehicle equipment codes and traffic laws (for example, I've been pulled over for "weaving"), one can assume that law enforcement officials daily witness countless potential violations they choose to overlook. Who hasn't sped past (or even driven next to) an officer while exceeding the speed limit by an amount below whatever discretionary threshold the officer is using to trigger a traffic stop, thereby avoiding interrogation? But assume that our hypothetical officer is eyeing Latina/o drivers and observes a violation. If that officer pulls over the Latina/o, the stop might thereby trigger legitimate further investigation— say, for example, if the officer were to observe evidence of criminal activity. In judging the legality of the stop, does it matter that the officer was motivated by his or her belief that the Latina/o occupants were more likely than Anglos to be engaged in criminal activity that the stop might uncover? Under current Supreme Court authority, it does not. The decision of *Whren v. United States*[77] considered and rejected a challenge to the constitutionality of a traffic stop on this basis. In *Whren,* officers patrolling a "high drug area" in the District of Columbia observed a truck with two Black occupants waiting at a stop sign for an unusually long time. The driver was looking into his passenger's lap. After the unmarked police car made a U-turn toward the truck, the truck turned without signaling and began traveling at an "unreasonable speed." While the truck was stopped at a traffic light down the road, one of the officers approached on foot and observed two large plastic bags of crack cocaine in the passenger's hands. Both occupants were arrested. Under the Fourth Amendment guarantee of protection against unreasonable searches and seizures, in order to make a traffic stop, police must possess probable cause to believe a traffic violation has occurred. Here, the officers had probable cause to believe that one or more traffic code provisions had been violated. The defendants argued, however, that the gauntlet of traffic laws is so staggering that it creates the potential for police to use traffic stops as a means of searching for other violations, for which no probable cause or legitimate suspicion exists at the time of the stop. In particular, officers might select motorists for stops based on the impermissible factor of the occupants' race. To protect against such racially motivated stops, the defendants urged that the constitutional standard under the Fourth Amendment ask whether a police officer, acting reasonably, would have made the same stop on the basis of the alleged traffic code violation. The Supreme Court, however, refused to allow proof of an impermissible motive to invalidate a search otherwise justifiable on the basis of probable cause. Because the driver had violated several traffic laws, the officer's motive in stopping him, even if attributable to the driver's race, did not invalidate the stop.[78]

In addition to traffic rules, other types of laws provide opportunities for subjective enforcement on the basis of impermissible racial or ethnic assumptions. In 1855, California adopted the Vagrancy Act, popularly known as the Greaser Act, addressing "all persons who are commonly known as 'Greasers' or the issue of Spanish and Indian blood . . . and who go armed and are not peaceable and quiet persons." Targeting the supposed "idle Mexican,"[79] the racist potential of this early antiloitering law survives today in loitering, antigang, anti–day laborer, and curfew statutes and ordinances that are racially neutral on their face yet give law enforcement officers great discretion in their application. Occasionally these discretion-oriented laws (such as curfews) go too far and are struck down as unconstitutionally vague under the due process clause of the Fourteenth Amendment.[80] A recent example is a Chicago ordinance against someone the police reasonably believe to be a gang member who loiters in any public place, "with no apparent purpose," and fails to obey an order to disperse.[81] Prior to its invalidation in 1999 by the Supreme Court because it failed to establish "minimal guidelines to govern law enforcement," this ordinance had served in just three years as the basis for over forty-five thousand arrests of mostly African Americans and Latinas/os.[82] As found by the Court, the primary flaw of the Chicago ordinance was in defining loitering as remaining in one place "with no apparent purpose," which gave police too much open-ended discretion. The Supreme Court has invalidated other loitering ordinances; often these laws had been applied by police in a racially discriminatory manner. For example, the Court struck down a loitering ordinance used in 1960s Birmingham, Alabama, against Blacks standing outside a store during an economic boycott.[83] Later, the Court invalidated a vagrancy statute that had been relied on to arrest two interracial couples for "prowling by auto."[84] In 1983, the Court nullified a California local ordinance demanding those loitering to produce identification to police on demand; the ordinance was employed to target a Black man who frequented White neighborhoods.[85]

Under current legal standards, in some instances law enforcement officers may permissibly use race or ethnicity as a factor in stopping and questioning or even searching someone. At ports of entry, such as the U.S.-Mexico border, the federal government may permissibly conduct warrantless searches for drugs and other contraband without probable cause and without regard to whether the search is motivated by ethnicity.[86] Further, racial profiling may be permissible beyond the border in immigration enforcement. In holding that Border Patrol agents may not rely solely on Hispanic appearance in conducting a vehicle stop on suspicion that the occupants are undocumented immigrants, the Supreme Court has stated that Hispanic (here Mexican) appearance nonetheless could be one factor in forming a reasonable belief that the occupants were undocumented:

> In this case the officers relied on a single factor to justify stopping respondent's car: the apparent Mexican ancestry of the occupants. We cannot conclude that this furnished reasonable grounds to believe that the three occupants were aliens. At best the officers had only a fleeting glimpse of the persons in the moving car, illuminated by headlights. Even if they saw enough to think that the occupants were of Mexican descent, this factor alone would justify neither a reasonable belief that they were aliens, nor a reasonable belief that the car concealed other aliens who were illegally in the country. Large numbers of native-born and naturalized citizens have the physical characteristics identified with Mexican ancestry, and even in the border area a relatively small proportion of them are aliens. The likelihood that any given person of Mexican ancestry is an alien is high enough to make Mexican appearance a relevant factor, but standing alone it does not justify stopping all Mexican-Americans to ask if they are aliens.[87]

Rejecting the probative value of Hispanic appearance for purposes of determining whether someone should be stopped for suspicion of being an undocumented immigrant, the federal Ninth Circuit Court of Appeals has diverged from the Supreme Court's apparent authorization of racial profiling in enforcing immigration laws.[88] Based on the changing demographics of the Southwest that reflect an enormous growth of the Latina/o population, the Ninth Circuit stated:

> Hispanic appearance is of little or no use in determining which particular individuals among the vast Hispanic populace should be stopped by law enforcement officials on the lookout for illegal aliens. Reasonable suspicion [under the Fourth Amendment] requires particularized suspicion, and in an area in which a large number of people share a specific

characteristic, that characteristic casts too wide a net to play any part in a particularized reasonable suspicion determination.[89]

As Kevin Johnson has argued:

The vast majority (roughly 90 percent) of the Latinas/os in the United States are lawful immigrants or citizens; therefore Latina/o ancestry is not a particularly good indicia of undocumented status. "That the Border Patrol targets persons of 'Hispanic appearance' almost invariably contributes to the fact that *close to ninety percent* of [all] removals [are of] Mexican and [Latin] American citizens, even though they constitute slightly more than one-half of the total undocumented population in the United States."[90]

Increased calls for border security after the September 11 terrorist attacks, as well as the practice of profiling Arab Americans traveling by airplane, may signal increased use of profiling against Latinas/os, particularly in the effort to intercept undocumented immigrants. Capturing popular sentiment, a friend with whom I had previously debated the propriety of profiling stated matter-of-factly that the events of September 11 justify racial profiling. As a Louisiana congressman put it, "If I see someone come in [the airport] and he's got a diaper on his head and a fan belt around that diaper on his head, that guy needs to be pulled over and checked."[91] Because most of the public, as well as many public officials, have no foolproof means of identifying Arabs or Muslims on sight, efforts to target them through profiling undoubtedly will ensnare Latinas/os, many of whom resemble Arabs. Shortly after September 11, for example, schoolchildren taunted both Latina/o and Arab students at some schools, apparently confusing Latinas/os with Arabs Americans or simply lashing out at any non-White students.[92]

Subsequent to initial racial- and ethnicity-motivated interrogatory stops (and searches), police and prosecutorial discretion tends to be applied to the detriment of Latinas/os. No doubt this discretion is exercised consistent with expectations of guilt, the ability to obtain the suspect's conviction, and the likelihood that the suspect will engage in further criminal conduct. Stereotypical conceptions of the criminally minded Latina/o work against them in this process. Latinas/os will be viewed as more likely to be guilty in the first instance and as inclined to commit future crimes. The potential for obtaining a conviction of the Latina/o defendant is enhanced by the likelihood that the judge or jury will hold similar perceptions of the Latina/o's criminal character. These circumstances may explain the results of a recent study of over seven hundred thousand plea bargains with prosecution that concluded that "whites as a group get significantly better deals than Hispanics or blacks who are accused of similar crimes and who have similar criminal backgrounds."[93] Illustrating the sometimes-abusive exercise of police and prosecutorial discretion is a case involving a friend of mine, Pete Gonzales, who was arrested, prosecuted, and convicted for the crime of harassment. Although Pete owns a knife, its purpose is solely for his passion of hunting and fishing. Pete's weapon was not his hobby knife, nor even his fists. The basis for the harassment charge was that Pete, in a business dispute, had spit at his competitor. The dispute occurred in a rough-and-tumble fishing town on the Oregon coast, where tavern-clearing brawls and drunken street fights are tolerated as an almost everyday occurrence. Yet mere saliva was enough for a responding officer to arrest Pete (who had no prior record in the county) and for the district attorney to seek a criminal prosecution and sentence against a Latino.

Latina/o defendants who reach trial face juries and judges whose prejudice sometimes imperils their life and liberty. A researcher has confirmed that a person accused of committing a stereotypical crime (in this study, a Latino accused of assault) is seen as more likely to be guilty than a nonstereotypical defendant.[94] American courtrooms reflect these findings. In a murder case arising in Portland, Oregon, a jury wrongfully convicted an eighteen-year-old Mixtec migrant worker, Santiago Ventura Morales, of killing another worker. Santiago's case garnered national attention when some of the jurors decided they had succumbed to group dynamics and made the wrong decision, initiating a five-year struggle that ultimately freed Santiago and cleared his name. Those group dynamics had assumed and assured Santiago's guilt from the outset. Santiago's trial was marred by the assumption that as a Latino who could not speak English, Santiago naturally spoke Spanish. In fact, his primary language, and that of the witnesses, was Mixtec, an indigenous language. By contrast to remarks of the arresting officer that the Mixtec and Spanish languages "go hand-in-hand in Mexican country down there," the defendant and witnesses knew little Spanish.[95] One juror viewed the judicial circus that resulted from the use of a Spanish-language interpreter as suggesting that Santiago and the witnesses were all "kind of guilty." Because Santiago's novice public defender had decided unilaterally that Santiago would not testify in his defense, another juror assumed he must boast a long criminal history. One of the jurors remarked after the trial that "[w]e don't need so many of 'em [Mexican migrant workers] running around here. . . . They're just here and they don't have anything to do. And people that don't have anything to do, they get into trouble."[96] Even the trial judge suggested the subhuman status of Santiago and the other Mixtecs testifying at trial by joking about their physical attributes—in response to the prosecutor's suggestion that he had a "short witness," meaning his testimony would be brief, the trial judge joked, "About 5-foot-1?" to which the prosecutor replied, "Less than that."[97] Those jurors who campaigned to free Santiago were moved to action when Santiago, who had been silent throughout his trial, began howling at the guilty verdict in what his public defender described as "horrible sorrow." Santiago, while imprisoned, described what had transformed those jurors: "They realized I was a human then."[98]

Historically, mistrust of Latinas/os by some prosecutors and government officials has contributed to the likelihood that Latina/o defendants will be tried before a jury of non-Latinas/os. A 1969 prosecution training memorandum included a warning from a Dallas prosecutor against letting "Jews, Negroes, Dagoes and Mexicans" serve on criminal juries.[99] Earlier, litigation in Texas in the 1950s established that although 14 percent of a county's residents had Latina/o surnames, for the previous twenty years not one person with a Latina/o surname had ever served on a grand jury or criminal jury in the county. In 1954, the Supreme Court concluded that Pete Hernandez, a Mexican defendant convicted of murder in this Texas county, had been denied his constitutional equal protection rights by this systematic exclusion of persons of Mexican descent from the county jury pool.[100] But almost forty years later, a New York prosecutor's exclusion of bilingual Latinas/os from the jury hearing a case against a Latino was upheld by the Supreme Court because the prosecutor offered a race-neutral basis for striking Latinas/os from the jury—he refused to trust that the bilingual juror candidates could accept the English translation of an interpreter over their own understanding of the testimony of anticipated Spanish-speaking witnesses.[101]

Prejudice against Latinas/os can influence their sentencing. Compared with Anglos, Latinas/os receive disproportionately heavy sentences, whether they are youthful offenders or adults subject to the death penalty. A study released in 2002 found that Latino youth arrested for drug offenses but never before detained were thirteen times more likely to be incarcerated than non-Latino White youth; these Latinos will also spend more than twice as much time incarcerated (306 days) as imprisoned White youth (144 days). The study concluded, "In the United States generally, Latino/a youth are disproportionately arrested, detained, and waived to adult criminal court. Their sentences are harsher and their commitments are for longer periods of time than those for White youth committing the same offenses."[102] One study of the imposition of the death penalty in a populous California county revealed that compared with Anglo offenders, Latina/o defendants were more than four times as likely to be charged with the special circumstances needed for imposition of the death sentence.[103] In Texas, which executes more prisoners than any other state, "future dangerousness" is an aggravating circumstance that can support a jury recommendation of the death sentence. In 1996, a prosecution expert there went so far as to suggest to a jury that they could infer future dangerousness to society from a defendant's Latino heritage. Victor Hugo Saldano had been convicted of killing a grocery-store clerk. At his sentencing, the prosecution's expert testified that Saldano's Argentine ethnicity "was a factor weighing in favor of future dangerousness." The Texas Court of Criminal Appeals decided this testimony did not constitute fundamental error. Before the U.S. Supreme Court, the Texas attorney general relented and confessed error, agreeing to a new sentencing hearing for Saldano and other Latino and Black death-row inmates targeted by similar testimony.[104] Yet, on remand to the Texas courts, the Court of Criminal Appeals denied Saldano his hearing, ruling that his lawyers had failed to object in a timely fashion to the admission of the expert's testimony at the original sentencing.[105]

The perception of Latinas/os as aggressive and dangerous criminals has often yielded a tragic end to police-Latina/o confrontations.[106] In several incidents, police have killed Latinos whom they perceived as a threat when a degree of force short of deadly shooting seemed more appropriate. In April 2001, Portland, Oregon, police officers killed twenty-nine-year-old José Santos Victor Mejia Poot in a hospital psychiatric unit with bullets to his head and chest. Poot had been taken to the hospital two days earlier by authorities after he had suffered an epileptic seizure on a city bus. Although he had no history of mental illness, he was taken to the psychiatric ward. Poot's father was unable to communicate with hospital officials in his native languages of Spanish and Maya in order to provide Poot with his epilepsy medication. Apparently frightened in his new surroundings, and without his medication, Poot broke out of his isolation room and knocked a staff member to the floor. At least twenty-five police officers responded to the hospital's call and initially used pepper spray and beanbag rounds to restrain Poot. When Poot allegedly tore off a metal rod from a door and advanced toward the army of police officers, he was killed. Poot's death galvanized the Portland Latina/o community and led to numerous protests and investigations. A county grand jury found no criminal wrongdoing by the Portland police officers,[107] who were later awarded a medal for their role in killing Poot, but a lawsuit against the Portland police claiming negligence and excessive force is planned.

In another incident, six Phoenix, Arizona, police officers together fired twenty-five rounds into Julio Valerio, a slight, 120-pound Mexican teenager armed with a kitchen knife, killing him. Officers had responded to a distress call from Valerio's mother, who alerted them that her son had left the house upset and had taken a kitchen knife. After unsuccessfully attempting to subdue Valerio with pepper spray, six of the ten officers who surrounded Valerio shot him. A Phoenix police investigation concluded that Valerio's killing was justified. According to one commentator, the Phoenix police were able successfully to construct the Latino criminal image in their defense, transforming Valerio

> from a thin Hispanic kid armed with a knife, wearing a dark shirt, and moving eastward from his home, to a drug-crazed-gang-member, wielding a butcher knife, threatening everyone in sight, and with the strength of a super-predator capable of killing armed officers by lunging forward or throwing a knife 13 feet.[108]

Examples abound of Latina/o suspects met with brutal, deadly force at the hands and trigger fingers of law enforcement officers. In the summer of 2001, in upscale Bellevue, Washington, police responded to a caller alleging that her cousin had brandished a kitchen knife and threatened her. The suspect, twenty-four-year-old Guatemalan immigrant Nelson Martínez Mendez, was leaving the apartment complex when his car collided at a slow speed with one of the responding patrol cars. In the ensuing commotion, Mendez allegedly reacted to an officer's orders by reaching for something in his waistband. He was shot and killed. A search of his waistband turned up only a wallet—a kitchen knife was found stowed under some clothing in the car's passenger seat. An inquest jury concluded the officer firing the shots had feared for his life and was justified in killing Mendez.[109]

The perception of Latinas/os as superhuman in their potential and capacity for violent aggression, used to justify deadly force in police-Latina/o confrontations, has also been invoked by private citizens in their encounters with the stereotypical Latina/o menace. In one example, a White man, William Masters II, encountered two Mexican American youths, Cesar Rene Arce and David Hillo, who were spray-painting support columns under the Hollywood Freeway in Los Angeles.[110] After Masters wrote down their vehicle license number, a confrontation ensued in which Hillo allegedly held a screwdriver in a threatening manner, prompting Masters to hand over the license number. As he walked away, Masters claimed he thought the youths were coming up behind him, so he fired at them with a loaded gun he carried without a permit in his fanny pack. Masters shot Hillo in his buttocks and shot Arce in the back, killing him. In exercising its prosecutorial discretion, the Los Angeles County District Attorney's Office declined to prosecute Masters, believing he had acted in self-defense in shooting the two boys. Masters was showered with public support, illustrated by a Simi Valley councilwoman who declared, "Kudos to William Masters for his vigilant anti-graffiti efforts and for his foresight in carrying a gun for self protection. If [Los Angeles] refuses to honor Masters as a crime-fighting hero, then I invite him to relocate to our town." Although Masters was later charged with a misdemeanor for carrying an unpermitted gun, he was sentenced to three years probation and only four days in jail, time he had already served while detained during the initial investigation. Masters's ability to dodge responsibility for the shooting placed him in the company of the most famous Anglo to invoke self-defense in justifying deadly force against persons of color—Bernhard Goetz, who shot four Black youths on a New York subway, paralyzing one permanently. Goetz was acquitted of all charges except carrying an unlicensed handgun. By contrast to the ability of Masters to avoid further jail time, David Hillo, who survived the encounter with Masters that killed his friend, was charged with vandalism and sentenced to two and one-half years in jail for accompanying probation violations, as well as a separate theft of eyedrops and cold medicine from a market.

The construction of Latinas/os as simultaneously superhuman, justifying deadly force against them in confrontations with police or with private citizens, and subhuman, depriving them of a fair trial, plagues Latinas/os in the criminal justice system. The images of superhuman Latina/o criminals in the minds of police and public are reminiscent of the media construction of Asian Americans—particularly of Japanese during World War II, who were represented as "monstrously large or strong; preternaturally cunning and devious; [and] resistant to pain."[111] Media have embraced this superhuman construction especially for Latina/o gang members. A *Time* magazine feature in September 2001, discussing the "nightmare" of Latina/o gangs in Los Angeles, explained that Latina/o "[g]angs, it turns out, can take more beatings and lock-down time than any humane society is prepared to deal out."[112]

The media and societal image of Latinas/os as criminally minded has caused harm beyond Latina/o encounters with the American criminal justice system. In the 2001 Los Angeles mayoral election, James Hahn stormed from behind in the polls on the strength of ads late in the campaign that depicted his rival, Antonio Villaraigosa, as a friend of drug dealers and drug users, perhaps even a user himself. One television commercial began with someone chopping cocaine with a razor blade and holding a crack cocaine pipe to a flame. It ended with the statement "Los Angeles can't trust Antonio Villaraigosa." At the same time, radio ads purchased by the Police Protective League portrayed Villaraigosa as soft on criminals and warned voters, "It's a matter of trust." These advertisements stemmed from a letter Villaraigosa wrote in 1996 to the White House on behalf of a convicted Latino cocaine trafficker, whose sentence was ultimately commuted by former president Clinton. Villaraigosa condemned the ads as "trying to imply cynically and wildly" that he somehow advocated crack cocaine.[113] Yet Hahn refused to pull the ads, which swept him to victory. Shortly after his election, Hahn rewarded the anti-Latina/o stereotype and sentiment by turning his focus to Latina/o gangs, announcing that the increase in certain violent gang-related crimes such as murders, felonious assaults, and attacks on police officers would be his top priority.

Texas politics also turned dirty in 2002 when Tony Sánchez, a Democratic challenger for the governor's office, was hit with campaign ads from incumbent Republican Rick Perry spotlighting the Sánchez family-owned savings and loan association, which was once used by Mexican drug smugglers in the mid-1980s to launder $25 million. The Sánchez family had long been cleared of any wrongdoing, but again, the opportunity to associate Latinas/os with drug crimes in the minds of voters proved irresistible; Sánchez lost the election.[114]

5

Mañana (Is Soon Enough for Me)
Fertility and Welfare

What do you call a taco with a food stamp inside it?
A Mexican fortune cookie.

What did the Mexican do with his first 50 cent piece?
He married her!

Why don't Mexicans like blow jobs?
Mexicans don't like any job that interferes with unemployment.

Latinas/os are perceived as lazy and as reluctant to work. At the same time, they are seen as fiery, passionate lovers, reflected in the male stereotype of the Latin lover and the less-flattering female stereotypes of the easy Latina, the fertile Latina, and the Latina whore. These images of the lazy yet sexually driven Latina/o underlie the related perception of Latinas/os as public charges who are complacent or even enthusiastic in receiving welfare and other public assistance.

Images of the lazy Latina/o, particularly of Mexicans, have dominated American media for decades. In popular music, Peggy Lee and Dave Barbour depicted the lazy Latina/o in their 1948 number-one hit "Mañana (Is Soon Enough for Me)":

The faucet she is dripping and the fence she's falling down . . .
My brother isn't workin' and my sister doesn't care. . . .
My mother thinks I'm lazy and maybe she is right
I'll go to work mañana but I gotta sleep tonight
Mañana . . . is soon enough for me.[1]

Appearing in *Looney Tunes* cartoons, "Speedy Gonzales," billed as the fastest mouse in all of Mexico, did seem to break the mold of media portrayals of the lazy Mexican. Yet, to balance this industrious image, Speedy's cartoon cousin, the sleepy-eyed Slowpoke Rodriguez, was dubbed the slowest mouse in Mexico. As two unfortunate "pussy-*gatos*" learned in the 1959 cartoon "Mexican Shmoes," Slowpoke compensated by carrying a large *pistola,* as would any stereotypical Mexican. Speedy himself was portrayed as lacking initiative in Pat Boone's 1962 novelty smash song "Speedy Gonzales":

[Voice of Speedy's love, Rosita:]
Stop alla your a-drinkin'
With that floozie named Flo
Come on home to your adobe
And slap some mud on the wall
The roof is leakin' like a strainer
There's loads of roaches in the hall
No enchiladas in the icebox
And the television's broke
[Voice of Speedy:]
Hey Rosita, come queek, down at
The cantina they givin' green stamps
With tequila![2]

Although it had suspended replay of Speedy Gonzales cartoons over concerns about Speedy's supporting cast of lazy, hard-drinking, señorita-chasing Mexican mice, the Cartoon Network began airing Speedy in the summer of 2002.[3]

In film, depictions of indolent Latinas/os date back to silent features such as 1923's *Why Worry?* set south of the border in "Paradiso," described by subtitles as "[a] drowsy city in a dreamy land. Rip Van Winkle's twenty-year sleep would be considered a nap down here." In Paradiso, dozens of Mexican natives are shown sleeping in their rocking chairs, on balconies, and on benches. Some even are laced with cobwebs that stretch from their napping heads to the walls.[4] This image of the sleeping Mexican was replicated on American-made pottery in the 1930s and 1940s and on the design once employed by Taco Bell under its bell.[5] I saw the infamous sleepy Mexican adorning pottery at a country fair last summer. In 2002, Tucson, Arizona, officials promoted a clean-air event with a public transportation advertising campaign urging residents to "give your car a siesta," depicting a green car snoring under a sombrero.[6] In my teens, as part of my mother's Mexican dance troupe, I had drawn on this stereotype in choreographing our production—when my cousin Joey Troncoso and I finished the traditional dance "Los Viejitos," we both retired to opposite sides of the stage to sleep under our sombreros until we "awoke" to perform in a later number. In the fall of 2002, a post office employee suggested to me that he deserved an afternoon siesta, "like down in Mexico, a shot of tequila and a siesta!" On television, a character of the comedy *Ed* explained in a 2002 episode that he always took a workplace siesta, as to do otherwise would disrespect his friends of Mexican heritage. Late comedian Freddie Prinze, costarring in the 1970s sitcom *Chico and the Man,* would express his aversion to hard work by remarking, "It's not my job." Appearing on the daytime television game show *Hollywood Squares,* Freddie responded to the question "Is it possible to teach a pig to bow?" with his catchphrase, "Eees not my job." In the aftermath of September 11, 2001, Representative J. C. Watts Jr., the chair of the House Republican Committee, ridiculed two Democratic leaders who took a weekend trip to meet with Mexico's president Vincente Fox while the House was grappling with the national economy: "This is not the time for the Democratic leadership to be skipping town. . . . Hey, Democrat leaders: No siesta for you."[7] The congressman's tirade implied that all south-of-the-border endeavors are mere frolics. In his book derived from his television show *Politically Incorrect,* Bill Maher addressed the subject of the productivity of American workers compared with Mexicans in a mocking commentary:

> Honestly, when you think of Mexican labor, the phrase "worker ants" doesn't leap to mind. But I'm here to say that the problem is not with the work habits of Mexicans but with the kind of thinking that posits any kind of work as the greatest virtue on the planet. Someone once defined work as whatever you'd rather not do, so who's out to lunch on this one? Well, the Mexicans are, and usually for three or four hours, but that's simply because they come from a different culture, one that lends nobility to the art of napping instead of scorn.[8]

The contrasting construction of Asian Americans as a model minority to be praised for their work ethic and industry has been used to enhance the view of Latinas/os as idle. Illustrating that this impression has taken hold in the public consciousness, a 1994 survey found that a majority of Whites felt that Latinas/os lacked "ambition and the drive to succeed."[9]

Further building on the perception of Latinas/os as lazy is the view and portrayal of Latinas/os as awash in alcohol, in contrast to a 1997 national study of youth aged twelve to sixteen that determined Latina/o youth drank alcohol at rates (22 percent— Latina; 20 percent—Latino) slightly less than those for White youth (23 percent for both sexes).[10] Several films have depicted the drunk Mexican. *Three Amigos* (1986) suggests that Mexican *bandidos* carry a personal bottle of tequila for frequent toasts and revelry, which they accompany by firing their pistols into the air. In the blockbuster *The Mexican* (2001), Brad Pitt encountered drunken Mexicans relieving themselves in the street, then stumbling on their way while shooting their pistols into the air. John Steinbeck's classic novel *Tortilla Flat* depicted Latinas/os as shiftless drunks whose sole ambition was finding an obliging *compadre* with a jug (or two) of wine. Liquor distributors have co-opted and commodified the Latina/o holiday Cinco de Mayo as an occasion to celebrate with drunken revelry (one beer distributor promoted Corona beer as "the Drinko for Cinco"). Few Anglos appreciate the historical significance of the celebration, which stems not from some reverence to tequila production but from a victory of Mexican forces over French troops in 1862, signaling the downfall of French intervention in Mexico. Although similar in historical significance to the Fourth of July, this official holiday in Mexico has been stripped of its historical understanding in the United States to become another basis for the construction of Mexican culture as one of fervent fiesta and frequent siesta.

The "Latin lover" image constructs Latinas/os as sexually driven. Latin lovers are familiar in American media—from former big-screen Latin stars such as Gilbert Roland, Ricardo Montalban, and Fernando Lamas to present-day singing sensations Ricky Martin and Enrique Iglesias. Obliging Latinas, too, are well represented in film and other media. Randy Anglos and virgin boys understand from these representations that they need only head south of the border to satisfy their carnal urges. In the film *Losin' It* (1983), Tom Cruise and his high school friends travel to the bordellos in "the nastiest, raunchiest . . . place in the whole world, Tijuana," to secure their manhood. Tijuana keeps its tawdry promise to the boys, even offering up a Latina-donkey sex show. Capturing Hollywood's unflattering conception of Latina sophistication and morals, the bordello piano player, who entertains the downstairs patrons while Tom Cruise and his buddies are upstairs, boasts in song:

> I know a señorita
> Her name's Rosanne
> She uses a tortilla for a diaphragm.

Tom Cruise returned to the cinematic Mexican whorehouses in *Born on the Fourth of July* (1989) as Ron Kovic, a paraplegic Vietnam veteran. On Ron's arrival in seaside Villa Dulce, another wheelchair-bound veteran (Willem Dafoe) advises him on the availability of Mexican prostitutes, urging, "Go into town, get yourself one. Fuck the shit out of you, even if you are paralyzed." In *The Mexican* (2001), Brad Pitt's mobster boss sent him to Mexico to retrieve a legendary pistol, instructing Brad that while there he could find "all the $10 hookers you can shake your stick at." The rock trio ZZ Top put the Anglo journey across the border to the lair of Mexican whores to music in "Mexican Blackbird":

> They all call her "puta" 'cause no one really knows her name.
> She works the cantina, dancin' and a-lovin's her trade.
> Her mama was Mez'can and her daddy was the ace of spades [Black].
> Oh, let's drive that old Chrysler down to Mexico boy. . . .
> Oh, this is gonna be so good.
> Mm, she's hot as a pepper but smooth as a Mexican brew.
> So head for the border and put in an order or two.
> The wings of the blackbird will spread like an eagle for you.[11]

ZZ Top's "puta" became the fictional Lupe in a song included in a UCLA college fraternity's *Associate Member Education Manual* for new members in the early 1990s, presumably to regale sorority members with humorous street song:

> Twas down in Cunt Valley, where Red Rivers flow
> Where cocksuckers flourish, and maidenheads grow
> Twas there I met Lupe, the girl I adore
> My hot fucking, cocksucking Mexican whore.

Earlier, in the late 1980s, UCLA's film school had screened a student film depicting a Mexican woman having sex with a donkey.[12]

In Larry McMurtry's 1966 novel *The Last Picture Show*, made later into a classic film, two small-town boys augmented their coming-of-age adventures in Texas with a road trip to Matamoros, Mexico. As they arrived, a boy jumped onto their pickup's running board and queried as their guide, "Girl? Boy's Town? Dirty movie?" Choosing dirty movies first, the Texas boys were shown a pornographic flick titled *Man's Best Friend*, in which a German shepherd dog and a man had relations with a woman. Later, the guide took the Anglo youths to Boy's Town, where one of them bargained for an all-night party with Juanita for twenty-five dollars. Once in the room where she led him, our Texas boy discovered Juanita was not only younger than she had looked in the cabaret but clearly pregnant with her third child. After a few minutes in bed, he simply stopped and fell asleep. When the boys reached their hometown the next day, its lights were reassuring after the "strangeness" of Mexico,[13] reinforcing perceptions not only of the unique decadence but of the foreignness of Mexico and Mexicans.

First published in 1956 and included later in his famous work *On the Road*, Jack Kerouac's quasi-autobiographical short story "A Billowy Trip in the World" recounts Jack's south-of-the-border adventures. Pulling into a gas station, Jack suggested to a vendor that although he was not interested in purchasing his wares, he would "buy" a señorita. "Sure, sure!" the young man replied, "I get you gurls, onnytime." After the young man's mother procured them some marijuana, which he rolled into "the biggest bomber anybody ever saw," he took them to a whorehouse, where Jack and his traveling companions eyed a sixteen-year-old "colored girl" and a fifteen-year-old with "almond colored skin." After several hours there of mambo and manhood, Jack remembered he "was in Mexico after all and not in a pornographic haseesh daydream in heaven" and headed back for the States.[14]

Songwriter John Hiatt's tune "Mexican Lover" comically blasts his woman for her ongoing south-of-the-border affair by conjoining images of the Latina prostitute and her Latino pimp. As Hiatt remarks to his unfaithful partner, his name is not Miguel, and he has no baby sister to "sell." Yet he can always "tell" when she travels to visit her Mexican lover because she shamelessly fails to hide their affair by leaving guacamole smeared on her fingers and tortillas covering her eyes, while still wearing the smell of her Mexican lover's "bean taco."[15]

One need not cross the border in American media to find an obliging Latina.[16] In the film *The Last American Virgin* (1982) she was Carmela, a suburban, middle-aged Latina willing to "entertain" three Anglo high-schoolers without charge until her lover, Paco, arrived from Puerto Rico to interrupt the festivities. As Carmela explains to the boys while taking an "intermission" from their afternoon orgy, she just loves "a little fiesta." The dedicated Latina student whom actor Samuel Jackson tutors in the thriller *187* (1997) nonetheless is portrayed as a slut—she tells Jackson in the classroom that he has a nice butt, strips naked for him at a late-night tutoring session and offers her body in gratitude, and is caught in the schoolyard utility shed "bustin' the train" with "five or six *cholos* lined up." *Colors* (1988) featured a Latina homegirl, actress Maria Conchita Alonso, who appeared to counter the promiscuous Latina stereotype in her budding relationship with Anglo cop Sean Penn by displaying her family values in caring for his partner's baby at a barbecue during their first date. But when Penn drives her home, she turns and walks back to his car, and in the subsequent frame, Penn and Alonso are naked, having sex. Later, after his brutal approach toward policing her barrio neighborhood imperils their brief relationship, Penn finds Alonso in the bedroom of a crowded gang party, putting on her clothes after apparently having had sex with a gang member released from prison that day. By contrast to her understated appearance on earlier dates, she is wearing a low-cut dress, high heels, and thick makeup. The previously shy Alonso calls attention to her transformation, yelling to Penn, "Look at me, Pacman. This is me too, man!"[17] In *Down and Out in Beverly Hills* (1986), the obliging Latina was an undocumented immigrant housekeeper willing to satisfy her wealthy married Anglo employer Richard Dreyfuss and, later, his Anglo street-bum houseguest. And in the musical motion picture *Grease* (1978) she was Cha Cha, the "best dancer" with the "worst reputation." Opting for the virginal charm of blonde Olivia Newton-John, John Travolta explained that he and Cha Cha didn't "go [steady] together," they just "went together"; in other words, it was lust, not romance.[18] In the film *The Professional* (1966), actor Burt Lancaster asked his Latina former girlfriend, Chiquita, "How's your love life?" "Terrific," she replied. "Don't you ever say no?" he asked. "Never!" Chiquita responded. "Anybody?" he pressed. Her reply—"Everybody!"[19]

Media images of the ever-willing Latina encompass Latinas of all origins—Madonna's fictional sexual fantasies and fetishes, detailed in her book *Sex*, include a whorish Cuban salesgirl, Lourdes, who drops to her knees in a department-store dressing room to take an apparently well-to-do customer in her "magnificent" mouth. After servicing him with her "genius" mouth, Lourdes tells the customer he must purchase the shirt she uses to wipe her face and rejects his request for lunch: "Oh, you don't owe me anything. Besides I have a boyfriend."[20]

Emerging from media representations of Latinas is their supposed desire for relations with Anglo men. As far back as the 1800s, a popular folk song went:

> Already the señoritas
> Speak English with finesse.
> "Kiss me!" say the Yankees,
> The girls all answer "Yes!"[21]

Conceptions of willing Mexican women and lazy Mexican men were conjoined in the 1846 poem "They Wait for Us," proclaiming:

> The Spanish maid, with eye of fire,
> At balmy evening turns her lyre
> And looking to the Eastern sky,
> Awaits our Yankee chivalry
> Whose purer blood and valiant arms,
> Are fit to clasp her budding charms.
>
> The man, her mate, is sunk in sloth—
> To love, his senseless heart is loth:
> The pipe and glass and tinkling lute,
> A sofa, and a dish of fruit;
> A nap, some dozen times a day;
> Sombre and sad, and never gay.[22]

One representative dime novel from 1886, *Little Lone Star*, featured a young Mexican woman threatened with rape by a Mexican *bandido* but rescued by a fair-haired Anglo cowboy, with whom the sexual relationship would be consensual.[23] Arnoldo De León has suggested that the construction of Latinas as sexually obliging and as favoring Anglos originated from the need of Anglo men to explain their otherwise inconsistent intolerance and mistreatment of Latinos and their sexual desire for Latinas:

> Thus, the position of the white men was that they had been lured across the racial line. Fornication could be justified on the pretense that it was

caused by Mexican women having a penchant for them. Contempt for *all* Mexicans, including "greaser women," and austere mores and taboos prohibiting intercourse with "mongrels," could then be overcome.[24]

Compounding their image of sexual availability, Latinas are constructed as excessively fertile.[25] Latina fertility was well depicted in a 2001 Degree deodorant commercial featuring a young Anglo couple returning from a trip to Mexico and having to confront Mexican customs officials. Attempting to explain the couple's discovered contraband of Cuban cigars, the woman conveys through words and arm-cradling that she is having a baby. At that moment, celebratory Mexican music begins to play and the three customs officials proudly display their wallet baby photos. One of the officials has at least nine photos, the other two at least seven each. To disabuse the notion that the pictures depict the same child, one of the officials begins counting in Spanish, "Uno, dos . . ." while pointing at his pictures. On boarding the plane, the Anglo woman tells her male partner that she may indeed be pregnant, evoking a reaction of surprise that suggests this will be the couple's first child. By contrast, the three Mexican customs officials lay claim to at least twenty-three children.[26] In one of his classic novels, *Tortilla Flat*, John Steinbeck includes the fictional account of Señora Teresina Cortez, a woman nearing thirty who lives with her nine children in Monterey, California. To feed her children during a season when the bean crop failed, four men came to her aid by stealing food. Before leaving Teresina's rescue to address other lessons of life and values in early Monterey, Steinbeck reveals that Teresina discovered she was pregnant again, causing her to "wonder[] idly" which one of the four men was responsible.[27]

The attention focused on the dramatic growth of the Latina/o population as reported in the 2000 U.S. Census likely heightens the view of Latinas as exceedingly fertile. This growth touched all geographic regions in America. Migration of Latinas/os toward jobs in the Southeast more than doubled the Latina/o population from 1990 to 2000 in states such as Georgia (299.6 percent increase), North Carolina (393.9 percent), and Tennessee (278.2 percent). Adding to the perception of a Latina/o population explosion was the realization that Latinas/os have become the largest minority group in the United States. Thus, members of other minority groups, particularly African Americans, began to question the implications of this population trend on issues from local politics to race relations.[28]

Viewing Latinas/os as lazy and Latinas as fertile, Anglos tend to regard Latinas/os as public charges who subsist on welfare. Reflecting this attitude, one early 1990s survey found that 74 percent of Anglos surveyed thought Hispanics were more likely than Whites to prefer welfare.[29] Further illustrating this attitude was a "poem" directed at Latina/o immigrants sent by a constituent and actually read into the California legislative record in 1993 by Republican assemblyman Pete Knight, which contained such verses as:

> Write to friends in motherland, tell them come as fast as can. . . .
> They come in rags and Chebby trucks, I buy big house with welfare
>   bucks. . . .
> Everything is mucho good, soon we own the neighborhood.
> We have a hobby, it's called breeding.
> Welfare pay for baby feeding. . . .
> We think America damn good place.
> Too damn good for white man race.[30]

The leading proponent of California's anti–bilingual education initiative Proposition 227, Ron Unz, contrasted Spanish-speaking immigrants in speaking favorably of his Jewish grandparents:

> [They] came to California in the 1920s and 1930s as poor European immigrants. They came to work and become successful . . . not to sit back and be a burden on those who were already here![31]

Perceptions of laziness are difficult to debunk. However, it bears noting that Latinas/os are employed disproportionately in professions that entail rigorous physical labor, such as agriculture, meatpacking, food service, and construction. Anglos have described strenuous physical labor jokingly as "Manuel labor," thereby expressing an association between Latinas/os and hard labor that seems to contradict the conception of Latinas/os as lazy and sedentary. Similarly, explosive growth of Latina/o-owned businesses in America runs counter to the view that Latinas/os lack initiative. For example, a report by the National Foundation for Women Business Owners in Washington, D.C., revealed that between 1987 and 1996, Latinas originated businesses in the United States at a rate more than four times that of the general population.[32] Regarding Latino men, data from the 2000 Census established that Latinos were more likely than Anglos to be working or looking for work—the year 2000 labor force participation rate for Latinos was 80.4 percent, compared with only 74.3 percent for non-Hispanic White men. At the same time, Latinas have increased their workforce presence over the years to a participation rate (56.6 percent) that now approaches that of non-Hispanic White women (60.8 percent).[33]

Although almost every American understands the Spanish word *siesta,* few appreciate that siestas are lore rather than practice among Latinas/os in the United States, and even among most Mexicans in Mexico.[34] Of my dozens of Latina/o friends and family, not one takes regular afternoon naps or otherwise has a sleeping pattern that differs from that of the typical Anglo. In 1999, the Mexican government officially outlawed long afternoon breaks by its government employees.[35] Even prior to their official abolition, siestas simply made the workday longer, as public employees would take a few hours off in the mid-afternoon heat and then return to work until 9 or 10 P.M.

On the subject of fertility, Latinas indeed exhibit a higher fertility rate than Anglo women. Still, the rate varies dramatically among Latinas of different origins. A study released in 1998 by the National Center for Health Statistics identified above-average fertility rates among Latinas of Mexican origin, particularly recent immigrants. The study estimated that Latinas of Mexican origin will average 3.2 births over their lifetimes, while Cuban American women will average 1.7 births and Puerto Rican women 2.2—rates that compare to those of non-Hispanic White women (1.7).[36] Later government research released in 2001 found that Anglo and non-Mexican Latina teen pregnancies declined between 1989 and 1999, but births to Mexican American teens increased from 94 babies for each 1,000 teens in 1989 to 101 in 1999.[37] Foretelling a reduction ahead in Mexican American birthrates, however, is the tremendous decline in fertility among women in Mexico. Having averaged 7 children per mother in 1965, Mexican women average only 2.4 today.[38]

Latinas are no more promiscuous than Anglo women. A 1997 national study determined that in the previous year, 19 percent of Latinas aged twelve to sixteen had engaged in sex, compared with 20 percent of White girls.[39] Rather than deriving from any heightened sexual drive,[40] promiscuous character, or desire to exploit welfare laws, high Latina fertility rates, particularly among Mexican Americans, stem from poverty, religion, and lack of education. Typically, Mexican American Latinas are raised under the Catholic religion, which does not condone most forms of birth control.[41] Moreover, sex education is often lacking.[42] Poverty is linked to high birthrates, as the poor may effectively be forced to bear large families as a means of obtaining wages through their children's labor or of obtaining care when elderly.[43] In Mexico, the steady decline in birthrates is projected to continue as more women work outside the home and pursue their education.[44]

Although Latinas/os maintain a higher welfare participation rate than Anglos, Americans tend dramatically to overestimate the number of Latinas/os collecting welfare in the United States. A nationwide study conducted in 1999 determined that more than one-third of the respondents believed at least half of citizen or documented Latinas/os receive welfare. Actually, only 6.9 percent of Latinas/os over age fifteen receive public assistance or federal disability payments; if housing assistance or Medicaid is included, the figure rises to only 25 percent.[45] A report on receipt of welfare by Latinas/os in Arizona concluded that fewer than 4 percent were receiving welfare, most of those children. Rebutting the perception that Latinas/os seek to maintain their grip on welfare benefits, the report determined that more than four-fifths of those Latinas/os receiving welfare had been doing so for less than two years. Most of those recipients had terminated their welfare payments at least twice before, but job loss or some other crisis led them to resume collecting benefits.[46] The same report also confirmed that despite their eligibility, Latinas/os rarely took advantage of certain state-funded programs such as food stamps, child-care subsidies, and child health care.

Much of the public perception of and outcry over Latina/o dependence on welfare is directed at Latina/o immigrants. In his controversial anti-immigrant book *Alien Nation,* Peter Brimelow included statistics that compared immigrant welfare participation rates in 1990 by national origin group. In these statistics, immigrants from Mexico had a welfare rate of 11.3 percent, those from Cuba 16 percent, and those from the Dominican Republic 27.9 percent, while immigrants from European countries all had welfare participation rates under 8 percent except for the former USSR, with 16.3 percent.[47] Despite the prevailing sentiment that immigrants are a financial drain on government resources, several studies have confirmed that immigrants pay more in taxes than they receive in government benefits.[48] This is particularly the case for undocumented immigrants, who must contribute to programs such as unemployment and Social Security through their payroll deductions even though they will not be eligible for any benefits because of their immigration status. Given their ineligibility for most welfare benefits, no doubt what lures undocumented immigrants to the United States is employment opportunity. As one observer concluded:

> There is no evidence whatsoever that the availability of health care or any other kind of public service in the United States is an important incentive for Mexicans contemplating a move to the U.S. Their motives are overwhelmingly income, job, and family-related. They come to the U.S. to work and get ahead, not to consume public services.[49]

Moreover, these immigrants have been educated elsewhere, with Mexico and other countries of origin bearing that cost to supply the United States with immigrants in their prime working years. As Juan Gonzalez has maintained:

> The cost of their education was thus borne by the governments of their homelands, yet the sending countries lost the benefits of that investment in human capital when many of their brightest, most ambitious and resourceful citizens immigrated to the United States. Meanwhile, the United States gained young workers in whose education it did not have to invest any money.[50]

Perceptions of Latinas/os as lazy, fertile, and thus dependent on welfare have fueled anti-immigrant agendas. These anti-immigrant attitudes were most pronounced in the 1990s and targeted Latinas/os, primarily Mexicans. The anti-immigrant sentiment was directed at both the number of immigrants coming to the United States and their access to government services once here. A Gallup poll in 1993 found that 65 percent of Americans favored a reduction in immigration. By contrast, the same pollster had determined that only 33 percent of Americans felt this way in 1965. A majority of respondents in 1993 believed that immigrants "cost the taxpayer too much by using government services like public education and medical services." The poll identified peculiar resentment toward Latina/o and Asian immigrants, as 62 percent of respondents felt there were too many immigrants from Latin America and Asian countries, while a majority felt the number of immigrants from Europe was "about right."[51]

Anti-immigrant sentiments have been particularly virulent in California. Californians overwhelmingly passed the citizen initiative Proposition

187 in 1994.[52] Despite strong opposition from Latina/o voters, Anglo voters ensured its passage by voting for the initiative at the rate of 63 percent.[53] Proposition 187 was, at bottom, an assault on Latina/o reproduction.[54] It excluded "illegal aliens" from state social services and health care, such as prenatal care. Most prominently, it excluded illegal aliens from public education, spanning elementary through postsecondary school. Each school district was required to undertake to verify the legal status of every student and parent; for every child unable to establish legal status in the United States, the initiative specified a ninety-day transition period before the student would be expelled, ostensibly to return to his or her country of origin for continued schooling.

The Proposition 187 media campaign focused on undocumented Latina/o immigrants. Some pro-initiative flyers urged Californians to "wake up and smell the refried beans."[55] The dominant media image created was one of a Latina/o collecting a welfare check with one hand while dealing drugs from the other. Media statements of one of the drafters of Proposition 187 conveyed this unfavorable construction of Latinas/os and other "illegal aliens":

> Illegal-alien gangs roam our streets, dealing drugs and searching for innocent victims to rob, rape, and in many cases, murder those who dare violate their "turf."[56]

This drafter also attacked the children of undocumented immigrants:

> You get illegal alien children, Third World children, out of our schools, and you will reduce the violence. That is a fact. . . . You're not dealing with a lot of shiny face, little kiddies. . . . You're dealing with Third World cultures who come in, they shoot, they beat, they stab and they spread drugs around in our school system. And we're paying them to do it.[57]

Hostility toward Latina/o reproduction was evident in the initiative campaign. One southern California mayor active in the campaign for Proposition 187 reportedly described the children of undocumented immigrants as "those little fuckers."[58] At the same time, Pete Wilson's successful reelection campaign for governor of California showed images of Mexicans running across the border en masse with an announcer warning, "They keep coming."[59]

Court action settled on appeal through mediation eventually gutted

Proposition 187, leaving intact only its criminal penalties for manufacture and use of false documents to conceal undocumented immigration status, already a crime under federal law.[60] Although this litigation curtailed Proposition 187's legal effects, its private enforcement by vigilantes was more pronounced. Proposition 187 by its terms envisioned enlisting thousands of schoolteachers, health care providers, and other government workers as operatives in the war against undocumented immigrants. It was a small and foreseeable step, then, for the rest of the public to join the fight, particularly since it was their own citizen initiative that enacted this anti-immigrant public policy in California. Anti-immigrant vigilantes in California targeted Latina/o adults and children, whether they were undocumented immigrants, immigrants with legal status, or even citizens. In several reported incidents sparked by the initiative, Californians confronted Latinas/os with suspicions about their legal status. The day after Proposition 187 was adopted, customers accosted a Latino cook, demanding to see his "green card" and declaring they were now in charge of "kicking out all illegals" under Proposition 187. While stopped next to a Latina permanent resident at a traffic light, a man demanded to know whether she was an "illegal." Service providers questioned the right of Latinas/os to receive services even while Proposition 187's enforcement was suspended by the pending court action. A doctor refused a Latina mother's request for a letter verifying her child's affliction with Down's syndrome to enable her to receive government assistance for his care, explaining that "Latinos should work if they want to be here" and demanding that she produce immigration papers. A fifth-grade teacher at Bell Gardens Intermediate School assigned her students homework to write about their parents' immigration status. Illustrating the blurred conception of public/private enforcement of the initiative, the owner of a dog that had bitten a Latina refused her money for medical treatment, claiming, "Illegals have no right to medical care, [Governor] Pete Wilson said so." When approached again regarding payment of hospital expenses, the dog owner reiterated his misguided understanding of the import of Proposition 187, responding that "I don't have to pay anything, Pete Wilson said it was the law."[61]

One of the evils of Proposition 187 was that in denying services to undocumented immigrants, it subjected all Latinas/os to scrutiny as to their entitlement to public education and social services. Sixty percent of the calls made to a discrimination hotline in California just after the adoption of Proposition 187 were from citizen or lawful permanent resident victims of discrimination.[62] As illustrated in "Cheech" Marin's poignant film comedy *Born in East L.A.* (1987), the common use of physical appearance by border enforcement authorities and by the public as indicative of alien status is flawed and subjects many documented and citizen Latinas/os to mistreatment and suspicion. Indeed, in the case of Proposition 187, this overbroad reach may have been by design. Although it explicitly targeted only undocumented immigrants, Proposition 187 proved to be an early step in California's initiative assault on Latinas/os generally, being followed in later years by initiatives affecting both Latina/o immigrants with legal status and Latina/o citizens in targeting affirmative action programs (in 1996) and bilingual education (1998).

Prompted by the success of California's Proposition 187, in the 1990s, Congress also aimed to confront the perceived abuses by immigrants of welfare laws. Federal law already barred undocumented immigrants from eligibility for most federal public services, such as Aid to Families with Dependent Children (AFDC), food stamps, and Medicaid. In the Personal Responsibility and Work Opportunity Reconciliation Act of 1996, Congress stripped other federal services, such as immunizations, school lunch programs, and housing assistance, from undocumented immigrants. The legislation went further, however, and barred most documented but noncitizen immigrants from eligibility for federal benefits such as AFDC, food stamps, Medicaid, and Social Security. The next year, in 1997, Congress did restore Social Security and Medicaid benefits to elderly and disabled documented immigrants.

Targeting children born in the United States to undocumented parents, California's then-governor Pete Wilson and others called in the 1990s for a federal constitutional amendment to deny citizenship by birthright to these children. These scapegoaters were concerned that undocumented Latinas, particularly Mexicans, were crossing the border into the United States to bear their children in order to secure their American citizenship —the citizenship clause of the federal Constitution's Fourteenth Amendment had been interpreted by the Supreme Court in 1898 to confer citizenship status on a child born in California to Chinese parents who themselves were barred from citizenship by the Chinese Exclusion Act.[63] The threat posed by the possibility that Mexican women, themselves violating immigration law, might unilaterally confer citizen status on their supposed abundant offspring was too compelling for many lawmakers to ignore. In 1993, some congressional representatives introduced a resolution to repeal and replace this constitutional citizenship protection with a provision reading, "All persons born in the United States . . . of mothers who are citizens or legal residents of the United States . . . are citizens of the United States."[64] By 1996, the Republican Party Platform Committee had endorsed a proposal abolishing, by constitutional amendment, the Constitution's expansive guarantee of citizenship to "all persons born or naturalized in the United States."[65]

The perception that Latinas enter the United States to bear children protected as American citizens was apparently to blame for the mistreatment in 1995 of a Mexican beauty queen at the hands of U.S. border agents. While seeking to enter the United States to attend her crown's annual conference, Ana Beatriz de Santiago, the queen of the U.S.-Mexico Sister Cities International Association, was detained at the border by Customs and Immigration and Naturalization Service officials who suspected her of being pregnant and of seeking to enter the country to deliver her baby. One official even lifted her dress and pressed on her stomach to ensure she was not pregnant. Santiago, who was not pregnant and indeed was a virgin, was detained for over two hours while being questioned and inspected.[66]

Perceptions of Latinas' fertility, as well as of their laziness and welfare abuses, led Congress and some states to tighten welfare laws as they applied even to citizen recipients. For example, the federal Personal Responsibility and Work Opportunity Reconciliation Act of 1996 placed a five-year lifetime limit on welfare payments and required that the family head be employed within two years.[67] In Massachusetts, sensationalized press coverage of a Puerto Rican mother's transgressions prompted welfare reform legislation deemed the nation's toughest. Claribel Ventura, the twenty-six-year-old single mother of six children, was pregnant with her seventh child when she was arrested on charges of child abuse for allegedly scalding her four-year-old son's hands "almost to the bone." Somehow, the story of Claribel Ventura transformed from that of one "extraordinarily aberrant 'bad mother' to one about welfare dependency," especially when further investigation determined that most of Ventura's sixteen siblings were receiving welfare or other public benefits.[68]

Stereotypes of Latina fertility have even helped propel anti-immigrant and anti-Latina/o animus in environmental organizations. John Tanton, the former president of the Zero Population Growth organization and a cofounder of U.S. English, once wrote about his fears of a "Latin onslaught," asking whether "the present majority peaceably [will] hand over its political power to a group that is simply more fertile?" and suggesting that, if so, "[p]erhaps this is the first instance in which those with their pants up are going to be caught by those with their pants down!"[69] In 1998, members of the Sierra Club organization were confronted with a ballot measure asking whether their club should adopt a comprehensive policy advocating zero population growth through a combination of reducing natural population increases and placing enhanced restrictions on immigration. Although this anti-immigrant measure was defeated, 40 percent of those members voting favored the proposal.[70] Anti-immigrant sentiments remain part of mainstream environmental strategies and movements. Some environmentalists view immigrants, particularly Latinas/os, as excessively fertile and as failing to value environmental quality.

This attitude that scapegoats immigrants for environmental ills is misplaced. It is well documented that environmental degradation stems from multiple causes that range from military activities to Americans' excessive consumptive behavior.[71] Environmental policies and strategies directed against immigrants at bottom favor ecosystems over the lives of Latina/o immigrants, particularly Mexicans. Even accepting the notion that to some extent long-term environmental quality takes precedence over the short-term treachery of these policies to humans, it is not fair to implement strategies that burden Latinas/os. Latinas/os already bear the brunt of the human consequence of pollution by their exposure to hazardous chemicals in the discriminatory siting of waste production and disposal facilities, and as farm workers exposed to pesticides in the fields. Legitimate strategies would address environmental ills through measures to reduce energy and consumer-goods consumption, as well as employing more humane strategies to reduce fertility rates such as working to eradicate poverty and making birth control products and information more accessible.

6

In the U.S.A., It's English or *Adiós Amigo*
Latinas/os and Assimilation

"No hablo inglés."
"Hablo Smith and Wesson?"
—dialogue between a Latino drug dealer and an Anglo narcotics
officer, played by Billy Crystal, who pulls his gun on the
dealer in the 1986 film comedy *Running Scared*

How are Mexicans like billiard balls?
The harder you smack 'em, the more English you get out of them.

Latinas/os are dogged by the stereotype that paints them as
foreigners who are unwilling or unable to assimilate into mainstream
American life and culture. Although assimilation is an indeterminate concept, for Latinas/os this perception focuses most prominently on their use
of the Spanish language instead of English.

The perception of Latinas/os as unassimilable is reflected in the remarks of diverse commentators, ranging from politicians and writers—
even Latinas/os—to a flamboyant rock musician. Senator Alan Simpson
has observed that "[t]he assimilation of the English language and other
aspects of American culture by Spanish-speaking immigrants appears to
be less rapid and complete than for other groups."[1] Former presidential
candidate Pat Buchanan railed against Mexican immigrants:

Unlike the immigrants of old, who bade farewell to their native lands
when they boarded the ship, for Mexicans, the mother country is right
next door. Millions have no desire to learn English or to become citizens.
America is not their home; Mexico is; and they wish to remain proud

Mexicans. They have [only] come here to work. Rather than assimilate, they create Little Tijuanas in U.S. cities, just as Cubans have created a Little Havana in Miami. . . . With their radio and TV stations, newspapers, films, and magazines, the Mexican Americans are creating a Hispanic culture separate and apart from America's larger culture. They are becoming a nation within a nation.[2]

Prominent conservative Latina/o spokespersons Linda Chávez and Richard Rodriguez have criticized the supposed reluctance of Latinas/os to learn English.[3] While touring in Texas during 2000, rock guitarist "Terrible" Ted Nugent preached to his audience, "If you're not gonna speak English, get the fuck out of America."[4] Media representations of the unintelligent Latina/o (addressed in Chapter 7) contribute to the impression that, in addition to the recalcitrant Latina/o, some otherwise willing Latinas/os simply are incapable of learning the English language and the other cultural, social, and political expectations and mores of Americans.

Peter Brimelow, author of *Alien Nation,* complained that even many assimilated Latinas/os, particularly Mexican Americans, are engaged in an antination process of reverse assimilation by retaining a preference for the Spanish language despite their proficiency in English.[5] When country/pop/rock singer Linda Ronstadt toured in support of her first Spanish-language album, *Canciones de mi padre,* in 1987, many of her Anglo fans were surprised to learn of her Latina heritage. At a Massachusetts show, hecklers chanted, "English, English." At one New York concert, a disgruntled concertgoer "grumpily stomped down an aisle [toward the exit] and shouted to no one in particular, 'Remember the Alamo, Mex!'"[6] One of the most cherished *Seinfeld* television series episodes suggests that bilingual Latinas/os are unwilling to forgo using Spanish, despite its apparent inadequacy in the mainstream of American commerce and culture. Kramer had validated the notorious behavior of the Soup Nazi merchant by suggesting that he should not tolerate anything less than perfection from his customers. The next customer asked for his soup, adding as a courtesy, "Por favor." The Soup Nazi questioned, "Por favor?" The customer replied, "I'm part Spanish." "Adiós!" demanded the Soup Nazi, sending him away without soup. I suppose the writers may not have meant any offense—perhaps they meant to portray the Soup Nazi as a bigoted Archie Bunker–type character whose views would be too extreme to resonate with the audience (an approach that backfired in the *All in the*

Family television series, when many Americans embraced Archie as a spokesperson for their views). Yet it strikes me as foul to suggest that it is imperfect to utter even a courtesy in Spanish, and that this marketplace imperfection is somehow comical. This episode is even more disturbing when viewed against the relative invisibility of Latinas/os throughout the running of this renowned television series set in New York City, an absence sustained by current New York–location sitcoms *Friends* and *Will and Grace*.

Views of Latinas/os as unassimilable are not limited to Mexican Americans. Salsa pioneer Willie Colón captured the popular sentiment toward Puerto Ricans by naming the band he leads Legal Alien. Cuban Americans in Dade County, Florida, were perceived by Anglos there as so resistant to accepting the English language that Floridians launched the modern Official English language movement, examined below.

The construction of Latinas/os as unassimilable extends beyond perceptions of their unwillingness or inability to learn English. Latinas/os are seen as unpatriotic—particularly as pledging their allegiance to another country and as desiring to "rewrite" history to introduce notions of colonialism, oppression, and discrimination not apparent from the Anglo vantage point. Peter Brimelow supposed that unchecked immigration from Mexico might lead to a movement to reclaim California and other southwestern areas for Mexico.[7] Linda Chávez points to Chicana/o activists in the 1960s who called for the reuniting of Mexico with the Southwest as part of a "Plan de Aztlán," thereby disavowing their European roots.[8] Another commentator charged that while forsaking the Pledge of Allegiance to the American flag, many Latina/o students in California give oath to "the Hispanic Cinco de Mayo" holiday.[9] Equally offensive to many Anglos were television images of Mexican Americans in California carrying the United Farmworkers and Mexican flags while protesting against Proposition 187. These images reinforced the speculation of Barbara Coe, one of the drafters of Proposition 187, that the "militant arm of the pro-illegal activists . . . have vowed to take over first California, then the Western states and then the rest of the nation."[10]

Related to the public's view of Latinas/os as unwilling or unable to assimilate is the widespread perception of Latinas/os as foreigners.[11] This perception encompasses even those Latinas/os born in the United States to immigrant parents, as well as Latinas/os of later generations. Speaking Spanish, whether by monolingual or bilingual speakers, is assumed to signify a recent immigration. Speaking English with an accent similarly triggers the assumption of foreignness. So pervasive is this view of Latinas/os as foreigners that physical appearance alone may be used to signal national origin. Many later-generation Latinas/os have fielded the question "Where were your parents born?" implying they are a mere generation removed from foreignness. In the fall of 2001, while teaching law school in downtown San Francisco, I rode a city bus daily into the Tenderloin district. One morning, an Anglo-appearing passenger who was intoxicated, mentally disturbed, or both was initiating loud conversations with passengers before they could retreat to another part of the bus. When three young Latino-appearing youth entered the bus, the animated Anglo managed to strike up a conversation with them, asking as his initial question "Are you guys foreigners?" "We live here," one replied in English. "Are you Spanish?" he asked. "Conquistadors?" "Bandits?" One replied, "We're college students." The Anglo pressed forward, now talking to himself, "What are you studying to be? Rock 'n' rollers? You know there aren't many Spanish rock stars. There is that one. . . ."

American media have contributed to the view of Latinas/os as foreigners unable to assimilate. In 1930, the *New York Times* opined that "[i]t is folly to pretend that the more recently arrived Mexicans, who are largely of Indian blood, can be absorbed and incorporated into the American race."[12] Particularly in the 1990s, journalistic coverage of Latina/o immigration invoked military and animal reproductive metaphors to portray Latinas/os as invading insect-like hordes traveling an unceasing trail stretching from Mexico to the United States.[13] These images establish and reinforce the public's perception that Latinas/os are immigrants and foreigners.

Political advertisements have also played a role in constructing Latinas/os as foreigners. One of Pat Buchanan's presidential campaign television advertisements in 2000 depicted a fictional man who chokes on a meatball on hearing of a government move to provide better access to federal programs to non-English-speaking citizens. After dialing 911, he dies while trying to navigate a multilingual menu. "Do you ever miss English?" asks the announcer, who suggests, "Immigration is out of control."

Media portrayals of Latinas/os living in the United States often exaggerate cultural differences between Anglos and Latinas/os and foster perceptions of foreignness. A videocassette summary of the motion picture *Fools Rush In* (1997) describes its plot as "A New York architect [Alex Whitman] working in Las Vegas meets and marries a beautiful Hispanic photographer [Isabel Fuentes, played by Salma Hayek] and experiences some culture shock with her family." Throughout the film, Isabel travels geographically between Mexico and Nevada, as well as linguistically between Spanish and English. The film thus situates her both as a foreigner and as culturally different from Americans. Isabel dances salsa while preparing dinner, lavishes affection on her Chihuahua, and "spices" up the couple's home with splashy colors and large religious crosses. She argues over the religion of the couple's baby. Weekend dinners at her family house in Las Vegas, where she had shared one bathroom with five brothers and three live-in cousins, are lively gatherings of about twenty-five people with a mariachi band playing. In his first social meeting with Alex's parents, Isabel's father suggests allegiance to a different flag when he points out angrily how "the West was stolen from Mexico."

crazy/beautiful (2001) tells the cinematic story of a Latino (Carlos) who buses from a Los Angeles barrio to a wealthy Pacific Palisades high school. There, Carlos falls for the Anglo daughter (Nicole, played by Kirsten Dunst) of a wealthy politician. The Anglo/Latino worlds depicted here are more than a two-hour barrio-to-burbs bus ride apart. When his Latino friends visit suburban Pacific Palisades, a racial confrontation ensues with his Anglo football teammates. When Nicole bumps into a Latina classmate at the high school, hostilities flare as the Latina threatens Nicole and then language-switches to Spanish to curse her. At an Anglo-hosted party in Pacific Palisades, a 1980s-style White punk rock band entertains, while back in the barrio, salsa music is the party favorite at the *quinceañera,* a coming-of-age celebration for fifteen-year-old Latinas similar to a "sweet sixteen" party. Illustrating the significance of the color line, Nicole remarks to Carlos how she likes their contrasting skin: "Look how good our skin looks next to each other."

Television's *Beverly Hills 90210* highlighted Anglo/Latina/o cultural difference by conjoining an aspiring Latino (Jesse) and one of the Anglo students (Andrea) in a relationship ending in Andrea's troubled pregnancy. Reflecting his religious beliefs against abortion, Jesse argued against ending the pregnancy, and the two fought over whether the baby would be raised Jewish or Catholic.

Debunking the perception that Latinas/os are unwilling or unable to learn English, studies confirm the desire of Latina/o immigrants to learn English, as well as their ability to learn English as fast or faster than past Anglo immigrant groups from Europe. In one study, over nine out of ten Latinas/os in each of the ethnicity groups of Mexican, Puerto Rican, and

Cuban agreed or strongly agreed with the survey question of whether "U.S. citizens and residents should learn English."[14] Another survey revealed that 93 percent of Mexican immigrants agreed that residents of the United States should learn English.[15] The traditional pattern of English-language acquisition by immigrants extends three generations: the first generation acquires some English ability but is mostly monolingual; the second is bilingual; and by the third generation, English is the dominant language.[16] Not only is Latina/o English-language acquisition consistent with this model, but one study points to a move among Latina/o immigrants toward a two-generation pattern of English acquisition.[17] My own family history supports the ready acceptance of English. My maternal grandfather (Fernando Troncoso) immigrated to Los Angeles from Chiapas in 1918, and my grandmother (Ramona Montes de Oca) left Guadalajara for California's Coachella Valley in 1921. Both learned English but spoke mostly Spanish at home. My mother speaks both English and Spanish fluently. Although I was born and raised in East Los Angeles, I spoke English at my Catholic elementary school and at home and know little Spanish. My mother and my Latino stepfather (Luis Acevedo) would speak Spanish to each other but switch to English when addressing me.[18]

Perceptions that Latinas/os are unwilling or unable to assimilate underlie the virulent English-language movement that originated in the early 1980s and has since secured the adoption of English-language laws in about half the states, including California, Colorado, Florida, Virginia, and most recently in Iowa in early 2002. These laws typically declare English as the state's official language. Some go further and purport to protect and preserve English as the state's official language, while a few others expressly prohibit government speech in languages other than English. Many cities have also adopted local government versions of these English-language laws.

Adopted by initiative in 1988, Arizona's law represented the most far-reaching of these English-language laws. In addition to elevating English as the "official language" of the state for "the ballot, the public schools, and all government functions and actions," the initiative required Arizona and all its political subdivisions to take "all reasonable steps to preserve, protect, and enhance the role of the English language as the official language of the state of Arizona." Further, Arizona and all political subdivisions were required "to act in English and no other language." A few exceptions were specified, such as when necessary to ensure public health or safety (presumably encompassing 911 operators) and to protect the rights of criminal defendants.[19] Litigation challenging the Arizona initiative in federal court was dismissed by the U.S. Supreme Court on the procedural ground that the Arizona state employee who had initiated the lawsuit had left her job. Ultimately, state court litigation reached the Arizona Supreme Court, which struck down the law in 1998 on the ground that it violated the First Amendment's guarantee of free speech by denying limited or non-English speakers the right to participate equally in the political process and by depriving elected officials and public employees of their ability to communicate with constituents and the public.[20] In recent years, both Utah and Alaska adopted English-language laws by initiative. As in Arizona, the constitutionality of these measures was challenged and is still pending in the courts—in Utah, by the American Civil Liberties Union and other groups,[21] and in Alaska, by Native groups and other plaintiffs. In 2002, an initiative petition seeking to adopt an English-language law in Oklahoma similar to that struck down in Arizona was aborted when the Oklahoma Supreme Court found the initiative constitutionally infirm under the free speech and due process guarantees of its state constitution.[22]

Introduced regularly in Congress since 1981, national Official English legislation has never been enacted, although in 1996 such legislation did pass the House. In the summer of 2001, President George W. Bush was developing a guest-worker proposal authorizing the entry of Mexican workers into the United States. Unlike prior proposals, the 2001 plan was to include a language component to require the learning of English. As one Bush aide described the English requirement, "Bush wants the American public to hear, 'These guys are coming here to work, not to be on the dole.'"[23] The September 11 tragedy derailed proposals to expand the number of documented immigrants, as the economy slowed and attention turned instead to heightened border security.

In recent years, the English-language movement, led by the national organization U.S. English, has shifted its emphasis from Official English and English-only laws to the legal eradication of bilingual education. Bilingual education programs do not follow a single model. Rather, they range from curriculum that intends to maintain Spanish (or other non-English) language fluency while teaching English skills, to models that emphasize English language acquisition. Latina/o conservatives Linda Chávez and Richard Rodriguez have long criticized education programs for limited or non-English speakers that entail anything but a "sink or swim" approach to learning the English language. In a presentation at the University of Oregon, Rodriguez blasted programs in which Latinas/os are taught English while they learn other substantive subjects in their native language of Spanish. Rodriguez explained, "Do you recall your French-language teacher in high school who spoke only French and disallowed English in the classroom?" He advocated immersion as the most effective means of teaching a new language. Indeed, my uncle José Troncoso, who taught Spanish at colleges throughout the West Coast for over thirty years, insisted that his native English-speaking students speak only Spanish in the classroom. Yet, when they left his class and headed to their sociology, psychology, and business economics courses, surely they reverted back to English. Otherwise they would sacrifice their understanding of those other courses in the single-minded pursuit of speedier proficiency in Spanish. Linda Chávez, too, has attacked schools whose bilingual education programs were not sufficiently emphasizing the English language and which dared to facilitate the Spanish language. She accused these programs of intending "not to assimilate Hispanic children . . . but to maintain and strengthen their ethnic identity by teaching them in their native language and by inculcating in them their native culture," thereby abdicating the assimilative function she demanded of schools.[24] Chávez and Rodriguez possess views that do not reflect those of Latinas/os generally—a 1998 national survey of Latina/o opinions concluded that Latinas/os overwhelmingly favor bilingual education programs designed to facilitate the learning of both Spanish and English. Seventy percent of Mexican Americans, 73 percent of Puerto Ricans, and 77 percent of Cuban Americans regarded the appropriate objective of bilingual education as enabling Latinas/os to learn two languages, as opposed to lesser percentages (15, 12, and 10 percent, respectively) who viewed the objective narrowly as learning just English, and even lower percentages who believed the goal should be to maintain Spanish language and culture (9, 8, and 5 percent, respectively).[25] Of the variety of bilingual programs, then, Latinas/os favor those designed to teach English while remaining respectful of the Spanish language and presumably not sacrificing proficiency in other substantive subjects in the single-minded interest of speedier English acquisition.

In contrast to many English-language laws that are primarily symbolic, the anti–bilingual education initiatives passed in California (Proposition 227, adopted in 1998) and Arizona (2000) directly affect the education of children with limited proficiency in English. These initiatives replace the local control, design, and choice of bilingual education programs with a state-mandated approach that places English learners in a classroom in which nearly all instruction is in English while providing a curriculum designed for children learning the language. This immersion is not normally intended to exceed one year, during which time the initiatives permit local schools to place together students of different ages with similar degrees of English fluency. In this "sink or swim" approach to assimilation, English acquisition is favored over all other substantive subject areas. Rather than learning subjects such as history and mathematics in their native language while also learning English, Latinas/os are exposed to these other subjects only as a training ground for English-language acquisition. Once returned to mainstream classrooms after their year-long immersion, the students presumably must compete with native English speakers who had the benefit of being educated in substantive subjects they were able to comprehend in their native language. Moreover, consider how non-English-speaking parents will be able to adequately assist with and oversee their immersed child's English-language homework assignments.

California's anti–bilingual education initiative has withstood constitutional challenge in federal court. Since federal courts have declined to construe the federal Constitution to require bilingual education,[26] the district court concluded that California voters were free to denounce the concept of bilingual education. Although the federal Constitution would not permit majority voters intentionally to discriminate against a minority, the initiative challengers did not demonstrate such discriminatory intent. Moreover, the court suggested that it could not discern any agenda of discrimination from the face of Proposition 227. It regarded the initiative as merely taking a nondiscriminatory position on the best method to educate children who are national origin minorities.[27] By contrast, some legal commentators contend that Proposition 227 was racially motivated against Latinas/os, pointing to the campaign's "near exclusive focus on the Spanish language, the history of discrimination against Mexican Americans in California, including the increase in anti-Latina/o and anti-immigrant animus in the 1990s, statements by the advocates of the initiative, and the racially-polarized vote."[28]

Ron Unz, the Silicon Valley software millionaire financing the California and Arizona anti–bilingual education initiatives, of late turned his attention to other states. In fall 2002, his initiative failed in Colorado but passed overwhelmingly in Massachusetts.

*

The adoption of English-language laws by state legislatures is complemented by the private implementation of English-language agendas by citizens. In the immigrant-rich states of Arizona, California, Colorado, and Florida, English-language laws were adopted by citizen initiative. Initiatives eradicating bilingual education were approved later in Arizona and California. But the role of citizen participation in anti-Spanish agendas goes beyond electoral support of initiatives. In private settings ranging from workplaces to places of relaxation, Spanish speakers have been confronted by language vigilantes motivated in part by their perceptions that Spanish-speaking Latinas/os are unwilling or unable to assimilate by learning and using English. In the mid-1990s, for example, a Washington tavern owner hung a sign over her bar demanding, "In the U.S.A. It's English or Adios Amigo."[29] She was sued by Spanish-speaking customers whom she had ejected for violating her policy.[30] To prevail in such actions under civil rights laws, the plaintiff normally must establish that the discrimination was purposeful. The trial judge ruled for the tavern owner because he believed the owner was acting to ensure the safety of others and her property by insisting customers speak a language she could understand to ensure no fighting words were being exchanged. Although the judge thought her condescending bar sign was "insensitive to minorities," he ruled it was not actionable discrimination.[31] The Washington tavern owner, validated by the courts, could thus continue to run her business as if she were *Seinfeld*'s Soup Nazi, free to give her Spanish-speaking customers a hearty *adiós* and a point toward the door, all in the ostensible interest of keeping the peace.

Other examples of language vigilantism abound. After communication problems arose with a Colombian couple, a Florida cooperative apartment building voted to deny residency to non-English (i.e., Spanish) speakers, justifying the policy as one intended to keep out "undesirables."[32] In California, a San Jose couple refused to rent their apartments to Spanish speakers who could not speak English.[33] The Ninth Circuit Court of Appeals let stand a jury verdict in favor of the landlords on the prospective tenants' Fair Housing Act claim while observing, on the issue of discriminatory intent, that the landlords had testified their purpose was to ensure effective communication in an emergency.[34] Throughout the country, several employers have adopted English-only rules requiring bilingual Latinas/os (and other bilingual workers) to speak only English on the job.[35] The world's largest online service, America Online, briefly imposed an English-only policy for its international sports chatroom, aiming to protect against vulgar language, but reversed its policy after uproar from Latinas/os and others.

In recent years, proponents of English-language laws have begun to couch their proposals in terms of their benefit to immigrants. One promotional advertisement for the U.S. English organization even suggests that the impetus for language regulation comes from immigrants themselves, stating, "Immigrants want and need to learn English. It's time politicians got the message."[36] One congressional language bill was titled the Bill Emerson English Language Empowerment Act of 1996 (but labeled the Linguistic and Voting Deprivation Act by opponents). Commentators have debunked this supposed benevolent justification that masks ill will toward immigrants.[37] Nor should private enforcement of assimilationist agendas be regarded as well intentioned; rather, language vigilantism often is driven by anti-Latina/o animus and sometimes has prompted or served as an outlet for hate crimes against Latinas/os. For example, a tavern in Forest Grove, Oregon, adopted a policy disallowing any foreign language in the bar. "Problem" customers—those who failed to speak English—were to be moved to a table away from the bar (as if to the back of the bus) and the jukebox turned on to drown out their conversation. The tavern owners justified their policy as relieving the friction between Anglo and Mexican American customers—the local Anglo population disliked the "foreigners" in their midst and suspected that the Mexican Americans were talking about them in Spanish. At the time, in 1972, the community of Forest Grove was home to about eighty-five hundred residents, more than two thousand of them Mexican Americans. One night, after Anglo customers had expressed their irritation, the tavern's bartender pulled the beers of three Latinos (all U.S. citizens) who were conversing in Spanish. Three Anglos, all regular customers, followed the Latinos out of the tavern and gave them a violent lesson in the American way and the subordinate status of Latinas/os— one of the Anglos was convicted in state court for striking one of the Latinos over the right eye with a fire extinguisher in his efforts to impress on them the importance of speaking English when in the United States.[38]

Sometimes, even judges have applied their assimilationist agendas against Latinas/os. In 1995, a Texas judge instructed a bilingual Latina in a child custody hearing that she was abusing her five-year-old daughter by speaking only Spanish with her:

[Y]ou're abusing that child and you're relegating her to the position of a housemaid. Now, get this straight. You start speaking English to this child because if she doesn't do good in school, then I can remove her because it's not in her best interest to be ignorant. The child will hear only English.[39]

As a local Spanish-language newspaper editor observed, the judge's edict so alarmed Latinas/os in Texas that they feared the government could take their children away if they spoke Spanish to them.[40] The judge's assimilative views brought to mind dialogue from a 1948 western, *Three Godfathers,* in which John Wayne chided the Latino helping Wayne to transport a newborn to town and safety: "Cut out that Mex lingo around the kid . . . first thing you know he'll be talking it. We got to raise him with good all-American habla [speech], like his ma."[41]

In Washington State, a municipal court judge routinely asked Latina/o defendants if they were "legal," ordered them to enroll in English classes, and sometimes threatened them with deportation.[42] An Anglo judge in Pennsylvania attracted attention in 1996 for his handling of two Latinos who pled guilty to selling cocaine to an undercover officer at a local tavern. As part of their sentence, the judge ordered them to learn to read, write, and speak English. The judge explained his purpose was "to stir them into learning English so they would know what jeopardy they were in." The local district attorney agreed, suggesting it makes sense to "make the defendant a better citizen and help him assimilate into society."[43]

Though seemingly incredible, in the most striking example of assimilationist pressures in America, a Latino in Texas was actually sentenced to prison because he was unable to speak English. The defendant, Aristeo Lira Flores, had been convicted of drunk driving. (Those readers judging his character from his conviction should recall that both President George W. Bush and Vice President Dick Cheney have been arrested for drunk driving.) Had Flores been able to speak and understand English, he would have been sentenced to attend a diversion program of alcohol education and therefore avoided prison time. Yet, because the program was unavailable in Spanish and Flores was unable to speak English, he was sentenced to one year in prison. Astoundingly, the Texas appellate court upheld his imprisonment as consistent with federal and state constitutional requirements of due process and equal protection. On appeal, Flores's counsel argued that his sentencing constituted race or national origin discrimination for which the government policy must undergo strict constitutional scrutiny. Yet the court refused to treat his inability to speak English as discrimination on the basis of race or national origin. The government's policy, which led to his imprisonment, thus survived the more lax standard for equal protection of whether the policy was rationally related to a legitimate government interest. Among the government interests typically cited in these language cases is the potential cost to a cash-strapped government to provide services and programs in languages other than English. But what "civilized" society could sanction imprisonment based on one's native language?

When challenges are made against state and federal governments providing services only in English to non-English speakers, the courts have overwhelmingly failed to recognize a constitutional duty (under the equal protection clause) to furnish services in native non-English languages such as Spanish. For example, the California Supreme Court held monolingual Spanish speakers had no constitutional right to receive notice in Spanish terminating or reducing welfare benefits.[44] The federal Second Circuit Court of Appeals rejected challenges to the federal government's failure to provide Social Security benefit forms and services in Spanish,[45] and the Sixth Circuit upheld a city employment exam administered in English to non-English speakers.[46] Claimants arguing under the equal protection clause must prove intentional discrimination. Courts usually regard the government's decision to provide services only in English as a facially neutral act that reflects a nondiscriminatory preference for English over other languages,[47] and these claims thus fail. Federal regulations promulgated under Title VI of the Civil Rights Act of 1964 permit disparate impact claims as an alternative to proving intentional discrimination under Title VI. But when a Latina invoked these regulations in a class action against the state administrators of an English-only driver's license testing policy, the Supreme Court rejected her action on finding Congress did not intend a private cause of action under the regulations.[48] These judicial outcomes stand in stark contrast to the overwhelming position of Latinas/os, as reflected in a 1989 national survey, in which 90 percent of Mexican Americans and 94 percent of Puerto Ricans and Cuban Americans agreed or strongly agreed that public services should be provided in Spanish.[49]

Facing these court decisions, non-English speakers presumably could attempt to obtain their own translations of government communications into their native language. Still, translators would not overcome government English-language testing requirements as a condition to obtaining a driver's or occupational license. Moreover, hypothesizing that Latinas/os could procure a translator does not address the expense and difficulty they face in actually obtaining an accurate and timely translation, particularly for government documents that impose stringent time deadlines for action. Because of the difficulty in obtaining translations, many non-English-speaking Latinas/os rely on their children to attempt to read often technical and private English-language communications. Going beyond the refusal to translate government documents into Spanish, legislation introduced in the 1990s in Mississippi sought to link receipt of government benefits to the recipient's English-language ability, thus prohibiting non-English speakers from obtaining benefits.[50] Building on that state's Official English law, the bill would have required any person receiving state public assistance, such as Aid to Families with Dependent Children and medical assistance services under Medicaid, to be proficient in English, presumably as some incentive toward assimilation or as punishment for failing to assimilate. But coercion is unnecessary to convince Latinas/os of the importance of learning English. As then–chief justice of the New Jersey Supreme Court suggested in dissenting from his court's denial of a constitutional challenge to the state's policy to send information on unemployment claim appeal rights in English to monolingual Spanish speakers:

> Some might think that the rule of the majority provides an incentive to learn English. No such incentive is needed, for every day of their lives provides Hispanic-Americans with innumerable, often devastating reminders of their disadvantaged position resulting from the language barrier they face. There is no carrot in this decision, only a stick.[51]

The so-called Americanization program of the early 1900s offers a historical example of efforts to assimilate Latinas/os through complementary government-sponsored programs and private efforts. Deployed in the Southwest, and particularly in California, this program targeted Mexican immigrants in a campaign that had previously been directed, with different tactics, at Native American children.[52] Operating through school curriculum aimed at children, particularly Mexican girls, as well as through labor-camp classes aimed at adults, the Americanization campaign sought to teach Mexicans to speak in English and to acquire "American" ideals. As the Los Angeles school superintendent explained the program in 1923, "We have these [Mexican] immigrants to live with, and if we Americanize them, we can live with them."[53] Americanization efforts focused primarily on the acquisition of English, as represented by the policy of the Arizona state superintendent's office that "every phase of school life [for Mexican children] should take part in promoting the meaningful use of English."[54] Americanization lessons extended beyond language to address stereotypical traits associated with Mexican immigrants, such as perceptions of their laziness and uncleanliness. For example, teachers urged Mexican children to make fun of their lazy Mexican classmates, and many schools subjected Mexican children to regular hygiene inspections and mandatory showering.[55]

California formalized its Americanization program by establishing, in 1916, a Division of Immigrant Education within its Department of Education.[56] Local school districts sometimes established similar departments, and school administrators in other southwestern states issued bulletins and guidelines for instructing Mexican students. Although during the Great Depression attention shifted from welcoming and assimilating immigrants to excluding and removing them, Latina/o immigration continued in the Southwest and elsewhere. "Americanization" lost favor as the popular and official term of reference for assimilation efforts, but those efforts continued unabated in government programs and through private endeavors. As one commentator observed, "Language and culture continued to be major educational concerns, and the identification of the Spanish language and Mexican culture as contradictory to educational success lost no ground in conventional theory and practice."[57]

My educational experience in Catholic elementary schools in the 1960s and early 1970s reflects these assimilationist priorities in American classrooms. Although I attended schools in East Los Angeles and neighboring Monterey Park with overwhelmingly Latina/o student bodies, the teachers and administrators were Anglos. Spanish was prohibited in the classroom and relegated to the play yard when students were out of the earshot of school officials. Classroom curricula had little or no recognition of Latina/o culture or history. My experience was not unique —both public and private schools, particularly those in the Southwest, harbor a notorious history of punishing children for speaking Spanish on the school grounds.[58] Even in 2002, an Arizona elementary school with an almost entirely Latina/o student body[59] allegedly instructed its teachers not to speak Spanish to students even outside the classroom and to encourage students to speak English in the hallways, cafeteria, and playground.

The perception of Latinas/os as foreigners has influenced both their legal and private treatment. Federal restrictions on immigration undoubtedly reflect the assumption that Latinas/os (and other groups) are unable to assimilate. In the post–World War I era especially, Anglos advocating restrictions on Mexican immigration have pointed to Mexicans' supposed inability to assimilate.[60] Further illustrating the link between assimilation stereotypes and immigration law are the remarks of Pat Buchanan, while a presidential candidate in 1992: "I think God made all people good, but if we had to take a million immigrants in, say Zulus, next year, or Englishmen, and put them in Virginia, what group would be easier to assimilate and would cause less problems for the people of Virginia?"[61] Even the Supreme Court invoked perceptions of immigrant inability to assimilate in upholding the Chinese Exclusion Acts, adopted by Congress in the late 1800s to prohibit Chinese immigration. The Court reasoned in 1889 that the Chinese "remained strangers in the land, residing apart by themselves, and adhering to the customs and usages of their own country. It seemed impossible for them to assimilate with our people or to make changes in their habits or modes of living."[62]

The view of Latinas/os as foreigners subjects Latina/o citizens to scrutiny as "illegal aliens" at border checkpoints and elsewhere. One of the evils of Proposition 187, California's initiative outlawing the delivery of government services to "illegal aliens," was the alien witch-hunt it launched against Latina/o children and adults in California. Under this law, those persons "reasonably" suspected as illegal aliens were to be denied public social services and expelled from public schools. Although the law targeted the delivery of services by public employees, private citizens purported to enforce the law in private settings. For example, recall that vigilantes demanded the "green card" of a Latino cook while he worked in a restaurant.[63]

The most dramatic illustration of the public's presumption that Latinas/os are foreigners came from Washington, D.C. In 1996, Congressman Luis Gutierrez, a Puerto Rican born in Chicago, was denied admission to the Capitol by a security aide who rejected his congressional credentials and told Gutierrez to "go back to the country where you came from." Supposedly because the congressman's daughter and niece were carrying small Puerto Rican flags, the aide assumed not only that Congressman Gutierrez was impersonating a U.S. congressman but that he was a foreigner.[64] In a strikingly similar episode in 2001 that reflects the construction of other groups, particularly Asian Americans, as "aliens," Oregon congressman David Wu, a Chinese American, was denied entry to the U.S. Energy Department, where he was to deliver a speech in celebration of Asian Pacific American Heritage Month. Security guards rejected his congressional identification and asked him twice whether he was an American. In Oregon, the successful Mexican American candidate for state school superintendent, Susan Castillo, was attacked during her campaign in 2002 by hate-radio commentators who questioned how she could be a U.S. citizen with the last name of Castillo.

The terrorist events of September 11, 2001, may both increase the pressure on Latinas/os to assimilate and transform what assimilation should entail. Those events and the ensuing military response have led Americans to emphasize unity in culture and values and to look with greater suspicion on immigrants and others considered to be foreigners. Under this new assimilationist regime, Latinas/os can expect increased hostility against the Spanish language as a marker of foreignness. The "eyes and ears of alert citizens" are looking for foreigners and listening for non-English languages. Calls for airline passengers to assist in detecting and preventing terrorist plots serve to deputize the public in the interdiction of terrorists. Because undocumented immigrants are now regarded as a national security threat, it is likely that the general public will see their role as extending to the enforcement of open-ended anti-immigrant agendas. In the case of language, these post–September 11 prerogatives to ensure national security and to detect terrorist plots are linked to justifications employed in the past to explain private language vigilantism. Tavern owners, for example, have defended against legal challenges to their English-language policies for customers by claiming that they were keeping peace in the bar by preventing "fighting words"—as one put it, "[I]f they're speaking Spanish, how is my bartender going to know if they're cussing?"[65] A similar justification led a Washington State trial judge to conclude a tavern owner had lawfully enforced an English-only policy against her customers to ensure the safety of her property and others in the bar. As one tavern customer maintained, "They start speaking their own language and we don't know what they're saying. They could be insulting us, making fun of our wives or figuring out a way to rob the place."[66] With the judge's finding of a nondiscriminatory purpose, the tavern owner was insulated from liability under civil rights laws that require proof of purposeful discrimination.[67] This fear of conspiracies crafted in Spanish was even reflected in the blockbuster film *Training Day* (2001), when undercover narcotics officer Denzel Washington warned his new partner that an ignorance of *español* would get him killed: "These [Latino] motherfuckers out here are plotting all kinds of shit behind your back." Employers, too, have relied on similar justifications (such as protection against conspiracies for theft) in imposing workplace English-only policies on their employees.[68]

No doubt the September 11 events will further legitimate these private language policies. Should a tavern be sued for its English-language policy applicable to its customers, the owner might claim the tavern was trying to facilitate the role of its employees and English-speaking customers to detect the makings of terrorist plots. Similarly, an airline or other transit service might adopt an English-language requirement for domestic travel to aid its passengers in detecting and preventing terrorist plans, as well as to ease the discomfort of some travelers who might view non-English speakers as dangerous foreigners conspiring toward disaster. Employers in the transportation or transportation-related industries, such as airline food caterers, as well as other vulnerable industries, such as power plant or chemical facilities, might also demand English from their employees in the interest of ensuring workplace security and safety. The legality of employer English-only policies tends to hinge on the degree of business necessity behind the policy. In challenges to these rules under Title VII of the Civil Rights Act of 1964, which prohibits employment discrimination on the basis of race, color, sex, religion, and national origin,[69] employers will suggest a legitimate business necessity to justify their policy. Although the standards for survival of employer English-language policies under Title VII disparate impact scrutiny are still emerging,[70] it seems apparent that language policies intended to ensure workplace safety for employees and customers are less likely to be invalidated than those not claiming a safety justification. For example, a compliance manual used by Equal Employment Opportunity Commission (EEOC) investigators suggests that a rule requiring all workers on an oil-rig deck to speak English to enable them to communicate quickly and respond effectively to emergencies would potentially be lawful.[71]

By contrast, the EEOC has viewed customer preference rationales as suspect and potentially illegitimate, at least where the employees are not speaking directly to the customer. The courts have upheld English-language policies addressing direct communication with customers. The most notable decision concerned the termination of a Latino disc jockey from a popular southern California radio station after he refused to stop mixing Spanish into his radio broadcasts; a consultant had found the disc jockey's bilingual format hurt ratings among Anglo listeners by "confusing" them about the station's programming.[72] But a tougher question is presented when language policies govern conversation between employees that customers or other employees might overhear.[73] The EEOC manual suggests it might be impermissible for a retailer to require English at all times because its customers object to overhearing its employees speaking Spanish.[74] Employers have sought to justify such rules in stressful environments such as hospitals and nursing homes, where hearing an unfamiliar language allegedly would intimidate an ailing patient. Thus the employer tries to portray customer preference, or even prejudice, as a safety issue.[75] Presumably, in the aftermath of September 11, some employers might ground their customer preference policies in terms of workplace, customer, and even societal safety through the detection of terrorist plots.

As a consequence of the terrorist attacks, decreased tolerance for Third World traditions and practices in the United States, particularly religious practices, may foretell disapproval and distrust among Anglos of so-called nontraditional Latina/o religions such as Santeria and religious observances such as Dia de los Muertos, which may be regarded as able to galvanize "foreigners" to engage in anti-American acts. The Mexican holiday Cinco de Mayo, however, now commodified by the American liquor and tavern industries into a Mardi Gras–like celebration of alcohol, is unlikely to be seen as a threat to patriotism. Reliance on attire to identify those persons with the will to commit anti-American acts suggests a centripetal force toward homogeneity in dress among Latinas/os and others desiring to avoid profiling as anti-American. Mere baggy-pants attire and "pachuco" haircuts were enough to prompt attack from Anglo servicemen and civilians in the Zoot Suit Riots in 1940s Los Angeles.

In schools, the terrorist events and specter of war will increase pressures on curriculum and on teachers to create a unifying cultural bond among students, not only with regard to language but also by suppressing curricula and historical lessons that could detract from the view of America and Americans as culturally and morally superior to enemies of the state. The risk of heightened subversion of history in public schools was brought home by the Pentagon proposal in February 2002 deliberately to plant false stories to influence foreign perceptions of the United

States in the interest of the war on terrorism.[76] By early 2002, U.S. Supreme Court justice Anthony Kennedy and the American Bar Association had launched a school curricular initiative, called "Dialogue on Freedom," under which lawyers and judges will visit high schools to instruct on core democratic values. Moved by his perception of a lack of moral outrage over the terrorist events by some high school students, Kennedy created the program to teach "fundamental values and universal moral precepts."[77]

Following the terrorist events of September 11, many called into question the patriotism of Latinas/os. Among the most pointed statements came from the head of a Utah anti–undocumented immigrant group, who justified the pre–Winter Olympics federal sweep of undocumented workers at Salt Lake City's airport:

> [I]f you go to an illegal Mexican working at the airport and he has access to airplanes, or he's manning a baggage check or whatever, and an Arab terrorist walks up to him and says, "I'll give you $10,000 if you plant a 9-millimeter on the airplane for me," well, here's an individual who's never stood up, held his hand over his heart and said, "I pledge allegiance to the flag and to the country for which it stands." You think that Mexican is going to head south with the 10 grand? You betcha.[78]

Doubting the patriotism of even documented but noncitizen Latinas/os and other immigrants, in the post–September 11 federal takeover of airport security, Congress imposed a citizenship requirement on airport screeners.[79] In addition to English-language policies, we can expect to hear increased calls for citizenship requirements, whether imposed by law or privately, in the transportation industry as well as in other vulnerable industries.

A national survey in 1990 found that 61 percent of Whites believed Hispanics were less patriotic than Whites.[80] Despite the recurrent questioning of Latina/o patriotism, Latinas/os boast a distinguished war record in World War II, Korea, and Vietnam. Gil Carrasco has expressed the loyalty of Latino soldiers fighting for the United States in World War II:

> Throughout the course of World War II, no Latino soldier was ever charged with desertion, treason, or cowardice. The bravery of Latino troops was recognized in the many medals awarded to Mexican Americans, including the Congressional Medal of Honor (the United States'

highest honor), the Silver Star, the Bronze Star, and the Distinguished Service Cross.[81]

As many as one-half million Latinas/os served in World War II, including fifty-three thousand Latinas/os from Puerto Rico.[82] Although Latinas/os served in the Vietnam War in disproportionate numbers, one writer was struck by their invisibility "in the histories, oral histories, and literary anthologies of the Viet Nam War era."[83] Latina/o service was also evident in the 2003 military campaign in Iraq, with several Latino soldiers killed.

At the same time that Latinas/os were dying abroad in Vietnam, some Latinas/os, particularly Chicanas/os in southern California, were rallying against the Vietnam War and the injustices they perceived, particularly that soldiers of color were being placed on the front lines and that the casualty rate for Mexican Americans in Vietnam was over 50 percent higher than their proportion to the total population in the United States.[84] Antiwar protests in East Los Angeles led to a police riot in late summer of 1970 that killed Rubén Salazar, a *Los Angeles Times* reporter writing about police brutality in the Chicana/o community.[85] The presence of Latino soldiers on the front lines while the Latina/o community back home both protested and supported the war reflects the diversity of the Latina/o experience. Supporters included my Mexican American mother and my Mexican American stepfather, ironically a police lieutenant obligated to quell the protests. At the same time, before my teens, I counted myself among those opposing the war.

Despite causing tension at times in my childhood household (I recall in particular a heated argument with my stepfather), this difference among Latinas/os in attitudes over the war was duplicated in the even more complex dynamics among Latinas/os with regard to assimilative pressures in American society. Some Latinas/os, well represented by conservatives Richard Rodriguez and Linda Chávez, advocate that Latinas/os should abandon their culture and embrace an Anglo vision of assimilation that includes a no-compromise adoption of English—in essence, jumping into the assimilation pool feet first. This fervent side of the assimilationist ideal spawns incidents such as that involving the Latino in Arizona who, within one week of September 11, shot and killed a bearded Sikh from India who wore a turban, shouting as he was arrested, "I stand for America all the way."[86] Other Latinas/os, particularly some activist Chicanas/os, want no part of the assimilation pool, preferring to plant their feet in a separatist vision of Aztlán, an independent Puerto Rico, or another sovereign nation dismissive of Americanization.[87] Chicano activist Corky Gonzales penned the anthem for this anti-assimilationist view in his 1960s poem "I Am Joaquín," in which he refuses to be "absorbed."[88] Yet, as Laura Padilla has observed, "neither of these extreme views of assimilation represent the views of most Latinos."[89] Rather, most Latinas/os hold a more practical attitude toward assimilation that keeps both cultures afloat. Their attitude is reflected by the 1998 national survey concluding that Latinas/os overwhelmingly favor bilingual education programs designed to facilitate the learning of both Spanish and English. Edward James Olmos, who played the conservative Latino patriarch Jess Gonzalez in the PBS drama series *American Family,* at first seemed to suggest the extremist view favoring assimilation when, while speaking in English, he denounced programs of bilingual education to a Latino customer sitting in his barbershop chair. But when Gonzalez continued, speaking in Spanish, "In the U.S. you need to speak English," it became clear through his ease of language switching that Gonzalez had mastered English while preserving the hallmark symbol of his Latina/o culture—his native language—thus representing the goal of most Latinas/os, immigrant and nonimmigrant alike. In this barbershop, at least, the sign might read "Bienvenidos Amigos" (Welcome Friends).

7

One of the Smart Ones
Latina/o (Un)Intelligence

"You talk pretty fancy."
Puerto Rican: "For a spic?"
"Yeah."

> —Dialogue between Anglo former police officer and a
> Harvard-educated Puerto Rican gangster in the
> film *Badge 373,* which drew protest from
> New York's Puerto Rican community
> for its portrayals of Puerto Ricans

As soon as cheap labor from Europe was stopped, many lines of
American industry which had been run on a cheap-labor basis
turned to the Mexican supply. For here, right at our doors, was a
great reservoir of the cheapest and most docile labor. The Mexican
"peon" (Indian or mixed-breed) is a poverty-stricken, ignorant,
primitive creature, with strong muscles and with just enough brains
to obey orders and produce profits under competent direction.

> —Lothrop Stoddard[1]

An Englishman, an American, and a Mexican are called upon to
take a lie detector test.
   The Englishman says: "I think I can empty 20 bottles of wine."
   Buzzzzzz goes the lie detector.
   "OK," he says, "10 bottles." And the machine is silent.
   The American says: "I think I can eat 15 hamburgers."
   Buzzzzzz goes the lie detector.
   "Alright, 8 hamburgers." And the machine is silent.
   The Mexican says: "I think . . ."
   Buzzzzzzzzzzzzzzzzzzz [extra long buzz] goes the machine.

Why wasn't Jesus born in Mexico?
They couldn't find three wise men and a virgin!

Several years ago, an Anglo insurance defense lawyer aware of my ethnicity told me he had been retained years earlier to defend a suit arising out of a faulty gas-tank design that spewed gas on the vehicle's occupants after a collision. The driver had burned to death in the fire that ensued. As the California lawyer explained to me, the driver was of Mexican heritage, and although "you wouldn't think that would cost you a lot of money," he conveyed his sense of his client's miserable luck that this "Mexican" (American) was a high-ranking executive in a major corporation. As he put it, the accident had claimed "one of the smart ones." This example drawn from casual conversation is but one reflection of the common belief that Latinas/os are less intelligent than Anglos. Indeed, an early 1990s survey confirmed that 55 percent of Anglos thought Hispanics were less likely than Whites to be intelligent.[2] In schools, where students' success hinges on their perceived intelligence, Latina/o students have been described variously over the years as "mentally retarded," as "linguistically handicapped," and, euphemistically, as "at-risk."[3]

Media have helped both to create and to reinforce this view of Latina/o lack of intelligence. Among the well-known characterizations of Mexican (un)intelligence is José Jiménez, a fictional persona created in the late 1950s by Bill Dana, a comedian of Hungarian heritage.[4] José appeared first on the Steve Allen television show, and later on the *Bill Dana Show,* as well as on several hit recordings. The running punch line in José's skits was to place this dim-witted, accent-thick Mexican in occupations and situations calling for intelligence and skills beyond his capacity. José assumed such diverse roles as a Shakespearian actor and a television engineer. The audience laughed along with the joke that a Mexican could attain these positions. Illustrating his shortcomings, when introduced in a skit as the secret head of the CIA and queried as to how he was doing, José, wearing a mask to protect his identity, nevertheless uttered his trademark line "My name, José Jiménez."[5] As a Broadway writer, he was asked by a mock interviewer whether he used a *nom de plume* or a pseudonym. José responded that he used a typewriter. As the naval submarine commander of the U.S. *Triton,* José was asked if he had a "specific" assignment. "No," he replied, "I have an Atlantic assignment." In his most famous role, as José the Astronaut, José Jiménez was introduced to laughter as the chief astronaut, a man who "could possibly be the most important man in any of our lives." When asked his expert opinion about the most important thing in rocket travel, José responded not with a technical answer but that to him it was the "blast-off." As José explained (in a comedy skit rebroadcast as part of the 1983 astronaut movie *The Right Stuff*), "I always take a blast [drink] before I take off."

A Mexican American was a series regular in the 1950s television comedy *The Real McCoys*. "Pepino" was loyal and likeable but always subordinate to the unsophisticated Anglo family that ran the farm and employed him. Once, Grandpa Amos McCoy chased Pepino away after Pepino had the audacity to suggest how Grandpa and his son might better construct the boat they were attempting to build. As Grandpa explained in scolding Pepino, boat building required "delicate hands and fine brains."[6] This dichotomy of the more capable Anglo and the subordinate Latino was revisited for laughs again in the 1970s television sitcom *Chico [little boy] and the Man*.

The necessity for hapless Mexicans to rely on Anglo intelligence was the theme of the film comedy *Three Amigos* (1986). The film cast two Anglo comedic actors, Chevy Chase and Steve Martin, both famous for their self-deprecating portrayals of dimwits (in *National Lampoon's Vacation* and *The Jerk*), in a role where they were called on to outwit a Mexican *bandido* who had terrorized an entire Mexican village. The *bandido*, "El Guapo" (good-looking), and his band of outlaws, ultimately are outmatched by the three Anglos (with Martin Short as the third Amigo), whose ingenuity as American silent-screen stars saves the village that had been unable to save itself. As all the village residents gathered in wait for El Guapo and his men, they turned to the Three Amigos for direction— "We want to defend ourselves, but how?" One of the Amigos replied, "By using the skills and the talents of the people of Santa Poco [the village]. Now what is it that this town does really well?" After a long round of head-scratching and comic "hmmns," one villager finally replied, "We can sew." The Three Amigos hatched a plan using the village sewing skills to confuse El Guapo in the climactic gun battle by dressing all the villagers in the costumes of the sharpshooting Three Amigos.

Anglo perceptions of suspect Latina/o intelligence were behind the rejection in 1982 by the Princeton Educational Testing Service of advanced placement calculus scores earned by students of Mexican heritage at Garfield High School in East Los Angeles.[7] No other high school in California yielded more passing scores that year. The testing service suspected cheating when it subsequently found an unusual similarity among the incorrect answers of the Garfield students. When forced to retake the test or lose their credit, the Garfield students all passed the exam again. Their ordeal to overcome Anglo prejudice was captured in the motion picture *Stand and Deliver* (1988). Playing Jaime Escalante, the students' Bolivian-born math teacher, actor Edward James Olmos confronted the testing service officials and declared the film's premise: "Those scores would have never been questioned if my kids did not have Spanish surnames and come from barrio schools." The real-life Jaime Escalante was a favorite of George Bush Sr. In his 1988 presidential campaign, Bush visited Garfield High School to tell the Latina/o students that they "don't have to go to college to achieve success. We need those people who build our buildings, who send them soaring to the sky."[8]

Common to both television and film portrayals of Latinas/os is the use of broken English ("I theenk") and thick accents by Latina/o characters. Frequently played for laughs, as by Ricky Ricardo (Desi Arnaz) in *I Love Lucy* ("Lucy, you got some 'splainin' to do"), broken English is often regarded by listeners as a marker of lesser education and intelligence. Although Americans tend to view those who speak with French (or British) accents as cultured and sophisticated, they often regard the Spanish accent as signaling a lack of education.[9] In fact, the Latina/o's accent is a signal of fluency in Spanish, English, and perhaps also an indigenous language. Unlike children in the United States, who tend to be monolingual in English, children in Europe are multilingual—members of the European Economic Union require trilingualism by graduating high school seniors. Unintentionally, a classic *I Love Lucy* episode illustrates the shortcomings of a monolingually minded education—in one instance, of Lucy, who finds herself in a French jail wrongfully charged with counterfeiting. The French sergeant at the jail cannot communicate with Lucy, who speaks only English. But the bilingualism of both her Latino husband Ricky and the Europeans supplies the language link that allows Lucy to explain her innocence—Lucy speaks English to Ricky, who translates her story into Spanish for a jailed but obliging drunk, who translates into German to a police officer, who, in turn, translates into French for the sergeant.[10]

Anglos also perceive the Spanish language as a mark of lesser intelligence. César Chávez recounted an episode from his childhood schooling in which a teacher hung a sign around his neck reading, "I am a clown; I speak Spanish."[11] A February 2003 advice column in *Vanity Fair* magazine by British comic Barry Humphries (as Dame Edna) dismissed Spanish as the language of the help and of leaf blowers. Recall the candidate for Washington State's top education post who declared in 1996 that "Spanish is the language of doormen, dishwashers, and fruit pickers." He went on to suggest that instead of learning Spanish, children should learn English, "the language of doctors, dentists, and lawyers." The candidate later apologized, claiming his remarks were meant to address economic reality and that he believed "Spanish is a noble language."[12] This episode bears a striking resemblance to the more widely publicized child custody hearing in 1995, mentioned previously, wherein a Texas judge chastised a bilingual mother for speaking only Spanish with her five-year-old daughter. The judge likened speaking Spanish to child abuse and opined that the mother was relegating her daughter "to the position of a housemaid." Because it was not in the child's best interest "to be ignorant," the judge commanded, "Now get this straight . . . the child will only hear English."[13]

Intelligence testing conducted between 1915 and 1950 consistently found that Mexican children scored below Anglo children. Many studies, particularly those in the 1920s and 1930s, pointed to heredity to explain this differential.[14] In their controversial book *The Bell Curve* (1994), Richard Herrnstein and Charles Murray observed that intelligence test results for Latinas/os tend to fall within half to one standard deviation below the national mean.[15] Latina/o immigrants score below native-born Latinas/os—more than one standard deviation below the national native-born mean for all groups.[16] Taking a position on the "nature" or "nurture" debate, those authors conclude that both genes and the environment account for intelligence-test performance differences.[17] Although this debate of nature and environment continues unresolved, the most recent significant study bearing on the science of race, conducted by the National Institutes of Health, unraveled the sequence of the human genome and declared in 2000 that, based on the relative absence of genetic difference among the societal constructs of race, a single genetic race exists—the human race.[18] In other words, there is no gene for race. Rather, race is a construction of the human imagination.

Plainly, statistics on educational attainment of Latinas/os in the United States paint a grim picture. The 2000 Census revealed that only 57 percent of Latinas/os in the United States age twenty-five and over had graduated from high school—Mexicans had only a 51 percent graduation rate, while rates for those of Puerto Rican (64 percent), other Central and South American (64 percent), and Cuban (73 percent) origin were higher. By contrast, the graduation rate for non-Hispanic Whites was over 88 percent. Further, 27.3 percent of Latinas/os had lower than a ninth-grade education, compared with only 4.2 percent of non-Hispanic Whites.

Only 10.6 percent of Latinas/os had earned a college degree, compared with 28.1 percent of non-Hispanic Whites.[19] Consistent with these numbers, Latina/o students are more at risk of not finishing high school than any other ethno-racial group.[20] The national dropout rate for Latinas is twice that of Blacks and over three times the rate for White girls—26 percent of Latinas leave school, compared with 13 percent of Black girls and 6.9 percent of White girls. The Latino youth dropout rate (31 percent) is more than double that for Black (12.1 percent) and White (7.7 percent) boys.[21] Surprisingly, school dropout rates are higher among the grandchildren of Latina/o immigrants than among the children of Latina/o immigrants.[22] One study suggested that the causes of the alarming Latina/o dropout rate are substandard school conditions, language barriers, and lowered institutional academic expectations for these Latina/o students.[23] Another attributed the dropout rate to negative interaction with teachers.[24] For example, in the 1960s, a researcher asked a California teacher why she had instructed an Anglo boy to lead her Mexican students from the classroom. She replied, "His father owns one of the big farms in the area and one day he will have to know how to handle Mexicans."[25] One Latina acquaintance, who ultimately enrolled in a master's program of Public Policy and Management after obtaining her college degree, recounted to me how a high school teacher during her sophomore year had told her she was "a stupid Mexican [she is Ecuadorian] who will never amount to anything, so why even try?" Although she views this statement as a defining moment that propelled her to college and beyond, others have had less success in overcoming the gauntlet of barriers—motivational, financial, language-based, and others—faced by Latina/o students.

Some observers blame Latina/o ethnicity and culture for these educational shortcomings. At bottom, they assume a widespread lack of intelligence among Latinas/os consistent with the prevailing stereotype, as well as a lack of cultural regard for educational rigor. In a widely publicized expression of this view given at a 1997 news conference announcing the formation of a new campus student group to oppose affirmative action in admissions, University of Texas constitutional law professor Lino Graglia remarked:

> Blacks and Mexican-Americans are not academically competitive with whites in selective institutions. It is the result primarily of cultural effects. They have a culture that seems not to encourage achievement. Failure is not looked upon with disgrace.[26]

Graglia was responding to the question of whether lower test scores of these groups stem from genetic or cultural differences. Although some believe Latinas/os suffer an inherent cultural defect that devalues education, studies have shown that Latina/o parents both value education and encourage their children to take advantage of it. For example, the rate of Latina/o children who reported that their parents wanted them to attend college was the same as for Anglo children—more than 90 percent.[27] A 1998 opinion poll found that 97 percent of Latinas/os place high importance on education.[28] Another study determined that Latina/o high schoolers were as likely as Anglo students to report that their parents check their homework, talk at home about their studies, and visit their classrooms.[29]

My own family experience underscores these results. I was raised in and near East Los Angeles by my Mexican American mother and my Mexican American stepfather. Although I typically received A's in most subjects, when I received poor grades in conduct and in handwriting while in Catholic elementary school, my parents would visit my teachers and dispense appropriate punishment. Once, while home from college during summer vacation, my grades arrived by mail. I had taken eighteen credit hours while working almost full time as a dormitory dishwasher. My grades, except for one B, were all A's. My mother's concerned response was "¿Qué pasó?" (What happened to cause me to receive a mere B?). My family experience is not unique. Michael Olivas, a law professor in Texas, has written about the strict educational standards maintained by his Mexican American father:

> Every year, he would take us to school the first day of classes, introduce himself to the teachers, and tell them that he expected homework for us every night or a note explaining that we had no take-home work. . . . Once, in high school seminary, I brought home a report card with my lowest grade, a 96 (out of 100) in Theology. Instead of being pleased, he was angry that my lowest grade was in Theology, my chosen field. Years later, when I recalled this incident, he reported that he had feigned anger just to motivate me.[30]

The root causes of Latina/o underperformance in the classroom and in standardized educational testing are mainly institutional—gross and systematic disparities in school funding and resources,[31] language barriers, attitudes and expectations of teachers, and poverty. Cultural values may also play a role, but not in the negative manner Lino Graglia has suggested. Rather, cultural studies have established that Latina/o families tend to value respect for authority over individual assertiveness and value most highly those achievements that benefit the collective. In the classroom, this submissive tendency may be regarded by teachers as apathy to be contrasted with the aggressive, "engaged" participation of Anglo students.[32] Because teachers tend to reward the most active class participants with positive feedback, superior grades, and recommendations, this culture of the American classroom contributes to the negative channeling of Latina/o students away from college and academic pursuits.

The cultural hegemony of the American classroom is repeated in the administering of standardized tests, whose reward of rapid-fire answering favors Anglo males over groups such as Latinas/os.[33] Latinas/os perform more poorly than Anglos on standardized ACT college entrance exams, which test the areas of English, math, reading, and science reasoning. Test results in 1998 revealed that Asian (21.8 score) and White (21.7) students perform best on the exam, while Puerto Rican/Cuban (19.6), Mexican (18.5), Native American (19.0) and Black (17.1) students do not perform as well.[34] Ironically, the overuse of standardized testing scores in college and graduate school admissions gives rise to the need to restore equality through affirmative action programs in admissions. Yet those who believe Latina/o (under)achievement in standardized testing results from ethnic and cultural shortcomings will view these programs as grouping intellectually inferior Latinas/os with Anglos, thus marginalizing the educational experience. No doubt, the pervasive view of a lack of Latina/o (and Black) intelligence (along with the stereotype of Latina/o fertility and other factors)[35] helped launch the assault on affirmative action in recent years.

The current move to eradicate affirmative action in the post–Civil Rights era is being conducted through litigation as well as by political means. Initiated by a right-wing organization, the Center for Individual Rights, lawsuits challenging the constitutionality of admissions programs targeted such institutions as the University of Texas Law School, the University of Washington Law School, and both the University of Michigan and its law school. These lawsuits necessarily confront the seminal Supreme Court decision on affirmative action programs in higher education, *Regents of the University of California v. Bakke,*[36] in which Allan Bakke, an Anglo, disputed the admissions program of the Medical School of the University of California at Davis. At the time of Bakke's unsuccessful applications for admission, the Davis Medical School maintained a special admissions program for candidates who identified themselves as

Black, Chicano, Asian, or American Indian. These applicants were eligible for separate consideration by a special admissions committee comprised of a majority of racial/ethnic minority members. Sixteen of the one hundred seats in the annual entering class were designated for applicants recommended by this special committee.

Joined by no other justice in its entirety, Justice Powell's decisive "swing vote" invalidated the Davis program under the equal protection clause of the federal Constitution, made applicable to state government by the Fourteenth Amendment, which guarantees: "No State shall . . . deny to any person within its jurisdiction the equal protection of the laws." Powell subjected the Davis admissions program to "the most exacting judicial examination" because the program distinguished persons on the basis of race.[37] Although Powell believed that the goal of attaining a diverse student body was a constitutionally permissible basis for a racial preference, the Davis Medical School admissions system was flawed because it guaranteed a certain number of seats to minority candidates and deprived nonminorities of the opportunity to compete for these seats. By contrast, Powell spoke approvingly of admissions systems that, while giving weight to racial or ethnic background in the pursuit of a diverse entering class, do not protect any seats from competition and countenance diversity established on nonracial and nonethnic grounds. Twenty-five years after *Bakke,* in 2003, the Supreme Court is expected to resolve lingering disagreement in the courts on the constitutionality of factoring race or ethnicity into admissions that seek a diverse student body.[38]

Outside the courtroom, the current assault on affirmative action programs in education and beyond has proceeded though citizen initiatives. Building on the abolition of affirmative action in higher education admissions, contracting, and hiring by the University of California Regents in 1995, Californians approved Proposition 209 in 1996 by a 54 percent majority, with 63 percent of Anglos voting favoring the initiative.[39] Proposition 209 establishes:

> The state shall not discriminate against, or grant preferential treatment to, any individual or group on the basis of race, sex, color, ethnicity or national origin in the operation of public employment, public education, or public contracting.

Two years later, in 1998, voters in Washington State approved a similar citizen's initiative. In addition to encompassing employment and government contracts, California's Proposition 209 went beyond the Regents' resolution to target financial aid and scholarships in public education.[40] The Ninth Circuit Court of Appeals upheld Proposition 209 against challenge under the equal protection clause, distinguishing between what the Constitution permits and what it requires. Although the Constitution permits those race-based preferences that survive a strict scrutiny analysis, it does not constitutionally compel these affirmative action programs: "The Fourteenth Amendment . . . does not require what it barely permits."[41] Under this analysis, although affirmative action programs using race or ethnicity stand a chance of constitutional survival, programs directed at marginalized groups may be snuffed by the political will of the majority.

The effect of the abolition of affirmative action by citizen initiative or the threat of litigation on enrollments of Latina/o undergraduate and law students has been dramatic. A study of public law school admissions in California revealed a drop in Latina/o enrollments from 13.4 percent of the class in the four years before Proposition 209 took effect (1993–1996) to 7.2 percent in 1997–2000. At the same time, African American and Native American enrollments dropped, but Asian American admissions remained steady and White enrollments increased substantially.[42] Proposition 209 effectively turned the clock back on race relations and progress toward diversity in the California schools—at the UCLA Law School, the entering class of 1997 brought the smallest enrollment of Latinas/os since the year 1968.[43]

In addition to serving as one basis for rallying opposition to affirmative action programs, the social construction of Latinas/os as less intelligent than Anglos has been used to justify oppressive and subordinating government policies toward Latinas/os. Most prominently, this construction underlies the U.S. treatment of Puerto Rico. As journalist Juan Gonzalez has pointed out:

> How else could the U.S. Government justify to its people the continued possession of a colony except by cultivating an image of Puerto Ricans as helpless and unable to care for themselves?[44]

Back in 1840, another commentator reflected the prevailing parallel sentiment toward Mexicans in frontier California, describing them as "an imbecile, pusillanimous, race of men, and unfit to control the destinies of that beautiful country."[45] Is there a pattern here?

8

No Mexicans or Dogs Allowed
Subhumanity

Their [Mexican] minds run to nothing higher than animal functions
—eat, sleep, and sexual debauchery. In every huddle of Mexican
shacks one meets the same idleness, hordes of hungry dogs, and
filthy children with faces plastered with flies, disease, lice, human
filth, stench, promiscuous fornication, bastardy, lounging, apathetic
peons and lazy squaws, beans and dried chili, liquor, general
squalor, and envy and hatred of the gringo. These people sleep by
day and prowl by night like coyotes, stealing anything they can get
their hands on, no matter how useless to them it may be. Nothing
left outside is safe unless padlocked or chained down. Yet there are
Americans clamoring for more of this human swine to be brought
over from Mexico.[1]

Go drink another beer, you fucking Mexican piece of shit.
　　—Retort caught on videotape of then Denver Nuggets basketball
　　　　　coach Dan Issel to a heckling fan in December 2001
　　　　　　　　(Issel apologized to the Latina/o community and
　　　　　　　　　　　　　　resigned two weeks later)

Did you hear they came out with a new Selena doll?
Ken and Barbie needed a maid!

Many Anglos regard and treat Latinas/os as a lesser class of
people, indeed, as less than human. The stereotypical conceptions described previously of idleness, promiscuity, failure to assimilate, criminal-
mindedness, and lack of intelligence all contribute to this perception.
However, this construction of Latinas/os as subhuman goes beyond those
supposed traits to encompass those associated with animals, particularly
dogs, and with a savage, primitive culture.

Latinas/os, particularly Mexicans, are regarded as dirty and disease-ridden. In 1955, the *Science News Letter* warned of the public health threat posed by Mexicans under the headline "Wetbacks Bring Insects."[2] Especially offensive is the belief that Latinas/os not only reside in but are content with such miserable environments. These views have persisted for decades. In 1920, *The Survey* wrote, "Having few standards to begin with, it is not surprising that the poor Mexican immigrant is content in the tenements with one toilet and one hydrant for fifteen families, four or five of these families living in one or two rooms."[3] Thus, Mexican Americans apparently are comfortable with overcrowded and unsanitary conditions. Reflecting the association of Mexicans with filth, the *San Antonio Express* newspaper editorialized in 1871 that "the hogs lived as much in the [Mexicans'] houses [as the Mexicans did] . . . and from the similarity it was hard to tell where the hogs left off and inhabitants began."[4]

These attitudes held sway in a popular guide to the Americanization of Mexicans through school homemaking curriculum. In her 1929 book *Americanization through Homemaking,* author Pearl Idelia Ellis opined:

> Sanitary, hygienic, and dietic measures are not easily learned by the Mexican. His philosophy of life flows along lines of least resistance and it requires far less exertion to remain dirty than to clean up.[5]

To remedy these deficiencies, she advised lessons in sanitation and hygiene:

> Teach them [Mexican girls] the importance of durable and clean underwear. They are apt to be lax in this respect. . . . Teach the importance of a daily bath. Mexicans are apt to be lax in this respect, giving rise to the term "dirty Mexican." Impress it upon the girl's mind that a clean body and a clean mind are the attributes of a good citizen. Many schools have shower baths and girls can have practice in taking them and experiencing the exhilaration and improved mental attitude which results from them.[6]

Schools throughout California and the Southwest subjected Mexican students to degrading flea and lice inspections.[7] A 1959 guidebook for employers of Mexican housemaids included tips to share with the maid for everyone's benefit:

> [I]f you stay clean, you will not only look better, but feel better. Your employer will show you where she wants you to bathe. She will want

you to take a bath or shower regularly, and wash your hands with soap. You will be furnished a washcloth and towel for your own use.[8]

These attitudes about deficient Latina/o sanitation have survived to the present. Recently, I overheard an Anglo man in Washington speak accusingly toward his wife that she should clean their house because they were "living like Mexicans." In 1994 a Michigan radio station held a Cinco de Mayo "contest" with the winner getting his or her "own personal Mexican." The "humorous" legal trailer added, "Members of the station and their families are not eligible to own Mexicans—bathing and delousing of Mexicans is winner's responsibility. Station assumes no responsibility for infectious diseases carried by Mexicans."[9] The view of Latinas/os as dirty people living in filth goes beyond personal hygiene. At a dinner party I attended a few years ago, a prominent Oregon environmentalist announced her belief that the most significant impending environmental crisis in the United States is the influx and breeding of Mexicans, who as a people display no regard for environmental quality. To her, Mexicans affirmatively choose to live in squalor and care nothing for the quality of their water, air, and soil. This Oregon environmentalist is no lone voice in the wilderness. The San Diego–based group Voices of Citizens Together has warned on its Web site, "When the Mexicans take over they're going to kick the crap out of the environmentalists and turn California into a cesspool."[10]

Contrary to the views held by Americanization programs, no character flaw lurks in Latinas/os that causes them to disregard sanitation and hygiene. Rather, the perception of Mexicans and other Latinas/os as dirty people often stems from the staggering poverty faced by Latina/o immigrants, who are met with discrimination and other mistreatment in the United States.[11] Today, as before, Latina/o migrant workers crowd into substandard housing out of necessity rather than some sense of enjoyment.

The belief that Latinas/os possess no regard for environmental quality is inconsistent with the reality that maquiladoras operated by U.S. and other multinational corporations are a significant source of degradation in Mexico. As journalist Juan Gonzalez has warned, these factories lining the U.S.-Mexico border emit and generate staggering amounts of toxic pollution, including the release by General Motors of xylene into the sewers of Matamoros, where the levels of this highly toxic industrial solvent are sixty-three hundred times that permitted by U.S. standards for drinking water.[12] Industrial waste turns border rivers, including the Rio Grande, into industrial cesspools.

Further, Latinas/os in the United States suffer the brunt of toxic waste and environmental hazards by working in pesticide-laden fields in rural areas and by living near environmental wastelands in urban industrial areas. Sixty percent of Latinas/os (and Blacks) live in a community with at least one unmitigated toxic waste site.[13] Exemplified most prominently by the United Farm Workers (UFW), formerly led by César Chávez, Latinas/os have not accepted these conditions without protest; pesticides in the fields helped precipitate national boycotts of grapes, spurred on by the UFW. Yet these environmental struggles by Latinas/os have tended to occur outside the framework of the mainstream environmental movement in the United States, which focuses primarily on the preservation of wilderness habitat while often ignoring urban and rural habitats of people of color. In recent years, legislative and citizen initiatives in California have demonstrated the environmental imperatives of Latinas/os, leading one journalist to label Latinas/os "the most devoted environmentalists in California."[14] His remarks were prompted by exit polls in early 2002 showing that 74 percent of Latina/o voters had approved Proposition 40, a $2.6 billion parks, open space, clean air, and clean water bond initiative in California. By contrast, just 56 percent of White voters approved the measure. Further, he noted that Latinas/os have been instrumental in passing other California open space, clean air, and clean water initiatives and legislation since the mid-1990s. Indeed, a 1999 survey by a San Francisco public policy organization revealed that 96 percent of Latinas/os agreed with the importance of preserving the environment. This staggering support suggests that mainstream environmental organizations would gain from ignoring calls to adopt anti-Latina/o and antihuman policies against immigration and from instead reimagining their strategies to incorporate the Latina/o vision toward healthier human habitats.

Constructions of Latinas/os as subhuman exhibit additional dimensions. The societal perception and media portrayal of Latinas/os as sexually promiscuous has been documented in Chapter 5. Building on that perception is the view of Latinos and Latinas as sexually perverted and dirty —even willing to perform sexual acts with animals. In the film comedy *Losin' It* (1982), one of Tom Cruise's buddies seeks out a donkey sex show in the Tijuana whorehouses. A shocking anti-Mexican hate-speech post that was widely distributed by e-mail included the following appalling description of Mexican women:

> To this day, Mexican girls practice animal sex acts in the tawdry bars and cabarets of Mexico's flesh emporiums. Tell me, do Mexican men find it appetizing to kiss a Mexican girl only to find out later that she just got through sucking the sperm from a donkey's dick. Excuse me. I have to VOMIT!

While a guest on the Howard Stern television show, singer Enrique Iglesias disclosed that he had a Latina girlfriend. Exhibiting his zeal for dwelling in America's sexual gutter, Howard suggested that those Latinas will do anything in the bedroom, including oral manipulation of the anus.

Adding to their reputation as criminally minded, Latinas/os are perceived as savage and bloodthirsty. Latinas/os have been portrayed by media as "primitive" and "savage" in the mold of Hollywood's Native Americans. In the 1935 film *Bordertown*, for example, renowned Anglo actor Paul Muni was cast as a Mexican American lawyer (Johnny Ramírez). After his disbarment in California for striking his opposing counsel, Ramírez drifted to a Mexican border town where a young Bette Davis pined for him. As the owner of a high-class casino there, Ramírez fell instead for debutante Dale Elwell. Yet Dale and her circle of upper-crust friends viewed Ramírez as representing a savage breed. One of her girlfriends inquired, "Out of what cave did you lure that fascinating brute?" Dale explained that her attraction to Ramírez emanated from the "prehistoric" in her. Ultimately, she rejected his marriage proposal as "out of the question," contending:

> [Y]ou belong to a different tribe, savage. I mean there's such a thing as equality.

The sports of bullfighting and cockfighting, which are legal in Mexico, add to the image of Latinas/os as inhuman and as cruel, particularly to animals. So does the Spanish-language film *Amores Perros* (2001), popular in America, which centered on underground dogfights in Mexico City, and the NBC miniseries *Kingpin* (2003), in which a Mexican drug lord agreed to arrange a dogfight for his Asian business associates. This conception of cruelty toward animals was suggested by Frank Norris in his 1901 novel *The Octopus,* describing a roundup of destructive jackrabbits:

Armed with a club in each hand, the young fellows from Guadalajara and Bonneville, and the farm boys from the ranches, leaped over the rails of the corral. . . . The Anglo-Saxon spectators round about drew back in disgust, but the hot, degenerated blood of Portuguese, Mexican, and mixed Spaniard boiled up in excitement at this wholesale slaughter.[15]

Santeria, a religion with origins in Africa, has many Latina/o practitioners in the United States, primarily among Cuban Americans and Puerto Ricans. The animal sacrifice ritual by Santeria adherents has led some to view this religion with revulsion. Among the animals subject to sacrifice, and often consumption, in the religious ceremonies are chickens, doves, ducks, goats, sheep, and turtles. The sacrifice of larger mammals, such as goats and sheep, is rare.[16] In 1980, the *New York Times* encouraged negative sentiment in its report of a police raid on a "primitive" Santeria "cult" ceremony:

Acting on a tip, a raiding party of police officers and agents of an animal protection society went to a tenement in the Bronx yesterday afternoon and interrupted a primitive religious rite involving the ritual slaughter of animals. . . . The people in the apartment acknowledged they were followers of a cult known as Santeria.[17]

In 1987, the city council of Hialeah, Florida, adopted ordinances targeting religious animal sacrifice among Santeria practitioners. Because the ordinances permitted almost all killings of animals except for religious sacrifice, thus placing a nonneutral burden on religious exercise without being narrowly drawn or advancing interests of the highest order, the Supreme Court invalidated them as violating the constitutional protection of the free exercise of religion.[18] For example, the ordinances failed to prohibit the killing of animals for sport by hunting or fishing, as well as infliction of pain through animal testing by scientists.

Apart from the legality of Santeria rituals, one Santeria adherent justified the religious sacrifice of animals on moral grounds against the backdrop of improper treatment of animals in Western culture:

Santeros [Santeria priests] think a society that condones the mass slaughter of animals, often under appalling conditions, to simply eat their flesh has no right to criticize the ritual slaughter of animals for religious reasons. Our present-day Western culture consistently practices what may be the most cruel and inhumane treatment of animals of any culture in re-corded history. The subjugation and exploitation of animals for research and the conditions of mass-breeding farms create a level of cruelty that is unimaginable and unconscionable in the eyes of indigenous cultures that over the ages have maintained a balance and sense of purpose in their hunting and animal sacrifice practices.[19]

Anglo culture has its own fair share of pastimes and practices that ar-guably should be seen as barbaric. In the United States, professional wrestlers celebrate savagery by using a variety of props and implements to feign brutal assault on another human. Television highlights of profes-sional hockey invariably focus more on vicious brawls and blood-letting on the ice than on displays of sporting skill. In 2002, television's USA Network aired a one-hour special of the best of cinematic combat (in-cluding fist-, street, gang, and "girl" fights) in its program *Ultimate Fights.* Helped by discussion on *The Howard Stern Show,* an Internet-only video called *Bumfights* has sold over three hundred thousand copies to viewers who revel in watching America's homeless stage brutal street fights and shocking stunts, such as pulling their teeth with pliers and jumping off a building into a dumpster.[20] Anglo audiences cheered Mel Gibson's gratuitous street fight with a ruthless heroin dealer in the finale of *Lethal Weapon* (1987), and rocker Ozzy Osbourne's career was re-vived in the early 1980s among Anglo heavy-metal fans when he bit the head off a live dove (and later a dead bat) in a publicity stunt.

Cockfighting originated as a European sport, as did dog fighting, which was once a sport of British "gentlemen." In London, noblemen would pit their roosters against those of other nobles for both reputation and money. The sport reached the Americas with colonists from Spain, Portugal, and other European countries. A 2001 poll in New Mexico, where cockfighting remains legal (as it does in Louisiana), revealed that 76 percent of Latinas/os favored outlawing the practice.[21]

The image of Latinas/os held by many Anglos and conveyed by the media is simultaneously one of an animal and one of an alien, inhuman being. The familiar reference in print media to undocumented Mexican and other Central American immigrants as "illegal aliens" bolsters the image of some type of inhuman creature. The companion reference to mi-grants as "wetbacks" also dehumanizes them. Common, too, is the asso-ciation of Latinas/os with dogs. Until recently, some taverns in the South-west displayed signs such as "No Mexicans or Dogs Allowed." Many

Anglo observers did not understand the outcry by some Latinas/os[22] over Dinky (aka Gidget), the cute taco-hawking Chihuahua in the late-1990s Taco Bell advertising campaign. Presumably the campaign had tried to overcome stereotypes by suggesting this Chihuahua was intelligent—an early commercial had Dinky stroll by a television in his quest for tacos and provide the question ("What is a logarithm?") to a *Jeopardy* game-show answer. Yet, as the most prominent Latina/o image in the media at the time, until replaced in the year 2000 by Ricky Martin and then, in 2001, by Jennifer Lopez, Dinky the Chihuahua was seen by some as suggesting that Latinas/os are interchangeable with dogs. One Internet joke site even pictured the Taco Bell Chihuahua with the caption "The World's Smartest Mexican."[23]

Bolstering the association of Latinas/os with animals has been the print media's use of animal and insect metaphors to describe such supposed characteristics of Latinas/os as their fertility, their criminal tendencies, and their migration patterns. In these images, Latinas/os come to the United States in "swarms," hang out in "wolf packs" of hoodlums, and breed indiscriminately as "dogs." As early as 1953, *Time* magazine quoted a Border Patrol worker who described Mexican immigrants with the remark, "They're swarming over the desert like ants."[24] The recent cable television movie *Thin Air* included references to Latinas/os as "cockroaches." Latinas/os are also presented by media as bloodthirsty and ruthless—as vicious animals. Set in the fictional South American country of Tecala, the blockbuster film *Proof of Life* (2000) offered no Latinas/os of any redeeming moral character and depicted Latinas/os as savage and heartless beasts. Most pointedly, one of the hostages of the Latino guerilla kidnappers lifts his gray hair to show his Anglo rescuer the bloody nub where his ear was chopped or bitten off, imploring, "They're animals. Look!"

Viewing Latinas/os as subhuman both prompts and justifies a variety of inhuman government policies and private actions against them. Often these government and private actions complement each other in a seamless oppressive campaign. Federal immigration policy represents a compelling example of how regard for the safety of Latinas/os too easily gives way to other priorities. Launched in October 1994 by the Clinton administration, the stepped-up border enforcement program known as Operation Gatekeeper has been responsible for the deaths of countless Latina/o immigrants. Several factors led to that administration's decision to support enhancing border enforcement—the hostile political climate in California and elsewhere toward undocumented immigrants, as evidenced by the passage of Proposition 187; the woes the economy was experiencing, which many U.S. citizens blamed on immigrants; and the upheaval to Mexico's economy expected under the North American Free Trade Agreement (NAFTA).[25]

Operation Gatekeeper (the name for border buildup near San Diego) was implemented through a combination of increased manpower, technology, and infrastructure. In the Illegal Immigration Reform and Immigrant Responsibility Act of 1996, Congress increased the number of Border Patrol agents by one thousand in each of the subsequent five years and mandated the deployment of these agents in areas of high need—in proportion to the level of illegal border crossings in the preceding fiscal year and as reasonably anticipated in the next. That act called for the installation of infrastructure such as physical barriers and for the removal of obstacles to the detection of "illegal entrants." The act provided for construction of a second and third fence extending fourteen miles eastward from the Pacific Ocean along the international border south of San Diego. The act also authorized the acquisition of advanced technology devices and equipment for use in interdicting undocumented immigrants, such as night-vision goggles and scopes and sensor units. From 1994 to 1998, the annual budget of the Border Patrol, the INS's enforcement arm, more than doubled, from $354 million to $877 million.[26] (As of March 2003, border enforcement is now overseen by the Bureau of Customs and Border Protection, as part of the new Department of Homeland Security.) During the same time period, in the San Diego sector alone, the length of fencing and walls increased from nineteen to over forty miles, the number of underground sensors from 448 to 1,214, and the number of infrared scopes from twelve to fifty-nine.[27]

The tragic flaw of this border buildup strategy is that because of beefed-up enforcement near urban centers such as San Diego and El Paso (where the buildup was known as Operation Hold the Line), would-be immigrants are diverted to remote areas to undertake a vastly more treacherous entry. In 1993, nine of ten undocumented migrants entered the United States at border cities. "Cheech" Marin's film *Born in East L.A.* (1986) had depicted this former pathway of migrant entry comedically, as an entire mountainside complement of Latina/o immigrants ran across the border near San Diego to the musical backdrop of Neil Diamond's "Coming to America." By 2000, two of three entries were crossings in isolated groups trekking through remote, treacherous areas.[28] Perhaps policy makers did not anticipate the lengths to which immigrants would go to reach jobs in the United States. Apparently the Border Patrol and INS officials expected the Gatekeeper strategy to cause would-be immigrants to forgo the heightened risk of entry across the mountains and desert. Yet, when the death toll accelerated, decision makers either ignored the obvious mounting tragedy or were slow to act.

A report released in 2001 by the University of Houston's Center for Immigration Research identified a clear correlation between the enhanced urban border enforcement and Latina/o immigrant death rates.[29] According to INS statistics, in 1998, for example, 261 U.S.-Mexico border deaths were counted; in 2000, there were 369.[30] More than 40 percent of the border deaths in 2000 resulted from exposure to heat or cold. One study compared the number of Latina/o immigrant deaths from exposure and drowning: 57 in 1994 (before Operation Gatekeeper was implemented) and 227 in the year 2000.[31] Especially chilling is the likelihood that the migrant fatality counts are vastly understated, due to the ruggedness of the terrain and the probability that only some of the deceased are discovered.

In May 2001, Border Patrol agents reaped the grim harvest of federal border enforcement policies—the bodies of fourteen Latino men and teenagers burned black and mummified from the desert heat near the Cabeza Prieta National Wildlife Refuge in the remote Arizona desert. The few survivors of this ill-fated group of migrant border crossers were treated and released to Border Patrol custody. They told a story of about two dozen immigrants who headed to the United States in search of jobs, facing a seventy-mile journey across the desert on foot to reach Interstate 8 in Arizona. The Cabeza Prieta Wildlife Refuge has no facilities of any kind for thirty miles in any direction. Within two days, the would-be immigrants had run out of food and water. Faced with blistering temperatures soaring above 115 degrees, they resorted to digging plant roots to eat and to drinking from cacti and their own urine in a desperate effort to survive.[32] Few did. Immigrant deaths have continued unabated—between Thursday, June 6, and Monday, June 10, 2002, Border Patrol officials announced that at least fifteen undocumented immigrants from Mexico died from dehydration on the Arizona side of the border. A spokesperson for the Mexican consulate in Tucson, Arizona, commented, "Nothing justifies that human beings, whose fundamental intention is to come to the United States to look for work, die in this manner."[33]

Of course, my point here is that many Anglos do not view these "illegal aliens" as human. With this alien, subhuman construction, migrant deaths do not warrant a change in national border policy, no matter the death toll.

Other grisly episodes of mass border deaths followed the bolstering of federal border enforcement. Water has claimed many victims. In the desert, rains can turn dry washes into rampaging torrents. In 1997, eight Mexican migrants drowned only a few yards inside Arizona when they were swept away by a fifteen-foot-high wall of water unleashed by a summer night downpour known in Arizona as a monsoon.[34] In Calexico, California, immigrants swim or float the New River in their journey from Mexicali, Mexico, to the United States. The eye-stinging New River is so steeped with industrial waste from maquiladora factories, raw sewage from Mexicali's overburdened sewer system, and agricultural pesticides that Border Patrol agents will not enter the water to retrieve the desperate migrants.[35] The swift-moving All-American Canal, which parallels the California border for eighty-two miles, took twenty-six migrant lives alone in 2000 and eleven more by early June 2001. In May 2001, this waterway claimed two migrants who, like many before them and after, were unidentified. They were buried unceremoniously in the United States as "John Does," with a small stone the size of a brick marking their resting place.[36] About one-third of the migrant dead have been buried as John and Jane Does in graveyards along the eighteen-hundred-mile border between the Pacific Ocean and Brownsville, Texas.[37] Their families in Mexico, in the United States, or elsewhere will never know their fate.

Freak snowstorms have claimed many migrants in recent years. A snowstorm in April 1999 brought over a foot of snow and temperatures in the twenties, and the exposure claimed eight migrants in the Cleveland National Forest twenty miles north of the Mexican border near San Diego.[38] Later, in March 2000, a snowstorm in nearby mountains and temperatures dropping into the low twenties killed three Mexican migrants traveling in lightweight clothes and sneakers.[39] National newspapers reported these tragedies with headlines such as "Three Suspected Illegal Immigrants Die"[40] and "Seven [Eight] Illegal Migrants Die in Snowstorm."[41] No doubt, public sentiment on deaths conveyed in these callous terms runs similar to that toward criminal suspects killed in police shootouts.

Many undocumented Latina/o immigrants have perished in tragic automobile accidents while traveling to reach their distant American field of dreams. In 1999, thirteen Latinos destined for work in the South were killed when their transport van slammed into the rear of a tractor-trailer stopped on an icy New Mexico highway. Mostly from the Mexican state of Chiapas, the men had just crossed the border through the Arizona desert a few days before on foot and had reached the suburbs of Phoenix, where they were loaded into the van for transport across the country. To avoid detection of these Mexican-appearing passengers, all seats in the van had been removed except for the driver and the front passenger seats, and the immigrants were huddled on the floor for the nonstop journey that snuffed out their young lives.[42] In June 2002, five undocumented Latinas/os were killed in California when their van, loaded with thirty-three people and traveling in the wrong lane without headlights to bypass a Border Patrol checkpoint, collided head-on with a car driven by another Latino, sending him plunging over a steep embankment to his death.[43] In October 2002, the skeletal remains of eleven Mexican immigrants were discovered in a sealed railcar in Iowa. In May 2003, eighteen Latino/a immigrants died by suffocation in a stifling truck trailer while being transported from Mexico to Texas.[44]

Highway pursuit of undocumented immigrants has often gone terribly wrong. April 1996 was a particularly bloody month for immigrant Latinas/os on American highways. In the premorning darkness on April 6, 1996, twenty-eight undocumented Mexican immigrants traveled north in a pickup truck and camper shell toward the strawberry fields of northern California. When a Border Patrol truck spotted the overloaded camper and gave chase, the "coyote" (smuggler) driver sped up. Some of the twenty-five migrants inside the camper shell managed to open a rear window and motioned frantically for the federal officers to give up the dangerous pursuit. Moments later, the truck failed to negotiate a curve and hurtled into a steep gully, landing roof first. Eight of the migrants died, nineteen were injured.[45] A friend of some of the victims remarked to journalist Rubén Martínez about the bodies returned to Mexico for burial:

> You should have seen the bodies. The Americans didn't even bother to wipe the blood off their faces. And the stitches from the autopsies! The Americans must have thought our boys were dogs.[46]

This tragedy bears a chilling resemblance to a "joke" I encountered on an Internet joke site:

The sheriff arrived at the scene of the horrible accident just as his deputy sheriff was climbing from the controls of a bulldozer. "Say, Bubba, what's going on?" he asked.

"A whole bus full of migrant workers went out of control and over the cliff. I just got through burying 'em," explained the deputy.

"Good work, Bubba," said the sheriff. "Pretty gory work. Were all of them dead?"

Bubba nodded gravely. "Some of 'em said they weren't, but you know how those Mexicans lie."

Just a few days before, on April 1, 1996, two sheriff's deputies in Riverside, California, were captured on news helicopter video savagely beating two Mexican immigrants after a high-speed chase. When a pickup truck carrying at least nineteen migrants had failed to stop at a Border Patrol checkpoint, authorities gave chase. During a high-speed pursuit on eighty miles of southern California freeways, the pickup's camper shell flew off, exposing its terrified human cargo. After the truck stopped on the freeway shoulder, its passengers began running for cover. As Alicia Sotero Vasquez struggled with her passenger-side door, then crawled out of the truck window, one of the officers clubbed her with his baton. Another struck her on the ground. When her companion Enrique Funes Flores came to her rescue, he, too, was clubbed; the blows continued even as he hunched to shield himself. Both were treated for injuries, Alicia Vasquez for a contusion. Many Americans blamed the Mexicans and felt they got what they deserved as lawbreakers and because their driver failed to heed the checkpoint.[47] One astoundingly vicious editorialist espoused little compassion for Alicia Vasquez and other "Mexican aliens" who invade the United States "like a plague of locusts":

> Despite what an assortment of pro–Mexican Americans and sob sisters in the media might want us to believe, try not to forget that wretched women such as Vasquez and her companions in that truck cross our southern border with every intention to take whatever they can garnish from our rich land—forget that they begin their march illegally. With the possibility of a [lawsuit against the police] . . . being bantered about by the liberal lawyers, I predict that even more caravans of Mexicans in broken-down trucks who hope to strike it rich beneath the blows of an American policeman's baton will soon be racing for the border.[48]

The federal government attributes these mounting migrant deaths to Mexican smugglers (coyotes) who fail to prepare their human cargo for the perils of the journey. Since the border buildup, immigrants are increasingly likely to rely on smugglers, and smuggler fees have risen to reflect the increased treachery of the journey. In the eighteen months of 1995 to mid-1996 alone, the percentage of migrants employing smugglers increased from 42 to 52 percent.[49] To deflect some of the blame, the INS and the Border Patrol have given some attention to safety and rescue efforts. The INS launched Operation Lifesaver in 1998 as a program of patrol flights to discover migrants in distress. The government erected signs on border fences warning of sun, rattlesnakes, and other hazards. The Border Patrol began to train its agents in search-and-rescue techniques. In 1999, 1,041 migrants were rescued; 2,054 were rescued in 2000.[50] In 2001, the Border Patrol announced plans to install six thirty-foot metal poles to enable desperate migrants to signal for help, with signs reading, in both English and Spanish, "If you need help, push red button. U.S. Border Patrol will arrive [to arrest you] in one hour. Do not leave this location." Recently, the Arizona Pima County Board of Supervisors approved funding to help a humanitarian group erect water tanks along routes known to be used by migrants. Opponents of the allocation had argued the tanks would encourage more illegal immigrants. Previously, some local residents had been threatened with arrest by the Border Patrol for offering water and other assistance to migrants.

Apparently, violating federal immigration laws justifies the slaughter of Mexicans and other Latinas/os by auto, sun, cold, and water. In decrying the pre–Operation Gatekeeper closure of two lanes of traffic on Interstate 5 north of the U.S.-Mexico border in order to curb deaths of undocumented immigrants crossing the freeway, one writer concluded:

> Thus, illegal aliens, committing an illegal act by entering the United States, became the reason for the closing of part of a superhighway on American soil—and all because Hispanic activists said that the traffic deaths of people entering the country illegally were murder![51]

A radio talk-show host in 1996 even suggested that southern California motorists receive sombrero-shaped bumper stickers as awards for hitting undocumented immigrants on the freeway.[52]

America's response to the terrorist events of September 11, 2001, will only increase the migrant carnage. Even prior to the terrorist attacks, President Bush supported increasing the number of Border Patrol agents. After the attacks, in his 2002 State of the Union address, Bush called for doubling the funding for national security, including border enforcement. Back in 1993, President Clinton had remarked at a press conference about the need to enhance border patrols to protect against terrorism:

> The simple fact is that we must not, and we will not, surrender our borders to those who wish to exploit our history of compassion and justice. We cannot tolerate those who traffic in human cargo, nor can we allow our people to be endangered by those who would enter our country to terrorize Americans. . . .
>
> Today, we send a strong and clear message. We will make it tougher for illegal aliens to get into our country.[53]

Despite the horrible toll resulting from border buildup, public opinion shortly before the September 11 tragedy nonetheless called for increased measures to hamper Mexican immigration. A Time/CNN poll in May 2001 determined that 53 percent of those sampled felt it should be made harder for people to cross the Mexican border into the United States, while only 15 percent favored easing restrictions.[54] As public sentiment after September 11 builds toward establishing even tougher immigration restrictions at the Canadian and Mexican borders, migrating workers from Mexico and Central America will face a more perilous gauntlet in their efforts to reach jobs in the United States.

> "Hold it man, you're going too far. They ain't Mexicans."
> —dialogue from film *Dudes* (1987); member of redneck outlaw gang urging others not to kill three White punk-rocker teenage campers they had just robbed in the Arizona desert

Vigilante violence directed at Latinas/os has a long history in the United States. A Texas historian has recounted the scores of lynchings and mutilations of Mexicans in Texas in the 1800s.[55] In the 1850s, many Mexicans were whipped, branded, or hanged by vigilantes who enforced laws in the California gold rush days.[56] One vigilante at the time proffered, "To shoot these Greasers ain't the best way. Give 'em a fair trial, and rope 'em up with all the majesty of the law. That's the cure."[57]

These attitudes of indifference toward Latina/o life have survived into the present day, with "wetbacks" and "illegals," or those perceived to be undocumented, as the primary targets of violence and threats of violence. In litigation in Arizona in the 1980s, a federal food-service facility supervisor challenged his job transfer after he circulated among his employees a mock set of State Game Commission guidelines for hunting and killing wetbacks.[58] Circulated nationally around that time as a "joke," these guidelines purported to authorize an official open season on the "South-Western Wet Back (known locally as Mexican, Greaser, Grease Ball, Spic, Mex., or Low Rider)." The mock game commission rules declared it unlawful to shoot a wetback in taverns because the bullet could "ricochet off the grease and injure a civilized white person." Further, "[t]raps may not be set in welfare offices." And, on seeing a wetback on the highway, "you may kill it, just don't pick the greasy bastard up."

In the mid-1990s, vigilante groups in California began to police the San Diego airport as the "Airport Posse" to search for and intimidate any suspected undocumented immigrants. The posse formed when a caller to a San Diego radio show complained about seeing a group of Hispanic men rushing onto a flight to Pittsburgh at the last moment before departure, when airport personnel were unable properly to check for government-issued photo identification. Angry callers lit up the switchboard, and the Airport Posse was born. Wearing blue-and-yellow T-shirts with the words "U.S. Citizen Patrol" and a Border Patrol–like logo, these vigilantes patrolled the airport, taking notes, reminding airport personnel to enforce the FAA rule requiring proper photo identification, and subjecting those with a Latina/o appearance to scrutiny as if they were a prison chain gang. One volunteer claimed that "illegal immigrants" from Mexico are easy to spot because they wait out of sight for the last boarding call before coming forward, wear out-of-style clothing, speak Spanish, and exhibit a "nervous appearance."[59] The Border Patrol and the INS took no official position against the patrols, with one INS spokesperson suggesting that "[they're] exercising their constitutional right to be at the airport, just like the guy playing his tambourine."[60] In the earlier but similarly minded "Light Up the Border" campaign in 1989 and 1990, vigilantes in southern California would gather at the border by the hundreds to shine their car headlights toward Tijuana to deter night crossings; eventually, they were met by counterdemonstrators holding up mirrors and reflective foil.[61]

Since 1994, federal border enforcement policies have directed migrants away from urban centers and freeways in southern California and toward the sparsely populated California, Arizona, and Texas deserts. This increased foot traffic led ranchers in Arizona to arm themselves and to initiate vigilante patrols—first as property owners, ostensibly to protect against property damage, and later as activists, to draw attention to what they viewed as a foreign invasion and a threat to national security.

The most prominent Arizona vigilante ranchers are brothers Roger and Donald Barnett, who patrolled a twenty-two-thousand-acre ranch with binoculars, an M-16 automatic rifle, and a tracking dog. In 2000, they boasted of capturing as many as 170 "illegals" in one day and turning them over to federal authorities. As Roger Barnett described his quarry:

> They move across the desert like a centipede, 40 or 50 people at a time. You always get one or two [of those caught] that are defiant. One fellow tried to get up and walk away, saying we're not Immigration. So I slammed him back down and took his photo. "Why'd you do that?" the illegal says, all surprised. "Because we want you to go home with a before picture and an after picture—that is, after we beat the shit outta you." You can bet he started behavin' then.[62]

Vigilante rancher meetings in Arizona attracted California anti-immigration groups, as well as a representative of the Ku Klux Klan. Years earlier, in the mid-1970s, the Klan had undertaken border enforcement duties in California and the Southwest, claiming the Border Patrol had failed its duties.[63] Therefore, it is not surprising that the Klan viewed the ranchers as acting in vigilante brotherhood. Although apparently rejecting the Klan's offer to help by sending the representative away, the ranchers solicited other volunteers. A leaflet surfaced in April 2000 that invited volunteers to park their recreational vehicles on border ranches and to help patrol them as part of the "American Way Team" while "enjoying the great southwestern desert at the same time."[64] This promotion has the flavor of the despicable mock State Game Commission guidelines for hunting and killing "wetbacks." Officials in Mexico have condemned the practices of Arizona ranchers as *cacería de immigrantes,* "immigrant hunting." In one such recent "sporting" confrontation, Miguel Angel Palafox was crossing the Arizona desert when one of two horsemen dressed in black shot him in the neck. After wrapping his shirt around the bullet wound, the young migrant crawled back to Mexico, where he reached help.[65]

Despite the attention focused in recent years on the Arizona vigilante ranchers, violence toward Latina/o immigrants in Arizona (and elsewhere) has a long history. One particularly notorious incident occurred in August 1976, when George Hannigan and his two sons, Patrick and Thomas, dispensed frontier justice to three Mexican undocumented workers who made the near-fatal mistake of crossing the Hannigans' Arizona border–side ranch on foot. The immigrants, Manuel Garcia Loya, Eleazar Ruelas Zavala, and Bernabe Herrera Mata, were held, stripped, and tortured with hot pokers, burning cigarettes, knives, and a shotgun filled with bird seed. Hours later, they were set free to return to Mexico naked and bleeding. An all-Anglo jury acquitted the two Hannigan brothers of charges of kidnapping, assault, and robbery; father George died before trial. Following strident protest, federal authorities ultimately charged the Hannigans with obstructing interstate commerce. Patrick Hannigan, but not his brother Thomas, was convicted and sentenced to three years' imprisonment.[66]

Vigilante strikes against undocumented Latina/o immigrants are not confined to Arizona. In May 2000, two young Mexican migrants reached an isolated Texas trailer home near the border and begged for water. When the elderly couple refused and threatened to call the Border Patrol, the migrants fled. The couple gave chase in their truck, and seventy-four-year-old Samuel Blackwood fired at the two Mexicans from behind, hitting one in the leg and severing an artery. Twenty-two-year-old Eusebio de Haro bled to death in the desert before help arrived. Blackwood was indicted by a grand jury on a charge of deadly conduct, but not for murder. Although convicted, Blackwood received a minimal sentence of 180 days of house arrest and a fine of $4,000. Two Latina/o commentators responded that apparently in America a dog's life is worth more than that of a Mexican—a California man had recently received a three-year sentence for killing a dog. But, for killing a Mexican, the penalty was "[l]ess than the price of a used car."[67] By contrast, consider the likely outcome in Texas had young Eusebio de Haro possessed a weapon and used it to defend himself from attack, shooting or even killing the elderly Anglo Blackwood. Haro might be alive but waiting his turn on death row for a lethal injection. The Mexican government condemned the lack of justice for Haro:

The Mexican government considers it unacceptable that a judicial system might allow that a person who was proven to have taken the life of another person by shooting him in the back not receive the severe sentence of incarceration that such a crime calls for.[68]

Despite this shooting, or perhaps inspired by it, in late 2000 volunteers in Texas formed the organization Ranch Rescue and solicited by flyer for "volunteers from all over the USA" to help protect border ranches from trespassing immigrants.[69]

Further illustrating vigilante hatred toward Latina/o immigrants and the trifling significance of Latina/o life in the American legal system is the murder of a twelve-year-old Mexican boy near San Diego in 1990. His killer, Dwight Ray Pannel, had been drinking beer and ingesting methamphetamine one morning while at a friend's house in suburban San Diego near the Mexican border. After target shooting from the balcony, he suggested, "Let's shoot some aliens." Pannel dropped to one knee and fired his high-powered rifle into the hills, piercing young Emilio Jiménez Bejinez in the forehead, killing him instantly. Bejinez had just crossed the border with three family members. Pannel pled guilty to involuntary manslaughter and received only a two-year jail sentence.[70]

A vicious beating on Long Island, New York, in September 2000 did bring a commensurate sentence. Tensions in several Long Island communities had surfaced over the influx of Latina/o laborers, who would wait on street corners for contractors and landscapers to hire them as day laborers for odd jobs. Community groups organized to oppose what they viewed as an invasion of undocumented immigrants, destroying their suburban quality of life with their salsa music and the like. Reflecting the violent attitudes toward these immigrants, a New York legislator remarked later in legislative hearings in August 2001 that if his town were to be inundated by illegal aliens, "we'll be out with baseball bats."[71] Against this backdrop of intolerance and lack of regard for Latina/o lives, two local skinheads, Christopher Slavin and Ryan Wagner, both etched with anti-Jew and other hate tattoos, posed one morning as contractors and offered work to Israel Perez and Magdaleno Estrada Escamilla, two undocumented immigrants. Wagner later testified that he was impaired by LSD and beer. Slavin and Wagner had vile intentions. They led Perez and Escamilla to the basement of an abandoned building where they attacked them. Slavin bludgeoned Escamilla in the head with a posthole digger, and Wagner slashed Perez with a knife. Although Perez nearly bled to death, the two men survived and eventually returned to Mexico. Both

Slavin and Wagner were convicted and each given a prison sentence of twenty-five years. At his sentencing hearing, Slavin wore a suit and an American flag tie.[72] In late September 2001, a lawsuit was filed on behalf of the two recovering laborers against several anti-immigrant groups, alleging they had influenced the skinheads by broadcasting a message of hate and violence.

Although immigrants have served as the primary targets of vigilante violence directed at Latinas/os, this violence reaches all corners of Latina/o life in the United States. In early 2002, for example, dozens of Latina/o lawyers, along with activists and community groups throughout the United States, received a hate letter ending with "And by the way, watch out for the white powdery stuff in this envelope."[73] Each envelope contained white powdery granules that tested negative for anthrax. Touching on almost every negative conception of Latinas/os, the hate letter is a testament to the resiliency of these images into the new century:

> You stupid, fucking, spic turds. . . .
>
> I am so sick of Hispanics—spics for short—complaining about being discriminated against, when in fact you owe all of what you have to the generosity and capable leadership of the white population at large. If it weren't for affirmative action, you would probably all still be bean pickers and prostitutes. Every time you try to do something on your own, you fuck up. Take bilingual education, for example. Now we are going to have to admit a whole generation of spics into college who will be even stupider than they would have been otherwise. . . .
>
> [S]ince you grease balls still can't run your own countries effectively, like rats escaping a sinking ship, we get more and more of your wet back asses to care for. If that isn't bad enough, your whore-women can't keep from getting knocked up and producing more mongrel-spics that the rest of us have to provide welfare for.
>
> I never had anything given to me for nothing, and I am college educated and own my own house that is big enough to hold an entire barrio of you useless drug pushers.[74]

Earlier, in 1991, Latina/o families with children attending California's Santa Monica High School received a similarly themed hate letter, implying violence in addressing an incident where two Latino youths had fired five rounds near the school:

Protect innocent, law respecting students from these brown animals. Mexicans [*sic*] students are inferior and dumb. If these animals can't learn to be responsible citizens, then they can't be treated in a civilized way. Mexicans are the most lazy and ignorant race in the world. . . . They don't want to be responsible citizens, they just want to steal. We are dealing with cruel and violent animals with no self control. Look at Rodney King. He'll think twice before robbing another store.[75]

As Gil Carrasco has observed, America's reliance on Latina/o labor, particularly that of Mexicans and Mexican Americans, has been an inexorable cycle of "invitation and exile" for people regarded more as agricultural beasts of burden than as human workers.[76] During times of need for cheap labor in labor-intensive industries such as agriculture, Mexican migrant workers have been summoned, put to work, shown their place in the labor hierarchy, and exploited but, through it all, tolerated grudgingly. When economies have worsened, however, Mexican migrant laborers have been scapegoated and shipped unceremoniously across the border. These invitations and exiles have been carried out by government actors, private vigilantes, and most often a combination of public and private coercion. Exclusionary tactics were evident in the 1930s during the Great Depression. Vigilantes throughout California and the Southwest forced Mexicans and even Mexican Americans to return to Mexico; in Oklahoma, the tactics were to threaten to burn Mexican laborers out of their homes; in Texas, signs warned Mexicans to leave town.[77] Motivated by the opportunity to delete an entire ethnicity from its welfare rolls during the rampant unemployment of the depression, local governments joined the oustings by coercing Mexicans and Mexican Americans into leaving the United States. Scholars estimate that between 350,000 and 600,000 Mexicans and Mexican Americans were sent to Mexico during the depression decade, many of them from southern California.[78] As part of this repatriation, even Latinas/os who were lawful permanent residents of the United States were caught in the net and uprooted from their homes and families.[79] Many families were separated, even to the point of separating children from their parents.

The onset of World War II tilted the labor market toward a shortage, and once again Latinas/os were summoned to serve America's economic needs. This time, Mexicans came pursuant to a formal labor immigration agreement reached in 1942 between Mexico and the United States that established the Mexican Labor Program, known more commonly as the Bracero Program. Bracero workers not only replaced Japanese workers who were imprisoned in the mass internments during World War II; they also replaced Mexican Americans drafted into the armed forces and sent to battle for the United States. Although it survived officially for over twenty years until its lapse in December 1964, the Bracero invitation gave way in the 1950s to tensions with labor unions and laborers who viewed Latina/o migrants as unfair competition. On June 17, 1954, the U.S. attorney general launched "Operation Wetback," a massive government-sponsored deportation of undocumented immigrants. Between 1954 and 1959, 3.7 million Latinas/os were deported, many of them American citizens caught in the deportation frenzy. Again, families were separated and workers uprooted.

Today, immigration policies continue to work in concert with employers and other private actors in the summoning and exiling of Latina/o immigrant laborers, without regard or respect for the bonds of familial relationships. Border-armoring policies such as Operation Gatekeeper, aided by border vigilantes terrorizing migrants, have increased the treacherousness of border passage and thus the likelihood that some family members will stay behind in Mexico and elsewhere in Central America. In past years, Latina/o migrants would return home after their seasonal farm labor had ended, as well as for holidays and familial events such as weddings. With the prospect of a perilous border crossing and the expense of hiring a coyote guide to better ensure safe passage through desolate areas, migrants are forced to remain in the United States longer and to be separated from their families left behind.[80] For other Latina/o migrants, family separation occurs differently, but with the same tragic outcome—some migrant families that journey together to the United States are severed by immigration raids at the workplace that may leave children orphaned behind. Sometimes, employers have engineered these raids to derail employee efforts to secure better wages and working conditions.[81] The threat of these raids is enough to keep most migrant workers subordinated and in their place.

American law provides scant protection against employers who use immigration laws as leverage against employees seeking to organize for fair working conditions. For example, the Second Circuit Court of Appeals held that a Latina union organizer could be deported even though her employer had turned her over to the INS to retaliate for her union activities.[82] In 2002, the Supreme Court established the primacy of immigration policy over worker rights by holding that an undocumented Mexican worker who used false papers to obtain a manufacturing job in California was not entitled to receive the same back pay as other workers to compensate for his unlawful retaliatory discharge for union organizing.[83] The employer's lawyer justified the Court's ruling, explaining that "employers should not be required to make windfall payments to illegal aliens."[84] Observers fear this precedent may affect the full range of rights that an undocumented immigrant might otherwise invoke—from damages for unlawful discrimination and harassment to redress of wage and hour violations.

Illustrating the slight regard under American law for the welfare of immigrant workers and their families are employment death-benefit laws in several states that discriminate against nonresident dependents. These laws often are prejudiced against U.S. immigrant workers' family members who stayed in Mexico or elsewhere. Kansas, for example, provided for payment of up to $200,000 for the dependents of workers killed while on the job. For those deceased employees without dependents who were citizens or residents of the United States, however, its Workers Compensation Act authorized payment of up to only $750 in death benefits. The Kansas statutory scheme was challenged by the family of Fermin Jurado, who died of massive head injuries while working for a Kansas construction company. Holding an engineering degree from Mexico, Jurado had moved to Kansas hoping to learn English and eventually to obtain employment as an engineer and bring his family to Kansas. His dependents, a wife and three young children, were still residents of Mexico when Jurado died. Entitled to only $750 in death benefits, Jurado's family successfully challenged the Kansas employment death benefits system as violating the constitutional equal protection rights of the deceased worker Jurado.[85] Yet, in other states such as Utah, discriminatory statutes of this nature remain operative, surviving constitutional challenge because the courts subject them to scrutiny from the standpoint of the constitutionally unprotected nonresident alien dependents rather than from the protected status of the resident decedent employee.[86]

In the old days, miners would carry birds with them to warn against poison gas. Hopefully, the birds would die before the miners. Farmworkers are society's canaries.   —César Chávez

What do you get when you cross a Mexican and an octopus?
Got me, but it can sure pick lettuce.

The construction of Latinas/os as subhuman fuels the perception that
they are docile and sedate workers—content to work at treacherous, punishing jobs for substandard wages and comfortable when living in deplorable housing. Latinas/os are disproportionately employed in dangerous occupations in construction (especially roofing), meatpacking,[87] agricultural, and other industries. Consistent with their employment in these
perilous industries are statistics that Latina/o immigrants suffer a much
higher death rate than other workers. Overall, the on-the-job death rate
for all Latinas/os is 20 percent higher than the rate for White or Black
workers.[88]

Agricultural workers in the United States are exposed to toxic pesticides that cause serious long-term health consequences. The agricultural
labor community is overwhelmingly Latina/o (about 79 percent), and almost all of these workers are of Mexican origin.[89] These workers face a
greater risk of pesticide exposure than workers in any other occupation.
In one particularly compelling incident that illustrates the dangers of
these poisons, José Antonio Casillas, a seventeen-year-old Mexican migrant farm worker in Utah, was accidentally soaked by pesticides sprayed
from a tractor in June 1998. The next day, emergency workers found
Casillas with white foam streaming from his nose. His cause of death was
listed officially as a brain hemorrhage.[90] From 1991 to 1996, an average
of 665 cases of occupational poisoning by agricultural pesticides were reported annually to the California Environmental Protection Agency's Department of Pesticide Regulation. Employer threats and retaliation, particularly against undocumented employees, keep these reported cases ar-
tificially low.[91] The federal Environmental Protection Agency (EPA) has
estimated that pesticides nationally cause between ten and twenty thousand illnesses each year for farm workers and their families.[92] Further,
an EPA study in 1991 concluded that almost half the children laboring
in the fields had been sprayed with pesticides at least once.[93] Actor/
comedian Paul Rodriguez has recounted being in the California fields
when a plane flew overhead, dousing his migrant family with pesticide,
while his mother yelled at him not to breathe as she covered him with her
shawl: "Those bastards wouldn't allow migrant farm workers an hour's
warning back then. God only knows how many miscarriages, how many

people are disabled, how many lives were lost—all brown lives—because of that."[94]

Apart from short-term health consequences of pesticide poisoning, agricultural poisons may explain the higher incidence of cancers among farm workers as compared with the general population, as well as the increased number of birth defects and stillbirths among children of farm workers. According to the National Migrant Resources Program, migrant farm workers claim a life expectancy of only forty-nine years; by contrast, the U.S. average is seventy-five years.[95] The perils faced by Latina/o and other farm workers in the United States are perhaps matched only by those of Latinas/os toiling in U.S. and other industrial nation owned maquiladoras just south of the Mexican border. There, birth defects have been linked to PCBs and other toxic chemicals in the workplace. Overall, Mexico's industrial accident and illness rate ranks among the world's highest, yet foreign companies are shielded from lawsuits for work-related injuries.[96]

Symbolizing the low regard for the welfare of American farm workers by the agricultural industry was *el cortito,* the short-handled hoe, known too as *el brazo del diablo*—"the devil's arm." The hoe was only twelve inches long, forcing farm workers to bend over and work close to the ground. Abundant medical evidence established that the hoe led to severe back injuries when used over a substantial period; in medical terms, the hoe caused abnormal degeneration of the spine, resulting in permanent disability and chronic back pain. Although replaced in most farming states by the long-handled hoe, growers in California continued to insist that their workers use the short-handled hoe in their lettuce fields. After noticing Latino farm workers walking with a rigid gait, a California Rural Legal Assistance lawyer began a seven-year struggle in the late 1960s to bury the short-handled hoe. Although the California Division of Industrial Safety by administrative regulation had outlawed the use by farm workers of "unsafe hand tools," the division interpreted its prohibition to encompass only those tools with inherent physical defects (such as a loose-headed axe), not those tools harmful because of the manner in which they were used. The legal battle, on behalf of several Latino farm workers, to outlaw the short-handled hoe eventually reached the California Supreme Court, which ruled the division had misinterpreted its regulation—a defectively designed tool causing injury through its regular use is just as unsafe as a defectively manufactured tool or a tool in poor condition.[97] Following this decision, California state regulators specifically prohibited the short-handled hoe.[98]

Despite the dangerous nature of their jobs, agricultural workers earn the lowest family income of any occupation surveyed by the Bureau of Census—$17,700 as of 1997, with the median income of individual workers only $9,828.[99] Not surprisingly, then, agricultural workers face the highest poverty rate of any surveyed occupation.[100] Contrary to the stereotype of being willing to work for substandard wages and to live in inadequate housing, Latina/o farm workers have long sought to be paid living wages. But many farm workers are excluded from federal and state statutory minimum-wage and overtime-pay protections. Further, in many states, farm workers are exempted from coverage under worker compensation laws[101] and unemployment insurance and are denied protection of their right to organize under the federal National Labor Relations Act.[102] Federal law also exempts child farm laborers from child labor restrictions. When the Chávez-led United Farm Workers union offered to California voters an initiative in 1976 adding farm-worker protections to the state constitution, including the right of organizers to enter the fields to talk with workers, opponents tapped into stereotypes to soundly defeat the measure. Presenting the measure as a threat to the property rights and personal safety of farmers from criminally minded Mexicans entering their ranch as union organizers, one ad opposing the measure showed a woman peering nervously from her window. As one observer put it, "They were giving the public a message that, in reality, read: 'Do you want a Mexican on your property attacking your daughter.'"[103]

Nationally, eight hundred thousand farm workers are believed to lack adequate shelter. A 1995 California study estimated that 250,000 farm workers and family members there had inadequate housing. That report found workers "packed 10 or 12 into trailers and sleeping in garages, tool sheds, caves, fields and parking lots."[104] Another study found farm workers living in abandoned automobiles and even underneath porches.[105] Many migrant labor camps have no electricity or running water. Laundry is done in polluted irrigation canals, and the workers sleep on beds of dirt or plywood. Some California migrant workers had spent four years living in a hole they had dug in the ground. These workers slept on cardboard and bathed when a ranch foreman hosed them down while he watered the crop.[106] Another California migrant worker opined that "the owners don't care how we live. We are like burros to them."[107] At one

Oregon migrant labor camp, the farm owner supplied housing to seventy workers, who slept together on the bare floor on thin pieces of carpet or on cardboard. They had no kitchen facilities (so that the laborers would resort to buying food prepared by the camp operator), only one working shower, and four outdoor overflowing port-a-potties.[108] One Mexican immigrant in California was housed by his rancher employer for ten years in a discarded metal horse trailer with no heat, water, or other facilities. He used an outdoor hose for a shower, even in the winter.[109] A 1998 *New York Times* report on national migrant housing detailed miserable conditions throughout the country. In Washington State, Mexican cherry pickers slept in crude tents. In Florida, a Guatemalan tomato picker was giving the journalist a tour of the trailer he shared with seven others when a rat scurried across the floor. In southern California, Mexican workers harvesting peppers and cucumbers shared huts built with tree branches, pieces of lumber, cardboard, and black plastic—enough to keep out the rain but not the rattlesnakes. Migrants bathed and did laundry in a nearby stream.[110] Confronted with these widespread accounts of abominable housing conditions, Americans must ask themselves which other group of workers in today's American economy is forced to live in cars, in tents, and in holes in the ground. Longtime activist and cofounder of the United Farm Workers union with César Chávez, Dolores Huerta, sums up the dynamic between the agricultural industry and its workers:

> Growers dehumanize their workers. Why would you refuse to give workers a toilet? Because if you don't give them a toilet, then they're not human beings. Why would you allow workers to be sprayed with pesticides? Growers view farmworkers as tools. . . . They don't consider the horrible poverty these workers suffer. Why? Because their goal is profit and they don't care about the people.[111]

Shantytown housing conditions for Latinas/os are prevalent not just for migrant farmworkers. In Texas, several hundred thousand people, more than 95 percent of them Latinas/os, live under abysmal conditions in unregulated *colonias* settlements. Many of these residents work in light manufacturing jobs, such as in the garment industry. Their residences in the *colonias* often lack clean water, sewers, paved roads, and other municipal services. Common sights in these *colonias* are "[d]ecrepit trailers, shacks made of wood slats, tin, or cardboard nailed onto scavenged pallets, and condemned homes moved from the city."[112] Only half the homes boast indoor toilets. Yet, justifying the plight of *colonia* residents living without municipal or clean water sources, an El Paso water utility official remarked, "You can bring these people water, but you can't make them bathe. They have to take pride in themselves."[113]

Latinas/os, as well as Blacks and other subordinated groups regarded as subhuman, routinely are treated as guinea pigs for American scientific experimentation, oftentimes government-sponsored. Searching for a link between brain chemistry and violence, the New York State Psychiatric Institute in the early 1990s administered a perilous drug to thirty-four Black and Latino boys aged six to ten. Fifty-six percent of the boys were Latinos, the rest Black; all the boys had older siblings regarded as juvenile delinquents. Scientists supposed that Blacks and Latinas/os were predisposed to violence due to low levels of serotonin in their brains. They hypothesized that they could increase serotonin levels by administering the drug fenfluramine in controlled doses through an intravenous catheter for five and one-half hour sessions, while drawing blood hourly. Federal Drug Administration studies led the FDA to ban this drug—it caused severe heart valve damage in 30 percent of adult users, and a single dose did long-lasting damage to the brain cells of rodents and monkeys. Although the federal Office of Protection from Research Risks exonerated the institute after an eighteen-month investigation, the institute's racially based research led to the introduction of legislation in New York requiring scientists to justify research based on ethnicity or sex to the state health commissioner and to warn parents of the possible side effects of experiments on children.[114]

These experiments harked back to the infamous "Tuskegee Study of Untreated Syphilis in the Negro Male," spanning forty years from the 1930s, in which 399 poor Black men, told they were to receive free medical treatment and burial, were actually left untreated, even after the discovery of penicillin, so that their resultant deterioration and death from syphilis could be studied in the interest of science.

Women in Puerto Rico were once used as laboratory rats for the testing of oral contraceptives. Of the 132 Puerto Ricans who took part in the 1950s experiment, many died and others suffered side effects that included cancer and urinary infections.[115] For several years up to the 1970s, women in Puerto Rico were also subjected to a coercive campaign of sterilization, funded by private U.S. agencies and federal funds and implemented by the Puerto Rican government through public health workers. By the 1970s, over one-third of women of childbearing age in Puerto Rico had been surgically sterilized. The horrifying legacy of coerced sterilizations was duplicated among Native American women in the 1970s[116] and African Americans in the South around the same time, reminding many of Hitler's compulsory sterilization laws implemented in 1934 against Jews and others in the pursuit of racial purity. During the 1950s and 1960s, legislators in the South had even considered conditioning the receipt of welfare benefits on sterilization of unwed mothers.[117]

During the development of the atomic bomb, an African American was used as a scientific receptacle for the testing of the effects of plutonium on humans. Until 2003, the U.S. Navy used the inhabited Puerto Rican island of Vieques (of which the navy controls twenty-six thousand of the island's thirty-three thousand acres) for military bombing exercises. (In 2003, the military announced it would halt its exercises in Vieques.) These bombs release uranium, lead, and other hazardous substances that affect health and increase infant mortality rates. The inhabitants of Vieques reside closer to a live firing range than any other U.S. citizens.[118] One commentator described the compelling consequences to the Vieques residents of the bombing: "According to those who want the Navy out, the rate of cancer in Vieques is much higher than the rest of Puerto Rico. The drinking water is contaminated. There is a higher incidence of lupus, asthma, scleroderma, telarquia,[119] kidney and heart disease and child mortality."[120]

Just as the U.S. government chose to locate its dangerous military testing in close proximity to Latinas/os, private companies have tended to site hazardous waste facilities in proximity to Latinas/os and other racial and ethnic minorities. An influential study in 1987 by the United Church of Christ's Commission for Racial Justice found race to be the most important variable in the siting of commercial hazardous waste facilities—communities with the most facilities had the highest percentage of nonwhite residents. Moreover, three of every five African Americans and Latinas/os live in communities with unmitigated toxic waste sites.[121] These findings helped fuel the environmental justice movement, which employs a combination of environmental and civil rights laws and strategies to confront racially motivated siting decisions. The defining victory in the environmental justice struggle has been the legal and grassroots effort that averted construction of a major toxic waste incinerator in Kettleman

City. Kettleman City is a small community in central California whose residents are overwhelmingly Latina/o and primarily farm workers. In the late 1980s, Chemical Waste Management, Inc., proposed building a hazardous waste incinerator at an existing waste facility near Kettleman City that would burn up to 216 million tons of toxic waste annually. After legal challenges to stall and derail the project, as well as community-based efforts by local Latinas/os, in 1993 the company withdrew its plans to construct the facility.[122]

The legacy of segregation in the United States includes Latinas/os and stems in part from conceptions of Latinas/os as unclean and subhuman. When Americans confront this country's experience of segregation and discrimination, typically they regard these practices as past events that our "enlightened" society has overcome. Moreover, many Anglos view the history of racial segregation and discrimination as having singled out Blacks without reaching other groups. Even conservative Latina writer Linda Chávez maintains that "Hispanics have not faced the same degree or intensity of discrimination in this [American] society as blacks."[123] But American society has long targeted Latinas/os and other groups for unfair or separate treatment, a practice that continues today for Blacks, Latinas/os, and others. For example, in the late 1800s and early 1900s many resorts, hotels, and clubs excluded Jews pursuant to a "No Hebrews" or "Gentiles Only" policy.[124] Although segregationist Jim Crow laws, particularly those in the South, tended to single out "Blacks," or "Colored" persons, segregation and discriminatory practices classified Blacks and Latinas/os on similar subhuman terms throughout the Southwest, especially in Texas and California. Latinas/os typically were not addressed in state statutes segregating Blacks from Whites,[125] but Latinas/os were the objects of informal segregation by public officials, such as park and school boards, as well as of discrimination by private businesses and individuals. A 1943 study determined that Mexican Americans experienced segregation in over 117 towns in Texas, both informally and in the form of *de jure* segregation laws.[126] For example, in the mid-1900s, a Texas public park sign read:

THIS PARK WAS GIVEN FOR WHITE PEOPLE ONLY.
MEXICANS AND NEGROES STAY OUT.
ORDER OF PARK BOARD.[127]

Similarly, a sign outside a Texas restaurant photographed in 1949 evidenced the reach of discriminatory practices beyond government action to private businesses, reading:

WE SERVE WHITE'S [*sic*] ONLY
NO SPANISH OR MEXICANS.[128]

In addressing the exclusion of Mexican Americans from juries in 1950s Texas, the Supreme Court observed, "At least one restaurant in town prominently displayed a sign announcing 'No Mexicans Served.' On the courthouse grounds at the time of the hearing, there were two men's toilets, one unmarked, and the other marked 'Colored Men' and 'Hombres Aqúi' ('Men Here')."[129]

One commentator described pervasive segregation against Latinas/os in California, prompted by stereotypical constructions of Latinas/os as unclean and subhuman:

> Two common examples of segregation were the movie theaters in the larger towns and the swimming pools in almost every community. The five theaters in downtown Santa Ana were segregated. Oscar Valencia remembered that, "the bottom [the main floor of the theater] was for the Americans, the top [balcony] was for the Mexicans. . . ." The "plunge," as the swimming pool in nearby Orange was called, had a "Mexican Day" on Mondays. It was the only day Mexicans were allowed to swim. The pool was drained that night and was closed on Tuesday for cleaning and re-filling.[130]
>
> Many organizations, businesses, and homeowners associations had official policies to exclude Mexicans, but in many instances it was more of a general social understanding among Anglos that Mexicans should be excluded.[131]

This account of "Mexican Day" at the local swimming pool is reminiscent of the film *The Ring* (1952), which depicted a young Mexican American couple being denied admission to a skating rink because it wasn't "Mexican Night."[132] Biographers of César Chávez detailed numerous examples of segregation and discrimination that César faced throughout his life. For example, at age twelve, César had ignored a "Whites Only" sign outside a California restaurant and ordered a hamburger. The waitress responded, "What's the matter, you can't read? Goddamn dumb Mex!"[133]

While on a seventy-two-hour leave from the navy, César seated himself in the Whites-only section of a movie theater, prompting his arrest.[134] Gil Carrasco has recounted stories of the discrimination directed at Latino Vietnam veterans on their return to the United States. A Texas funeral parlor refused to bury a decorated Latino veteran, Félix Longoria, because of his Mexican heritage. Another Latino veteran, Sergeant Macario García, recipient of a Congressional Medal of Honor, was arrested for defending himself against a restaurant proprietor who tossed him from the diner because he was a "Mexie."[135]

Although segregation often targeted Mexican Americans, other Latinas/os did not escape exclusion. For example, a San Bernardino, California, public swimming pool in the 1940s barred all Latinas/os from entry—not just Mexicans but "people from the score or more Latin American Republics and from Italy, Spain and Portugal."[136] Indeed, one of the plaintiffs in litigation challenging this exclusion was Eugenio Nogueros, a Puerto Rican. Cuban baseball players, such as Martín Dihigo in the 1920s and 1930s, were barred from the American major leagues. As a Black Latino, Dihigo was forced to play instead in the Negro Leagues.

Schools, too, were prompted to adopt segregation policies by constructions of Latinas/os as subhuman, dirty, and unintelligent. School officials sometimes attempted to justify so-called Mexican schools by suggesting that, given their inability to speak English and their lesser performance on intelligence tests, Mexican and Mexican American students could not compete with Anglo children.[137] Others expressed concern that poor Mexican American children might "feel inferior [to Anglos] because of their clothing they have to wear."[138] This reminds me of how my mother told me she used to hide her usual lunch, a bean taco (now called a burrito), from the other children at her school in East Los Angeles by keeping the bag wrapped tightly around the taco. Other school officials revealed the dehumanizing stereotypes often used to justify educational segregation of Anglos and Mexican American children. As one California superintendent wrote:

> Because of (1) social differences between the two races; (2) much higher percentage of contagious disease (among Mexican children); (3) much higher percentage of undesirable behavior characteristics; (4) much slower progress in school, and (5) much lower moral standards, it would seem best that . . . Mexican children be segregated.[139]

Records from school board meetings in Oxnard, California, illustrate the calculated intent to discriminate against children of Mexican heritage. These records reflect debate on the feasibility of staggered recess periods to keep Anglo and Mexican American students, already taught in separate classrooms, from playing with each other. The board also decided that the "brightest" and the "cleanest" of the Mexican American children could be placed in classrooms with White students if the White class was small and the Mexican class too large.[140]

Utilizing the same strategy as Blacks used to confront government segregation policies and practices, Latinas/os began to sue school districts and educational authorities to desegregate their schools. Outcomes in this litigation revealed the pervasive government design to segregate Latinas/os in schools throughout California and the Southwest. For example, the federal Fifth Circuit Court of Appeals concluded that "Mexican-American students in Austin had received an education inferior to that of their Anglo counterparts and that this was the result of ethnic segregation,"[141] and further, that "the Austin School Board, Austin Independent School District (AISD), engaged in acts showing a pervasive intent to segregate Mexican Americans."[142] Also, a federal court concluded that for several years the Arizona school district in Tolleson had by design segregated students of Mexican or Latin heritage from schools attended by Anglo children.[143]

Latina/o challenges to segregated schools predated the Supreme Court's seminal decision in *Brown v. Board of Education*. As early as 1931, Latinas/os had prevailed in lawsuits against segregation. That year, Mexican parents in Lemon Grove, California, challenged a school board decision to construct a separate school for Mexican Americans, netting a superior court ruling integrating the local schools.[144] In the most significant pre-*Brown* decision involving Latinas/os, the federal Ninth Circuit Court of Appeals ruled in 1947 that the segregation of Mexican and Anglo children in Orange County, California, public schools was unconstitutional.[145] In 1896, the Supreme Court had issued its infamous "separate but equal" ruling in *Plessy v. Ferguson,* treating separate accommodations for the races as constitutionally valid as long as the facilities were equal.[146] Homer Adolph Plessy, who was one-eighth Black and seven-eighths White, resisted state law that segregated Black and White railroad passengers. In upholding Louisiana's law against Plessy's challenge under the Thirteenth Amendment (which prohibits slavery and involuntary servitude) and the equal protection clause, the Court acknowledged that school segregation was "recognized as within the competency of the state legislatures in the exercise of their police power." Fifty years later, Orange County school officials invoked the legacy of *Plessy* in contending that Mexican American schoolchildren were furnished with facilities fully equal to those available to Anglo students. Yet, assuming the facilities were equal, and without questioning the precedent of *Plessy,* the Ninth Circuit managed to distinguish that authority and outlaw the segregated schools in Orange County. Although requiring segregation for Native American children, as well as for Chinese, Japanese, and Mongolian children, California statutes did not segregate Mexican American children. Because Orange County's segregation program came not from legislative act but from local administrative action, the Ninth Circuit distinguished *Plessy* as having upheld only segregation by legislation. Ironically, then, the Ninth Circuit was able to concede that although the California legislature could legally enact a law authorizing segregation of Mexican American schoolchildren, its failure to do so rendered the local practice constitutionally invalid. Of course, this convoluted decision was not the definitive expression of judicial policy against Latina/o segregation that activists desired.

The *Plessy* "separate but equal" regime began to unravel around this time, as its artificiality became apparent. In the 1930s and 1940s, the National Association for the Advancement of Colored People (NAACP), represented by Thurgood Marshall, a future Supreme Court justice, brought a series of lawsuits that undermined *Plessy.* One of those lawsuits challenged the accommodations made by the State of Missouri to compensate Blacks barred from its all-White state law school. Lloyd Gaines, an African American graduate from Missouri's Black college, wanted to attend law school. The state's only law school, the University of Missouri, barred admission of Blacks, but state law gave Gaines the accommodation of a scholarship to attend law school in a neighboring state that would admit Blacks. The Supreme Court rejected the government's argument that Gaines could receive an equally sound legal education in the adjacent states of Kansas, Nebraska, Iowa, and Illinois, all of which would admit non-resident Blacks. Rather, the constitutional inquiry under the equal protection clause was internal to Missouri—having furnished Whites with a legal education, Missouri could not deny a legal education within its boundaries to Blacks solely on the basis of color.[147] Later, Marshall sued the University of Oklahoma, seeking the admission of a Black woman to the state's only public law school. In response to the

Supreme Court's order that she be admitted,[148] Oklahoma simply took a small part of the state capitol building, assigned a few law teachers, and declared this the new state law school for Blacks.[149] Later that year, the Supreme Court concluded that Oklahoma had fulfilled its obligation to provide equal, albeit separate, facilities.[150] Protest over this artificial accommodation by over a thousand White students and faculty at the University of Oklahoma[151] suggested a decline in public acceptance of the separate-but-equal facade. Two years later, the Supreme Court ruled that the equal protection clause required the University of Texas Law School to admit a Black applicant, rejecting the contention that the separate facilities in Texas for legal education of Blacks were equal in character and caliber to the distinguished University of Texas.[152]

Ultimately, in 1954's decision of *Brown v. Board of Education,* these challenges yielded a new constitutional direction that acknowledged the intangible detriment of segregation on subordinated groups in generating a "feeling of inferiority as to their status in the community that may affect their hearts and minds in a way unlikely ever to be undone." Applying the equal protection clause, the Supreme Court ruled that "in the field of public education the doctrine of 'separate but equal' has no place. Separate educational facilities are inherently unequal."[153] Although *Plessy* had addressed segregated trains and the *Brown* decision schools, over time the Supreme Court extended its ruling in *Brown* to other government facilities such as beaches, buses, and parks.

Although removing the stigma of state sponsored (*de jure*) segregation, *Brown* failed to improve the educational quality for subordinated groups such as Latinas/os or to remove the reality of segregation in fact (*de facto*).[154] As a result of such influences as housing discrimination, Latinas/os and other subordinated groups tend to live in segregated neighborhoods within urban areas[155] such as East Los Angeles, where I grew up. When courts began fashioning remedies to integrate previously segregated schools—for instance, by busing Anglo children to schools with disproportionate enrollments of students of color, or the reverse—Anglo parents responded by fleeing the cities for the suburbs. There, behind gated communities with zoning restrictions against low-income housing developments, Anglo parents could escape the reach of court-ordered desegregation plans.[156] Those parents remaining behind in the urban "jungle" could send their children to private school while campaigning to undermine the funding structure of public education, such as by California's citizen initiative Proposition 13, which slashed property taxes and thus defunded local schools. In the 1970s, the Supreme Court ruled against a class action brought by Mexican Americans in Texas that challenged the property tax system for funding public schools as a violation of the equal protection clause.[157]

On occasion, though, Latinas/os gained minor victories in post-*Brown* desegregation litigation, being recognized by the Supreme Court as constituting an identifiable class for purposes of the constitutional guarantee of equal protection[158] and sometimes prevailing in litigation (such as a lawsuit against the San Jose, California, school district) that challenged more benign segregation tactics and policies, such as the siting of new schools to perpetuate segregation caused by racially or ethnically imbalanced neighborhoods.[159] But, overall, *Brown* was largely a symbolic victory for Blacks, Latinas/os, and other groups, as reflected by the remarks in 2000 by National Education Association president Bob Chase:

> As we commemorate that pivotal Supreme Court ruling, we also recognize that millions of students of color are still segregated into rundown schools, with overcrowded classrooms, less experienced teachers, outdated textbooks and outmoded technology. Instead of correcting historical school finance inequities over the past 46 years, regressive political forces have designed new schemes to divert even more public money away from public schools.[160]

These segregated classrooms and communities only increase the influence of media representations of Latinas/os and other subordinated groups. In the absence of intergroup contact, particularly in schools where social attitudes and prejudices take shape, the media gain precedence as the primary window on race and ethnicity in America.

Because the equal protection clause is limited in reach to government action, *Brown* failed to address private discrimination in settings such as restaurants and businesses and in housing rentals and sales. Prior to *Brown,* a Texas appellate court in 1944 had upheld the right of private swimming pool operators to exclude those of Mexican or Hispanic descent in the absence of state or federal civil rights legislation to the contrary.[161] In the 1960s, however, Congress finally enacted civil rights laws that prohibited discrimination and segregation in privately operated settings held open to the public. For example, Title II of the Civil Rights Act of 1964 outlawed discrimination or segregation on the basis of race, color, religion, and national origin in places of public accommodation such as hotels, restaurants, gas stations, theaters, and other places of entertainment.[162] The federal Fair Housing Act of 1968 barred discrimination in real estate transactions on the basis of race, color, religion, sex, national origin, disability, and familial status.

Despite these laudatory congressional and complementary state legislative efforts to address private discrimination, legislative inaction since the Civil Rights heyday of the 1960s has left Latinas/os and other groups unprotected against new, retooled strains of discrimination. One of the many virulent mutations of segregationist and discriminatory mind-sets uses language policy to injure those Latinas/os who do not speak English. Viewing language as a mutable characteristic distinct from one's immutable race, national origin, or color, those discriminating on the basis of language contend that federal and state civil rights laws are not invoked. Moreover, they rely on the typical requirement for proof of purposeful discrimination by pointing to some supposed business justification for the language policy. Illustrating the many variants of covert language discrimination are examples from sites of overt private and public discrimination and segregation on the basis of race and ethnicity—housing, public accommodations, and schools. Consider these examples, mentioned previously as stemming from the construction of Latinas/os as unwilling to learn English. In Florida, a cooperative building voted to deny residency to non-English (i.e., Spanish) speakers.[163] Similarly, a San Jose, California, couple refused to rent to a Mexican American family that did not speak adequate English. The Ninth Circuit Court of Appeals let stand a jury verdict in favor of the landlords on the prospective tenants' Fair Housing Act claim, noting on the question of discriminatory intent that the landlords had testified their purpose was to ensure effective communication in an emergency.[164] Sued for enforcing an English-only rule against her Latina/o tavern customers, as announced by a sign over the bar reading "In the U.S.A. It's English or Adios Amigo," a Washington tavern owner prevailed because the trial judge believed her policy sought to ensure safety in the bar rather than to purposefully discriminate.[165] Decisions such as these send the message to landlords and business owners, as well as to employers, that although they cannot overtly discriminate on the basis of race or national origin, they might rely on some pretextual nondiscriminatory rationale, particularly one related to safety, to adopt valid language rules in order to exclude Latinas/os unable to speak English.

In the American marketplace, merchants sometimes prey on the inability of some Latinas/os to understand English. For example, a New York landlord duped a Salvadoran couple who spoke only Spanish into signing a separate lease for parking, although they had no car.[166] In Oregon, a car dealer used Spanish-speaking employees to entice Latina/o immigrant customers to sign contracts written in English that sold them unwanted extras such as extended warranties and credit insurance. Another Oregon auto dealer misrepresented to a monolingual Spanish-speaking customer that an "as-is" warranty meant the customer had fifty days to rescind the purchase as desired. In 1994 a spokesperson for the National Council of La Raza announced that Latinas/os were being targeted for telemarketing fraud because they may lack English language ability. By emphasizing a duty to read the contract, American contract law has been slow to address this widespread language fraud in the marketplace.[167]

Finally, language discrimination in the classroom is resurgent with the passage of the anti–bilingual education initiatives in California (1998), Arizona (2000), and Massachusetts (2002). Under these initiatives, control over bilingual education programs at the local level is replaced by a one-year sink-or-swim English immersion program. One might naively view this abolition of bilingual education as consistent with the school desegregation effort—the bilingual education classroom presumably would be filled with students of color (Latinas/os and Asians) in a throwback to the segregated schools and classrooms that preceded the decision in *Brown*. But bilingual education, though perhaps requiring a segregated classroom, does not demand a segregated school. As early as 1951, in a challenge by children of Mexican/Latina/o descent to the practice of an Arizona school district to segregate these children from Anglos in separate schools with inferior facilities, a federal judge observed:

> The only tenable ground upon which segregation practices in the respondent school district can be defended lies in the English language deficiencies of some of the children of Mexican ancestry as they enter elementary public school life as beginners, but such situations do not justify the general and continuous segregation in separate schools of the children of Mexican ancestry from the rest of the elementary school population as has been shown to be the practice in the respondent school district.[168]

Of course, the aftermath of *Brown* is no success story—due to White flight to suburbs and to private urban schools, Latinas/os today are no less likely to be educated in a segregated school. Presumably, then, the maintenance of bilingual education, rather than separating Anglos from Latinas/os and Asians, merely isolates the children of Latina/o and Asian immigrants from the Latina/o and Asian children of later generations. More important, to abolish bilingual education programs invites the same fundamental evil in segregated schools that the *Brown* decision sought to overcome. The Supreme Court observed in *Brown* that to separate children "solely because of their race generates a feeling of inferiority as to their status in the community that may affect their hearts and minds in a way unlikely ever to be undone."[169] As Kevin Johnson and George Martínez have contended, "[B]y banning teaching in the native language of Spanish-speakers, [California's Proposition 227] creates a similar stigma for Latinas/os. It suggests that Spanish and other languages are inferior to English and not fit for education."[170] Indeed, Johnson and Martínez argue that California's anti–bilingual education initiative contravenes the equal protection clause because it discriminates against Latinas/os and other groups in using language as a proxy for race discrimination.

One of the ironies of the anti–bilingual education measures is their displacement of local school board control in deciding the most appropriate method for teaching non-English-speaking students. Historically, school boards played a significant role in segregation of schools—for example, in 1984, the Ninth Circuit Court of Appeals held that San Jose's school board intentionally maintained segregated schools to the detriment of Latinas/os.[171] Yet, manifesting their fear that the local school districts will actually aid non-English-speaking Latinas/os by adopting bilingual education programs, the anti–bilingual education measures strip local districts of this power. Although California law generally permits local school districts to seek a waiver from the program requirements of California's Education Code, a California appellate court made clear this loss of local control in rejecting an attempt by the Oakland, Berkeley, and Hayward school districts to employ this procedure to request a waiver from compliance with Proposition 227.[172]

Texas, which does not presently outlaw bilingual education, had criminalized the speaking of Spanish by teachers in its public schools for most of the last century. In 1970, for example, a Mexican American teacher in the Crystal City school district was indicted for teaching a U.S. history class in Spanish, although the indictment was later dismissed. Extending beyond teachers, any student who violated the no-Spanish rule was "corporally punished, shamed, threatened, fined, suspended and expelled from school by Texas school administrators."[173] As a federal district judge in Texas concluded:

> The presence of a statutorily mandated and rigorously enforced policy preventing a child from speaking [in] his native tongue the language which he and his parents may have spoken all of their lives, the language which is often spoken in their home, the language of their ethnic and national heritage[,] is calculated to produce the stigma of inferiority so soundly condemned in Brown v. Board of Education.[174]

9

Gringos in the Latina/o Imagination

What do you call a person who speaks three languages?
A polyglot.
Two?
Bilingual
One?
Gringo.[1]

pardon the lag
in writing you

we were left
with few
words

in your home
we were cast
as rugs

sometimes
on walls
though we

were almost
always
on the floor

we served
you as
a table

a lamp
a mirror
a toy

if anything
we made
you laugh

in your kitchen
we became
another pan

even now
as a shadow
you use us

you fear us
you yell at us
you hate us

you shoot us
you mourn us
you deny us

and despite
everything
we

continue
being
us

America
understand
once and for all—

we are
the insides
of your body

our faces
reflect
your future
                    —Francisco X. Alarcón[2]

The Latina/o reference to Anglos as "gringos" (and "gringas")
dates back at least as far as the derogatory reference to Latinas/os as
"greasers." Although the "greasers" label is always demeaning, the

"gringo" reference is sometimes humorous, other times intended or taken as derogatory, and often meant to be merely descriptive of Anglos and perhaps other Americans of non-Latina/o origin, such as Asian Americans. Pedro Malavet has best researched the unsettled origin of *gringo*:

> One [account] argues that it comes from "green coats," thus, a reference to the uniforms worn by U.S. soldiers during the Mexican War. Another story argues that the term originated in a bastardization of the song "Green Grows the Grass" allegedly sung by U.S. soldiers invading Mexico in 1847. . . . As early as the eighteenth century, the word was reportedly used in Spain as a bastardization of the word "griego" (Greek) and was used to refer to anyone speaking a foreign tongue or with a foreign accent. The usage is thus analogous to the American phrase "it's Greek to me." . . . But English dictionaries uniformly define it as a word used "disparagingly" or as a "contemptuous" reference to English-speakers generally and U.S. citizens in particular.[3]

Other slang terms among Latinas/os for Anglos include *blanquitos* and *gabachos*. Related to the reference to Americans, particularly Anglos, as gringos, is the reference among Mexicans to Whites as *los güeros* (those White people) or as *bolillos* (white bread). Indeed, some Mexican Americans who are regarded as overly acculturated—for example, by their inability to speak Spanish—might be called *gabachos* or *pochos* by other Mexicans or Mexican Americans as a derogatory reference.

To contrast the spectrum of Latina/o stereotypes in the imagination of the American media and public, it is useful to consider how Latina/o media productions and Latinas/os view Anglos (or gringos). Some of the stereotypical views of Anglos held by Latinas/os are slight and humorous, notably the conception shared by Blacks that Anglos possess no rhythm and cannot dance. Others are more substantial. Latinas/os, many of whom are fluent in both English and Spanish, tend to view Anglos as monolingual English speakers. As determined by the 1990 U.S. Census, over 96 percent of native-born non-Hispanic Americans (which includes many Asian and African Americans) speak only English. Regarding family, a 1990s study of Mexicans and Mexican Americans in the United States revealed their perception that Anglos were "much colder to their children in terms of family unity."[4] Some Latinas/os also bristle at the practice of Anglos placing their elderly parents in nursing home facilities, believing this disrespects the elderly. Latinas/os often tend to be group oriented, willing to sacrifice individual success for community advancement; Latinas/os perceive Anglo culture, by contrast, as geared toward rugged individualism. Anglos also are seen as overly materialistic; for example, in 1900, Uruguayan author José Enrique Rodó wrote that compared to the materialism in North America, South Americans were more "spiritual."[5] Also, some Latinas/os have suggested that Anglo culture is bland and would profit from the "spice" of Latina/o cultures and that of other ethno-racial groups. Author Alfredo Vea captured this sentiment in his novel *La maravilla* (1993), when a grandfather explained his grandson's rich mestizo (Spanish and Indian—Yaqui) heritage by contrast to the culture of the "gringos," who "have no stories. They have no tribe. Their camp fire is the goddamn television."[6]

The most significant perception of Anglos or gringos in the Latina/o imagination is the racist Anglo. Latinas/os often view Anglos as Archie Bunker types, particularly when they are authority figures such as a job supervisor (*el patrón*), police officer, judge, politician, teacher, or principal. Several Latina/o media productions depict the racist gringo as regarding Latinas/os as subordinate and inferior and as discriminating against Latinas/os in settings such as schools and the workplace. Julia Alvarez's novel *How the García Girls Lost Their Accents* (1991) includes a confrontation where a neighbor yells at García and her four daughters, all Dominican immigrants, "Spics! Go back to where you came from!"[7] Gregory Nava's film *Selena* (1996) depicts the refusal of a Texas beachfront club owner to audition Selena's then-youthful father Abraham's vocal group, the Dinos. Calling his booking agent, the owner decries, "They're a bunch of Mexicans. . . . I can't have that in my club. This club is Whites only." Directed by Edward James Olmos, *American Me* (1992) conveys the animosity toward Latinas/os that preceded the Los Angeles Zoot Suit Riots by showing an Anglo streetcar passenger changing seats when a Latina sits next to him. Later, the Latina is raped by Anglo sailors in the Zoot Suit Riots, while other sailors are beating and stripping pachucos. In Ramon Menendez's film *Stand and Deliver* (1998), actor Edward James Olmos charged advanced-placement testing officials with racism in the company's rejection of his students' test scores: "Those scores would have never been questioned if my kids did not have Spanish surnames and come from barrio schools." Luis Valdez's acclaimed film *La Bamba* (1987) included a racist Anglo father who refused to let his blonde daughter Donna date the Mexican American Ritchie Valens, who played "goddamn jungle music." As Donna's mother explained to her daughter, she

had best not lead Ritchie into thinking they could undertake a relationship—"you know how your father is."

The Latina/o conception of Anglos as racist is long-standing. A famous
street ballad, or *corrido,* during the Great Depression period ("Los de-
portados"—the deported ones) contended that Anglos were treating Lati-
nas/os unfairly by scapegoating them during the economic turmoil:

> The Anglos are very bad fellows
> They take advantage
> And to all the Mexicans
> They treat us without pity
>
> Today they bring great disturbance
> And without consideration
> Women, children, and old ones
> They take us to the border,
> They eject us from this country
>
> Goodbye dear countrymen
> They are going to deport us
> But we are not bandits
> We came to toil.[8]

Perceptions of Anglos as racist are widespread in the Latina/o community. A 1996 poll of Latina/o immigrants revealed that 80 percent
felt they were treated with racism or contempt by Anglos.[9] Further, Lati-
nas/os tend to view Anglo institutions as unfair, as reflected by a 1992
survey for the California Judicial Council that found a majority of Lati-
nas/os (and African Americans) believe that courts do not ensure racial
fairness.[10] That many Latinas/os regard gringos as racist may surprise Anglos; indeed, a 1994 survey determined that most Whites do not believe
they act on any prejudice to discriminate against Blacks or Hispanics
today.[11] The few media spokespersons for Latinas/os, at least those who
hold national attention, generally tend to voice sugar-coated, Ricky Mar-
tin-ized views of relations between Latinas/os and Anglos. Surely Anglos
do not perceive today's crossover Latina/o pop music singers as rebellious
or subversive. Instead, they are inviting Anglos to party with them in pursuit of *la vida loca.* Republicans have co-opted these optimistic messages
by employing Ricky Martin's "La copa de vida" (The Cup of Life) as the

theme song for the 2000 Republican National Convention in a gesture toward racial inclusiveness; later, Ricky Martin performed the song at George Bush's inauguration. George Bush also benefited from help on the campaign trail by a prominent Latino media figure, listed as one of *People* magazine's one hundred most eligible bachelors—his all-smiles nephew George Bush, son of his brother Jeb and Jeb's Mexican American wife Columba.

By contrast to Ricky Martin and the Latino George Bush, most Latina/o media messengers outside the mainstream, past and present, have conveyed their impression of Anglos as racist and the American system as unjust. Latina/o artists such as the band Ozomatli have denounced police brutality against the Latina/o community, singing about police bullets "that don't deserve to connect."[12] In his narrative *The Revolt of the Cockroach People*, "Gonzo" Chicano lawyer Oscar Zeta Acosta suggests that while some urban Chicanas/os hold a favorable opinion of gringos, other Chicanas/os view them properly as an enemy who regards the Chicana/o as a "lowdown cockroach."[13] In the late Puerto Rican Miguel Piñero's award-winning drama of prison life, a prisoner indicts America's criminal justice system, mocking the fairness of the "white man['s]" court and defining justice as "'Just us' . . . white folks."[14] César Chávez is said once to have publicly decried a Coachella City Council decision that closed a park where his farm-worker organizational meetings were held as "gringo justice," which he later said was the only time he could recall using the term *gringo* in anger.[15] Chicano poet and activist Rodolfo "Corky" Gonzales proposed "El Plan Espiritual de Aztlán" in 1969, which evinces hostility toward Anglos based on their historical treatment of Latinas/os, particularly the "brutal 'gringo'" invasion of Chicana/o territory and the destruction of Chicana/o culture by the foreigner "gabacho."[16]

Unlike the weighty legal impact of negative Latina/o constructions by Anglos, the perception by many Latinas/os that Anglos are racists has less legal significance because Latinas/os hold little or no political or legal clout in the American legislatures, courts, and elsewhere that could be directed against Anglos. Although White-on-Brown hate crime has been rampant throughout the modern history of the United States, Brown-on-White hate crime flowing out of perceptions of the Anglo as racist seems to have been less vicious, less organized, and less sustained. Nevertheless, some criminal manifestations of Latina/o rebellion against Anglos are evident. One example is the origin of the Mexican *bandido* image, which derived from Mexicans responding to their physical, legal, political, cultural, and social displacement in the Southwest during the U.S.-Mexico war and its aftermath.[17] Another is the gang violence between Puerto Rican and Anglo gangs in New York City, best known to Anglos, apart from media representations such as *West Side Story,* from the 1959 incident in which Salvador Agron (while wearing a cape) and other Puerto Rican gang members stabbed to death two White teens in a New York City playground, mistaking them for rival Irish gang members.

While debunking many of the negative conceptions of Latinas/os held by Anglos, at the same time I have documented a staggering legacy of legal and private abuse of Latinas/os that continues unabated, and I posit that the image of Anglos as tending to be racist has significant historical and current legitimacy. Anglo treatment of other subordinated groups, such as African, Asian, and Native Americans, adds other voices to validate this construction.

The fallacy of stereotypes is that they judge people as a group rather than on their individual merits. Many, if not most, Anglos would contend that they are being mislabeled as racists. The reality depends in large part on how racism is defined. Racism transcends attitudes and cannot be rebutted by attitudinal evidence in the vein of "I have a Mexican friend and I eat regularly at Mexican restaurants, so I'm not racist." Racism also takes the form of retention of the benefits of so-called White privilege[18] and institutional racism. Varieties of institutional discrimination and unfairness include systemic underfunding of urban and rural schools with disproportionate student bodies of color, as well as reliance in advanced education admissions on standardized testing.[19] Not simply passive, racism is also manifested in such actions as the overwhelming majorities of Anglo voters supporting recent initiatives to eradicate affirmative action and bilingual education.

In subsequent chapters, I address strategies to overcome both the negative construction of Latinas/os in the American imagination and the deleterious legal consequences that flow from that perception. Here, briefly, I suggest what must occur for Anglos to defeat their construction as racist in the Latina/o imagination. Among the paths toward racial healing are eliminating stereotypical depictions from media, particularly the virulent conceptions of Latina/o immigrants espoused on hate radio and elsewhere. In imagining a unified America post–September 11, Latinas/os must be embraced in a multicultural vision of a diverse America that respects its cultural composition. Yet mere attitudinal advances will fail to address institutional barriers that hold Latinas/os back and cause them to question the integrity of the criminal justice system and other valued American institutions. For example, instead of eradicating bilingual education and eliminating local control over educational choices, our educational system must consider Latina/o voices in deciding how best to educate non-English-speaking children in both English and substantive subjects. Local police departments, too, must engage and respect Latina/o voices in addressing enforcement practices that impact Latina/o communities, such as antigang policing. Only by including Latina/o voices toward solving problems, rather than continually blaming communities of color for social ills, will Anglo-Americans overcome the perception among Latinas/os that Latina/o participation in charting America's future is unrespected and undervalued.

10

Latinas/os in the Mirror
Intra-/Interethnic Glimpses

A couple walking the beach stumble upon a young Latina gathering crabs and placing them in a bucket with no lid. When the couple asks the girl whether she is worried that the crabs might climb out of her bucket and crawl away, the girl replies there is no need for concern, as "these are Latino crabs, if one of them tries to move up the bucket, the others are sure to pull it back down."

—Latina/o folklore repeated to me on many occasions to explain intraethnic jealousies[1]

Previously, I mentioned the potential for Latinas/os to internalize their media-driven negative stereotyping into feelings of inadequacy, self-hatred, and despair.[2] Their derogatory social construction may prompt another dimension of internalized oppression—the potential for Latinas/os to direct their self-hatred toward others who occupy an equally subordinate, or perhaps even an inferior, station in American society. At the same time, the influences of internalized oppression through negative social constructions compel these other marginalized groups to view and treat Latinas/os on similar terms, leading to intra-/interethnic conflict and tensions that, ironically, impede the cooperation and coalition necessary to confront media and societal stereotyping and consequent subordination.

Although one might expect tension among Latinas/os of Cuban, Puerto Rican, and Mexican heritage, thus far the geographic separation of these groups has dampened the potential for conflict. A national political survey revealing that Puerto Rican, Cuban, and Mexican Americans "felt closer" to Anglos than to other Latina/o groups exposed the distance, both geographically and otherwise, among these ethnic communities in the United States.[3] In theory, at least, one potential flashpoint between Cuban Americans, who are often anti-Castro, and Mexican Americans is the support of the Chicano movement for the Cuban Revolution. Politically, many Cuban Americans are Republicans, while most Mexican Americans and Puerto Ricans are Democrats.

Latinas/os have directed their social oppression internally within the Latina/o community toward the group even further marginalized in society—Latina/o immigrants. Most prominent among the sites of intraethnic tensions between Latina/o immigrants and later-generation Latinas/os is Los Angeles. Here, conflicts have occurred between Mexican Americans and immigrants from both Mexico and Central America. Rhetoric between these groups centers on jobs, culture, and class. Some Mexican Americans voice concern over the potential of losing jobs to cheaper immigrant labor.[4] Echoing the sentiment of many Anglos, some Mexican Americans also charge Latina/o immigrants with a reluctance to assimilate, particularly an inability to speak English. Countering this rhetoric, some Latina/o immigrants criticize Mexican Americans for Americanization that abandons their heritage and leaves them unable to speak proper Spanish, if any at all.[5]

A 1992 survey revealed that more than three of four Mexican Americans agreed that "there are too many immigrants."[6] As one political scientist explained the phenomenon of internalized oppression at work, "[T]he assimilated people feel embarrassed by the poverty and rural ways of the immigrants. Mexican-Americans want to fit into the American culture and do not want to be associated with immigrants."[7] Many of my Mexican American friends tell stories of how their relatives distinguish themselves from immigrants, either by denigrating immigrants as "wetbacks" or by renouncing their own identity by claiming to be Spanish, Italian—"anything but Mexican."[8] After having lived in East Los Angeles for most of her life, my Mexican American mother once lamented to me on moving to Oregon that East L.A. had become "*puros Mejicanos,*" her reference to an overwhelming influx of immigrants whom she viewed as bringing crime, drugs, and poverty. My mother's attitudes on that occasion reflected those of the character Mercedes Cruz in the film *Lone Star* (1995). A successful Texas restaurant owner, Cruz complained incessantly about immigrants from Mexico, bemoaning that "we're up to our ears in them," referring to immigrants as "wetbacks," insisting her Mexican restaurant employees speak English ("[T]his is the United States, we speak English"), and opining that "[e]ither they get on welfare, or they become criminals."[9]

The negative attitudes of some Latinas/os toward Latina/o immigrants are manifested through gang warfare, discriminatory treatment, and anti-immigrant voting. California's Proposition 187 (outlawing public benefits to "illegal aliens") and Proposition 227 (barring bilingual education) both garnered considerable backing from Latina/o voters, despite the fact that the propositions targeted both Latina/o immigrants and the presence of Spanish in public education. About one in four Latina/o voters supported Proposition 187.[10] Although support declined from early polls, nearly 40 percent of Latina/o voters still favored Proposition 227 on Election Day; among the initiative's proponents was the East Los Angeles Latino math teacher who inspired the film *Stand and Deliver.*[11]

Tensions in New York between long-settled Puerto Ricans and immigrants from Mexico have led to hate violence—in one 1998 incident, a group of Puerto Ricans attacked two Mexican immigrants with baseball bats in Queens while hurling ethnic insults.[12] In Phoenix, Mexican immigrant students formed gangs to protect themselves from harassment by more established Mexican American gangs.[13] Conflict in the Los Angeles area has created rivalries even among Latina/o immigrant groups. For example, in 2000, rivalries between Salvadoran and Mexican immigrants in Newbury Park culminated in a drive-by shooting at a condominium complex that killed nineteen-year-old Edgar Cruz.[14] Probably the most prominent example of mistreatment of Latina/o immigrants by other Latina/o immigrants is the family ring that forced deaf, undocumented Mexican immigrants through torture to sell trinkets in New York subways in the 1990s.[15] A more sustained example is the mistreatment of Latina/o undocumented immigrants at the hands of some coyotes.

African Americans and Latinas/os tend to hold negative stereotypical views of each other. A 1994 poll found that half of Blacks believed that Latinas/os "tend to have bigger families than they can support," while half of Latinas/os thought that Blacks "are more likely to commit crimes and violence."[16] About one in four Latinas/os surveyed felt that "Blacks want to live on welfare," and the same number of African Americans agreed that Latinas/os "lack ambition and drive to succeed."[17]

Hollywood depicts, or perhaps even helps incite, Black-Brown tensions in urban communities through movies such as *Colors* (1988), where gang warfare occurs on racial and ethnic lines and leads Black gang members to shoot up a predominantly Latina/o house party. In the thriller *Freeway* (1995), a carload of Latinos kill Reese Witherspoon's Black boyfriend in a drive-by shooting. Latina/o students in Los Angeles terrorized Black substitute teacher Samuel L. Jackson in the drama *187* (1997)—one gang member declaring that "once we go in [Jackson's house] we don't come out till that nigger's dead"—while Cuban and Black high school students fought each other in the Miami-based film *The Substitute* (1996). Written by Black rapper/actor Ice Cube, the film comedy *Next Friday* (2000) displayed the hostilities toward Blacks of three Latino brothers running a cocaine operation next door to Cube's fictional uncle.

Relations between African Americans and Latinas/os have been most strained in areas of geographic convergence between these two groups. In the South Central Los Angeles area, Latinas/os—primarily immigrants from Mexico, El Salvador, and Guatemala—now far exceed the population of African Americans.[18] Latinas/os also outnumber Blacks in Watts. A 1992 survey revealed the intensity of the conflict in finding that Blacks in Los Angeles were more likely to feel close to Whites than to Hispanic Americans.[19] A 1991 poll found 67 percent of Latinas/os in Los Angeles identifying Blacks as the group that "Hispanics have most trouble with."[20] Tensions between Latina/o immigrants and Blacks are duplicated in Washington, D.C., by conflict between Blacks and Central American immigrants, as reflected by rioting in 1991 after the acquittal of an African American police officer who shot a Salvadoran immigrant. Hostilities in Miami between mostly Democratic African Americans and the majority community of mostly Republican Cuban Americans stem in part from alleged police brutality—particularly the 1989 killing of a Black motorcyclist by a Cuban police officer,[21] which sparked riots in poor, Black neighborhoods—and from the refusal in 1990 of Miami's then Cuban mayor Xavier Suarez to meet Nelson Mandela because of Mandela's unwillingness to denounce Fidel Castro.[22] In New York, Black and Latina/o communities have fought over political redistricting.[23] Although most are racially Black, Dominican immigrants in Harlem have drawn resentment from some African Americans who blame them for West Harlem's reputation as a local drug epicenter.[24]

Stepping away from particularized conflicts, the sources of tensions between Blacks and Latinas/os nationally tend to derive from perceptions that Latina/o immigrants compete unfairly for jobs and social services, and that Latinas/os are situated on the color line so that they should be legally classified as White and thus ineligible for affirmative action programs or other redress for discrimination. The executive director of the Black Leadership Forum, a confederation of civil rights groups, has observed, "A large number of Hispanics are white. The issues that resonate with people of color may not resonate throughout the Hispanic population."[25] Another commentator suggests that Blacks "often see Latinos/as as a racially mobile group capable of leapfrogging them, with access to whiteness and all [the privilege] that it entails."[26] Some Blacks view Mexican Americans and other Latinas/os as free riders[27] who attempt to share in the hard-fought Civil Rights victories of African Americans for desegregation, affirmative action, political rights (under the Voting Rights Act), and other programs and protections. An African American sociology professor at Harvard has pointed to the vast numbers of Latinas/os eligible for affirmative action as a major factor in the loss of political support for these programs among the American public.[28] Regarding job competition, some Blacks view Latina/o immigrants as unfairly competing through their sheer numbers and their willingness to work for less money. One commentator addressed attitudes of African American farm workers in the South toward the influx of Latina/o migrant workers there: "Latino immigrants are often seen as working too hard for too little. Some [Black] workers complain that immigrants have the unfair advantage of using their wages to support families living in distant countries, where the dollars they earn go further than in the United States."[29] At the same time, some Latina/o leaders have complained that Blacks are overrepresented in the federal government and in military leadership positions.[30]

In Los Angeles, the divide between Black and Latina/o communities was reflected politically in the astounding outcome of the 2001 mayoral election, in which 80 percent of Latina/o voters went for Antonio Villaraigosa while 80 percent of African American voters helped elect Anglo candidate James Hahn.[31] Latino comedian Paul Rodriguez acknowledged on stage the anger Blacks felt when the newly elected Hahn refused to support the reappointment of Bernard Parks, the city's Black police chief: "I was disappointed in my African American friends. They voted for Jimmy Hahn. But that's okay, because then he turned around and [fucked] you like a plantation master!"[32] Previously, California's divisive Proposition 187 political campaign aimed to convince Blacks that Latina/o (and Asian) immigrants were taking their jobs and government services.[33] Although their support was less than that of Anglo voters, 47 percent of Black voters ultimately backed the initiative.[34]

At the relational crossroads of these Black-Brown tensions lies the potential for coalition on two of the most vital issues for the sustainability and development of Black/Brown communities—confronting policing issues that encompass police brutality, the war on drugs, and racial profiling,[35] and addressing the sorry state of public education funding in America, where the poorest urban and rural schools are dominated by Black/Brown students.

As with African Americans and Latinas/os, tensions between Asian Americans and Latinas/os tend to erupt in areas of geographic convergence, such as South Central Los Angeles, where Latina/o immigrants, Koreans, and Blacks reside in substantial numbers. The dynamics of conflict between Asians and Latinas/os, though, are somewhat different from those between Latinas/os and Blacks. Fault lines emerge from the feelings of some Asian Americans that Latinas/os are a drain on taxpayers and unfairly advantaged by affirmative action programs, contrasted by the attitudes of some Latinas/os that Asian Americans, as merchants and employers, treat them harshly or without respect, as depicted in the film drama *The City (La ciudad)* (1999), in which Asian managers mistreated Latina/o garment workers. In one study, 60 percent of Asian Americans rated Latinas/os as less intelligent than members of their own group, and 72 percent thought Latinas/os prefer to live off welfare.[36] A 1994 poll determined that Asian Americans identified themselves most closely with Whites instead of with Latinas/os or Blacks.[37] Asian American attitudes toward Latinas/os were reflected in the strong Asian support for California's Proposition 187, with 47 percent of Asian American voters (the same percentage as Blacks) voting for the initiative. Exit polls revealed that 57 percent of Asian American voters had approved California's anti–bilingual education initiative.[38] Illustrating the complex anti-immigrant tensions between these groups, shortly after the passage of that education initiative, a group of Asian men assaulted two Latinos at a California convenience store, yelling, "What are you wetbacks doing in here?"[39] Conversely, in the 1992 South Central Los Angeles riots, some Latinas/os targeted Korean-owned stores for looting, with one Latino interviewed on television explaining, "Because we hate 'em. Everybody hates them."[40] The film *Luminarias* (1999), directed by José Luis Valenzuela, evidenced this tension between Koreans and Latinas/os in southern California with a plotline that included a Korean-Latina romance; her surprised Latina girlfriends warned, "You know how Koreans feel about Mexicans."

Distinct from the grounds for coalition building between African Americans and Latinas/os, the basis for coalition between Asian Americans and Latinas/os centers on the large numbers of recent immigrants that comprise both groups and the consequent perception of foreignness they share.[41] Thus, Asians and Latinas/os might seek convergence on such issues as federal immigration policy and the procedural rights of undocumented immigrants in custody, as well as language policy, such as preserving the legality of bilingual education programs and resisting Official English/English-only laws, as occurred in Monterey Park, California, through an Asian/Latina/o coalition.

Relations between Native Americans and Latinas/os have been examined less thoroughly than those between Latinas/os and other groups. Although the relative absence of significant urban contact between Latinas/os and Natives has spared them from the inflammatory urban confrontations between other groups, tensions between Latinas/os and Natives have nonetheless resulted in violence, as when dozens of Latina/o and Native high school students scuffled at a San Diego area school in May 2000. This school violence apparently was prompted by long-standing perceptions among Natives that Mexican American students believe they stand higher in the pecking order than Natives.[42] Dating back to mistreatment of Natives at the hands of Spanish colonizers in the missions of the Southwest, many Natives share this sentiment that Mexican Americans consider Natives a lower class of people. One of my Latina research assistants remembers derogatory remarks from family members directed at Papago Indians in the Tucson area, such as "She looks like she just walked off the reservation." Natives and Latinas/os possess some mutual policy concerns toward coalition, particularly the impact of official and vigilante English-language policies and other assimilative expectations on these groups.[43] Sharing indigenous heritage, Natives and most Latinas/os also maintain a stake in resisting derogatory stereotypes of indigenous culture as subhuman.

11

Eradicating Stereotypes
Community-Based Strategies of
Media Counterspeech and Protest

Given my contention that derogatory stereotypes contribute to the unfavorable legal and social treatment of Latinas/os in the United States, it will surprise no reader that this book adds to the call for eradicating stereotypes. But determining an effective means to eliminate and to counteract media and societal stereotypes is daunting. Moreover, even if media were to routinely present authentic constructions of Latina/o ethnicity and culture, it would not ensure that negative stereotypes that exist in the collective public consciousness could be erased in the same generation. Still, many of the strategies suggested below confront stereotypical media productions. Even if one were to concede that media possess no influence in creating or perpetuating negative constructions, which I do not, other reasons counsel targeting negative media representations. Most important of these is the impact of derogatory media images on the self-esteem of Latinas/os themselves.

In the struggle against stereotypical constructions of Latinas/os, arguably the most important objective is to seize control of the means of production, in this case the ownership of communicative media. Communicative control would enable Latinas/os to begin to tell their counter-stories[1] to mainstream audiences as a form of counterspeech to the body of derogatory stereotypical works that exist.[2] Lisa Iglesias has suggested:

> [T]he "means of communication" have become as central to the structure of power/lessness in our postmodern, hyperlinked, globalized, mass media society as the "means of production" were central to the class struggles of modernizing industrialism.[3]

Relying on media as currently governed to rid themselves of stereotypes is unrealistic. Mass media generally tend to ignore Latinas/os. When

169

Latinas/os are relevant to the production, media typically present them in a negative light. Indeed, many Latinas/os are so starved for inclusion and relevancy in media's portrayal of American society that they will accept questionable characterizations through cartoon images (the long-retired Frito Bandito) and dogs (Dinky/Gidget the Taco Bell Chihuahua) as better than invisibility. When Latinas/os cross over into the mainstream of American media, it is typically as a "flavor of the month" commodification, with no more longevity in the American cultural record than the short-lived macarena dance craze. More often than not, Latinas/os play only an incidental role in mainstream productions, even those centered in ethnic "locations." Anglos apparently are needed to serve as ethnic tour guides. For example, while documenting the American drug trade and pointing the blame at Mexico, the film *Traffic* (2000) relied on its Anglo star, Michael Douglas, to set its moral and legal tone. Julia Roberts and Brad Pitt supplied the star power to carry the film *The Mexican* (2000)— while Mexican locations dominated the plot, no Mexican characters had significant roles. Asians and other subordinated groups suffer the same syndrome—the film *Snow Falling on Cedars* (1999), which used the vantage point of an Anglo journalist to tell the story of a Japanese American wrongfully accused of murder, led one observer to question, "Why do filmmakers generally seem to assume that a mainstream audience wants, indeed needs, a white character as an avenue into any story about an Asian American, or for that matter any other minority community?"[4] A 2001 study by Children Now and the National Hispanic Foundation for the Arts identified a related phenomenon in which the primary recurring Latina/o characters on prime-time television tended to be cast as assistants or "sidekicks" who deferred to an Anglo superior for direction (in the tradition of the 1970s sitcom *Chico and the Man*).[5]

The staggering negativity of the Latina/o image in the United States has led many Latinas/os to mask their ethnicity and culture when able. Lighter-skinned Latinas/os may be particularly able to accomplish this cultural and ethnic erasure by "passing" as White and thereby contributing to the invisibility of Latinas/os. The film and music industries evidence the long-standing tendency of Latinas/os to Anglo-cize their names in order to shed their image as a foreigner, as well as the negative baggage of other social constructions that Latinas/os carry with them. Actor Martin Sheen, born to an Irish mother and Spanish father, previously was Ramón Estévez. One of his actor sons, Charlie, took the name Charlie Sheen though born Carlos Estévez. Actress Raquel Welch, daughter of a

Bolivian-born father, changed her last name from Tejada. Examples from the music industry include Baldemar Huerta (country/pop singer Freddy Fender) and Florencia Bisenta de Casillas Martínez Cardona (Vikki Carr). Recent transformations include those by Enrique Martin Morales (Ricky Martin), Marco Antonio Muñiz (Marc Anthony), and Juan Secada (Jon Secada). The eliding of ethnicity to prompt mainstream audience acceptance is sometimes orchestrated by entertainment agents. The movie *La Bamba* (1987) portrays the involuntary cultural transformation of Richard Valenzuela to Ritchie Valens at his manager's insistence to appeal to Anglo record buyers—"Look, it could have been worse, you could have been Ricky Zuela."

To begin to alter public opinion through more authentic and sustained constructions of Latina/o identity, Latinas/os will need to acquire the means of media communication through ownership, as well as through securing management and production positions in the spectrum of media that ranges from television, film, music, and radio to the print media. In television, for example, the impetus for Latina/o productions will come from Latina/o producers, as television is a producer-driven medium.[6] Spanish-language print media, television networks, and radio stations, although important to provide Latinas/os with positive self-images and role models, will not fully counter the inadequacies of American media. It is vital that authentic constructions reach mainstream audiences as well. This must be accomplished by mainstream media productions in English that feature Latinas/os in prominent counterstereotype roles.

Latinas/os who acquire ownership, management, or production roles need to ensure they do not misuse their influence. Equally, Latina/o actors, singers, and other performers must refuse to participate in projects that they believe negatively portray Latinas/os and perpetuate derogatory stereotypes. This will be challenging, especially for lesser-knowns, as Latina/o actors are few, and many of the roles offered them perpetuate stereotypes. For example, Latinas are routinely cast on television and in film as maids; the Black actress who received an Academy Award for playing a maid in *Gone with the Wind* once put it bluntly: "It's better to get $7,000 a week for playing a servant than $7 a week for being one."[7] Further, the film industry has demonstrated its willingness throughout its history to substitute Anglos for Latinas/os in stereotypical roles, ranging from *bandidos* to gang members. For example, Paul Newman played a *bandido* in *The Outrage* (1964), and Robbie Benson portrayed a Latino gang member in *Walk Proud* (1979), eliciting protest from the Chicana/o community and even prompting recognition of the resultant furor in a "protest" anthem sung by Richard "Cheech" Marin in the film comedy *Cheech and Chong's Next Movie* (1980):

Mexican Americans
Don't like to go to movies
Where the dude has to wear contacts to make his blue eyes brown,
And don't it make your brown eyes blue.

Other notable examples in Hollywood history of Anglos standing in for Latinas/os include actor Paul Muni playing a Mexican American lawyer in *Bordertown* (1935) and, later, Mexico president Benito Juárez in the film *Juárez* (1939). Italian American Al Pacino played a reformed Puerto Rican heroin dealer in *Carlito's Way* (1993) and a ruthless Cuban American cocaine dealer, Tony Montana, in *Scarface* (1983). Italian American Marisa Tomei's casting as a Cuban immigrant in *The Perez Family* (1994) brought objection from Latinas/os, as did Charlton Heston in brownface makeup as Mexican narcotics agent Ramon Miguel "Mike" Vargas in *Touch of Evil* (1958).

The Cheech and Chong drug comedy films of the late 1970s and early 1980s illustrate the failure of a Latino with writing and production control, Richard "Cheech" Marin (a straight-A student in high school, despite his drug-stupefied entertainment image), to steer the project clear of negative stereotypes. Among the most prominent representations of drug dealing and drug use in contemporary cinema, Cheech's self-deprecating movies such as *Up in Smoke* (1979) and *Nice Dreams* (1981) helped to situate and center Mexicans and Mexican Americans in the public consciousness on America's drug problem. Such Latina/o-controlled productions as Gregory Nava's film *My Family/Mi Familia* (1995), Luis Valdez's *La Bamba* (1987),[8] and the Edward James Olmos–directed *American Me* (1992) portray Latino drug dealers in California. Thriving in another medium, Latino David Gonzales has generated controversy with his toy figurines, "Homies," which include caricatures of Latinos with gang-member appearances and names such as "Big Loco" and "8-Ball" (a drug reference).[9] Latina/o literature has often centered on gang culture—for instance, Yxta Maya Murray's novel *Locas*,[10] and Luis Rodriguez's more hopeful autobiographical account *Always Running, La Vida Loca: Gang Days in L.A.*[11] *Locas* is an unflinching fictional account of a Chicana gang in Los Angeles, with leader Lucía "jumping in" new members in bloody slugfests, using her switchblade to seal their comraderie with blood drawn from their arms, and orchestrating muggings of Latina immigrants and then White folks "for the real money"—at least, when her girls weren't busy transforming shiny sixth-graders into cocaine addicts for their Chicano gang boyfriends to supply.[12]

Most other Latina/o productions or media with Latina/o cast members have been marred by derogatory references toward or constructions of Latinas/os. In the short-lived sitcom *A.K.A. Pablo* (1984), comedian/actor Paul Rodriguez opened the show with a stand-up comedy routine about his carrying the "Mexican Express Card"—a knife.[13] The television comedy *The George Lopez Show* (debuting 2002) reminded viewers of the image of Latina/o foreignness when George joked about his daughter skipping swim class: "Why does she have to know how to swim? We're already here."[14] Even the heralded PBS drama series *American Family* featured a Latina heroin addict as the former girlfriend of a reformed parolee who became a fireman and compassionate father.

Several Latina/o musical artists have perpetuated or confirmed negative societal constructions in their records targeting mainstream audiences. On his hip-hop single "We Thuggin'," Puerto Rican rapper Fat Joe (Joe Cartagena) extols the virtues of such party favors as alcohol and the drug Ecstasy ("I'm on E feeling ready and hot"). Jennifer Lopez's smash hit "I'm Real" begins with a shout-out to marijuana (rapper Ja Rule's verse "Blowin' back on this Mary Jane"). The overarching lyrical theme of Cuban American rappers Cypress Hill is the legalization of marijuana; their gold-selling song "Insane in the Brain" blasted "cops" who came to snatch their "crops." Puerto Rican–Black rapper Noreaga (Victor Santiago) has glorified gang membership.[15] Productions meant for Latina/o record buyers also are not free from negative constructions. One of the late Selena's Spanish-language hits manages to portray (her audience of) Mexicans and Mexican Americans as lazy, drunken tortilla eaters:

If y'all come to dance . . . well, let's go enjoy ourselves
If y'all come to sleep, get out of here!
Because this song is not for any lazy one . . .
Look at Juan,
He can't even move
Well his shoes weigh a lot
He must have mud on them

> Look at Maria
> She's moving from her chair
> That's what always happens to you if you eat a lot of tortillas
> Look at José because he's only sitting
> He drank a lot of beer and
> Now he's walking sideways.[16]

Popular in Mexico and also among some Latinas/os in the United States, *"narcocorridos"* celebrate the lifestyle and adventures of drug traffickers in the mold of gangster rap glorifying the gangster life and of earlier *corridos* lionizing *bandidos*. One representative *narcocorrido* depicts the fictional adventures of two murderous Latinas, dressed as nuns, crossing the border with cocaine disguised as powdered milk for an Arizona orphanage.[17] These musical artists defend their questionable themes by suggesting that they are not drug dealers or users themselves but are just trying to make a living. Further, one suggested, "If by getting rid of corridos you can get rid of drugs, go to it! We'll retire."[18]

The renowned stage comedy trio Culture Clash, which reaches both Latinas/os and mainstream audiences by blending English and Spanish dialogue, frequently uses marijuana as a prop in representing the diverse tapestry of Latinas/os and Latina/o culture in America. When I saw their otherwise brilliant presentation in 2002 at the Berkeley Repertory Theatre, the Latino cast members thanked the mostly Anglo audience and joked about there being Mexicans seated in the upper balcony, "warning" the Mexicans not to steal anything on their way out.

For African Americans, rap music illustrates vividly the missed opportunity for a racial/ethnic group to seize on its control of media for positive ends. A 2001 national survey of African Americans revealed that 48 percent thought hip-hop, rap music, and rap culture had a mostly negative influence on young Blacks, while only 18 percent saw a mostly positive impact.[19] Although African Americans sometimes control the means of production for rap music, even owning several record labels, most of the momentum and direction of rap music perpetuates stereotypes of Black Americans. Many popular rap performers have glorified violence, gang membership, and drug use (the Luniz's hit "I Got 5 on It," referring to five dollars on a weed purchase, and Afroman's "Because I Got High"), as well as sexual infidelity, fertility (for example, Notorious B.I.G.'s anthem "Big Poppa" urged his associates not to "shoot up" the nightclub because he saw "some ladies tonight that should be having [his] baby"), and welfare abuse (the Bone Thugs-N-Harmony hit song "1st of tha Month" extolled the pleasures of cashing welfare checks toward liquor and drugs).

To confront the predominance of negative media constructions of Latina/o-ness, Latina/o-controlled productions must offer projects that are subversive and antisubordinating works. These counterstories may fall into several categories. One variety meant primarily for a Latina/o audience warns off Latinas/os from perpetuating stereotypes by engaging in harmful behaviors such as gang membership or substance abuse. In 1992, several Latino rappers sampled music from the multicultural band War to declare "war" on gang violence (against the background of War's "Why Can't We Be Friends?") and drugs (because "if you smoke dope, you're at war with yourself").[20] Popular too among Black rappers, this cautionary message from Black artists has targeted Black-on-Black crime, gang violence, bicoastal hostilities, drug use, and domestic violence.[21]

A related subversive production aimed at Latinas/os celebrates Latina/o-ness, particularly by delivering a message of ethnic pride to raise Latina/o self-esteem and by disrupting the dominant paradigm of assimilationist ideals and Angloness. The college-radio hit "Brown and Proud" (1999) from Los Mocosos and the rap "Mexican Power" (1992) by Proper Dos exemplify this approach, following in the tradition of such Black Pride anthems as James Brown's hit "Say It Loud—I'm Black and I'm Proud" (1968).

Another variety of rebellious production exposes and challenges discrimination against Latinas/os. For example, the film *Stand and Deliver* (1988), directed by Ramon Menendez, confronted discriminatory attitudes of the standardized testing industry. The coupling of Latino rappers and War rhythms in 1992 decried racial profiling of Latinos as gang members by law enforcement.[22] Similarly, Black rappers have challenged discriminatory policing practices and such symbols of oppression as Arizona's reluctance to establish a state holiday for Martin Luther King's birthday.[23] Even Anglo artists have questioned the Anglo establishment through punk music in the late 1970s and 1980s[24] and through songs addressing discrimination against long-haired hippie youth, such as the 1971 hit "Signs." If seeking a mainstream audience, these confrontational projects must face the potential for backlash that sometimes accompanies the airing of Latina/o grievances in the media. For example, some critics in New York reacted negatively toward the Broadway staging of *Zoot Suit,* a Latina/o production that depicted the racial injustice in 1940s Los Angeles of the Sleepy Lagoon murder prosecution and the Zoot Suit Riots. One critic blasted the play as "a slanted neo-rabble-rouser, abrading ethnic emotions, presented in unnecessary hyperbole, terminal exaggerations. . . . The plot is almost totally stereotypically anti–American establishment."[25]

Perhaps the most important category of counterproductions are those aimed at mainstream American audiences that contradict social constructions by depicting Latinas/os in roles that run against societal expectations. The high school students in the film *Stand and Deliver* (1988) were capable of outperforming Anglo takers of the National Advanced Placement Calculus Exam. The film *La Bamba* (1987) depicted the efforts of an enterprising Latina in propelling her son Ritchie toward mainstream musical stardom—debunking a talent manager's assumption that the family spoke only Spanish, Ritchie's mother informed him in English that she also spoke "business." Similarly, the film *Selena* (1996) focused on a father's role in orchestrating his family's entertainment business. The film *Born in East L.A.* (1987) highlighted the assimilative distance between later-generation Mexican Americans and Mexican nationals in their native languages and other cultural flashpoints. *American Family,* the PBS series that debuted in 2002, depicted Latinas/os as lawyers, business owners, and firemen—the post–September 11 profession of heroism.[26] *American Family* cast a Latina immigration lawyer (who balanced the anti–undocumented immigrant attitudes of the conservative family patriarch and reflected the political diversities among Latinas/os), while the Showtime cable series *Resurrection Blvd.* includes a Latina law student. The film *Luminarias* (1999) featured several Latina professionals, including a divorce attorney; *Tortilla Soup* (2001) included a young Latina offered the chance to manage an international start-up technology company.

These Latina/o productions convey the diverse range of the Latina/o experience in the United States, including the oft-ignored Latina/o middle class. A 1992 study of television programming revealed that three of four Latina/o characters were from the lower socioeconomic class (for instance, the stereotypical Latina maid); in contrast, only 17 percent of Whites were so represented.[27] As George Hadley-Garcia has observed:

> Hollywood had failed to look for the varieties of Hispanidad, at real-life Hispanics who are affluent, educated, middle- or upper-class, who are creative or light-skinned, who are gay or don't speak Spanish, who have

1.5 (not 5.1) children or are blond or Jewish or don't have "Spanish-sounding" surnames. These roles and stories remain to be written, and most likely will have to be written by Hispanics.[28]

Ironically, however, it is possible that such portrayals will pose the same risk that some researchers discovered in studying the impact of *The Cosby Show* on White audiences. Instead of reducing their prejudices, the show left a number of White viewers believing that Blacks could succeed in the United States as the Huxtables had, if only they would work hard enough.[29]

Some Latina/o commentators have posed the question of whether Latina/o media productions should portray the Latina/o community "warts and all, showing drugs, crime, and gangs," rather than focusing solely on the positive attributes of this community.[30] One Latino writer asked a similar question directed at mass media productions generally: "[W]ill we really be happy if all Latinos in movies are successful doctors and lawyers with problem-free families?"[31] Still, I believe Anglo media productions, with their dominant focus on derogatory depictions of Latinas/os, must be countered with Latina/o-originated narratives accenting the positive and showing the reaches of the Latina/o community, such as its middle and upper class, that have been ignored by the dominant gaze's fixation on Latino gangsters (whose wealth, if any, is ill-gotten) and unsophisticated Latina maids and women of easy virtue.

Finally, situated in the media spectrum between derogatory constructions and subversive works are facially neutral Latina/o endeavors that elide ethnicity. In these productions, presumably the film actor, television character, or musical artist, although a Latina/o, could have been Anglo or any ethnicity, as ethnicity is downplayed in the role or lyrics. An example from television is Erik Estrada's role as motorcycle officer Frank Poncherello on the long-running 1970s television series *CHiPs*. Although Frank's Latino ethnicity was rarely mentioned, the casting of a Latino as a good-natured, witty police officer surely enhanced the image of Latinas/os. Cameron Diaz's role as Mary in the hit film comedy *There's Something about Mary* (1998) is another example of an ethnicity-neutral production. Directed by Robert Rodriguez, the popular film *Spy Kids* (2001) followed the adventures of the children of Latina/o international spies who have to rescue their parents but made their ethnicity incidental, leading one journalist to comment, "By placing Latino characters at the forefront and not depicting them as outside the mainstream, Rodriguez may achieve more than he would by raising a cinematic fist for racial equality."[32] On occasion, Latina/o actors have even been cast to play prominent Anglos. Actor Martin Sheen (born Ramón Estévez) has twice portrayed Anglo presidents—John F. Kennedy in the TV movie *Kennedy* (1983) and fictional Irish Catholic president Josiah Bartlett in the television drama series *The West Wing*.

American pop music serves up several examples of facially race- and ethnicity-neutral odes to love and life. The latest iteration of Latina/o pop (or LatPop) artists, including Ricky Martin, Christina Aguilera, Jennifer Lopez, Enrique Iglesias, Marc Anthony, and Shakira, lyrically and musically fall into this category of homogenized productions. These artists are notable for giving visibility to Latinas/os in mainstream culture and serving as a source of cultural pride for Latinas/os. Ricky Martin, for example, is far removed from the *West Side Story* image of Puerto Ricans as knife-wielding gang members. His English fluency helps dispel the impression that Latinas/os are unwilling or unable to learn English. Yet, despite these subtle positive influences, the LatPop artists tend to reflect the dominant social paradigm in their glorification of heterosexual relationships and in the subordination of women to men.[33] Spanish TV network programs replicate these images by sexualizing and objectifying women. Sadly, the Latina/o culture tends to vilify homosexuality and to be patriarchal. Still, Latino male dominance, patriarchy, authoritarianism, and spousal abuse, sometimes labeled machismo,[34] in fact differ little from the subordinate treatment of women under Anglo culture.

Complementing efforts to acquire and effectively wield control of media production for positive ends, Latinas/os and other concerned groups should continue to rely on the sometimes fruitful strategy of protest against stereotypical media productions. Latina/o activists have employed protest over the years in campaigns such as those by César Chávez and the United Farm Workers, seeking fair wages and collective bargaining, and more recently in the struggle against environmental racism. Latinas/os have also directed the technique of protest against stereotypical media productions.

Latinas/os have protested negative constructions in a variety of media, such as television (*Chico and the Man*), radio (*The Howard Stern Show*, for his disparaging comments about Selena, Mexican Americans, and "Spanish" people who possess "no depth"), film (*Boulevard Nights*— Mexican American protests; *Badge 373*—Puerto Rican protests; *Walk*

Proud—Mexican American protests; *Fort Apache, The Bronx*—Puerto Rican and African American protests), and theater (prompting cancellation of a high school production of *West Side Story* after protest from the Puerto Rican community).[35]

Other subordinated groups similarly have campaigned against their media constructions. Gay activists challenged the portrayal of gay men as perverse and abnormal in the film *Cruising* (1980), as well as the portrayal of lesbians in *Basic Instinct* (1992) as man-haters.[36] Feminists protested the violence against women in the slasher film *Snuff* (1977), whose poster ads intersected Latina/o stereotypes in heralding *Snuff* as "[t]he film that could only be made in South America . . . where Life is CHEAP!"[37] Native Americans have struggled to eradicate derogatory "Indian" mascots of athletic teams, and activism by Asian American students led clothier Abercrombie and Fitch to discontinue shirts demeaning Asians with such slogans as "Two wongs can make it white," poking fun at the supposed inability of Asians to speak English correctly and at their stereotype as laundry laborers.

Although protest by Latina/o activists has helped to end several stereotypical campaigns and productions, it is less evident whether the strategy of protest is effective in the first instance to dissuade the creation and issuance of stereotypical productions. Issues surrounding the use of protest as a tool[38] against stereotypical media include the need to determine the protest objective. Is the goal to halt exhibition, or to prompt more sustained reform by the hiring and use of diverse producers, actors, and industry executives? What should trigger media protest—should protest target the release of a specific stereotypical product, or does the overwhelming presence of negative constructions in media or the nature of the protest objectives warrant a preemptive approach? Who should protesters target—the actors, originators, and producers of the project; facilitators of the media broadcast, such as movie theaters or television stations and the businesses that purchase advertising; or media consumers, by calling for product boycotts of movies and other media? Should innovative techniques be used, such as targeting the licenses of broadcasters? What role should lawyers and lawsuits play in facilitating protest and achieving the objectives sought? Will protest be counterproductive by increasing viewership through the free publicity that controversy generates? Will protest serve an educative function about the detriment of unfavorable social constructions and their influence on unfavorable legal and social treatment of Latinas/os?

Grassroots protest by Latinas/os prevailed against José Jiménez, the dim-witted Latino comic persona created by Bill Dana, a comedian of Hungarian heritage. After ten years of performances on television, on record, and on stage, Bill Dana bowed to pressure and announced in April 1970 to ten thousand Mexican Americans attending a Chicano pride extravaganza at the Los Angeles Sports Arena that "after tonight, José Jiménez is dead."[39] Of course, by that time José was past his prime. Moreover, after the furor had subsided, Dana revived José on occasion, such as for a recent CD greatest-hits compilation and, before that, a cassette compilation on which José (Bill), in an effort to be trendy, turned in perhaps the most anemic rap performance ever recorded.

In 1999, a protest initiated by students at Santa Monica High School in California, which later gained the support of the Mexican American Legal Defense and Educational Fund (MALDEF) and others, prompted the Walt Disney company to alter its hot-selling *Toy Story 2* video game to remove a *bandido* character. The game had employed a Mexican *bandido*-looking figure (replete with sombrero, droopy mustache, ribbons of bullets, and Spanish music accompaniment) as the first human target for players to shoot after they had dispatched monsters, robots, and animals.[40]

The Frito Bandito advertising campaign witnessed the use of grassroots protest in combination with legal measures to end images of a cartoon Mexican *bandido* selling Frito-Lay Corn Chips. Launched in 1967, the Frito Bandito advertising campaign prompted the formation in 1968 of two Mexican American groups to challenge racist stereotypes—Involvement of Mexican-Americans in Gainful Endeavors (IMAGE) and the National Mexican-American Anti-Defamation Committee (NMAADC). Faced with the threat of product boycotts orchestrated by these groups, the Frito-Lay Corporation toned down its *bandido*'s presentation.[41] IMAGE and NMAADC ultimately approached broadcasters and secured the agreement of some to boycott the ads. At the same time, NMAADC turned to legal measures, announcing its intention to lodge a regulatory complaint with the FCC under the fairness doctrine and, later, to file a $610 million lawsuit against Frito-Lay Corporation, its advertising agency, and the television networks CBS and ABC. The lawsuit would claim $100 on behalf of each Mexican American in the United States "for the fictitious defamation" of their character. Ultimately, Frito-Lay decided to terminate its *bandido* campaign.[42] As discussed in Chapter 13, lawsuits of this nature are effectively barred under current law, and challenges to stereotypical media generally must be waged outside the courtroom.

Activists confronted a stereotypical episode of the *Seinfeld* television series that suggested the Puerto Rican community has a mob mentality. The episode depicted the character Kramer accidently setting fire to the Puerto Rican flag during the Puerto Rican Day parade and stomping on it to extinguish the flames. When a group of incensed Puerto Ricans retaliated by vandalizing his friend Jerry's car, Kramer remarked, "It's like this every day in Puerto Rico." The National Puerto Rican Coalition, as well as other Latina/o groups, called for a public apology to air during the series finale episode, withdrawal of the disparaging episode from syndication, and a restructuring of the NBC network's Broadcast Standards and Content Policy Department.[43] NBC later agreed to drop the episode from reruns that year. What made this portrayal of New York's Puerto Rican community so offensive and negative was that Puerto Ricans had been previously invisible in the *Seinfeld* series, despite its New York City location. Related to criticism of *Seinfeld* were concerns leveled against Paul Simon's Broadway production of *The Capeman*. One might ask, what harm was done by a talented Anglo (Simon) telling a factual slice of Puerto Rican life in New York City? The answer stems from the insignificance and illegitimacy of Latina/o stories in the culture of American mass media. Anglo borrowing of Latina/o influences and Anglo telling of Latina/o stories would be more tolerable and even welcome if they occurred against a backdrop of Latina/o relevancy and positive visibility. Surely, stereotypical images will lose their sting if they are balanced by a steady depiction of Latina/o characters in honorable roles. Against such a backdrop, *West Side Story* would not be the only media representation of Puerto Ricans, and thus their portrayal as a murderous but perhaps misunderstood thug in *Capeman* (or as an unruly mob in *Seinfeld*) could be viewed more properly as one man's misdirected life than as a cultural blueprint for Puerto Ricans and other Latinas/os.[44]

Apart from whether they have been portrayed positively or negatively, Latinas/os and other minority groups have been largely absent from the pivotal media of network television. Feliz Sanchez, president of the National Hispanic Foundation for the Arts, remarked recently that "[f]or many Latinos, our under-representation on television and in film—both in front of and behind the camera—is tantamount to segregation in the digital age and the civil rights issue to address for this century."[45] In 2000,

Latinas/os comprised only 2 percent of the prime-time television characters on the six major broadcast networks, portrayed only eight recurring
characters, and were relegated to incidental roles consisting mostly of
criminals and blue-collar workers. Despite the burgeoning Latina/o population, the representational numbers were down from 1999, in which
3 percent of prime-time television characters were Latina/o.[46] In the
2001–2002 season, the numbers were slightly better but still bleak—
imagining the cast of the 2001–2002 prime-time television season as
a room of one hundred people, you would find only four Latinas/os in
the room.[47]

Film industry numbers are equally disturbing. In 2000, Latinas/os had
4.9 percent of all roles cast, well below their 2000 Census population of
12.5 percent. By contrast, African Americans, roughly equal in population with Latinas/os, were cast in 14.8 percent of film roles. In 1999,
Latina/o film directors worked 1.1 percent of the total director days
worked, compared with African American directors, who worked 4.6
percent of the directorship hours in 1999.[48] That year, a coalition of national Latina/o groups initiated a campaign directed at both film and
network television for the overall invisibility of Latinas/os and the absence of positive portrayals. The coalition called for a one-week boycott
("brownout") of network television, as well as for a federal study on the
impact of media imagery on Latina/o self-esteem.[49] Other measures to be
pursued included meetings with advertisers and purchases of stock in
order to assert presence and power in publicly owned company shareholder meetings.

In planning strategies toward positive and sustained portrayals of Lati-
nas/os, activists should be mindful that opposition to media stereotyping
has been most successful when the appeal is financially oriented rather
than morally based, targeting industry's conscience. For example, inflammatory images in early Hollywood films led the Mexican government in
the 1920s to prohibit the importation of films that portrayed Mexicans
unfavorably. Other Latin American countries imposed similar bans, outlawing films that offended Mexico. Given the substantial market there for
American films, this threat ultimately moved Hollywood to act. At the
same time, uproar over perceptions of immorality and indecency in Hollywood films posed the risk of boycott by Catholic filmgoers in the United
States and of censorship by states and the federal government at a time
when the Supreme Court had left cinema unprotected under constitutional free speech guarantees.[50]

These influences combined in 1934 to prompt adoption by the film industry's Production Code Administration (PCA) of an industry watchdog standard (considered censorship by many) that policed the depiction of Mexicans and other financially vital groups, while also ensuring morality of cinema in areas as diverse as sex, obscenity, profanity, and crime (for example, by not presenting criminals in a sympathetic light).[51] Overseeing portrayals of Mexicans and other protected groups, this code provided:

> No picture shall be produced that tends to incite bigotry or hatred among peoples of differing races, religions, or national origins. The use of such offensive words as Chink, Dago, Frog, Greaser, Hunkie, Kike, Nigger, Spic, Wop, [and] Yid should be avoided.[52]

Presumably, without the PCA's blessing, a film would encounter distribution problems, as the movie studios that controlled the theaters agreed not to distribute films lacking the Production Code Seal.[53] Under the supervision of the PCA, Hollywood scripts were forced to abandon derogatory references toward Mexican characters as "greasers," both in film titles and in dialogue.

The 1935 film *Bordertown,* starring Paul Muni and Bette Davis, well illustrates the PCA's influence in cleansing most negative Latina/o images from film. Its screenplay was written initially by author Carroll Graham, based on his novel *Border Town.* Faithful to his novel, Graham's screenplay followed fugitive farm laborer Johnny Ramírez south of the border to Mexicali after Ramírez had gunned down a California ranch owner and his foreman with a stolen army revolver. Taking up with a French prostitute there, Ramírez makes his fortune by smuggling drugs and then rum across the border during Prohibition and perishes in an auto accident while being chased by authorities in a final run for the border. On behalf of the PCA, its head Joseph Breen rejected this ignoble portrayal of Mexicans as murderous smugglers.[54] Warner Bros. studios fired Graham and rewrote the script to appease the PCA by portraying Johnny Ramírez as a fiery-tempered lawyer rather than a desperado. Still, the PCA exercised rigid oversight of the new script, demanding removal of all references to Ramírez as a "greaser" and even instructing the studio to tone down any suggestion of excessive drinking by Ramírez. In the film, Ramírez, though plagued by his foul temper, was ambitious enough to graduate from night law school and later to open a successful casino in Mexicali.

Alterations suggested by the PCA to the draft script for film classic *The Treasure of the Sierra Madre* (1948) included these:

> Page 20: In handling these Mexican girls, please avoid any direct suggestion that they are prostitutes. Page 44: In this sequence, please make it clear that the bandits are attempting to rob the woman and nothing more. There should . . . be no suggestion of attempted rape.[55]

The PCA's authority grew even more compelling with the impact of World War II on European film markets and with the emergence of wartime government-based pressures (the Good Neighbor Policy) to maintain relations with supportive countries. But PCA influence began to wane after World War II and in the 1950s, following the introduction of television, the legal breakup of the anticompetitive hold of movie studios on distribution and theaters, and the Supreme Court's recognition that films are protected under the First Amendment and thus substantially immunized from government censorship.[56] By 1961, even the Mexican "greaser" was back in the saddle of Hollywood films, beginning with the western *One Eyed Jacks*.

Despite its success in ridding Hollywood temporarily of the most extreme negative portrayals of Latinas/os, the PCA's influence was problematic. Aside from trying to keep the favor of our "good neighbors" to the south (and elsewhere), the PCA was also zealously committed to protecting Americans from infiltration of Communist sentiments. At the same time that the PCA attempted to ensure favorable depictions of groups such as Latinas/os, the PCA would not tolerate films that called American institutions into question and thereby, it was assumed, ushered in Communist alternatives. Thus films addressing institutional discrimination or injustice against Latinas/os were censored. For one script involving Latino boxers, the PCA warned that "it would not be good to infer that the police discriminate against these boys because of their nationality."[57] In another instance, the PCA contended that a script was a disservice to America that would enable its enemies to point to the "shocking manner" in which the film heaped injustices on "the confused, but innocent, young American of Mexican extraction."[58]

Ultimately, Hollywood bowed to its morality critics with an industry movie-rating system that replaced PCA self-censorship with public notice through voluntary ratings. Ironically, while depictions of sex, violence, drug use, or immoral behavior tend to garner rating advisories for more mature audiences, negative images of Latinas/os and other subordinated groups do not appear to influence ratings. In the late summer of 2001, President Bush floated a government initiative, called Communities of Character, that included encouraging news organizations to "increase reporting on good news" and Hollywood to promote movies that undermine racial stereotypes.[59] The terrorist events of September 11 soon redirected government priorities; moreover, this proposal for government intervention to police against stereotypical portrayals was attacked as running counter to the anti-interventionist, pro-market sensibilities of Republicans.[60]

Looking to the recording industry, which responded to threats of federal regulation by adopting warning labels on explicit music (signaling explicit sex, strong language, violence, or substance abuse), the film industry, recording industry, and other media might embrace a standard of disclosure that is less restrictive than censoring productions with negative racial/ethnic images. Presumably, this system would entail some form of disclaimer of the potential for a production to offend, perhaps with a statement that the portrayal is intended as entertainment and is not meant to represent the particular group. Such disclaimers have been added to several films as concessions to group protest—including *Fort Apache, The Bronx* (1981), which cast the late playwright/poet Miguel Piñero as a Puerto Rican junkie who shoots up a hospital emergency room;[61] *Cruising* (1980) (gay protest);[62] and *Year of the Dragon* (1985) (Asian American protest).[63] Yet, mere disclaimers are unlikely to be effective. The film *Scarface* (1983) portrayed Cuban Americans as ruthless drug dealers and murderers, yet included the following postscript to soften its derogatory images:

> *Scarface* is a fictional account of the activities of a small group of ruthless criminals. The characters do not represent the Cuban/American community and it would be erroneous and unfair to suggest that they do. The vast majority of Cuban/Americans have demonstrated a dedication, vitality and enterprise that has enriched the American scene.

One Latino observer recalled the audience laughter this disclaimer drew at a screening.[64] Given their overwhelmingly negative image in the history of media, Latinas/os deserve and need more than disclaimers of ill intent. Derogatory representations must be eradicated while strategies are pursued to counteract that history with positive productions.

Recently, the National Council of La Raza called on media to adopt a self-policing code of ethics against stereotyping.[65] Media, particularly television and Hollywood, should adopt voluntary content guidelines that embody the spirit of the former PCA code to avoid productions tending to "incite bigotry or hatred among peoples of differing races, [ethnicities,] religions, or national origins," while forgoing the tendency of that former self-censorship body to withhold indictments of American institutions. Cinema, television, and the American public can manage without one more murderous Latino drug dealer, Latina maid, Latino *vato loco* spray-painting barrio walls, Latina junkie or whore, or Latina/o relying on Anglo ingenuity or defense lawyers to save the day. As researchers have observed, stereotypes are particularly difficult to eradicate in a climate of societal tension.[66] Therefore, this campaign must be continuous, taking advantage of lulls in tensions toward Latinas/os that tend to coincide with periods of economic prosperity.

12

Mi Familia as Counterspeech

[T]o write the story of my family, I have to begin where millions
of stories have begun. In a small village in Mexico, a long, long
time ago.
> —Narrator/writer Paco in the film *My Family/Mi Familia*

Directed and cowritten by Latino Gregory Nava, the film
drama *My Family/Mi Familia* (1995) offers a compelling multigenera-
tional account of one Latina/o family's struggle for an economic and cultural foothold in California. Their odyssey begins in 1926, when José
Sánchez leaves Michóacan, Mexico, on foot, headed for Los Angeles,
where his great-uncle lives. Once there, José meets Maria, a housekeeper
for a wealthy family on the West Side of the Los Angeles River, while
working as a gardener. Maria had journeyed from central Mexico to become a U.S. citizen. José and Maria marry and raise six children—two
daughters and four sons. One of their daughters, Antonia, becomes a nun
but later leaves her order to work as an activist for immigrants. Their
other daughter, Irene, owns a Mexican restaurant. José and Maria's four
sons are Guillermo, a UCLA law student and later a lawyer using the
Anglo name William; his brother Paco, an aspiring writer who served in
the U.S. Navy and later narrates the family history; and Chucho and
Jimmy. In the late 1950s, Chucho is the leader of a Latino gang, "one of
the baddest pachucos on the whole East Side," and a dealer of *mota* (marijuana). But, unlike media's typical Latina/o gang leader or drug dealer,
Chucho's character is developed as a compassionate lover of family, especially of his younger brother, Jimmy, whom he teaches to mambo along
with the other neighborhood children. Hunted by police after he kills a
rival gang member in self-defense with his knife at a dance, Chucho is
shot to death by pursuing officers in front of Jimmy. Jimmy can't escape
his own demons from watching his brother die—as a young adult, he is

arrested for armed robbery. Although no one was hurt, Jimmy's "lack of money and bad attitude" got him prison time. Later, when Jimmy's immigrant wife dies while giving birth, Jimmy's demons renew their compulsion, and he is jailed again for burglarizing a jewelry store. His jailer welcomes Jimmy: "I knew you'd come back. Your kind always comes back." As commentator Ediberto Román observed, even such a well-intentioned and richly crafted movie as *My Family/Mi Familia,* overseen by a gifted Latino director, played into the stereotypical roles of a pachuco drug dealer and a recidivist convict who assuages his pain with crime and self-destruction.[1]

Although lacking the Hollywood drama of dueling switchblades and police gunfire, my own family story nonetheless adds to the developing body of narrative works that counter notions of the stereotypical Latina/o family. Like José Sánchez in the film *My Family/Mi Familia,* my grandfather Fernando J. Troncoso had his own California dream, at the age of eighteen leaving Chiapas, Mexico, in 1918 by train for Los Angeles. There he attended Frank Wiggins Trade School and earned a living as a car painter, a musician (playing the flute and marimba at Olvera Street clubs in downtown Los Angeles and traveling to Alaska with a cruise-ship orchestra), and later an electrical switchboard mechanic. In 1921, at the age of twelve, my grandmother Ramona Montes de Oca left Guadalajara, Mexico, with her mother and three siblings for California's Coachella Valley. Ramona worked in the fields with her family as a child and suffered the loss of her mother, Refugio Santana de Montes de Oca, who succumbed to cancer in her early forties. Ramona and Fernando, both fluent in English and Spanish, met and lived near Olvera Street until they moved to East Los Angeles in the early 1930s to raise a family.

My grandparents Ramona and Fernando had five children—Virginia, Fernando Jr., Irene (my mother), José, and the youngest, David. None was a drug dealer, a pachuco gang member, an armed robber, or even a thief, although one of my uncles while a young boy did exhibit a penchant for sticking his head into the local corner grocer's ice-cream freezer and swallowing an ice-cream bar whole while pretending to sort through the confections. All of them were educated, fluent in both English and Spanish, and a testament to the enterprise and *corazón* of the Latina/o community.

A graduate of Garfield High School in East Los Angeles, as were all five siblings, my aunt Virginia Troncoso was an accomplished pianist. She played in Latin bands with Sal Chico and Hector Rivera in Los Angeles.

Virginia began working for a local doctor at age fifteen, and decided she wanted to attend medical school. Unfortunately, Virginia developed severe health problems in her youth that she battled throughout her life; ultimately, she died in 1996 after contracting hepatitis from a blood transfusion. Most of my memories of Tía Virginia are from hospital room visits and of her suffering from poor health and facing constant surgery. Although she graduated from East Los Angeles Junior College (now East Los Angeles College) and attended UCLA and USC as a pre-med student, her health problems kept her from finishing her studies and becoming a doctor. She was able to spend several years as a hospice volunteer in Las Vegas before she died.

The second child of Ramona and Fernando, Fernando Jr., is an accomplished musician, playing the guitar, violin, stand-up bass, electric bass, and synthesizer with several bands, musicians, and vocalists such as Martin Denny, Manny Lopez, Leslie Uggams, and Don Tosti. In the 1950s, when *My Family/Mi Familia*'s fictional Chucho was selling *mota* and leading a gang of pachucos, Fernando was serving as a radar instructor in the U.S. Air Force. He graduated from East Los Angeles Junior College with a degree in music and spent three years at California State University at Los Angeles. Later, he spent a year as a police officer for the City of El Monte, California, leaving because of injury. Fernando's life passion, however, is bow hunting. He honed his skills hunting rabbit and game in the hills above East Los Angeles in the early 1940s. By the late 1950s, Fernando had established himself as one of the top archers in the history of the sport, winning state championships in both California (1959, 1962), and Colorado (1983, 1984) and later holding numerous Senior Olympic gold medals and gaining election to the National Bow Hunter Archery Hall of Fame and the California Archery Hall of Fame in 1992. His wife, my *tía* Eva, also is a champion archer, who was inducted into the California Archery Hall of Fame in 1984. Fernando has written technical columns for *Archery* magazine for twenty-five years and conducted seminars around the world. Evidencing his ingenuity and his enterprise, Fernando's archery inventions, marketed through his company Golden Key-Futura, Inc., which he founded in 1968, have revolutionized the sport.

My grandparents' third child, José, is the most accomplished scholar of the *familia*. After obtaining a general studies degree from East Los Angeles Junior College and a philosophy degree in 1961 from California State University at Los Angeles, José gained his teaching credentials in

Spanish and French and began teaching in the Los Angeles School District. From 1964 until 1968, José worked as a language instructor for the U.S. Peace Corps at California State University at Los Angeles. Ultimately earning a master's degree in Spanish from Eastern Washington University, with a minor in French, José became an assistant professor of Spanish at Eastern Oregon University; later, he taught for thirteen years at Mt. Hood Community College in Oregon, where he received a distinguished teaching award in 1996. Like the rest of the family, José is a gifted musician, having played the electric bass, vibraphone, and classical guitar throughout Los Angeles with such musicians as Sal Chico and Bobby Gill. Also a composer, José's arrangements have been recorded by artist Rick Foster. Most of my youth, I remember José practicing his classical guitar religiously for several hours each evening.

Ramona and Fernando's last child, David Troncoso, is a nationally renowned Latin jazz musician. After attending East Los Angeles Junior College for over a year, David's zeal for the stand-up bass and electric bass led him to a distinguished career that continues with the recent release of his Latin jazz CD *Meant to Be*. In the mid-1960s, David played bass with famed Latin pianist Eddie Cano. Eddie Cano had recorded a national Top 40 hit album, *Eddie Cano at P.J.'s*, in 1962. In 2001, the Rhino company rereleased an elegant Eddie Cano/David Troncoso composition from 1965, "His Groove," on its CD compilation *¡Saoco! Masters of Afro-Cuban Jazz*. By 1968, David was touring with Donovan (of "Mellow Yellow" recording fame) and playing bass on the national Top 20 album *Donovan in Concert*. In the early 1970s, David toured and recorded with pop/jazz/classical pianist Peter Nero, who scored a gold album and a crossover pop hit in late 1972 with "Summer of '42." I recall several occasions when our family would gather to watch my uncle David perform with Peter Nero on such national television venues as *The Tonight Show*. David also performed as a studio musician for an eclectic array of artists, from timbalist Willie Bobo and vibraphonist Bobby Hutcherson to vocalists Debby Boone and the "Father of Chicano Music," Lalo Guerrero. He has accompanied such luminaries as Celia Cruz. In the late 1970s, David released a solo jazz album that was a local hit in Los Angeles. In the 1980s, David reunited with Latin jazz pianist Eddie Cano; they played with such acclaimed musicians as Pancho Sanchez until Cano's fatal heart attack in 1988.

My mother, Irene, the third of the five children, was born in 1935. Although she, too, is a musician and played the cello for six years in both the junior high and Garfield High School orchestras, her artistic passion is traditional Mexican and Spanish dance. At age nine, she began taking Mexican and Spanish dance lessons from dancers Lily Aguilar and Corina Valdez. My mother danced at local parks, at school auditoriums, and at church functions for Cinco de Mayo and other celebrations. As a dancer, she fronted her family band, the Troncosos, which performed throughout Los Angeles at many functions and nursing homes. Later, in eastern Oregon, she organized a dance troupe that performed for many years. My mother designed and helped make costumes for her dancers and took the stage herself with her castanets. While in Los Angeles, she attended business college and then worked for a year as a stenographer in the U.S. Attorney's Office before beginning a sixteen-year career as a legal secretary in downtown Los Angeles.

When I was seven years old, my mother married Luis Acevedo. Their backgrounds were similar; Luis was born to parents (Pedro Carlos Acevedo and Maria Inocencia De La Torre) who had both emigrated from Mexico to the United States around 1922. Luis graduated ten years before my mother from East L.A.'s Garfield High School and was fluent in both English and Spanish. In contrast to my mother, Luis was born in Kansas City, where his father, Pedro, worked as a railroad laborer. Eventually Luis's family went to join his great-grandparents in Los Angeles, where Pedro found work as a ditchdigger and later as the owner of a small store across the street from Belvedere Junior High School. After serving two years in the U.S. Air Force, Luis was hired by the Los Angeles County Sheriff's Department as a deputy. Working in the sheriff's offices in East Los Angeles and then in Temple City, Luis advanced to lieutenant.

Born in 1960 shortly after my grandfather Fernando died, I spent the first fourteen years of my life with my mother in the East Los Angeles area, initially attending Catholic grade school in East L.A. I never lived with my late father, whose ethnicity was German, Irish, and Scots-Irish. In the late 1960s and early 1970s, I attended Catholic grade school in adjacent Monterey Park, sometimes riding my bike to nearby Mark Keppel High School. During that time, Luis Rodríguez (author of *Always Running, La Vida Loca: Gang Days in L.A.*) was surviving gang life while becoming a Chicano activist at Mark Keppel. As a seventh- and eighth-grader, I played tennis almost daily with a Mark Keppel varsity tennis player who predicted I could make their varsity team as a freshman. But I left Los Angeles with my mother in 1974 for eastern Oregon, to live near my uncle José's family after my stepfather Luis suffered a fatal heart attack while playing basketball with me. I've lived most of my life in Oregon since then, although I did spend five years in Phoenix working for a major law firm representing, as I jokingly describe them, later "failed or jailed" savings and loan clients from the mid-1980s. Having taught law school in Oregon and California for the last thirteen years, I'm sure that academia is more my calling than musicianship, but I do play congas and Latin percussion in a local band of law professors and lawyers, and I'm still jealous of my uncle David, who has performed with the premier international *conguero* Poncho Sanchez.

Although the story of my mother's *familia, mi familia,* may lack Hollywood drama, it does run counter to most every Latina/o stereotype of criminal-mindedness, anti-assimilationism, proclivity toward welfare, unintelligence, and lack of enterprise. Besides, it would offer a catchy beat that you can dance to.

13

Eradicating Stereotypes
The Collision of Legal Strategies with the First Amendment

The right of a [wo/]man to the protection of [her/]his own reputation from unjustified invasion and wrongful hurt reflects no more than our basic concept of the essential dignity and worth of every human being—a concept at the root of any decent system of ordered liberty. —Former Supreme Court justice Potter Stewart[1]

Whether contesting particular stereotypical productions, seeking more mainstream visibility for Latinas/os through positive portrayals, or urging the adoption of self-policing codes of media ethics on group imagery, protestors face a peculiar challenge in today's crowded media market. Now, even financial arguments against media stereotyping must be constructed carefully. Simply pointing to the burgeoning Latina/o population (in the United States or elsewhere) and suggesting that this audience may be lost to stereotypical productions may no longer be a compelling strategy. In the network television market, at least, the proliferation of programming choices on cable and other competing media has created a viewer mind-set of decreased tolerance for diverse programs. More than ever, viewers want shows that resonate with their narrow, self-oriented world. Because Anglos still comprise a majority of the network television audience, the networks tend to appease these viewers and to target their narrow preferences.[2] In this environment, financially driven arguments seeking diversity of programming and positive images may need additional support.

Legal and litigation strategies may be warranted to supplement moral and financial appeals to entertainment media. Unfortunately, courts are hostile to the enforcement of statutes and to the maintenance of litigation directed at derogatory group stereotypes. The present state of the law stands in stark contrast to that in the early to mid-1900s, in which all the states came to adopt laws criminalizing libel—the defamation of one's reputation. These laws were prompted by racial, ethnic, and religious tensions surrounding Blacks and immigrant groups such as Jews.[3] Although defamation law tends to redress damage to an individual's reputation, some of these laws were group-oriented and targeted false depictions of racial and religious groups. Further, they confronted injurious stereotypical depictions with criminal prosecutions and sanctions. Representative of this expansive and potentially powerful assault on group racial defamation were the statutes of Illinois and Massachusetts. Massachusetts law imposes a fine of $1,000, one year's imprisonment, or both on "whoever publishes any false written or printed material with intent to maliciously promote hatred of any group of persons in the commonwealth because of race, color, or religion." This Massachusetts law remains in effect today.[4] Adopted against a backdrop of racial tension and race riots in Chicago and the Midwest, particularly violence toward Blacks, the Illinois statute proscribed the exhibition in any public place of

> any lithograph, moving picture, play, drama or sketch, which publication or exhibition portrays depravity, criminality, unchastity, or lack of virtue of a class of citizens, of any race, color, creed or religion which said publication or exhibition exposes the citizens of any race, color, creed or religion to contempt, derision, or obloquy or which is productive of breach of the peace or riots.[5]

The promise of these laws to address blatantly false and negative stereotypical media, as well as racist hate speech, was never realized. Few prosecutions were brought under the statutes, and the laws were challenged as contravening the guarantees of freedom of speech under the federal Constitution, as well as under state constitutions.[6]

Despite these setbacks, events in early 1950s Chicago suggested the potential for these laws to aid in the struggle for truth and dignity in the societal dialogue on race. Joseph Beauharnais, president of the hate group White Circle League, had distributed leaflets soliciting membership in his association by calling on Chicago's White residents to

PRESERVE and PROTECT WHITE NEIGHBORHOODS!
FROM THE CONSTANT AND CONTINUOUS INVASION, HARASSMENT AND ENCROACHMENT BY THE NEGROES.[7]

The leaflets urged the "self respecting white people in Chicago" to unite, adding that "if persuasion and the need to prevent the white race from being mongrelized by the negro will not unite us then the aggressions . . . rapes, robberies, knives, guns and marijuana of the negro, surely will."[8] Beauharnais was convicted of violating Illinois's misdemeanor criminal libel statute, quoted above, and given the maximum fine of $200. Reaching the U.S. Supreme Court, his legal challenge was grounded in the guarantee of free speech under the federal Constitution's First Amendment, made applicable to the states under the Fourteenth Amendment. Although some observers felt the Illinois statute went too far in prohibiting the dissemination of false racially charged speech, the Supreme Court reminded that certain narrow categories of speech, such as lewd and obscene speech, "fighting words," and "the libelous," may be prohibited and punished without contravening the guarantee of free speech. As the Court reasoned, "such utterances are no essential part of any exposition of ideas, and are of such slight social value as a step to truth that any benefit that may be derived from them is clearly outweighed by the social interest in order and morality."[9] In upholding Beauharnais's conviction, the Court accorded states constitutional leeway to criminalize group defamation as a means of easing racial tension:

> [W]e cannot deny to a State power to punish the . . . [defamatory] utterance directed at a defined group, unless we can say that this is a wilful and purposeless restriction unrelated to the peace and well-being of the State.[10]

The *Beauharnais* decision in 1952 thus marked the high-water potential for the criminalization and legal disrepute of malicious stereotypical productions—the confluence of a statute targeting group racial defamation, the willingness of local officials to pursue a criminal prosecution under this law, and the recognition by the Supreme Court of constitutional latitude for such laws to function. The promise of *Beauharnais* soon dissipated, however, as later Supreme Court and circuit court decisions chipped away at the unprivileged status of libelous speech that *Beauharnais* had recognized. Some commentators have even questioned whether *Beauharnais* survived the assault. At the same time, criminal libel laws were either repealed or left unenforced in the states. Today, only a handful of states retain these laws. Most of the remaining statutes have abandoned any explicit reference to race or religion.[11] Further, the surviving statutes are oriented toward defamation of individual character, as few seem to contemplate prosecution of defamation targeting groups.[12]

Subsequent to its decision in *Beauharnais,* the Supreme Court began to apply a First Amendment standard under which content-based restrictions are presumptively invalid and rarely upheld.[13] The Court has stated that "above all else, the First Amendment means that the government has no power to restrict expression because of its message, its ideas, its subject matter, or its content."[14] Of particular relevance to criminal libel statutes, this content analysis will guard against content discrimination (underinclusive or selective prohibition) of otherwise unprotected speech. In *R.A.V. v. St. Paul,*[15] the Court struck down a municipality's disorderly conduct ordinance prohibiting the placing "on public or private property [of] a symbol, object, appellation, characterization or graffiti, including, but not limited to, a burning cross or Nazi swastika, which one knows or has reasonable grounds to know arouses anger, alarm or resentment in others on the basis of race, color, creed, religion or gender." Although the ordinance had been construed to regulate content that inflicts injury or incites immediate violence, thus falling under the "fighting words" exception from free speech protection, the Court viewed the ordinance as impermissibly engaging in content discrimination—the government can proscribe fighting words, but it cannot selectively outlaw just those fighting words evincing group hatred, at least not without showing that the regulation is narrowly tailored to serve a compelling state interest. Here, the Court believed that an ordinance outlawing all fighting words would have been equally effective as one limited to speech targeting race, religion, or gender. Since the only purpose served by enacting a more narrow prohibition of fighting words was to convey the municipality's special hostility toward certain race- and group-based content, its ordinance fell outside the scope of the fighting words exception.

Applied to the criminal libel statute in *Beauharnais,* which regulated portrayals of depravity, criminality, unchastity, or lack of virtue of a class of citizens of any race, color, creed, or religion, the Court's subsequent disallowance of content discrimination could be problematic. Although the *Beauharnais* statute does not appear limited to race- or religion-based discrimination (presumably, for example, it could outlaw a depiction of gay men as sexually unchaste), it does single out certain potentially libelous depictions—depravity, criminality, unchastity, or lack of virtue—to the exclusion of others. For example, portraying a group as lacking intelligence, though potentially libelous and damaging to the group, would not appear to fall within the statutory prohibition. Still, the potential constitutional defect of content discrimination might be readily remedied by drafting the state's criminal libel statute to target all varieties of libel, so that it could not be said to single out certain libelous content.

The Supreme Court's assault on libel actions began in earnest in 1964 with *New York Times v. Sullivan,* conditioning a civil (noncriminal) libel action brought by a public official against critics of his official conduct on the plaintiff proving that the defamatory statement was false and made with "actual malice," defined by the Court as "knowledge that it was false or . . . reckless disregard of whether it was false or not."[16] Libel, the Court said, could claim no "talismanic immunity from constitutional limitations." Later that year, the Supreme Court extended its holding in *Sullivan,* a private libel action, to the prosecution of a district attorney under Louisiana's criminal libel statute for his disparagement of eight criminal judges (public officials) there. The Court believed that "[w]hether the libel law be civil or criminal, it must satisfy relevant constitutional standards."[17] Subsequently, the demanding *Sullivan* standard requiring proof of actual malice was applied by the Court beyond libel of public "officials" to actions for libel brought by public "figures."[18]

Some commentators have suggested that the rationale for greater protection accorded speech about public officials and figures in *Sullivan* and its progeny—the access these victims enjoy to the media for counter-speech and the implied consent public figures and officials give to media discussion—applies equally to groups such as Mexican Americans, who are represented by organizations such as MALDEF that supposedly possess access to the media to rebut libelous remarks.[19] This contention is flawed because it assumes an already overburdened organization is positioned to counterspeak. Moreover, the staggering history of negative stereotypes directed at Mexican Americans and other Latinas/os has dampened the ability of such organizations to be taken seriously in the public marketplace of ideas. Finally, organizations such as MALDEF, if indeed public figures, are reluctant public figures pushed forward by a discriminatory society; these organizations are not those who, in the Supreme Court's words, have "thrust themselves to the forefront of particular public controversies in order to influence the resolution of the issues involved."[20]

By contrast to the demanding standard in *Sullivan,* in a defamation action brought by a private figure against a media defendant, the Court allows slightly more constitutional leeway, requiring a showing of some fault on the defendant's part but giving the states latitude to define the appropriate standard of fault.[21] Thus, consistent with federal constitutional constraints, in actions by private figures, state defamation law could specify a liability standard of mere negligence of the statement's falsity. Adding to the thicket of constitutional free speech jurisprudence in defamation actions, the Supreme Court held later that in actions by a private figure against a media defendant implicating "speech of public concern," the plaintiff cannot recover damages without bearing the burden of establishing that the media statements were false.[22] In this decision, the offending newspaper article addressed a matter of public concern in suggesting the plaintiffs had links to organized crime that they wielded to gain favorable corporate treatment in the state legislature.

Compared with the standards under *Beauharnais* in 1952, civil and criminal defamation actions today would demand far more stringent proof. In *Beauharnais,* Illinois law recognized truth as a defense. But, in addition to establishing truth, the defendant also had to demonstrate the publication was made "with good motives and for justifiable ends."[23] Presumably, then, even true statements could be actionable under *Beauharnais* absent a showing by the defendant of good-faith purpose. Now, truthful criticism would not be actionable.[24] Moreover, not only must the plaintiff establish the requisite standard of the defendant's fault, but for speech of "public concern" published by media defendants, the plaintiff must also bear the burden of proving the statement's falsity. Placing the burden of proving falsity and fault on the plaintiff could prove challenging and decisive.[25]

Consider the challenge of requiring the plaintiff to establish the falsity of broad ethnicity- or race-related statements directed at an entire group —for example, a statement suggesting that Latinas/os are less intelligent than Anglos. Many such statements are so far-fetched and amorphous that they are difficult to disprove. Or consider a statement comparing Mexicans to dogs or cockroaches. Again, determining how to disprove such a hurtful but absurd statement could be vexing. Recall dialogue from the television sitcom *Seinfeld,* where, on finding his friend Jerry's car vandalized by Puerto Ricans, Kramer suggested, "It's like this every day in Puerto Rico." How might the plaintiff establish that the atmosphere in Puerto Rico was described falsely? If just one instance of car vandalism occurs on average in Puerto Rico each day, arguably this dialogue could escape challenge. Adding to the problem of establishing media representations as defamatory is that dialogue and depictions often tend to impugn Latinas/os through indirect negative connotations rather than direct untruthful statements. For example, the 1960s Frito Bandito commercials did not state explicitly that Mexicans are all lawless, gun-brandishing bandits. Also, in depicting South American kidnappers as "animals," the film *Proof of Life* (2000) did not explicitly contend that all Latinas/os are subhuman. In depicting some Cuban American Mariel boat refugees as murderous drug dealers, the film *Scarface* (1983) explicitly disclaimed any suggestion that its characters represented "the vast majority of Cuban Americans."

A related concern in challenging media or other communicative matter as defamatory is whether the alleged defamatory statements could find constitutional protection as statements of opinion rather than as unprotected assertions of fact. Because little difference in harmful impact stems from statements phrased as opinion ("In my opinion, all Mexican American youth are gang members") and those constituting assertions of fact ("All Mexican American youth are gang members"), the Supreme Court properly has resisted any artificial fact/opinion distinction. Recognizing that expressions of opinion often imply an assertion of objective fact, the Court has held that the First Amendment does not compel a constitutional privilege for defamatory statements that can be categorized as "opinion" rather than as "fact."[26] Yet the Supreme Court has applied the First Amendment to protect several types of communications that it recognizes as somehow failing to include a false assertion of objective fact.

For example, parodies tend to escape attack on the basis that no listener would honestly believe that the comedic communication meant to state an assertion of fact. In the most notorious parody case, founder of the Moral Majority, Jerry Falwell, sued publisher Larry Flynt and *Hustler* magazine for *Hustler*'s mock advertisement suggesting Falwell's first sexual encounter was with his drunk mother in an outhouse. The parody mimicked an actual advertising campaign for a spirits company that featured celebrities recalling their first time tasting the liquor. The jury had rejected Falwell's defamation claim by deciding that *Hustler*'s mock advertisement could not be understood as describing actual facts about Falwell or actual events in which he participated. But the jury awarded Falwell damages under the tort of intentional infliction of emotional distress, known also as outrageous conduct. Applying the First Amendment, the Supreme Court held that the Constitution barred a damages claim for publishing an advertisement parody that "could not reasonably have been interpreted as stating actual facts about the public figure involved."[27] This parody ruling will constrain challenges to media representations, whether brought as defamation or as outrageous conduct actions, that are seen as parodies and thus not as sufficient assertions of fact. The *Falwell* case could effectively insulate most communications made in the context of "comedy" media as not reasonably capable of being taken seriously. For example, recall that in 2002, tourism officials in Rio de Janeiro threatened to sue the producers of the animated television sitcom *The Simpsons* for falsely depicting that city's image. In the episode "Blame It on Lisa" (a takeoff of the 1984 film *Blame It on Rio*), the Simpsons travel to Rio to find a missing orphan whom Lisa Simpson had sponsored. While there, the Simpsons encounter a gauntlet of perils and unsavory characters—Homer is kidnapped by a taxi driver and held for ransom; Bart is swallowed whole by a boa constrictor; the family is assaulted by begging children, then by violent monkeys; and Marge has trouble getting help from local police.[28] These outrageous exaggerations, made in the context of an animated sitcom, seem to fall within the constitutional protection of parody because representations in this setting could not reasonably be interpreted as stating actual facts about Rio.

Other Supreme Court decisions indicate the apparent broad scope of communicative matter that is not actionable in defamation or otherwise as a false statement of objective fact. One decision stemmed from a union newsletter that described the nonunion plaintiffs as scabs and included a literary definition of a scab, attributed to author Jack London, providing in part:

> A scab is a two-legged animal with a corkscrew soul, a water brain, a combination backbone of jelly and glue. Where others have hearts, he carries a tumor of rotten principles.
>
> When a scab comes down the street, men turn their backs and Angels weep in Heaven, and the Devil shuts the gates of hell to keep him out.
> ... [A] SCAB is a traitor to his God, his country, his family and his class.

The newsletter's reference to the plaintiffs as scabs was not actionable—the plaintiffs were indeed scabs, as the Supreme Court defined this term, since they were nonunion members. The newsletter's offensive definition of scabs, referring to the plaintiffs as "traitor[s]" and as "rotten," was protected in the marketplace of ideas because such words were "obviously used here in a loose, figurative sense to demonstrate the union's strong disagreement with the views of those workers who oppose union-ization."[29] Similarly, referring to a real estate developer's negotiation with city authorities as "blackmail" was held not to constitute defamation because "even the most careless reader must have perceived that the word [blackmail] was no more than rhetorical hyperbole, a vigorous ep-ithet used by those who considered [his] negotiating position extremely unreasonable."[30]

Yet another constitutional limitation may apply to defamation actions. Although the Court's decision in *Beauharnais* recognized the link be-tween criminal libel statutes and breaches of the peace, the Court seemed to suggest that the libelous speech need not pose a clear and present dan-ger of any violence or uprising.[31] Yet later decisions can be read to require that criminal libel statutes (by contrast to civil defamation actions) must be drawn narrowly to target defamatory statements likely to incite immi-nent lawless action. In invalidating Louisiana's criminal libel law in 1964, the Court criticized that statute as not being narrowly drawn to reach speech tending to cause a breach of the peace or speech especially likely to lead to public disorder.[32] The Court's decision in *Brandenburg v. Ohio* in 1969 is cited by some as requiring a showing of imminent lawless ac-tion or clear and present danger in the criminalizing of libel—more than just a showing that the libel had a tendency to induce violence.[33] *Bran-denburg* reversed the conviction of a Ku Klux Klan leader under Ohio's Criminal Syndicalism statute that proscribed advocating "crime, sabo-tage, violence, or unlawful methods of terrorism as a means of accom-plishing industrial or political reform," as well as the voluntary assembly "with any society, group, or assemblage of persons formed to teach or ad-vocate the doctrines of criminal syndicalism."[34] The Court struck down the statute as inconsistent with free speech; the Constitution does not per-mit a state to forbid "advocacy of the use of force or of law violation ex-cept where such advocacy is directed to inciting or producing imminent lawless action and is likely to incite or produce such action."[35] Given the connection between false constructions of Latina/o identity and violence by vigilantes and government against them, it is possible that this linkage could be established. Even so, having to demonstrate the potential for imminent lawless action seems inapposite for criminal libel prosecutions. Obscenity is criminalized without the need for any showing of an immi-nent breach of the peace flowing from the obscene production. Like ob-scenity, false statements should be criminalized because they "are no es-sential part of any exposition of ideas."[36]

Despite the formidable constitutional setbacks subsequent to the *Beauharnais* criminal libel action, opportunities remain for further scholarly examination, litigation, and optimism in both criminalizing and maintaining civil actions against defamatory stereotypes. These include the likelihood that an action for libel, whether criminal or civil, still survives constitutional scrutiny, at least where the state's libel action does not discriminate by regulating only certain types of defamatory content, and also subject to requirements for establishing falsity and the requisite fault.

Aside from this eroding exception for libelous speech, hurtful stereotypes might be regulated by categorizing them as exempt from First Amendment protection on other grounds.[37] The Supreme Court has stated as a "bedrock principle" that government cannot "prohibit expression of an idea simply because society finds the idea itself offensive or disagreeable."[38] Yet the Court has recognized several categories of speech that are unprotected. Obscene speech, for example, is excluded from the constitutional prohibition of content-based regulation. Unfortunately, the courts define obscene material narrowly as that "which deals with sex in a manner appealing to prurient interest."[39] Further, the obscenity standard focuses on "contemporary community standards" in asking whether the work appeals to the prurient interest in a patently offensive way while, overall, lacking serious literary, artistic, political, or scientific value.[40] Although they may not appeal to the prurient interest, hurtful racial and ethnic stereotypes might offend community standards and lack any overall value. Yet the judicial limitation of obscenity to expression that is "in some significant way, erotic"[41] effectively precludes reliance on the obscenity exception to proscribe racial and ethnic stereotypes.

Limited to those words "inherently likely to provoke violent reaction,"[42] the "fighting words" exception from constitutional protection appears to demand a degree of immediacy that stereotypical depictions would not attain. Similarly, the fighting words exception has not saved university hate speech codes from constitutional invalidation.[43] The related exception to constitutional protection for speech inciting violence similarly demands immediacy. In striking down the Ohio statute used to convict a Ku Klux Klan leader for advocating violence, the Supreme Court insisted in *Brandenburg v. Ohio* that speech advocating violence is unprotected only if "directed to inciting or producing imminent lawless action."[44]

Recognizing the limits of these established exceptions to protected speech under the First Amendment, some commentators urge regulation of racist hate speech—which should encompass some negative stereotypes and racial defamation[45]—as a *sui generis* acknowledgment of its special harm. Mari Matsuda has contended that racist speech presenting "an idea so historically untenable, so dangerous, and so tied to perpetuation of violence and degradation of the very classes of human beings who are least equipped to respond" should be held "outside the realm of protected discourse."[46] Matsuda proposed criminalizing speech carrying a message of racial inferiority that is directed at a historically oppressed group and that is persecutory, hateful, and degrading.[47] Among other differences, stereotypical speech can differ from racist hate speech in its target audience. Although hate speech often is directed at the members of the racial or other hated group, stereotypes in media tend to be aimed at a wider audience, analogous in their most virulent forms to the speech at a Ku Klux Klan rally. Arguably, negative stereotypes as a type of racist hate speech are more dangerous than speech directed at the target group—although hate speech directed at Latinas/os may cause severe emotional harm, negative stereotypes meant for Anglo audiences are intended to or may spark physical retaliation or harmful legal consequences against Latinas/os.

Short of outlawing negative stereotypical depictions, constraints on the time, place, and manner of communicating such messages may survive constitutional scrutiny where narrowly tailored to further a compelling governmental interest. These time/place/manner restrictions stand the best chance for validity when imposed against broadcast speech. Relying on a rationale of the scarcity of broadcast frequencies (which some contend is no longer viable, given technological advances), the Supreme Court has accorded broadcasters the least First Amendment deference among speakers.[48] Among content-based restrictions upheld where limited in time and designed to protect compelling interests is the ban of indecent speech from afternoon radio programming, permitting the midday censoring of George Carlin's "Seven Filthy Words" comedy monologue, in which he elaborated on the sexual and excretory meanings of "shit" and "fuck."[49] The afternoon broadcast was during a time when impressionable children were likely to be among the listening audience. Patricia Worthy has argued that the governmental interest of protecting children from racial stereotyping is sufficient to justify imposing restrictions on the hours within which racially stereotypical programming could be aired by broadcast media, as well as to permit laws requiring warnings before and during such programming.[50]

Addressing objections over violent media programming reaching children, the federal Telecommunications Act of 1996 required that new televisions carry "V-chips," permitting parents to block violent programming.[51] As long as the media industry controls the labeling of which broadcasts are unsuitable for children, constitutional free speech concerns should be avoided. Many Americans quick to defend the First Amendment are ignorant of its limited scope reaching government, but not voluntary industry, restrictions on speech. For example, in decrying the recent announcement of the NBC network to reverse its decision to air hard-liquor advertisements, one editorialist condemned NBC's ban on liquor ads as running "roughshod over the distillers' First Amendment rights."[52] Notwithstanding such errant views, media could constitutionally adopt self-censoring restrictions against programming that includes derogatory racial or ethnic content.

Flowing from the lesser protection accorded broadcast speech, broadcasters may be unable to retain their licenses if regulators (the Federal Communications Commission) determine that denial would serve the public interest.[53] Although the FCC once engaged in significant content-based programming review when deciding which among two or more competing broadcast license applicants would best serve the public interest, license review today is far less substantive, having been described as a rubber stamp.[54] Nevertheless, Latina/o and other civil rights organizations have continued to contest the licensing of media outlets based on their hiring records of Latina/o employees and their coverage, or lack of coverage, of Latina/o issues.

In addition to the lesser protection accorded broadcasters, commercial advertising speech has enjoyed less constitutional protection than political speech. Government regulation of commercial speech may be upheld where the regulation directly advances a substantial government interest and is narrowly tailored to serve that interest.[55] For example, legislation targeting stereotypical advertising images such as the Frito Bandito might be scrutinized under this less-stringent constitutional standard that may permit content-based regulation if sufficiently compelling interests are at stake. In her examination of the impact of advertising on race, however, Deseriee Kennedy speculated that the decreasing reliance on overtly stereotypical and demeaning images in advertising today would pose a challenge to those establishing a link between these images and any discriminatory effect. Therefore, regulation outlawing stereotypical advertising might not survive constitutional scrutiny as directly advancing the substantial government interest in nondiscrimination.[56]

Despite the urgency for legal means to combat stereotypes as a complement to protest and counterspeech efforts, some commentators have offered policy arguments against group defamation/libel laws as applied to racist hate speech and stereotypes. One such argument is that prohibiting this speech enlists the government as a censor, with no assurance that racial and ethnic minorities could protect their own speech from being targeted if government priorities shifted. As Mari Matsuda recounted this argument, "Admitting one exception will lead to another, and yet another, until those in power are free to stifle opposition in the name of protecting democratic ideals."[57] One Jewish commentator warned about the dangers to the Jewish community in embracing statutory protection against speech targeting Jews:

> Because we Jews are uniquely vulnerable, I believe we can win only brief respite from persecution in a society in which encounters are settled by power. . . . I want restraints which prohibit those in power from interfering with my right to speak, my right to publish, or my right to gather with others who also feel threatened. . . . To defend myself, I must restrain power with freedom, even if the temporary beneficiaries are the enemies of freedom.[58]

The argument here, then, is one telling racial and ethnic minorities to be careful not to burn any constitutional bridges in pursuing dignity, as minorities may need to invoke constitutional protections for counterspeech in reaching their goals. In the marketplace of American ideas, supposedly all speech, including such counterspeech, will be heard, dutifully considered, and the public will then make rational decisions about whether the racist speech is founded on falsehoods. But historical racial experience exposes the flaws in such paternalistic, tough love–minded approaches to constitutional interpretation. An analogous failing is when those viewing affirmative action programs as contrary to the goal of race neutrality in society urge a "color-blind" interpretation of the Constitution.[59]

In the case of the First Amendment, at the same time that media are riddled with hurtful stereotypes, Latinas/os are hampered in their counterspeech by their lack of access to mainstream media. Given their invisibility in public debate, Latinas/os might be willing to risk stifling their future counterspeech in return for the immediate cessation of this barrage of negative, harmful constructions of Latina/o ethnicity in Anglo-dominated media. For a brief moment in the 1960s, hope existed for media visibility of Latina/o concerns by invoking the "fairness doctrine" to compel licensed broadcast media to provide free access to those presenting opposing viewpoints on matters of public import. In the doctrine's heyday, the Supreme Court upheld its constitutionality,[60] and a federal appeals court in 1968 construed the doctrine to force broadcasters to run anti-smoking public service advertisements.[61] In 1969, the National Mexican-American Anti-Defamation Committee, along with other groups, invoked the fairness doctrine in threatening to contest the FCC's refusal to allow it free time on San Antonio television stations to respond to the Frito-Lay company's Frito Bandito commercials.[62] But the FCC soon narrowed its interpretation of the fairness doctrine to remove entertainment programs and commercial product advertising from its scope, and finally the FCC repealed the doctrine in 1987.[63]

Heidi Kitrosser has argued against analogous regulation of hate speech and pornography on the basis that permitting extreme manifestations of racial and gender hatred and bias will expose and highlight more benign biases in society that, while less extreme, are pervasive and deeply held. Presumably, once the public realizes their daily bombardment from these rampant benign images, they will confront both the extreme and the benign with private forces such as protest and counterspeech. Instead of coming from the voices of a few marginalized activists, the counterspeech would be more comprehensive and effective. Further, Kitrosser contends that "the generally undetected nature of such biases represents a particular danger in regulation of their more extreme manifestations; specifically, that such regulation will be seen to have effectively targeted and solved the problem, while the more 'benign' manifestations of the problem, and indeed, the larger problem [of societal subordination] itself, remain."[64]

Yet both extreme and benign manifestations of inferiority have plagued Latinas/os for decades without any comprehensive and sustained public uprising to confront either the extreme or the benign. Any conception that these images stir the public to action to suppress them is laughable, given the resiliency of these images and their continued inclusion in recent blockbuster media productions such as the films *Proof of Life, Training*

Day, Blow, and *The Mexican.* Indeed, despite the continuance of abhorrent images and the absence of regulation, much of the public nonetheless believes that problems of racial and ethnic subordination are long vanquished in our modern society. Moreover, this rationale holds nothing for those activists who "see" the depth of the benign portrayals and desire government regulation to complement their targeting of offensive speech by regulating against the extreme while the activists' private campaign challenges and educates about the benign. Further, rather than exposing the embedded images, legal tolerance of the extreme serves to create a safe space within which the benign may thrive. Regulation directed at extreme and obvious racial and ethnic falsehoods represents a welcome step toward making media and other speakers sensitive to derogatory stereotyping and perhaps causing them to interrogate even benign representations. In a legal climate that does not recognize remedies for extreme portrayals, enlightened activists who challenge the benign are accused of overreacting by Americans who too often exhibit little sense of historical perspective when it comes to racial and ethnic stereotypes. Latina/o outcry over the Taco Bell Chihuahua was seen by most Anglos as ludicrous—how could these people object to a cute Mexican dog selling tacos? Yet many Latinas/os, remembering signs in the Southwest equating Mexicans with dogs and excluding both from taverns and other establishments, saw the Taco Bell Chihuahua as subtly reminding Americans of this atrocious association.

Another commentator who researched the historical shift among Jewish organizations from supporting to opposing group libel laws pointed out that as Jews assimilated, organizations such as the American Jewish Committee came to doubt the propriety of these laws and to value individual rights over group rights.[65] Criminal libel laws that focus on group defamation admittedly are oriented toward group rights.[66] Nevertheless, such laws are well suited for Latinas/os, who tend to value the welfare of their community over individual interests. Indeed, the Supreme Court has recognized the connection between individual dignity and group rights, stating in *Beauharnais* that "it would . . . be arrant dogmatism . . . for us to deny that the Illinois legislature may warrantably believe that a man's job and his educational opportunities and the dignity accorded him may depend as much on the reputation of the racial or religious group to which he willy-nilly belongs, as on his own merits."[67] The link between group membership and individual reputation is particularly strong for Latinas/os and other subordinated groups. Anglos tend to be judged on their individual merits—few Anglos viewed Timothy McVeigh or teenage school gunman Kip Kinkel as suggesting Anglos are inclined as a group toward terrorism or mass murder. By contrast, Latinas/os often are depicted and regarded in group terms, so that the depiction of a Latino as a murderous, soulless drug dealer is taken to represent all Latinas/os, and the reputation of individual Latinas/os is affected by each such image. With the connection between Latina/o group and individual reputation, it is fitting that defamation laws embody a group orientation.

Given the need to establish the falsity of the particular libelous statements, Jewish organizations also became concerned that trials against those who libeled Jews could cause further harm by turning courtrooms into forums to debate such issues as whether Jews are truly subhuman.[68] The possibility of a courtroom battle over such issues as the criminal character of Latinas/os should not devalue these criminal libel laws. Prosecutions for rape, for example, might suffer the possibility of personal attack against the accuser in the interest of individual and societal redress for the subordination of women. Moreover, criminal enforcement prerogatives are often a matter of societal preference and influence. Presumably, then, enforcement authorities would be unlikely to initiate a criminal libel prosecution without some outcry from the victimized group, which will have weighed the potential for embarrassing proof in coming forward to seek justice.

The strongest argument for regulation of stereotypes, and at the same time for survival of this regulation against constitutional scrutiny, is that negative racial and ethnic stereotypes simply occupy no place in legitimate public debate. One commentator has powerfully distinguished racial defamatory speech from political speech that deserves legal protection:

> Racial defamation often looks like political speech. One need scratch barely beneath the surface, though, to recognize that racial defamation offers no ideas, opinions, or proposals—nothing of substance or merit. It may be more accurately perceived as linguistic abuse. . . .
>
> It is difficult to envision anything about racial defamation that would justify its participation in the marketplace of ideas.[69]

Another commentator makes an analogous argument against the legitimacy of campus hate speech by pointing out the similarities between hate speech and obscenity:

[T]he Supreme Court denies First Amendment protection to obscenity, in large part, because obscenity appeals to a prurient, rather than an intellectual or deliberative interest in sexual matters. Because the appeal of obscenity is so far removed from the intellectual process, its residual value is outweighed by such competing interests as the quality of life or public safety. Similarly, because individuals direct hate speech on campus at prejudiced audiences who generally accept the expression as true without conscious or rational deliberation, such speech does not contribute to the marketplace of ideas.[70]

The Supreme Court recognized too in *Beauharnais* that racial defamation was no part of the marketplace of protected ideas for public debate— "such utterances are no essential part of any exposition of ideas, and are of such slight social value as a step to truth that any benefit that may be derived from them is clearly outweighed by the social interest in order and morality."[71] Speaking to the broader issue of the societal bankruptcy of false ideas, the Court also has stated that "there is no constitutional value in false statements of fact. Neither the intentional lie nor the careless error materially advances society's interest in 'uninhibited, robust, and wide-open' debate on public issues."[72]

In carving out "exceptions" to the constitutional protection of speech, the Supreme Court has recognized certain societal values that trump a literal reading of the First Amendment prohibiting any government impediments on free speech.[73] As Richard Delgado and David Yun have reminded, many of these exceptions from First Amendment protection tilt toward powerful interests, such as the exceptions for regulation of false advertising, copyrights, disrespectful speech directed at a judge, and words of business monopoly.[74] Why should the First Amendment be balanced only to protect powerful societal forces but not subordinated, defenseless groups and individuals? By demonstrating the often devastating linkages among racial/ethnic defamation, legal consequences, and vigilante action, I have made the case for a weighty interest in curbing speech that propagates a false social imagination of Latinas/os.[75]

As noted previously, although laws criminalizing racial defamation may survive scrutiny under free speech guarantees, these laws have been repealed in several states, in many instances out of concern of constitutional impingement. In those states where they remain effective, criminal defamation laws have rarely been enforced. Given the diminished potential of public enforcement against virulent racial stereotypes in the media, activists must consider the viability of civil enforcement against such images through private defamation actions for libel (written defamation) or slander (oral defamation).[76] Although private defamation actions will trigger constitutional scrutiny under free speech guarantees, as examined above, arguably any constitutional roadblocks of proving falsity and fault can be navigated. An additional constitutional hurdle applicable to private actions—that any defamation plaintiff unable to establish the defendant's knowledge of the falsity or reckless disregard for the truth is limited to recovery for actual injury, not any presumed injury, to reputation[77]— also will not prohibit such private actions entirely. Yet it is not the Constitution but state doctrinal restraints on civil defamation actions that render these actions unusable for private redress of group racial or ethnic defamation.

Anglo-American law has long protected an individual's reputation from injury against falsehoods by recognizing the tort of defamation to remedy reputational harm caused by false statements. These civil defamation actions tend to be individual-oriented, demanding that plaintiffs establish that the false statement refer to them. When the defamatory statement is directed at a large group to which the plaintiff belongs (such as all Latinas/os, all Mexicans, or all Latina/o or Mexican immigrants), the party best suited to maintain the action would seem to be a representative of the group targeted. Recall that in 1971 the National Mexican-American Anti-Defamation Committee announced its intention to file a $610 million lawsuit against Frito-Lay Corporation, its advertising agency, and the television networks CBS and ABC for their role in propounding the Frito Bandito as the cartoon spokesperson for Fritos Corn Chip products. The lawsuit would claim $100 on behalf of each Mexican American in the United States "for the fictitious defamation" of their character. Although never filed, this lawsuit would have encountered substantial doctrinal impediments. Courts have prevented large organizations from maintaining a group defamation action where the defamatory statements do not address the organization. For example, if one targeted a Latina/o organization, such as the student activist group MEChA (Movimiento Estudiantil Chicano de Aztlán), with a defamatory statement that MEChA members all belong to criminal gangs, presumably that organization could maintain an action for its injuries as an organization—but not for injuries to its individual student membership.[78]

In the case of the Frito Bandito advertising campaign, those injured by the defamation of *bandido* criminality were all Mexicans, perhaps all Mexican Americans, and maybe even all Latinas/os. (It is unclear whether the image of a male cartoon gunslinger could be shown to include Latinas as well as Latinos.) Treating the reputational reach of this imagery as affecting all Mexican Americans, the threatened lawsuit was of dubious validity. In light of the above hypothetical involving MEChA, the National Mexican-American Anti-Defamation Committee (the potential Frito Bandito plaintiff) was not itself the object of the defamation and thus would lack standing. Perhaps the leading case rejecting an organizational claim for defamation without a showing that the statements targeted the organization was the Sixth Circuit's decision in *Michigan United Conservation Clubs v. CBS News,*[79] dismissing a claim against CBS brought by a Michigan organization representing hunters. CBS had broadcast two documentaries, *The Guns of Autumn* and *Echoes of the Guns of Autumn,* that the plaintiffs alleged defamed game hunters. The defamation, however, was aimed at game hunters, not the organization representing them. Similarly, a Massachusetts Appeals Court ruled that a defamation action brought by the Polish-American Guardian Society against the makers of the film *The End* (1978) was properly dismissed, since the society was not the object of the alleged cinematic defamation; rather, the apparent victims were persons of Polish descent.[80] In 1983, a New York court dismissed a defamation action against the CEO of a major corporation who, in his appointed capacity as chairperson of President Ronald Reagan's Private Sector on Cost Control, allegedly slandered Puerto Ricans. In an official presentation on "The Problem of Big Government," the CEO stated that the nine hundred thousand Puerto Ricans living in New York are "all on food stamps, so this [government] food stamp program is basically a Puerto Rican program." Five Puerto Rican nonprofit community organizations sued for defamation, claiming his statement was slander jeopardizing their ability to raise funds. Dismissing the claim, the court stated the remarks could not justify an action on behalf of the nonprofits because the remarks did not refer to them, nor could these organizations sue on behalf of Puerto Ricans in a representative capacity.[81]

Presumably, if defamatory remarks target a group of individuals rather than a particular organization representing them, the individuals could sue in their personal capacity. Thus, any Mexican American (at least Mexican American males) might have sued Frito-Lay and the media defendants. Yet the courts restrict such lawsuits by demanding again that the defamatory statement refer to the individual plaintiff. As summarized by the influential Restatement (Second) of Torts:

> One who publishes defamatory matter concerning a group or class of persons is subject to liability to an individual member of it if, but only if, (a) the group or class is so small that the matter can reasonably be understood to refer to the member, or (b) the circumstances of publication reasonably give rise to the conclusion that there is a particular reference to the member.[82]

As applied by the courts, this requirement generally precludes actions brought by individual members of a defamed group or class that exceeds twenty-five people. As the Restatement explains:

> The extreme example is the statement of David that "All men are liars," which in a sense defames all mankind and yet could not reasonably be taken to have any personal reference to each member of the human race. On the same basis, the statement that "All lawyers are shysters," or that all of a great many persons engaged in a particular trade or business or those of a particular race or creed are dishonest cannot ordinarily be taken to have personal reference to any of the class.[83]

Relying on this rule, a Massachusetts Appeals Court upheld the dismissal of a defamation action brought by an individual plaintiff against the makers of the film *The End*—the alleged defamation had targeted the large group of persons of Polish descent, rather than the plaintiff individually. A federal district court in New York invoked the Restatement standard to dismiss a defamation action contending that a TV movie about World War II, *The Dirty Dozen: The Next Mission,* was defamatory toward American citizens and armed forces. The film's premise was that the Allied forces at some point came to prefer that Hitler remain in power, so they commissioned an American commander to protect Hitler. Applying the standard that the defamation must be of and concerning the plaintiff, the plaintiff's claim (presumably as an American citizen and a former member of the armed forces) was unfounded because the movie in no way mentioned, depicted, or otherwise referred to him personally.[84] The Sixth Circuit used the same reasoning to reject a claim by game hunters as individuals for two allegedly defamatory television documentaries: "Vague, general references to a comparatively large group do not constitute actionable defamation."[85]

Because group defamation targets all group members, arguably an action for redress should lie with the group itself in the form of a class action. Therefore, the Frito Bandito claim could have been brought by a class representative on behalf of the class of Mexican Americans, instead of by a Mexican American organization that was not itself the direct target of the negative imagery. Nevertheless, courts have disallowed class actions sought to be maintained on behalf of a large group of defamed individuals. Dismissing litigation against the makers of the film *The End,* the Massachusetts Appeals Court reasoned that styling the defamation lawsuit as a class action on behalf of all persons of Polish descent did not rescue the claim. Because no single member of the class had a claim (since the defamation did not refer to individuals), all of them together similarly were claimless.[86] A federal district court judge in New York dismissed a claim brought by an individual Nigerian as a class action on behalf of all Nigerians engaged in international business with U.S. citizens, a group of about five hundred. The class claim arose out of alleged defamatory statements on a CBS *60 Minutes* broadcast that stated, "Nigerians engaged in international business with United States citizens are fraudulent and deceitful." Because the statements did not concern any particular plaintiff, neither the individual class representative nor the class of Nigerians had a claim.[87]

The upshot of these judicial limitations on private defamation actions is that, in the absence of criminal libel laws, one apparently can broadcast or publish false, harmful statements about Latinas/os, Latina/o immigrants, Mexican Americans, or other large subclasses of those of Latina/o origin with legal impunity. In the case of a defamatory statement directed at, say, Mexican Americans, neither a Mexican American organization such as MALDEF, a Mexican American individually, nor a Mexican American representing a class of Mexican Americans, could pursue a claim. This approach seems illogical and wrong, a legal catch-22 in which no one is left with standing to pursue the claim. One commentator cataloged the multiple rationales relied on by courts to reject these private claims stemming from group defamation—"First, there is a feeling that, as the size of the group increases, the harm to any individual member is diluted 'until at some point the harm falls below the threshold of legal recognition.'"[88] Yet many consumer class action claims have effectively been employed to redress claims of very small individual damage amounts. Although some contend that only the lawyers benefit from these actions, they nonetheless serve to deter harmful conduct that has such a diffuse influence on the individual class members that none could be expected rationally to personally bear the brunt of maintaining an individual action. Second, the commentator points out that "courts have worried that allowing claims by the members of large groups would unduly encroach on freedom of speech." Related to this argument, he suggests that for large groups, "the possibility exists for more effective counterspeech." Indeed, some courts have relied on constitutional free speech guarantees to dismiss a group defamation class action. An action brought in a California federal district court in 1980 sought damages arising from the television movie *Death of a Princess* that allegedly defamed all Muslims, an international class exceeding 600 million at the time. In dismissing the claim, the court explained that permitting the action would damage the media and "render meaningless the rights guaranteed by the First Amendment to explore issues of public import,"[89] citing the Supreme Court's decision in *New York Times v. Sullivan*. Dismissing a slander action brought by Puerto Rican organizations against the presidential appointee who suggested that all New York Puerto Ricans receive food stamps, a New York court also invoked the First Amendment guarantee:

> Actions seeking to restrict discussion, or even attacks, on racial or ethnic groups must be strictly scrutinized. To do otherwise might inhibit the free and open discussion of matters of public interest and conflict with First Amendment guarantees. . . .
> . . . It is in the cleansing light of public examination, and not in the court, that his insensitive insults will receive the criticism they deserve.[90]

Given the many restrictions imposed on criminal and civil defamation actions by the Supreme Court, no justification supports an additional constitutional standard that says, essentially, "We are so concerned that the potential for catastrophic liability would chill your speech that we will immunize you from such claims." Enough protection resides in legal standards that require a showing of the statement's falsity and some fault in ascertaining that falsity. If such reasoning were to dominate law, then, for example, legislatures should confer blanket tort immunity on automakers and other manufacturers because otherwise the potential for tort claims in negligence might stifle innovative design. A fair and just society will take such risks, and little persuasive argument can be made that speech should be immune from all scrutiny.

The argument that large groups are well equipped to counterspeak effectively is belied by the historical Latina/o experience and that of other subordinated groups who, lacking ownership and other status in the media hierarchy, are invisible in the public debate and possess little means apart from protest to challenge harmful stereotypes. These groups and their representative organizations boast no funds adequate to confront abusive media stereotypes with effective and comprehensive counterspeech. How might Mexican Americans have counterspoken against the Frito Bandito image? By airing countercommercials, purchasing counterbillboards, or purchasing rebuttive space on the supermarket shelves? At what outrageous expense?

Still more justifications are offered for the legal rejection of private group defamation claims—"individual claims for group references could foster a multiplicity of lawsuits."[91] Of course, that threat would be minimized considerably if the action was allowed to proceed on a class action basis, or if an organization was permitted to represent the defamed group. Alternatively, even if courts denied standing to all potential plaintiffs of group defamation claims seeking damages, they might authorize actions seeking injunctive relief. Injunctive actions would prevent a multiplicity of lawsuits, as multiple actions could be consolidated, and also would eliminate concern over the diffuse damages incurred by a large group. Yet claims for injunctive relief from group defamation, or defamation generally, do not appear to have fared well in the courts.

Courts typically withhold such equitable remedies for defamation as injunctions by reasoning that damage remedies furnish adequate relief.[92] For example, a New York federal district court refused to enjoin the showing of a motion picture allegedly defaming the plaintiff as disloyal and traitorous. The court believed that the plaintiff had an adequate remedy in a suit for money damages, as well as the possibility to urge prosecution for criminal libel (in 1939, when most states had such laws).[93] The procedural and practical limits of reliance on group defamation actions and criminal defamation enforcement have been documented above, undercutting this rationale against injunctive relief for defamation targeting a large group such as Latinas/os. Yet, because of courts' concern that prior restraints chill speech, special constitutional restrictions under the First Amendment come into play where injunctive relief is sought.[94] This fear that injunctions operate as a prior censure led a Pennsylvania court to refuse to enjoin the film *Fort Apache, The Bronx* (1981) in an action brought by representatives of the New York Puerto Rican and Black communities, who contended that the film portrayed them as "violent savages, prostitutes, and criminals."[95]

Finally, three related justifications are suggested against group defamation actions—"with a large group, reasonable persons are less likely to take the statement seriously"; "with large groups, most people have already formed their baseline opinions"; and "the large size of the group may suggest that the statement is one of opinion rather than fact."[96] Any fact/opinion distinction in law can be applied in each particular case without altogether denying standing to assert defamation claims in the first instance. Further, although the public may have formed its opinions already, it is likely that media have a hand in the perpetuation, if not the initial creation, of these impressions. Also, the pervasive historical record of stereotypes of Latinas/os, coupled with their injurious treatment in the legal system and through vigilante violence, counters any argument that Americans will not take negative depictions of Latinas/os seriously.

Given the paucity of criminal libel laws and enforcement priorities, the constitutional limitations on such enforcement, and the procedural and constitutional limitations on private defamation actions, innovative legal strategies must be envisioned. One such strategy would invoke the lesser constitutional protection accorded speech that is properly regarded as conduct. For example, while a hate group espousing the racial superiority of Anglos over Latinas/os arguably might be constitutionally protected, the Anglo skinheads who lured two Mexican day laborers into an abandoned Long Island warehouse and then savagely brutalized them with a posthole digger and a knife would in no sane society gain constitutional refuge for their atrocities by arguing they were merely expressing their dislike for their victims. This distinction between speech and conduct suggests the possibility of deploying tort theories in an expansive pursuit of hate groups and even media for playing a causal role in influencing physically injurious vigilante action against Latinas/os. Already, some lawsuits have succeeded in attributing the crimes of hate-group members to the organization itself—including one brought by the Southern Poverty Law Center against the Aryan Nations for physical assaults by some of its membership on Jews.[97] Lawyers should pursue such organizations and other facilitators of hate speech, even where physical assaults occur outside their official "membership," if hate speech, through Web sites and other media productions, can be shown to have spurred the vigilantes to action. Employing this theory, lawyers in New York filed an action in 2001 on behalf of the brutalized Mexican day laborers against several local anti-immigrant hate groups, claiming they had influenced the skinheads.

Here, too, the First Amendment guarantee of free speech may derail recovery for all but the most egregious examples of media incitement. In striking down an Ohio statute used to convict a Ku Klux Klan leader for advocating violence, the Supreme Court insisted that to escape constitutional protection, speech advocating violence must be "directed to inciting or producing imminent lawless action."[98] This immediacy has proved challenging for lawsuits seeking to hold media responsible for ensuing violence. Perhaps the most famous case implicated rocker/reality-TV star Ozzy Osborne, sued by the parents of a teenager who shot and killed himself allegedly because he was urged to do so by Ozzy's song "Suicide Solution." Ozzy claimed that rather than meaning to promote suicide, he was referring to abuse of alcohol (a liquid solution) as the self-inflicted means that killed his rocker friend Bon Scott of the band AC/DC. Under the Supreme Court's standard, in order to prevail against Ozzy, the family had to meet the almost insurmountable burden of establishing that Ozzy intended to cause the imminent suicide of listeners and that his music was likely to cause suicide.[99] Lawsuits brought against filmmakers and television networks contending that violent images prompted real-life violence similarly have failed. A judge dismissed a 1979 lawsuit brought against the three major television networks urging that pervasive violence in programming led a teenager to murder his eighty-three-year-old neighbor.[100] Similarly, a father failed in his efforts to sue the film studio that released *The Warriors* (1979), a gang drama allegedly causing the murder of his son, knifed by a filmgoer who imitated dialogue from the film: "I want you, I'm going to get you." Applying the Supreme Court's daunting standard for incitement, the appellate court concluded:

> Although the film is rife with violent scenes, it does not at any point exhort, urge, entreat, solicit, or overtly advocate or encourage unlawful or violent activity on the part of viewers. It does not create the likelihood of inciting or producing "imminent lawless action" that would strip the film of First Amendment protection.[101]

Another unsuccessful lawsuit claimed that a gunman who shot a young girl outside a San Francisco movie theater was lured by its screening of the gang film *Boulevard Nights* (1979). By contrast to the above media incitement lawsuits contending some media production had prompted violence, this lawsuit against the film producers claimed their movie foreseeably would attract persons predisposed to violence; thus, it alleged the defendants owed a duty to warn theatergoers and to provide adequate protection. This creative approach failed to assuage the court's First Amendment concerns—in dismissing the lawsuit, the court was moved by the lawsuit's potential chilling effect on the content of film, allowing the lawless among us in society in effect to dictate what would be shown in theaters, out of fear a particular film would lure their lawless side.[102]

Innovative legal campaigns against media stereotypes might employ the insider approach of purchasing stock in the target media corporation and then pursuing a derivative shareholders action based on the hurtful productions. In 1999, a coalition of national Latina/o groups initiated a campaign directed at both film and network television for the overall invisibility of Latinas/os and the absence of positive portrayals.[103] Among the strategies to be employed was purchasing stock of publicly owned companies in order to influence shareholder meetings. Yet shareholder lawsuits might also be considered against harmful stereotyping. The legal theory in these derivative actions would contend that the corporate decision makers failed to exercise due care in allowing such programming or, in the case of a Frito Bandito–like campaign, permitting such a derogatory advertising campaign, and thus breached their fiduciary duty to the corporation. Despite avoiding most constitutional constraints, these lawsuits would confront many obstacles. Particularly daunting, most jurisdictions provide latitude to corporate decision makers under the so-called business judgment rule that insulates against liability in the absence of conflicts of interest and grossly uninformed decision making. Even if the shareholder successfully demonstrates an actionable absence of care, proving damages will be difficult when measured by lost profits to the corporation. Should the company become the target of protest by activists complementing the litigation, however, damages might be measured by the lost profits flowing from a boycott.

Any strategy of purchasing stock in target companies and then submitting shareholder resolutions to management as well carries legal and practical shortcomings. Although federal Securities and Exchange Commission (SEC) rules require publicly traded companies[104] to include certain shareholder resolutions in their annual proxy statement at the corporation's expense, often companies can exclude these proposals without a practical risk of legal challenge. SEC regulations specify a number of potential exceptions to the company's obligation to finance the inclusion of the resolution in its annual elections proxy statement. A resolution addressing derogatory stereotypes has little or no chance of navigating these exclusions. Even should the proponent gain inclusion of the resolution in the company's proxy materials, shareholder resolutions cannot bind the company, even if approved by a majority of the voting shareholders (in practice, shareholder resolutions tend to garner less than 5 percent of the vote); under the laws of most states, the resolutions can only be precatory—suggestive to management—and cannot compel action by company management.[105]

The primary basis for excluding resolutions that implicate a company's policy toward stereotypes has been the SEC's exclusion of proposals that relate to the conduct of ordinary business.[106] Proposals addressing product advertising are particularly susceptible to this exception. For example, in 1988 a shareholder sought inclusion in the Kellogg Company's proxy material of a proposal requesting that Kellogg ensure that product advertisements present "in a non-prejudicial manner any members of groups victimized by hate crimes, including racial, religious and ethnic minorities as well as lesbians and gay men." One of the company's cereal commercials appears to have prompted the proposal—a campaign for Nuts n' Honey cereal, in which several men pull handguns on a man they believe called them "honey." Relying on the ordinary business exemption, the SEC issued a no-action letter to Kellogg.[107] Other no-action letters were given for similar proposals, such as one targeting advertising by the Tootsie Roll company that offends Native Americans[108] and one asking the Quaker Oats Company to review all advertising for content that demeans or slanders on the basis of race, ethnicity, or religion.[109] Based on these results, a hypothetical proposal requesting that a company avoid product advertising that is defamatory or demeaning to Latinas/os would stand little chance of inclusion in the proxy materials at company expense for a shareholder vote.

Shareholder proposals concerning the programming of media companies have similarly been regarded as excludable under the ordinary business exception. The SEC allowed the General Electric Company, owner of the NBC television network, to exclude a proposal requesting it exercise special sensitivity for material relating to sex, race, color, age, creed, religious rites, and national or ethnic origin. The proposal was triggered in part by an episode of *The John Laroquette Show* using the derogatory term *Polack* in its dialogue.[110] Other such proposals included one directed at the Time company, seeking to remove all anti-Polish denigrations from the film *The End* before it aired on the cable channel Cinemax,[111] and a proposal asking the same company to research whether Warner Bros. cartoon characters, such as Porky Pig, encourage teasing and bullying of other children.[112] In a related product-line determination, the SEC viewed a proposal urging Kmart to stop selling soft-porn magazines as involving the company's ordinary business and issued a no-action letter.[113]

An intriguing limitation on the exclusion of proposals addressing a company's ordinary business operations is the possibility for the SEC to declare a particular subject matter as "extraordinary" in importance, thus transcending the "ordinary" business exception. At bottom, this appears to demand a policy decision by the SEC that the proposal concerns a matter of such importance that the need to provide a practical means of democratic communication by shareholders outweighs the expense to the company and the intrusion into its sphere of management. Thus far, the most analogous variety of proposal that the SEC has found extraordinary is that addressing affirmative action policies. In the media context, inclusion of proposals to CBS and NBC was compelled where the proponent requested a report on affirmative action programs and statistics. These proposals also included a request for a report on the steps taken to increase the number of writers, producers, and directors who are female or ethnic minorities and on the procedures used to make program content more responsive to concerns of women and minorities.[114]

Facing the constitutional, doctrinal, and other obstacles to legal challenges to the perpetuation of negative stereotypes of Latinas/os by media, activists wishing to confront stereotype and subordination with tactics incorporating legal remedies might focus their legal efforts instead on the outcome of negative social attitudes. In prior chapters, I have examined the linkages between derogatory media and social images of Latinas/os and such legal and societal policies and practices as Official English and English-only laws and initiatives, Proposition 187 and other anti-immigrant laws, welfare reform, the eradication of bilingual education and affirmative action by laws and initiatives, as well as racial profiling and discrimination in employment, housing, and elsewhere. Lawyers possess a variety of constitutional, statutory, and common law weapons with which to confront these subordinating laws and practices. Yet a number of circumstances have hampered their efforts, both doctrinally and institutionally. First, several forces operate to impede the education, encouragement, and advancement of students committed to progressive lawyering for social change in the Latina/o community. Ironically, one of the products of negative stereotyping, the move to eradicate affirmative action programs, foretells a decline, or at least a slowing of growth, in the ranks of Latina/o lawyers. Spiraling debt loads from underfunded public institutions and inadequate salaries of public-interest lawyers place financial pressures on students intending to pursue public-interest careers. The deculturing forces at work in legal education that elide race and ethnicity in the teaching of legal doctrines fail to prepare these students for the challenges that await the progressive lawyer in devising innovative legal, political, and social strategies to confront oppressive laws and subordinating institutions.[115] One of the handful of law schools in the United States devoted to training progressive lawyers for subordinated communities, the Peoples College of Law in downtown Los Angeles, is not accredited by the American Bar Association, and thus its graduates may be unable to practice law in many states.

Once in practice, the progressive lawyer who aspires to use law as a means to achieve and ensure social justice for Latinas/os will find a legal wasteland marked by the increasing conservatism of judges in construing constitutions and statutes, and in halting the development of innovative common law theories. Moreover, lawyers must overcome the chilling of civil rights actions through legislative tort reform measures, through the dismantling or stagnation of statutory guarantees originating in the Civil Rights era, and through the doctrinal challenge under existing antidiscrimination laws to establish purposeful discrimination when the defendant asserts some pretextual business purpose for a discriminatory employment, housing, or other policy.[116]

Separate from undertaking to eliminate stereotypes by litigation, protest, and counterspeech, and from employing legal strategies to confront law and social policy that result from negative social constructions are efforts to eradicate or dampen the connection between stereotype and law. This book suggests the existence of a direct link among media stereotypes, collective prejudicial beliefs, private discrimination and vigilantism, and legal policy as applied to Latinas/os. To break this cycle demands that legal actors acknowledge the role of stereotypes in law and recognize their power to neutralize stereotypical influences and constructions in their policy and decision making.

One significant opportunity to employ this informed legal decision making occurs when courts entertain challenges to initiatives that tap into negative stereotypes. Most challenges to state initiatives proceed under open-ended federal constitutional doctrines, such as equal protection, that allow judges the leeway in balancing detriment and benefit to consider the misplaced motivations of citizens in adopting the initiative. In litigation against Arizona's now-defunct English-only initiative, an amicus brief filed by a Florida group had argued that the initiative process is the "quintessence of participatory democracy" and the most appropriate mechanism for addressing tensions between cultural pluralism and efforts to encourage assimilation, and had urged that courts exercise exceptional care in reviewing citizen-based initiatives.[117] Rather than deferring to these initiatives as the democratic will of the citizenry, judges should realize, as has been demonstrated above, that these initiatives are often the product of highly charged and misleading media campaigns that tap into long-held and often false prejudices. Sylvia Lazos Vargas, too, has urged that courts review with skepticism those initiatives impinging on minorities' civic participation rights, interrogating such factors as the effects of the initiative on the target group's day-to-day participation in civil society, on its political participation, and on the group's stigmatization through the initiative's official encouragement of private discriminatory acts against them.[118]

Margie Paris has suggested that moral resources that enable people to act humanely are diminished in the aftermath of crime, a phenomenon that imperils the human rights of criminal defendants and compels judges to "call people to their senses" by interpreting the Constitution in an instructive manner that erases societal legal misconceptions, sets a moral tone for society, and embodies a commitment to human rights.[119] As with the public frenzy attendant to criminal proceedings, the social image of Latinas/os is so deteriorated that moral resources protecting them against inhumane action are depleted. To combat this breakdown of moral safeguards, judges must embrace a commitment to human rights in interpreting constitutions, statutes, and common law.

Further, in criminal proceedings, judges must be wary of the potential for juries to allow their stereotypical conceptions to overcome presumptions of innocence. Judges must set appropriate examples by treating Latina/o defendants with respect and dignity, ensuring fair proceedings. Recall that in the trial of Santiago Ventura Morales, a migrant worker wrongfully accused of murder, the trial judge had joked about his diminutive stature and that of the other Mexican Mixtec Indians testifying at the trial—in response to the prosecutor's suggestion that he had a "short witness," meaning his testimony would be brief, the trial judge joked, "About 5-foot-1?" to which the prosecutor replied, "Less than that."[120] In sentencing proceedings, the judge must ensure that evidence is unique and personal to the individual defendant. (Revisiting an example from Chapter 4, in Texas, where "future dangerousness" can support a jury recommendation of death, a prosecution expert suggested to jurors that they could infer future dangerousness to society from an Argentine defendant's Latino heritage.)

Given the likelihood that jurors might harbor implied assumptions about dangerousness and criminality based on race or ethnicity, criminal defense lawyers might consider whether to seek admission of an instruction that the jury should not assume future dangerousness or criminality because of the defendant's Latina/o ethnicity and that such perceptions are stereotypes without objective basis in fact. Some legal commentators have urged use of such instructions; additional study is needed to confirm whether antistereotype jury instructions increase the rationality and fairness of criminal and civil proceedings.[121]

As legal actors, legislators should recognize that some subjects of legislation will tap into public prejudice and trigger vigilante action against Latinas/os. For example, assume that a legislature enacts a law conditioning the delivery of public benefits on the recipient's ability to speak and understand English—the Mississippi legislature has considered such a requirement. The legislature must appreciate that this law would send two derogatory messages to the public about Latinas/os—that they are otherwise unwilling to learn English, and that they are so dependent on and driven to receive welfare and other public assistance that their recalcitrance would be overcome. Similarly, even seemingly benign English-language laws that declare English the official language of the state have sparked injurious private vigilantism against Spanish speakers and Latinas/os generally. Since many of these English-language laws have been adopted by citizen initiative, American voters, too, as legal actors, must be sensitive to the legal and private effects of initiatives that might be used by some to justify abusing Latinas/os or other subordinated groups. Examples from Colorado[122] and Florida,[123] where Official English language laws were added to the state constitution by citizen initiative, demonstrate the potential for these laws to be misconstrued and misapplied by the citizenry. Providing simply that English was the official language of the states, the Colorado and Florida initiatives in no way could be construed to regulate nongovernment speech. Yet, after adoption of the Florida initiative, reports emerged of Latinas/os being told by residents, "Speak English. It's the law now." In Colorado, a schoolbus driver told his young passengers that the new language initiative made it illegal for them to speak Spanish on the bus. And, suggesting how young children interpret these laws, schoolchildren in Colorado told their Spanish-speaking Latina/o classmates they were now "unconstitutional" and had to leave the country.[124]

14

Beyond Stereotype
Movement toward Social Change

This book has advocated a multidimensional attack on the propagation of stereotypes by using law and litigation, voluntary industry standards and hiring practices, counterspeech, and community-based protest as its tools. Moreover, it has suggested ways in which enlightened judges, legislators, and the public can help dampen the effects of stereotype on the adoption and enforcement of law. Further, it has considered legal challenge to laws prompted by negative social constructions of Latinas/os and other subordinated groups. Yet endemic shortcomings exist in these approaches, particularly those dependent on law and lawyers, that go beyond the many obstacles I have mentioned previously. Increasingly, progressive legal commentators, such as Kevin Johnson, have pointed out the limitations of litigation and lawyer-based strategies for social change.[1] Rather, "the most penetrating changes in society have occurred when litigation complemented a mass political movement, such as the civil rights struggle of the 1950s and 1960s."[2] The nonlegal measures I have advocated are similarly constrained. These strategies tend to target media and assume that societal attitudes can soften and change through eliminating negative imagery and by presenting counterstories by Latina/o artists and Latina/o media productions. Yet the Black experience reveals the inadequacy of media as a vehicle for transformative societal change. Despite the increasing presence of African Americans in mainstream media as athletes, as television stars who play doctors and other professionals, as Academy Award–winning film stars, and as singers and musicians, societal barriers remain entrenched against Black America. In a recent article, I posed the question whether we are any closer to a Black president just because a Black actor has portrayed one in the movies.[3]

Even facially rebellious media productions hold little bite. Exposing the limitations of Black artistry that is overtly political but disconnected from an oppositional political culture, bell hooks contends:

Who can take seriously [rap group] Public Enemy's insistence that the dominated and their allies "fight the power" when that declaration is in no way linked to a collective organized struggle. When young black people mouth 1960s' black nationalist rhetoric, don Kente cloth, gold medallions, dread their hair, and diss the white folks they hang out with, they expose the way meaningless commodification strips these signs of political integrity and meaning, denying the possibility that they can serve as a catalyst for concrete political action. As signs, their power to ignite critical consciousness is diffused when they are commodified. Communities of resistance are replaced by communities of consumption.[4]

All the strategies I have suggested, then, while vital as interim or complementary measures, must be linked to a transformative political movement for social and redistributive change. Here, my analysis of societal attitudes and societal institutions comes full circle, in recognizing that attitudes and institutions are related in ways that demand dismantling and redirection of both, if Latinas/os and other subordinated groups are to experience meaningful progress toward equal dignity.

A political movement for Latinas/os toward the goal of ensuring their legal, economic, and societal well-being must address Latina/o youth, poverty, and immigration. To overcome structural barriers, the movement must foster educational and employment opportunities through both local and national efforts. Nationally minded strategies are necessary when confronting federal immigration policies that value border buildup over Latina/o lives and dignity. Although I do not undertake to articulate fully the strategy for building this transformative political movement, I recognize that it holds the best potential for eradicating stereotypes and breaking the chain of attitudes, institutions, and vigilante action toward Latinas/os.

The primary goal of a transformative political movement should address Latina/o poverty. An examination of poverty faced by many Latinas/os reveals the role of institutional disparities in the creation of negative attitudes, which in turn foster the perpetuation of institutional inequities. Latinas/os are disproportionately poor. In 1999, the Latina/o poverty rate of 22.8 percent was contrasted by that of 7.7 percent for non-Hispanic Whites; Latina/o families are among the poorest of American families, with one in five being poor in 1999 while only one in twenty Anglo families were impoverished. Latina/o full-time workers are more likely than any other racial or ethnic group to be poor.[5] Agricultural workers, who are primarily Latina/o, earn the lowest family income of any occupation surveyed by the Bureau of Census—$17,700 (as of 1997) with the median income of individual workers only $9,828.[6] In sum, agricultural workers suffer the highest poverty rate of any surveyed occupation. Poverty faced by Latinas/os contributes to behavior and circumstances that help fuel negative stereotypes of Latinas/os. Poverty places Latina/o children in substandard schools, deprives them of opportunities in higher education, and generally spurs them to drop out at the highest rate of any racial or ethnic group. The lack of Latina/o education thus fosters their construction as unintelligent. Poverty promotes criminal behavior, contributing to the perception of Latinas/os as criminally minded. Poverty also creates the despair that drives some Latina/o youth to seek refuge in gang affiliations. Lack of an educational future and economic necessity also prompt the establishment of alternate urban economies in the drug trade, which do not demand traditional education for advancement. Poverty is the key predictor of adolescent pregnancy, which increases reliance on government aid.[7] Poverty also is the obvious determining factor in receipt of government aid, fueling the perception of Latinas/os and other underpaid groups as welfare-minded. Poverty forces some Latinas/os, many of them farm workers, into overcrowded living conditions that engender the societal image of Latinas/os as dirty and subhuman. One poor California agricultural town near Bakersfield, for example, houses an average of 5.6 people, most of them Latinas/os, in every crumbling bungalow and deteriorating mobile home.[8] Poverty even retards assimilation by impeding the ability of Latinas/os to enroll in classes necessary to acquire proficiency in English. Thus progressive political movements might focus on antipoverty measures, such as broadening and increasing minimum-wage protections to all Latina/o workers and restructuring the financing of public education.

Less ambitious, although still daunting, goals that a progressive political movement for transformative change might pursue include resisting laws fueled by negative social constructions, such as anti-immigrant laws, and initiatives and legislation to eradicate affirmative action and bilingual education, to establish English as the official language and to prohibit other languages in government, and to reform and toughen welfare laws. Other campaigns would target abusive law enforcement practices such as racial profiling, as well as prompt reconsideration of existing law enforcement priorities, such as the costly war on drugs.[9]

Of course, political campaigns organized by Latinas/os face considerable historical, legal, financial, and other obstacles. In the 1970s, when the César Chávez–led United Farm Workers offered an initiative to California voters adding farm worker protections to the state's constitution, opponents relied on anti-Latina/o stereotypes and imagery to help soundly defeat this Latina/o foray into state politics. Similarly, Antonio Villaraigosa's campaign for mayor of Los Angeles faltered when his Anglo opponent tapped in to stereotypes to depict Villaraigosa as favoring cocaine dealers and users. Further, Latina/o political organizations are the target of frequent vigilante backlash, as in 2002, when Latina/o activist groups and lawyers were sent a threatening letter with fake anthrax.[10] Restrictions in many states on noncitizen voting impede Latina/o political organizing, as does the youth of the Latina/o population, with many too young to vote. Puerto Ricans on the island cannot vote in U.S. presidential elections, despite their citizenship; nor do they possess voting representation in Congress.[11] Disfranchisement of felons disproportionately affects primary targets of racial profiling, such as Latinas/os and African Americans. Failures to form effective coalitions with Asian and African Americans and other subordinated groups have further hampered the political participation of Latinas/os.

Complementing a progressive political movement for the societal and legal betterment of Latinas/os, a social movement must emerge to influence the social image of Latinas/os and to create support for the political and institutional reforms needed for transformative change. Among the goals for such a social movement are to look beyond the media to address other potential petri dishes in the propagation of negative stereotypes—influences from family, friends, schools, workplaces, and communities. For example, only through integrated schools, with diverse student bodies and faculty, will students enjoy the opportunity to make their own decisions about the value of Latinas/os and other groups in the American social fabric.[12] Measures to integrate workplaces and neighborhoods will dampen the influence of media and allow alternative conceptions of Latinas/os to emerge among adults too.[13]

Further, the social movement I envision can galvanize public sentiment against hate speech, whether in the form of negative media images or confrontational racial and ethnic slander. This movement must expose hate speech and hate violence against Latinas/os and other subordinated groups as terrorism, since such hate attacks the foundation of what being an American should come to mean—a commitment to equality and thus a commitment against subordination of any group and an embrace of the diversity that is coming to define America.

Facilitating the embrace and celebration of diversity in American society is an educational strategy for all students that constructs a new vision of Latinas/os and other subordinated groups through bi-/multicultural education. Such a program would counter prevailing stereotypes with information debunking false conceptions. Once alerted to the range of stereotypes and counterevidence, students would view media representations, such as films depicting Latinas/os and other groups in false or demeaning terms, and then discuss their perceptions. Going beyond education about misleading social constructions, this instructional model would bridge cultural gaps through language-acquisition programs that would follow the lead of European education in insisting that students learn two or more languages. As the most spoken language in the United States after English, Spanish seems a natural choice for such programs. Besides helping to ease racial tensions, such a cultural and linguistic program in the United States, producing a population ultimately fluent in both Spanish and English, would serve as a cultural centerpiece and link among the Americas.

Children are well situated for such bilingual/bicultural education. Not only are children better able to learn a second language than adults, but they are also more malleable in their formation and abandonment of societal prejudices. Targeting adults with bi-/multicultural instruction is more challenging, particularly given the scarcity of positive Latina/o representations in mainstream culture. In 1998 the Mexican American Legal Defense and Educational Fund (MALDEF) initiated an ambitious media campaign to counter the attitudes of Anglo adults in southern California, in response to a survey in which a majority disapproved of Latinas/os. Airing during evening news programs, a MALDEF television commercial attempted to address the perception of Latinas/os as foreigners unconcerned with American values by depicting Latinas/os engaged in civic and educational activities, with the messages "We are Hispanic Americans" and "We are part of you, America."[14]

Apparent in the American racial and ethnic experience is the fluidity of stereotypes. As Kevin Johnson has observed, "At different historical moments, German, Irish, Jewish, and Italian immigrants all were deemed to be of different and inferior racial stock. Benjamin Franklin, for example, decried the settling of German immigrants in Pennsylvania and considered them to be of a different 'race' than the English."[15] In his writings, Benjamin Franklin had questioned, "Why should Pennsylvania, founded by the English, become a colony of aliens who will shortly be so numerous as to Germanize us instead of Anglifying them, and will never adopt our Language or Customs any more than they can acquire our complexion?"[16] These views toward certain White immigrant groups, treating them as non-White, were reflected as well in media and social expression, for instance, by jokes targeting the Polish and other White groups. These societal perceptions of inferiority translated to legal action, particularly in the form of immigration laws that employed a national quota system from 1924 to 1965.[17] The current Official English and English-only movements targeting Latinas/os and also Asian Americans possess roots in xenophobic attitudes in the early 1900s toward immigrants from southern and eastern Europe. Nebraska's 1920 constitutional amendment declaring English the state's official language grew out of anti-German sentiment. By 1923, thirty-four states had declared English the official language of school instruction.[18] Over time, these stereotypical attitudes of inferiority and the concomitant superiority of certain White groups over other White groups subsided, and the focus of immigration laws and the English-only movement shifted more toward Latinas/os.

This experience of fluidity of stereotypes and their legal consequences arguably may hold some promise for Latinas/os and other subordinated groups. Rather than being seen as immutable, race and ethnicity might be regarded more accurately as social constructions adopted to serve purposes such as meeting labor needs of industry and justifying U.S. military and expansionist policies. Presumably, then, when the motivations diminish, the stereotypical cloud will lift. As Kevin Johnson noted:

> Classifying European immigrants as nonwhite becomes understandable only with the realization that race is a social and legal creation. The social assimilation, or "whitening," of various immigrant groups, such as the Irish and Jews, which occurred slowly over time, reveals how concepts of races are figments of our collective imagination, albeit with real-life consequences.[19]

Latinas/os, many of whom classify themselves racially as White, and indeed many of whom are viewed by other subordinated groups as White, may be situated as the European groups once were to escape their subhuman social construction and move toward the light. Yet grounds exist for being much less optimistic about the prospects for evolution of the negative stereotypes and treatment of Latinas/os absent legal, political, and societal reform. These reasons suggest the potential for permanency of these derogatory constructions and of racism toward Latinas/os. One is the proximity of Mexico and other countries of Latina/o immigration to the United States, coupled with their political and economic instability. The continued "threat" of immigration suggests that the Latina/o experience may be different from that of European groups whose immigrant numbers tapered off and who then came to be accepted as White and as American.[20] Although the threats of geographic proximity and of sustained immigration do not explain the persistence of the view of African Americans as inferior, perhaps their mistreatment might be seen in part as stemming from the "threat" of their growth in numbers by miscegenation and birthrate rather than by immigration. Still, this fails to explain the continued mistreatment of Natives, who are not taken to pose the same risk of expansion in population. Explanations I suggest as relevant for Latinas/os and other groups include the need in a capitalist economy for a permanent lower-class pool of workers without rights or voice. Further, as with Natives (and the analogous standing of Blacks seeking reparations), Latinas/os alarm many Anglos with their unresolved claims to land and workplace reparations[21] and the quest of some Latinas/os for sovereignty, particularly those Chicanas/os seeking recognition of Aztlán and those Puerto Ricans seeking independence. These forces driving abusive social conceptions and oppressive treatment of Latinas/os unfortunately appear far from resolution.

As I have shown, political coalitions among Latinas/os, African Americans, and Asian Americans are fragile and heightened by tensions among these groups—for example, African Americans may view Latina/o immigrants as unfairly competing in the labor pool, and some Asian Americans consider Latinas/os to be overly dependent on government social services. The political experience of interethnic coalitions with Latinas/os is also marked by failures—in California, for example, although Latinas/os opposed Proposition 187 in large numbers, Asian and African American voters were more split in their support and opposition, and the initiative passed with a strong showing from Anglo voters.

The confluence of stereotypical attitudes and oppressive legal consequences and societal institutions suggests new grounds for coalition among subordinated groups. American society constructs Latinas/os,

Natives, Blacks, and Asians in similar terms. Although subtle differences emerge among these groups in their constructions, such as Blacks not willfully resisting assimilation and Asians to some degree not seen as lacking intelligence, overall these groups are imagined as inferior and subordinate. In urging political coalition, commentators have tended to focus on discrete issues that instigate coalition—racial profiling linking Blacks, Latinas/os, and, particularly in the aftermath of September 11, Arab Americans;[22] Official English and English-only movements that rally Latinas/os and Asian Americans; and defense of affirmative action as uniting Blacks and Latinas/os.[23] My study suggests additional political organizing forces that have not been fully realized. One is the potential for groups constructed in similar negative terms, such as Blacks and Latinas/os, to confront and contest these images through coalition. Solutions toward eliminating negative stereotypes in the media and in society, whether by pursuing enactment of criminal libel laws or by media boycotts and protest, might best be sought through coalition. Toward this end, in 1999 the NAACP outlined an ambitious coalitional agenda to confront network television's exclusion of minority actors and issues, addressing its claims on behalf of not just Blacks but other excluded groups. The NAACP-led coalition struck diversity agreements with network television that addressed minority hiring and other areas of concern.[24] In summer 2002, the Multi-Ethnic Media Coalition, consisting of the Asian Pacific American Media Coalition, the American Indians in Film and Television, and the National Latino Media Council, issued report cards grading the four major networks on their progress toward diversity, with all receiving Cs or Ds.[25] Much work is left toward media diversity and the dividends that diversity will pay in helping to ensure authentic media constructions of subordinated groups.

Mutual interests against demeaning stereotypes in media and society may also galvanize Latinas/os of different political affiliations and disparate geographies. Whether a conservative Cuban in Florida or a liberal Mexican immigrant in California, no Latina/o wants to suffer Latinas/os constant group depiction and construction as subhuman. The National Latino Media Council, part of the Multi-Ethnic Media Coalition, is itself comprised of twelve Latina/o organizations spanning Cuban American, Puerto Rican, and Mexican American interests.

Further, intra- and intergroup coalitions should be created to target the root institutional and socioeconomic causes of the resiliency and apparent permanency of negative social constructions.[26] Such a coalition might move beyond isolated manifestations of subordination, such as racial profiling and English-language laws, to causes of broader societal dysfunction in which capitalism, globalization, and other social, cultural, political, and economic systems and norms may fall under scrutiny and challenge. Whether coalitions among subordinated groups can form and thrive to confront these broader institutional and international challenges is unclear. In pursuing a more just society in which social constructions of race and ethnicity and their consequences disappear, Latinas/os must also explore the potential for coalition with Anglos, particularly those Anglos once constructed on the non-White side of the color line, such as Jewish and Irish Americans. These groups are uniquely situated, in their cultural memory, to aid in developing a multiethnic democracy that imagines all groups on equal terms with an equal voice in the reshaping of a diverse American vision.[27]

> One thing you must remember is that people, no matter how poor, how disadvantaged, still have the same aspirations as you do, for their children, for the future.
> —César Chávez

Compared with the rest of the population, Latinas/os are disproportionately young. According to the 2000 U.S. Census, more than one-third (35.7 percent) of Latinas/os in the United States are under eighteen years old. A significant number of these youth are poor—in 1999, three of ten (30.3 percent) Latina/o children were impoverished, while fewer than one in ten (9.4 percent) of White non-Hispanic children lived in poverty.[28] By the year 2030, Latina/o children will comprise 25 percent of the national school population.[29] Latinas/os already see their future, and America's— a 2002 poll found education flagged by more than half of registered Latina/o voters as their most important issue.[30] To properly educate Latina/o children, we will need to invest in our collective futures by funding and valuing education over other spending priorities. Should we fail to do so, these children, already beset with a lack of positive images and role models in their development, will be hard pressed to break out of the vicious cycle of poverty and the lack of education that Latinas/os endure in disproportionate numbers. Whether we view our burgeoning Latina/o youth as an opportunity for collective growth or, through the lens of stereotype, as a fiscal and moral burden, may come to define our time in American history.

Notes

NOTES TO THE PREFACE

1. Luis Reyes and Peter Rubie, *Hispanics in Hollywood: A Celebration of One Hundred Years in Film and Television* (Hollywood: Lone Eagle, 2000), 5.

2. Arnoldo De León, *They Called Them Greasers: Anglo Attitudes toward Mexicans in Texas 1821–1900* (Austin: University of Texas Press, 1983).

3. Luis Angel Toro, "'A People Distinct from Others': Race and Identity in Federal Indian Law and the Hispanic Classification in OMB Directive No. 15," *Texas Tech Law Review* 26 (1995): 1219, 1274 n.162.

4. Darren Lenard Hutchinson, "Ignoring the Sexualization of Race: Heteronormativity, Critical Race Theory and Anti-Racist Politics," *Buffalo Law Review* 47 (1999): 1, 87. One writer suggests the term *greaser* as applied to Mexicans originated from the sight of Mexican laborers carrying undried cowhide bundles on their heads onto ships headed north. Alfred Charles Richard Jr., *The Hispanic Image on the Silver Screen: An Interpretive Filmography from Silents into Sound, 1898–1935* (New York: Greenwood Press, 1992), xxxvii.

5. Oftentimes I distinguish between Mexicans and Mexican Americans, reserving the latter reference for those persons of Mexican origin who are U.S. citizens. Occasionally I use the reference "Chicanas/os" to refer to Mexican Americans who have been politicized by their participation in the Chicano movement.

6. These laws are discussed at Chapter 4.

7. George Hadley-Garcia, *Hispanic Hollywood: The Latins in Motion Pictures* (New York: Citadel Press, 1993), 36–37.

8. Ibid., 36.

NOTES TO CHAPTER I

1. Consistent with mass media's and the public's tendency to refer to the United States as America, as used herein the term *America* does not encompass Central or South America.

2. Charles Ramírez Berg, *Latino Images in Film: Stereotypes, Subversion, Resistance* (Austin: University of Texas Press, 2002); Frank Javier Garcia Berumen, *The Chicano/Hispanic Image in American Film* (New York: Vantage Press, 1995);

Rosa Linda Fregoso, *The Bronze Screen: Chicana and Chicano Film Culture* (Minneapolis: University of Minnesota Press, 1993); Hadley-Garcia, *Hispanic Hollywood*; David R. Maciel, *El Norte: The U.S.-Mexican Border in Contemporary Cinema* (San Diego: Institute for Regional Studies of the Californias, 1990); Chon Noriega, ed., *Chicanos and Film: Essays on Chicano Representation and Resistance* (New York: Garland Publishing, 1992); Arthur G. Pettit, *Images of the Mexican American in Fiction and Film* (College Station: Texas A&M University Press, 1980); Reyes and Rubie, *Hispanics in Hollywood*; Richard, *Hispanic Image on the Silver Screen*; Alfred Charles Richard Jr., *Censorship and Hollywood's Hispanic Image: An Interpretive Filmography, 1936–1955* (Westport, CT: Greenwood Press, 1993); Alfred Charles Richard Jr., *Contemporary Hollywood's Negative Hispanic Image: An Interpretive Filmography, 1956–1993* (Westport, CT: Greenwood Press, 1994); Clara E. Rodríguez, ed., *Latin Looks: Images of Latinas and Latinos in the U.S. Media* (Boulder, CO: Westview Press, 1998); *The Mask of Zorro: Mexican Americans in Popular Media* (Los Angeles: Gene Autry Western Heritage Museum, 1994).

3. John F. Dovidio, John C. Brigham, Blair T. Johnson, and Samuel L. Gaertner, "Stereotyping, Prejudice, and Discrimination: Another Look," in *Stereotypes and Stereotyping,* ed. C. Neil Macrae, Charles Stangor, and Miles Hewstone (New York: Guilford Press, 1996), 276, 311 (demonstrating by research focusing on African Americans that stereotypes are "significantly related to both prejudice and discrimination," and finding that "Whites' prejudice systematically predicts discrimination against Blacks").

4. Stereotypes of other ethno-racial groups are examined in Chapter 3.

5. E.g., Robert M. Entman, "Representation and Reality in the Portrayal of Blacks on Network Television News," *Journalism Quarterly* 71 (1994): 509; Robert M. Entman and Andrew Rojecki, *The Black Image in the White Mind: Media and Race in America* (Chicago: University of Chicago Press, 2000), 147 (discussing research where students primed with stereotypical representations of Blacks as lazy, unintelligent, and aggressive were more likely to contend that Rodney King brought about his beating by police than students primed with a counterstereotype, as well as a study finding that the more White college students watched television news, the more likely they were to perceive Blacks as deviant).

6. Sissela Bok, *Mayhem: Violence as Public Entertainment* (Reading, MA: Addison-Wesley, 1998), 57 (stating that the vast majority of studies agree that media violence can cause short- and long-term debilitating effects and citing a 1993 report by the American Psychological Association that "[t]here is absolutely no doubt that higher levels of viewing violence on television are correlated with increased acceptance of aggressive attitudes and increased aggressive behavior"). One critic of media violence points out the potential for violent images to lead children to accept "a degraded environment that devalues everything—a shadowy world in which our kids are breathing an awful lot of poison without knowing

that there is clean air and sunshine everywhere. They are shaped by the media as consumers before they've had a chance to develop their souls" (ibid., 75).

7. Richard C. Ausness, "The Application of Product Liability Principles to Publishers of Violent or Sexually Explicit Material," *Florida Law Review* 52 (2000): 603, 632–633.

8. Ian M. Ballard, Note, "See No Evil, Hear No Evil: Television Violence and the First Amendment," *Virginia Law Review* 81 (1995): 175, 176.

9. Ausness, "Application of Product Liability," 633–634 (collecting the diverging studies). See also *American Booksellers Association, Inc. v. Hudnut*, 771 F.2d 323, 329n.2 (7th Cir. 1985) (noting that national commissions on obscenity in the United States, the United Kingdom, and Canada have been unable to demonstrate "a direct link between obscenity and rape or exhibitionism").

10. See Gloria Sandrino-Glasser, "Los Confundidos: De-Conflating Latinos/as' Race and Ethnicity," *Chicano-Latino Law Review* 19 (1998): 69, 121–122; Pedro A. Malavet, "Puerto Rico: Cultural Nation, American Colony," *Michigan Journal of Race and Law* 6 (2000): 1.

11. Michael B. Salwen and Gonzalo R. Soruco, "The Hispanic Americans," in *U.S. News Coverage of Racial Minorities: A Sourcebook, 1934–1996*, ed. Beverly Ann Deepe Keever, Carolyn Martindale, and Mary Ann Weston (Westport, CT: Greenwood Press, 1997), 147, 157 (quoting a journalist writing in the *New Republic*).

12. Patricia M. Worthy, "Diversity and Minority Stereotyping in the Television Media: The Unsettled First Amendment Issue," *Hastings Commercial/Entertainment Law Journal* 18 (1996): 509, 535.

13. "A Different World: Children's Perceptions of Race and Class in Media" (1998), at http://www.media-awareness.ca/eng/issues/minrep/resource/reports/dworld.htm (last visited Oct. 2002); see also Rhonda G. Hartman, "Revitalizing Group Defamation as a Remedy for Hate Speech on Campus," *Oregon Law Review* 71 (1992): 855, 885n.154 (compiling studies linking minority and religious stereotypes with a stigmatizing effect on group members).

14. Richard Delgado, "Words That Wound: A Tort Action for Racial Insults, Epithets, and Name Calling" in *Words That Wound: Critical Race Theory, Assaultive Speech, and the First Amendment*, ed. Mari J. Matsuda, Charles R. Lawrence III, Richard Delgado, and Kimberlé Williams Crenshaw (Boulder, CO: Westview Press, 1993), 89, 90.

15. Ediberto Román, "Who Exactly Is Living *La Vida Loca*? The Legal and Political Consequences of Latino-Latina Ethnic and Racial Stereotypes in Film and Other Media," *Journal of Gender, Race and Justice* 4 (2000): 37, 65.

16. "A Different World," 12.

17. Daniel Romer, Kathleen H. Jamieson, and Nicole J. de Coteau, "The Treatment of Persons of Color in Local Television News: Ethnic Blame Discourse or Realistic Group Conflict?" *Communication Research* 25 (1998): 286, 294.

18. Eric K. Yamamoto, "Critical Race Praxis: Race Theory and Political Lawyering Practice in Post–Civil Rights America," *Michigan Law Review* 95 (1997): 821, 842.

19. Thomas Joo provides an even more compelling example of the cause-and-effect influence of law on social constructions of Asian Americans. He describes the perception of Asians as foreigners as stemming from discriminatory immigration laws that restricted Asian immigration and caused them to be permanently foreign. Thomas W. Joo, "Presumed Disloyal: Executive Power, Judicial Deference, and the Construction of Race Before and After September 11," *Columbia Hu-man Rights Law Review* 34 (2002): 1.

20. See Steven W. Bender, "Sight, Sound, and Stereotype: The War on Terrorism and Its Consequences for Latinas/os," *Oregon Law Review* 81 (2002).

NOTES TO CHAPTER 2

1. De León, *They Called Them Greasers,* 21.

2. See Truman Clark, *Puerto Rico and the United States 1917–1933* (Pittsburgh: University of Pittsburgh Press, 1975), 152–153.

3. Frederick B. Pike, *The United States and Latin America: Myths and Stereotypes of Civilization and Nature* (Austin: University of Texas Press, 1992), 291–292.

4. Garcia Berumen, *Chicano/Hispanic Image,* 14 (describing the film *Why Worry?* (1923)).

5. "Mañana (Is Soon Enough for Me)," written by Dave Barbour and Peggy Lee. Copyright © 1948 © Renewed 1976 Criterion Music Corp. Used by permission, International Copyright Secured, All Rights Reserved. See generally George Archuleta, "Racial Slurs in Music Didn't Start with Gangsta' Rap," *Denver Post,* Dec. 18, 1997, B7.

6. Richard Delgado and Jean Stefancic, "Images of the Outsider in American Law and Culture: Can Free Expression Remedy Systemic Social Ills?" *Cornell Law Review* 77 (1992): 1258, 1275.

7. Richie Pérez, "From Assimilation to Annihilation: Puerto Rican Images in U.S. Films," in Rodríguez, ed., *Latin Looks,* 146.

8. Melissa Therrien and Roberto R. Ramirez, *The Hispanic Population in the United States* (2001) (using U.S. Census Bureau data, *Current Population Survey,* March 2000).

9. LatCrit is a multi-ethno-racial group of law professors, academics, lawyers, activists, writers, artists, and others whose anti-subordination agenda represents a vibrant scholarly and social movement. Published LatCrit symposia are listed on the LatCrit Web site at http://www.latcrit.org.

10. Fernando Peñalosa, *Chicano Sociolinguistics: A Brief Introduction* (Rowley, MA: Newbury House, 1980), 24.

11. "Report on 1990 Census Results," *SourceMex Economic News and Analysis on Mexico,* March 18, 1992.

12. Sandra Sanchez, "Misdiagnosed Patient Freed after 2 Years," *USA Today,* June 17, 1992, A3. The Trique language is also referred to as Triqui.

13. E.g., Martha Menchaca, *Recovering History, Constructing Race: The Indian, Black, and White Roots of Mexican Americans* (Austin: University of Texas Press, 2001).

14. Anthony M. Stevens-Arroyo, "The Latino Religious Resurgence," *Annals of the American Academy of Political and Social Sciences* 558 (July 1998): 163, 172 (citing a 1993 source by Barry Kosmin and Seymour Lachman); David Maldonado Jr., "The Changing Religious Practices of Hispanics," in *Hispanics in the United States,* ed. Pastora San Juan Cafferty and David W. Engstrom (New Brunswick: Transaction Publishers, 2000), 97.

15. Chris L. Jenkins, "Islam Luring More Latinos: Prayers Offer a More Intimate Link to God, Some Say," *Washington Post,* Jan. 7, 2001, C1.

16. *Church of the Lukumi Babalu Aye, Inc. v. City of Hialeah,* 508 U.S. 520, 525 (1993).

17. William Booth, "Gore, Bush Try to Woo Electorate That Defies Labels," *The Oregonian,* Feb. 28, 2000, A6. A 2002 survey by the Pew Hispanic Center and the Henry J. Kaiser Family Foundation produced similar results, finding that 49 percent of Hispanic registered voters identified themselves as Democrats, 20 percent as Republicans, and 19 percent as Independents. Gregory L. Giroux, "Parties Have Room for Growth among Hispanics," Oct. 3, 2002, http://www.washingtonpost.com (last visited October 2002).

18. Steven W. Bender, "Will the Wolf Survive? Latino/a Pop Music in the Cultural Mainstream," *University of Denver Law Review* 78 (2001): 719.

19. "Candidate Tenders Apology for Remarks about Spanish," *Eugene Register Guard,* June 30, 1996, 4C (reporting remarks of Anglo candidate Ron Taber).

20. Chon A. Noriega, *Shot in America: Television, the State, and the Rise of Chicano Cinema* (Minneapolis: University of Minnesota Press, 2000), 73.

21. Leonard Pitt, "The Foreign Miner's Tax of 1850: A Study of Nativism and Anti-Nativism in Gold Rush California" (unpublished M.A. thesis, UCLA, 1955).

22. Scott B. Vickers, *Native American Identities: From Stereotype to Archetype in Art and Literature* (Albuquerque: University of New Mexico Press, 1998), 40–44 (pointing out the detriment in the Noble Savage characterization).

23. Arthur Brice, "Bias Backlash May Be Building in U.S.," *Atlanta Constitution,* March 3, 1994, A6.

24. Therrien and Ramirez, *Hispanic Population in the United States* (using U.S. Census Bureau data, *Current Population Survey,* March 2000).

25. Kevin R. Johnson, "'Melting Pot' or 'Ring of Fire'? Assimilation and the

Mexican-American Experience," *California Law Review* 85 (1997): 1259, 1301–1302.

26. Ricky Martin, "Shake Your Bon Bon," on *Ricky Martin* (Sony/Columbia 1999).

27. Proposition 187 is examined in Chapter 5.

28. E.g., Cheryl Martinis, "Latino Parents Call School Lecture 'Racism,'" *The Oregonian*, May 10, 2000, E17.

29. Cheryl Martinis, "Three Latino Teens Sue Schools, Claim Bias," *The Oregonian*, Oct. 18, 2000, E1.

30. Jenny Rivera, "Domestic Violence against Latinas by Latino Males: An Analysis of Race, National Origin, and Gender Differentials," *Boston College Third World Law Journal* 14 (1994): 231 (examines the role of Latina/o stereotypes relevant to understanding domestic violence in the Latina/o community).

NOTES TO CHAPTER 3

1. *Baker v. Nelson*, 191 N.W.2d 185 (Minn. 1971) (holding Minnesota law does not authorize marriage between persons of same sex).

2. *Bowers v. Hardwick*, 478 U.S. 186 (1986) (Georgia's sodomy law does not violate constitutional rights of homosexuals). In 2003, the Supreme Court heard argument against a Texas statute prohibiting sodomy among same-sex couples. See *Lawrence v. State*, 41 S.W.3d 349 (Tex. Ct. App. 2001) (upholding conviction).

3. Gilbert Paul Carrasco, *Sexuality and Discrimination: A Rights and Liberties Perspective* (forthcoming 2004), chap. 4.

4. *Lofton v. Kearney*, 157 F.Supp. 2d 1372 (S.D. Fla. 2001) (upholding Florida's law against constitutional challenge).

5. Carrasco, *Sexuality*, chap. 2.

6. Hutchinson, "Ignoring the Sexualization of Race."

7. Richard H. Chused, "Married Women's Property Law: 1800–1850," *Georgetown Law Journal* 71 (1983): 1359. In a Supreme Court decision upholding the refusal of Illinois to confer a license to practice law on a married woman, a concurring justice preferred that the inability of a woman to contract without her husband's consent helped justify the state's decision that a married woman was incompetent fully to perform the duties of an attorney. Moreover, that justice explained, "[t]he natural and proper timidity and delicacy which belongs to the female sex evidently unfits it for many of the occupations of civil life," and the states may properly ordain which positions must be filled by men, the "sterner sex." *Bradwell v. State*, 83 U.S. 130, 141–142 (1872) (Bradley, J., concurring).

8. Catharine A. MacKinnon, "Pornography as Defamation and Discrimination," *Boston University Law Review* 71 (1991): 793.

9. Caroline A. Forell and Donna M. Matthews, *A Law of Her Own: The Rea-*

sonable Woman as a Measure of Man (New York: New York University Press, 2000).

10. Julie Brown, "Cuz I'm a Blonde" (1989) (song lampooing blondes' alleged lack of intelligence).

11. *Legally Blonde* (2001).

12. Floyd D. Weatherspoon, "The Devastating Impact of the Justice System on the Status of African-American Males: An Overview Perspective," *Capitol University Law Review* 23 (1994): 23, 28.

13. Leonard M. Baynes, "Paradoxes of Racial Stereotypes, Diversity and Past Discrimination in Establishing Affirmative Action in FCC Broadcast Licensing," *Administrative Law Review* 52 (2000): 979, 983.

14. "Poll Finds Whites Use Stereotypes," *New York Times,* Jan. 10, 1991, B10; David K. Shipler, "Challenge Is to Confront Camouflaged Racism in National Debate," *Star Tribune,* Oct. 20, 1997, 13A.

15. Farai Chideya, *Don't Believe the Hype: Fighting Cultural Misinformation about African-Americans* (New York: Penguin Books, 1995), 3. Rooney was suspended by CBS for three weeks in the resultant controversy; he has denied making these comments, which were reported in a newspaper for gays in Los Angeles.

16. Robert Blauner, *Racial Oppression in America* (New York: Harper & Row, 1972), 163–164.

17. Chideya, *Don't Believe the Hype,* 155–156.

18. Baynes, "Paradoxes of Racial Stereotypes," 983.

19. Worthy, "Diversity and Minority Stereotyping," 509, 536.

20. See Devon A. Mihesuah, *American Indians: Stereotypes and Realities* (Atlanta: Clarity, 1996).

21. Ward Churchill, *Fantasies of the Master Race: Literature, Cinema and the Colonization of American Indians* (San Francisco: City Light Books, 1998); Rennard Strickland, *Tonto's Revenge: Reflections on American Indian Culture and Policy* (Albuquerque: University of New Mexico Press, 1997).

22. Delgado and Stefancic, "Images of the Outsider," 1269.

23. Churchill, *Fantasies of the Master Race,* 184–185; Delgado and Stefancic, "Images of the Outsider," 1270.

24. Ward Churchill, *A Little Matter of Genocide: Holocaust and Denial in the Americas 1492 to the Present* (San Francisco: City Light Books, 1997).

25. Keith Aoki, "'Foreign-ness' and Asian American Identities: Yellowface, World War II Propaganda, and Bifurcated Racial Stereotypes," *UCLA Asian Pacific Law Journal* 4 (1996): 1, 64.

26. Ibid., 33, 39.

27. Ibid., 29.

28. Ibid., 20.

29. Gabriel Chin et al., *Beyond Self-Interest: Asian Pacific Americans toward*

a Community of Justice (Los Angeles: UCLA Asian American Studies Center, Leap Public Policy Institute, 1996), 13.

30. Keith Aoki, "No Right to Own? The Early Twentieth-Century 'Alien Land Laws' as a Prelude to Internment," *Boston College Law Review* 40 (1998): 37.

31. Ibid., 39.

32. Leti Volpp, "'Obnoxious to Their Very Nature': Asian Americans and Constitutional Citizenship," *Citizenship Studies* 5 (2001): 57.

33. Ibid.

34. Robert S. Chang, "Toward an Asian American Legal Scholarship: Critical Race Theory, Post-Structuralism, and Narrative Space," *California Law Review* 81 (1993): 1242 (ironically, Chin was a Chinese American whom the autoworkers had assumed was Japanese).

35. Joo, "Presumed Disloyal." Wen Ho Lee was indicted on dozens of felony counts and held without bail for several months. Later given an apology by a federal judge, Lee pled guilty to one count of violating nuclear security statutes and was released with a sentence of time already served.

36. Jack G. Shaheen, *Reel Bad Arabs: How Hollywood Vilifies a People* (New York: Olive Branch Press, 2001), 11; see also Natsu Taylor Saito, "Symbolism under Siege: Japanese American Redress and the 'Racing' of Arab Americans as 'Terrorists,'" *Asian Law Journal* 8 (2001): 1; Seth Hilton, "American Conceptions of the Middle East and Islam," *University of California at Davis Journal of International Law and Policy* 1 (1995): 355.

37. Joo, "Presumed Disloyal," 33.

38. Michael Paulson, "US Attitudes toward Arabs Souring, according to Poll," *Boston Globe,* Sept. 29, 2001, A5.

39. Leti Volpp, "American Mestizo: Filipinos and Antimiscegenation Laws in California," *University of California at Davis Law Review* 33 (2000): 795.

40. Román, "Living *La Vida Loca,*" 53.

41. Peter Matthiessen, *Sal Si Puedes (Escape if You Can): Cesar Chavez and the New American Revolution* (Berkeley: University of California Press, 1969), 14 (quoting Pacific Rural Press in 1936).

42. Researchers have noted a social distinction between "positive" and "negative" group constructions that labels the positive as generalizations and the negative as stereotypes. Yet, as discussed below, some seemingly positive constructions are unwelcome by the target group. Thus one researcher defined stereotypes more precisely as group generalizations that elicit controversy. David J. Schneider, "Modern Stereotype Research: Unfinished Business," in Macrae et al., *Stereotypes and Stereotyping,* 419, 429–430. By referring to stereotypes in this book as "negative," I realize I may be using a redundant reference, yet I am assuming that some readers may view positive generalizations as stereotypes as well.

43. Alfredo Mirandé, *Gringo Justice* (Notre Dame, IN: University of Notre Dame Press, 1987), 160.

44. Chin et al., *Beyond Self-Interest,* 18; Rodolfo F. Acuña, *Anything but Mexican: Chicanos in Contemporary Los Angeles* (London: Verso, 1996), 132.

45. Berta Esperanza Hernandez Truyol, "Building Bridges—Latinas and Latinos at the Crossroads: Realities, Rhetoric and Replacement," *Columbia Human Rights Law Review* 25 (1994): 369; Kevin R. Johnson, "Puerto Rico, Puerto Ricans, and LatCrit Theory: Commonalities and Differences between Latina/o Experiences," *Michigan Journal of Race and Law* 6 (2000): 107, 123–124.

46. Kevin R. Johnson, "Comparative Racialization: Culture and National Origin in the Latina/o Communities," *Denver University Law Review* 78 (2001): 633.

47. Ibid.

48. The English-language movement and bilingual education are discussed at Chapter 6.

49. See Leslie Espinoza and Angela P. Harris, "Afterword: Embracing the Tar-Baby—LatCrit Theory and the Sticky Mess of Race," *California Law Review* 85 (1997): 1585 (examining arguments for "black exceptionalism").

50. Rodríguez, *Latin Looks,* 17.

NOTES TO CHAPTER 4

1. Keith Liddle, Note, "Affirmative Action for Certain Non-Black Minorities and Recent Immigrants—'Mend It or End It?'" *Georgetown Immigration Law Journal* 11 (1997): 835, 853 n.120.

2. Mirandé, *Gringo Justice,* 160. The comparison of Latinas/os to Asians in this report illustrates the dangers of the model-minority construction discussed at Chapter 3.

3. Pearl Idelia Ellis, *Americanization through Homemaking* (Los Angeles: Wetzel Publishing, 1929), 26.

4. Lillian Jiménez, "Moving from the Margin to the Center: Puerto Rican Cinema in New York," in *The Ethnic Eye: Latino Media Arts,* ed. Chon A. Noriega and Ana M. López (Minneapolis: University of Minnesota Press, 1996), 23.

5. National Council of La Raza, "Out of the Picture: Hispanics in the Media," in Rodríguez, *Latin Looks,* 29.

6. Ibid., 27.

7. Ibid., 32.

8. Darlene Superville, "Stereotypes of Hispanics Still on TV, Study Shows," *Fort Worth Star-Telegram,* April 20, 1996, A38.

9. Robin Dougherty, "Study: TV News Promotes Stereotypes of Hispanics," *Arizona Republic,* June 13, 1996, C5.

10. Charles Ramírez Berg, "Stereotyping in Films in General and of the Hispanic in Particular" in Rodríguez, *Latin Looks,* 113.

11. Hadley-Garcia, *Hispanic Hollywood,* 43–44.

12. See Berumen, *Chicano/Hispanic Image,* 104.

13. Noriega, *Shot in America,* 35–37.

14. Mirandé, *Gringo Justice,* 17.

15. Robert S. Chang, "Los Angeles as a Single-Celled Organism," *Loyola Los Angeles Law Review* 34 (2001): 843, 847.

16. David G. Gutiérrez, *Walls and Mirrors: Mexican Americans, Mexican Immigrants, and the Politics of Ethnicity* (Berkeley: University of California Press, 1995), 124.

17. *People v. Zammora,* 152 P.2d 180, 237 (Cal. Dist. Ct. App. 1944).

18. Gutiérrez, *Walls and Mirrors,* 125; Citizen's Committee for the Defense of Mexican-American Youth, "The Sleepy Lagoon Case," in *The Mexican American and the Law,* ed. Carlos E. Cortés (New York: Arno Press, 1974), 9.

19. Carey McWilliams, *North from Mexico: The Spanish-Speaking People of the United States,* 2d ed. (New York: Praeger, 1990), 226.

20. Mauricio Mazón, *The Zoot Suit Riots: The Psychology of Symbolic Annihilation* (Austin: University of Texas Press, 1984), 75.

21. Chang, "Los Angeles," 846.

22. Carlos E. Cortés, "Who Is Maria? What Is Juan? Dilemmas of Analyzing the Chicano Image in U.S. Feature Films," in Noriega, *Chicanos and Film,* 83, 94–95.

23. An additional cinematic depiction of Puerto Rican gangs comes from *Saturday Night Fever* (1977).

24. Alberto Sandoval Sánchez, "West Side Story: A Puerto Rican Reading of 'America,'" in Rodríguez, *Latin Looks,* 164.

25. Alberto Sandoval-Sánchez, "Paul Simon's *The Capeman*: The Staging of Puerto Rican National Identity as Spectacle and Commodity on Broadway," in *Latino/a Popular Culture,* ed. Michelle Habell-Pallán and Mary Romero (New York: New York University Press, 2002), 147.

26. Angela Ginorio and Michelle Huston, *¡Sí, Se Puede! Yes, We Can: Latinas in School* (Washington, DC: AAUW Educational Foundation, 2001), 28.

27. Ibid.

28. "1997 National Longitudinal Survey of Youth," in *Minorities in the Juvenile Justice System* (Washington, DC: U.S. Department of Justice, Dec. 1999), 5.

29. See generally Mirandé, *Gringo Justice,* 192–193.

30. Terry McCarthy, "L.A. Gangs Are Back," *Time,* Sept. 3, 2001, 46.

31. Margaret Ramirez, "'Seinfeld' Scene Angers Latinos," *Newsday,* May 9, 1988, A3.

32. See Victorino Matus, "The Media Mob vs. Cuban Americans," *Weekly Standard,* May 8, 2000, 13 (describing the "special contempt" among the press for Cuban Americans); William Saletan, "Us and Them," *New Republic,* May 22, 2000, 6.

33. Robert Fresco, "Cubans Seize GA Prison," *Newsday,* Nov. 24, 1987, 5.

34. My friend Professor Pedro Malavet suggests this depiction is untrue, as the entry was largely quiet and bloodless.

35. "Ricky Needs an Agent," *I Love Lucy,* first aired May 16, 1955.

36. "Black Eye," *I Love Lucy,* first aired March 9, 1953.

37. The Latino and his drinking companions were played by the members of the Latino comedy troupe Culture Clash.

38. "Poll Finds Whites Use Stereotypes," *New York Times,* Jan. 10, 1991, B10.

39. "Hispanic Groups Ask GM Gillick for Apology," *Baltimore Sun,* May 24, 1998, C8.

40. See Richard, *Hollywood's Negative Hispanic Image,* 363.

41. MTV, Nov. 10, 2001.

42. Albor Ruiz and Bill Hutchinson, "David Letterman Issues a Rare Apology for Comedy Bit," *Wichita Eagle,* May 17, 2001, B5.

43. *Prime Time for Latinos: Report II: 2000–2001 Prime Television Season* 8 (Washington, DC: National Hispanic Foundation for the Arts, Sept. 2001).

44. Tim Padgett and Elaine Shannon, "The Border Monsters," *Time,* June 11, 2001, 69.

45. "Meth Plague of Conference," *Columbian,* Aug. 7, 2001, C2 (reporting the comment as borders rather than border, thus referring to Canada as well as Mexico; in a television news broadcast from the conference, I heard Hutchinson refer to "border," in the singular).

46. Niko Price, "Fox: Don't Blame Mexico for Drugs," *Miami Herald,* Nov. 27, 2000, A17.

47. "Editorial Humor/It's the Mexicans!" March 20, 1999 (e-mail on file with author).

48. David Cole, *No Equal Justice: Race and Class in the American Criminal Justice System* (New York: New Press, 1999), 144.

49. Substance Abuse and Mental Health Services Administration, U.S. Dept. of Health and Human Services, *National Household Survey on Drug Abuse: Preliminary Estimates from 1995* (Washington, DC, 1997), 13.

50. Hang Lee, Jared Strote, Henry Wechsler, and Jeana Gledhill-Hoyt, "Increased Use of Marijuana and Other Illicit Drugs at US Colleges in the 1990s: Results of Three National Surveys" (abstract), *Addiction* 95 (2000): 1655–1667.

51. U.S. Department of Justice, "1997 National Longitudinal Survey of Youth," in *Minorities in the Juvenile Justice System* (Washington, DC, Dec. 1999), 5.

52. Tracey Eaton, "Mexican Drug Sellers Add Convenient Walk-up Windows," *Arizona Republic,* April 19, 1998, A11.

53. Cole, *No Equal Justice,* 152–153.

54. One of many portrayals of Latina junkiedom comes from the 1982 film *Fort Apache, The Bronx,* in which cop Paul Newman discovers heroin needle track marks on the leg of his Latina girlfriend, a nurse. Similarly, *Badge 373* (1973) includes a prostitute-junkie Latina who is slain in her bed.

55. Peter Andreas, *Border Games: Policing the U.S.-Mexico Divide* (Ithaca, NY: Cornell University Press, 2000), 43. A militaristic attitude toward drug enforcement was depicted in the film *Clear and Present Danger* (1994), in which the fictional president stated, "These [Colombian] drug cartels represent a clear and present danger to the national security of the United States," prompting him to launch a covert military operation against Colombian cocaine operations.

56. Office of National Drug Control Policy, "National Youth Anti-Drug Media Campaign Links Drugs and Terror," press release, Feb. 3, 2002, at http:// www.whitehousedrugpolicy.gov/news/press02/020302.html (last visited September 2002).

57. Nick Gillespie, "Poor Results, Risky Tactics, a Good Time to Re-evaluate Border Policy," *Arizona Republic,* June 30, 1997, B5; "Marines Delayed Calling Medical Aid in Border Shooting, Texas Ranger Says," *Arizona Republic,* June 21, 1997, A4.

58. Bradley T. Winter, "Invidious Prosecution: The History of Seditious Conspiracy—Foreshadowing the Recent Convictions of Sheik Omar Abdel-Rahman and His Immigrant Followers," *Georgetown Immigration Law Journal* 10 (1996): 185, 190–191.

59. Ibid.

60. Lisa Napoli, Note, "The Puerto Rican Independentistas: Combatants in the Fight for Self-Determination and the Right to Prisoner of War Status," *Cardozo Journal of International and Comparative Law* 4 (1996): 131, 156.

61. Malavet, "Puerto Rico," 70–73.

62. News reports on the number of Americans killed in the raid on Columbus, New Mexico, differ; some put the number at seventeen, others eighteen.

63. Ollie Reed Jr., "Villa the Terrorist?" *Albuquerque Tribune,* Feb. 28, 2002, A1.

64. While some press reported Padilla's membership in the Chicago street gang the Latin Kings, others suggested his former affiliation with the Chicago gang Maniac Latin Disciples. "Suspect's Journey from Brooklyn to Al-Qaida a Mystery," *Times Union* (Albany), June 11, 2002, A6; Daniel de Vise and Larry Lebowitz, "Terror Suspect's History Details Embrace of Crime," *Miami Herald,* June 16, 2002, A1.

65. Stewart M. Powell, "Terror Recruits in U.S. a Danger," *Times Union* (Albany), June 15, 2002, A1.

66. Ignacio M. García, *Chicanismo: The Forging of a Militant Ethos among Mexican Americans* (Tucson: University of Arizona Press, 1997), 106–107.

67. Carlos Villarreal, "Culture in Lawmaking: A Chicano Perspective," *University of California at Davis Law Review* 24 (1991): 1193, 1214.

68. Marc Mauer, "The Intended and Unintended Consequences of Incarceration-Based Sentencing Policies," *Thomas M. Cooley Law Review* 16 (1999): 47.

69. "Race and Incarceration in the United States," Human Rights Watch Press Backgrounder, Feb. 27, 2002, at http://hrw.org/backgrounder/usa/race/ (last visited September 2002).

70. Ibid., table 5.

71. U.S. Department of Justice, "Criminal Offenders Statistics," at http://www.ojp.usdoj.gov/bjs/crimoff.htm#lifetime (last visited September 2002) (these statistics for drug offenses address inmates of any race or ethnicity).

72. Chideya, *Don't Believe the Hype*, 192–193.

73. *United States v. Thomas*, 787 F.Supp. 663 (E.D. Tex. 1992) (rejecting the contention of defendants charged with drug offenses that they were targeted improperly by an officer who had seen this training film), aff'd, 983 F.2d 1062 (5th Cir. 1993). Of course, Puerto Ricans, although regarded in American society as foreign, are U.S. citizens.

74. David A. Harris, "The Stories, the Statistics, and the Law: Why 'Driving While Black' Matters," *Minnesota Law Review* 84 (1999): 265, 296.

75. Maria Soledad Loven, "Racial Profiling: They Are at It Again," Oct. 18, 2000, available at http://www.quepasa.com (last visited October 2000).

76. Shelan Y. Joseph, "Six Flags Magic Mountain: A Family Entertainment Park, but Only if You Wear the Right Clothes," *Loyola Los Angeles Entertainment Law Journal* 16 (1995): 359, 360 (quoting amended complaint in legal action filed in California Superior Court, *Hernandez v. Six Flags Magic Mountain, Inc.*); see also Margaret M. Russell, "Entering Great America: Reflections on Race and the Convergence of Progressive Legal Theory and Practice," *Hastings Law Journal* 43 (1992): 749.

77. *Whren v. United States*, 517 U.S. 806 (1996).

78. See Kevin R. Johnson, "U.S. Border Enforcement: Drugs, Migrants, and the Rule of Law," *Villanova Law Review* 47 (2002): 897, 900 (observing that the Supreme Court left open the possibility that such conduct would violate equal protection but noting that equal protection claims are notoriously difficult to prove because of the requirement of establishing discriminatory intent).

79. See Tomás Almaguer, *Racial Fault Lines: The Historical Origins of White Supremacy in California* (Berkeley: University of California Press, 1994), 57.

80. Kim Strosnider, "Anti-Gang Ordinances after *City of Chicago v. Morales*: The Intersection of Race, Vagueness Doctrine, and Equal Protection in Criminal Law," *American Criminal Law Review* 39 (2002): 101.

81. *City of Chicago v. Morales*, 527 U.S. 41 (1999).

82. Harris, "The Stories, the Statistics," 292–293.

83. *Shuttlesworth v. City of Birmingham*, 382 U.S. 87 (1965).

84. *Papachristou v. City of Jacksonville,* 405 U.S. 156 (1972).

85. *Kolender v. Lawson,* 461 U.S. 352 (1983); see generally Strosnider, "Anti-Gang Ordinances."

86. Kevin R. Johnson, "The Case for African American and Latina/o Cooperation in Challenging Race Profiling in Law Enforcement," *Florida Law Review* 55 (2003): 341.

87. *United States v. Brignoni-Ponce,* 422 U.S. 873 (1975).

88. *United States v. Montero-Camargo,* 208 F.3d 1122 (9th Cir. 2000) (viewing the Supreme Court's suggestion that ethnic appearance may be a factor in determining reasonable suspicion as *dictum* for which the Court had relied on now-outdated demographic information).

89. Ibid., 1134.

90. Johnson, "African American and Latina/o Cooperation," 348 (emphasis in original).

91. "Apology from Congressman," *New York Times,* Sept. 21, 2001, A16 (U.S. Representative John Cooksey).

92. Marlon Vaughn, "Parent: Hispanic Daughter Has Been Subject of Taunts," *Flint Journal,* Sept. 15, 2001, A5.

93. Ian F. Haney López, *White by Law: The Legal Construction of Race* (New York: New York University Press, 1996), 139.

94. G. V. Bodenhausen, "Second-Guessing the Jury: Stereotypic and Hindsight Biases in Perceptions of Court Cases," *Journal of Applied Social Psychology* 20 (1990): 1112.

95. Peter Carlin, "What Becomes of the Resurrected?" *Los Angeles Times Magazine,* March 8, 1992, 20.

96. Barnes C. Ellis, "Ventura Sees Racism in Courts," *The Oregonian,* April 21, 1991, C1. This juror's attitudes are reminiscent of those of the prejudiced juror in the film drama *Twelve Angry Men* (1957), who voiced these prejudices against the young Latino defendant who allegedly murdered his father with a switchblade:

You know how these people lie. It's born in them. . . .
They don't need a real big reason to kill someone either. . . .
They get drunk . . . and someone's lying in the gutter. . . .
That's the way they are, by nature . . . violent.
Human life don't mean as much to them as it does to us.

97. Carlin, "What Becomes of the Resurrected?"

98. Steven W. Bender, "Silencing Culture and Culturing Silence: A Comparative Experience of Centrifugal Forces in the Ethnic Studies Curriculum," *Michigan Journal of Law and Race* 5 (2000): 913, 917–919.

99. John Gibeaut, "Issues That Don't Go Away," *American Bar Association Journal* (Nov. 2002): 40, 41.

100. *Hernandez v. Texas,* 347 U.S. 475 (1954). See also Ian F. Haney López,

"Institutional Racism: Judicial Conduct and a New Theory of Racial Discrimination," *Yale Law Journal* 109 (2000): 1717 (indicting the institutional racism in the Los Angeles County grand juror selection system, resulting in the 1960s in Mexican Americans accounting for one of every fifty-eight grand jurors while accounting for one in seven persons in local population, a ratio that, while somewhat reduced, continues today), Ian F. Haney López, *Racism on Trial: The Chicano Fight for Justice* (Cambridge, MA: Belknap Press of Harvard University Press, 2003).

101. *Hernandez v. New York,* 500 U.S. 352 (1991).

102. "¿Dónde está la justicia? A Call to Action on Behalf of the Latino and Latina Youth in the U.S. Justice System," available at http://www.buildingblocksforyouth.org/latino_rpt/fact_eng.html (last visited July 2002). Approved by California voters in 2000, Proposition 21 allows prosecutors to try juveniles as young as age fourteen in adult criminal court, without a fitness hearing in juvenile court before a judge, merely by alleging an offense that is "gang-related" or another specified type of major offense. See generally Jennifer Taylor, "California's Proposition 21: A Case of Juvenile Injustice," *Southern California Law Review* 75 (2002): 983.

103. Robert Garcia, "Latinos and Criminal Justice," *UCLA Chicano-Latino Law Review* 14 (1994): 6, 14.

104. Diana L. Hoermann, "Why the Injection of Race in *Saldano v. State* Constitutes Fundamental Error," *St. Mary's Law Review on Minority Issues* 4 (2002): 261; Mark Hansen, "Deadly Race Cards?" *ABA Journal* (Sept. 2000): 18; Juan A. Lozano, "Psychologist Discussed Race in Death Row Cases," *Charlotte Observer,* June 10, 2000, A4; Steve Lash, "Texas Death Case Set Aside," *Houston Chronicle,* June 6, 2000, A1.

105. *Saldano v. State,* 70 S.W.3d 873 (Tex. Ct. Crim. App. 2002) (*en banc*).

106. For additional confrontations, see Carmen T. Joge and Sonia M. Pérez, *The Mainstreaming of Hate: A Report on Latinos and Harassment, Hate Violence, and Law Enforcement Abuse in the '90s* (Washington, DC: National Council of La Raza, 1999).

107. Maxine Bernstein, "Kroeker Writing Up Response to Mejia Death," *The Oregonian,* May 22, 2001, B3; Maxine Bernstein, "Police Slaying of Man at Psychiatric Hospital Brings Questions," *The Oregonian,* April 4, 2001, D4; John Enders, "Mental Health Officials Investigate Shooting of Mexican Man," AP wires, April 4, 2001.

108. Mary Romero, "State Violence and the Social and Legal Construction of Latino Criminality: From El Bandido to Gang Member," *University of Denver Law Review* 78 (2001): 1081.

109. E.g., Margaret Taus, "Bellevue Marchers Call for Justice in Fatal Shooting of Hispanic Man," *Seattle Post-Intelligencer,* Aug. 17, 2001, B1.

110. This account comes from Cynthia Kwei Yung Lee, "Race and Self-

Defense: Toward a Normative Conception of Reasonableness," *Minnesota Law Review* 81 (1996): 367, 445–448.

111. Aoki, "'Foreign-ness' and Asian American Identities," 33.

112. McCarthy, "L.A. Gangs Are Back," 49.

113. Beth Shuster, "Villaraigosa Backers Decry Hahn Ad as Unfair," *Los Angeles Times,* May 29, 2001, B1; Patt Morrison, "Hahn Pulls Ahead of Villaraigosa in the Polls, but by What Methods?" *Los Angeles Times,* May 30, 2001, B3.

114. Jason Thompson, "Dirty Money, Dirty Politics," *Washington Post,* July 31, 2002, available at http://www.washingtonpost.com (last visited August 2002).

NOTES TO CHAPTER 5

1. "Mañana (Is Soon Enough for Me)," written by Dave Barbour and Peggy Lee. Copyright © 1948 © Renewed 1976 Criterion Music Corp. Used by Permission, International Copyright Secured, All Rights Reserved.

2. Archuleta, "Racial Slurs in Music" (supplying these lyrics).

3. "Speedy Reaches the Finish Line," available at http://www.foxnews.com/story/0,2933,55675,00.html (last visited June 2002).

4. Berumen, *Chicano/Hispanic Image,* 14–15.

5. Roberto Rodríguez and Patrisia Gonzales, "We Smell a Stereotypical Rat," Sept. 22, 1995, at http://www.eece.unm.edu/staff/larranag/www/stereotyprat.html (last visited Nov. 2002).

6. "Tucson Officials Pull Ad Promoting Clean Air Event," *Charleston Daily Mail,* March 30, 2002, A9 (reporting that city officials eventually pulled the advertisements as offensive).

7. Dave Boyer, "Mexican 'Siesta,' GOP 'Trick' Fuel Partisan Feuding on Hill," *Washington Times,* Nov. 16, 2001, A4 (Watts is African American).

8. Bill Maher, *Does Anybody Have a Problem with That? Politically Incorrect's Greatest Hits* (New York: Villard, 1996), 101.

9. National Conference of Christians and Jews, *Taking America's Pulse: The National Conference Survey on Inter-Group Relations* (New York, 1994).

10. U.S. Department of Justice, "1997 National Longitudinal Survey of Youth," in *Minorities in the Juvenile Justice System* (Washington, DC, Dec. 1999), 5.

11. Thanks to my *compadre* Pete Gonzales for suggesting I include this song.

12. Acuña, *Anything but Mexican,* 296.

13. Larry McMurtry, *The Last Picture Show* (New York: Dial Press, 1966), 130–141.

14. Jack Kerouac, "A Billowy Trip in the World," in *Gringos in Mexico,* ed. Edward Simmen (Fort Worth: Texas Christian University Press, 1988), 269.

15. Lyrics taken from http://www.xs4all.nl/~devet/hiatt/html/other.htm (last visited January 2002). A popular Phoenix rock station frequently played a slightly different version of this song, performed, I believe, by the group Buck Naked and the Bare Bottom Boys, which changed the last verse to the even more derogatory lyric "I can always smell when you've been seeing your Mexican lover."

16. The 1991 movie *The Last Prostitute* follows the summer adventure of two teenage boys who travel from Ohio to the Southwest to meet a legendary prostitute named Maria. Played by Latina Sonia Braga, the "best [prostitute] in the world" is now retired. Although she refuses the boys' advances, she puts them to work at her horse-breeding farm, and the film suggests that she may have "initiated" one of the boys.

17. See Kimberlé Williams Crenshaw, "Beyond Racism and Misogyny: Black Feminism and 2 Live Crew" in Matsuda et al., eds., *Words That Wound,* 111, 117–118. The film *Fort Apache, The Bronx* (1982) also portrayed the good Latina/bad Latina (or virgin/whore) juxtaposition, this time a shy Latina nurse who dated and slept with Paul Newman. Newman finds needle track marks on her body and questions whether she is a junkie. The Latina explains that "smack's like a vacation for me" and later overdoses. Yet another example of the transformation from "good" to "bad" Latina comes from the 1961 film *Young Savages,* in which the innocent-appearing sixteen-year-old sister of a slain blind Puerto Rican boy is revealed to be a prostitute, helping her family make ends meet.

18. Carlos E. Cortés, "Chicanas in Film: History of an Image," in Rodríguez, *Latin Looks,* 133.

19. Berumen, *Chicano/Hispanic Image,* 152–153.

20. See Madonna, *Sex* (New York: Warner Books, 1992); see also bell hooks, *Outlaw Culture: Resisting Representations* (New York: Routledge, 1994), 20 (describing a fictional passage from *Sex* in which Madonna takes a young Puerto Rican boy: "He was fearless. He would do anything. . . . [I]t was probably the most erotic sex I ever had. But he gave me crabs").

21. Almaguer, *Racial Fault Lines,* 61.

22. Ibid.

23. José E. Limón, *American Encounters: Greater Mexico, the United States, and the Erotics of Culture* (Boston: Beacon Press, 1998), 135–136.

24. De León, *They Called Them Greasers,* 43.

25. The 1982 film *Fort Apache, The Bronx* depicted a fourteen-year-old Latina giving birth.

26. I am indebted to my undergraduate student Monica Hildebrand from my "Chicanas/os and the Law" class for suggesting this example.

27. John Steinbeck, *Tortilla Flat* (New York: Penguin Books, 1935), 144–153.

28. Megan Twohey, "Role Reversal Jolts Blacks, Hispanics," *National Journal,* April 14, 2001, 1122.

29. Stanley D. Miller, "Racial Stereotypes Proving Stubborn," *Akron Beacon*

Journal, Jan. 9, 1991, A8. This survey conducted by the National Opinion Center also revealed that 56 percent of Whites thought Hispanics were more likely than Whites to be lazy.

30. Thomas D. Elias, "California in a Frenzy of Immigrant-Bashing," *Rocky Mountain News,* July 2, 1993, A44.

31. Mark Z. Barabak, "GOP Bid to Mend Rift with Latinos," *Los Angeles Times,* Aug. 31, 1997, B8.

32. Anne Chen, "Latinas Lead the Nation in Entrepreneurs," *The Record* (Northern New Jersey), May 30, 1999, 5.

33. National Council of La Raza, statement of Raul Yzaguirre on the Hispanic Census Report, March 6, 2001.

34. Jerry Pacheco, "U.S. Firms Have False Perception of Mexico," *Albuquerque Journal,* May 8, 2000, 5.

35. "Siesta Gets Rude Awakening," March 17, 1999, at http://news.bbc.co.uk/hi/english/world/americas/newsid_298000/298349.stm (last visited Nov. 2002).

36. Steven A. Holmes, "Hispanic Births in U.S. Reach Record High," *New York Times,* Feb. 13, 1998, A12 (discussing findings in National Center for Health Statistics report "Births of Hispanic Origin," 1989–95).

37. "Bad News for Hispanic Girls," *USA Today,* April 20, 2001, A14.

38. Mary Jordan, "Fall in Births, and Maybe Migrants," *Washington Post,* Aug. 9, 2001, A1.

39. U.S. Department of Justice, "1997 National Longitudinal Survey of Youth," in *Minorities in the Juvenile Justice System* 5 (Washington, DC, Dec. 1999).

40. One scientist who codiscovered DNA recently suggested a highly dubious biological link between skin color and sex drive, thus providing a scientific basis for so-called Latin lovers. Michelle Locke, "Sex Theory Generates Some Heat," *Denver Post,* Nov. 25, 2000, A1.

41. See generally Joel E. Cohen, *How Many People Can the Earth Support* (New York: W. W. Norton & Co., 1995), 287–291; Laura M. Padilla, "Latinas and Religion: Subordination or State of Grace?" *University of California at Davis Law Review* 33 (2000): 973.

42. "Bad News for Hispanic Girls."

43. Paul Harrison, *The Third Revolution: Environment, Population and a Sustainable World* (New York: I. B. Tauris & Co., 1992).

44. Jordan, "Fall in Births."

45. Michael A. Fletcher, "Latinos See Bias in Elgin's Fight against Blight," *Washington Post,* May 29, 2000, A1.

46. Karina Bland, "Hispanic Stereotype Shot Down," *Arizona Republic,* Jan. 16, 1999, A1.

47. Peter Brimelow, *Alien Nation: Common Sense about America's Immigration Disaster* (New York: Random House, 1995), 287–288.

48. David Cole, "Five Myths about Immigration," *The Nation,* Oct. 17, 1994, 410.

49. Wayne A. Cornelius, *The Future of Mexican Immigrants in California: A New Perspective for Public Policy* (La Jolla: University of California, San Diego Press, 1981), 47.

50. Juan Gonzalez, *Harvest of Empire: A History of Latinos in America* (New York: Penguin Group, 2000), 198.

51. Raymond Tatalovich, "Official English as Nativist Backlash," in *Immigrants Out! The New Nativism and the Anti-Immigrant Impulse in the United States,* ed. Juan F. Perea (New York: New York University Press, 1997), 78, 94.

52. The invalidation of Proposition 187 by the courts is discussed *infra.*

53. Laura M. Padilla, "'But You're Not a Dirty Mexican': Internalized Oppression, Latinos and Law," *Texas Hispanic Journal of Law and Policy* 7 (2001): 59, 79.

54. See also Ruben J. Garcia, Comment, "Critical Race Theory and Proposition 187: The Racial Politics of Immigration Law," *Chicano-Latino Law Review* 17 (1995): 118 (suggesting further that Proposition 187 stemmed from assimilationism).

55. Richard Delgado and Jean Stefancic, "California's Racial History and Constitutional Rationales for Race-Conscious Decision Making in Higher Education," *UCLA Law Review* 47 (2000): 1521, 1555.

56. Barbara Coe, "Keep Illegals Out of State," *USA Today,* Oct. 12, 1994, 12A (op-ed).

57. Pamela J. Podger and Michael Doyle, "War of Worlds," *Fresno Bee,* Jan. 9, 1994, A1 (remarks of Barbara Coe).

58. Kevin R. Johnson, "An Essay on Immigration Politics, Popular Democracy, and California's Proposition 187: The Political Relevance and Legal Irrelevance of Race," *Washington Law Review* 70 (1995): 629, 656.

59. Ibid., 652.

60. "Agreement Neutralizes Referendum," *Beacon Journal,* July 29, 1999, A6. Applying constitutional principles of supremacy, a federal district court judge in California had concluded in 1995 that many of Proposition 187's provisions were preempted by federal law. *League of United Latin American Citizens v. Wilson,* 908 F.Supp. 755 (C.D. Cal. 1995). Although the judge invalidated the provisions of Proposition 187 that governed classification of persons as "illegal aliens" and required notification of federal authorities, the judge left intact its provisions denying benefits. The judge did invalidate Proposition 187's refusal to educate undocumented immigrants, finding its denial inconsistent with the Supreme Court's decision in *Plyler v. Doe* (457 U.S. 202 (1982), which had applied the equal protection clause to prohibit states from excluding undocumented immigrant children from their public schools. Later, in 1997, following the federal government's enactment of the Personal Responsibility and Work Opportunity

Reconciliation Act of 1996, which barred undocumented immigrants from federal services such as immunizations, school lunch programs, and housing assistance, the California federal judge ruled that the benefit-denial provisions of Proposition 187 were meant to be preempted by Congress. *League of United Latin American Citizens v. Wilson,* 997 F.Supp. 1244 (C.D. Cal. 1997). Only the ancillary provisions of Proposition 187 addressing manufacture and use of false documents survived invalidation.

61. Nancy Cervantes, Sasha Khokha, and Bobbie Murray, "Hate Unleashed: Los Angeles in the Aftermath of Proposition 187," *Chicano-Latino Law Review* 17 (1995): 1.

62. Ibid., 20.

63. *United States v. Wong Kim Ark,* 169 U.S. 649 (1898).

64. Haney López, *White by Law,* 41–42.

65. Robert Pear, "Citizenship Proposal Faces Obstacle in the Constitution," *New York Times,* Aug. 7, 1996, A13.

66. Randy Kull, "Hostile Welcome, Beauty Queen Held at Border," *Phoenix Gazette,* Aug. 10, 1995, A1.

67. Dorothy Roberts, *Killing the Black Body: Race, Reproduction, and the Meaning of Liberty* (New York: Random House, 1997), chap. 5.

68. Marie Ashe, "'Bad Mothers' and Welfare Reform in Massachusetts: The Case of Claribel Ventura," in *Feminism, Media, and the Law,* ed. Martha A. Fineman and Martha T. McCluskey (New York: Oxford University Press, 1997), 203.

69. Leo R. Chavez, *Covering Immigration: Popular Images and the Politics of the Nation* (Berkeley: University of California Press, 2001), 166.

70. Jane Kay, "Sierra Club Sidestep on Immigration," *San Francisco Examiner,* April 26, 1998, A1.

71. Christopher Martinez, "The Greening of Hate," *Boston Globe,* July 22, 2001, A8.

NOTES TO CHAPTER 6

1. Walter P. Jacob, Note, "Diversity Visas: Muddled Thinking and Pork Barrel Politics," *Georgetown Immigration Law Journal* 6 (1992): 297, 303.

2. Patrick J. Buchanan, *The Death of the West: How Dying Populations and Immigrant Invasions Imperil Our Country and Civilization* (New York: St. Martin's Press, 2002), 125–126.

3. See Michael A. Olivas, "Torching Zozobra: The Problem with Linda Chavez," *Reconstruction* 2 (1993): 48.

4. Mark Davis, "Nugent Makes Noise, and LULAC Makes More," *Fort-Worth Star Telegram,* April 19, 2000, 13.

5. Brimelow, *Alien Nation,* 218, 273.

6. Bender, "Will the Wolf Survive?" 724–725.

7. Brimelow, *Alien Nation,* 193–195.

8. Linda Chavez, *Out of the Barrio: Toward a New Politics of Hispanic Assimilation* (New York: Basic Books, 1991), 72–73.

9. Georgie Anne Geyer, *Americans No More* (New York: Atlantic Monthly Press, 1996), 143.

10. Carol Byrne, "Proposition 187's Uproar," *Star Tribune,* Oct. 20, 1994, A7.

11. "White Men Rule Corporate America," *St. Petersburg Times,* March 16, 1995, A1 (reporting results of study of corporate executive opinions by the Glass Ceiling Commission that reflected a perception of Hispanics as recently arrived in the United States, arrogant, and unwilling to learn English).

12. Joseph Nevins, *Operation Gatekeeper: The Rise of the "Illegal Alien" and the Making of the U.S.-Mexico Boundary* (New York: Routledge, 2002), 105.

13. E.g., Timothy Christenfeld, "Wretched Refuse Is Just the Start," *New York Times,* March 10, 1996, §4, 4.

14. Ronald Schmidt Sr., *Language Policy and Identity Politics in the United States* (Philadelphia: Temple University Press, 2000), 78. A 1985 survey of Latina/o parents in Dade County, Florida, revealed that 98 percent agreed their children should "speak and write English perfectly." Sylvia R. Lazos Vargas, "Judicial Review of Initiatives and Referendums in Which Majorities Vote on Minorities' Democratic Citizenship," *Ohio State Law Journal* 60 (1999): 399, 444.

15. Roberto Suro, "Hispanic Pragmatism Seen in Survey," *New York Times,* Dec. 15, 1992, A20.

16. Antonio J. Califa, "Declaring English the Official Language: Prejudice Spoken Here," *Harvard Civil Rights and Civil Liberties Law Review* 24 (1989): 293, 312–317.

17. Carol Schmid, Comment, "Language Rights and the Legal Status of English-Only Laws in the Public and Private Sector," *North Carolina Central Law Journal* 20 (1992): 65, 71 (describing the 1988 Veltman study).

18. An Anglo practice that my mother's parents adopted for her was to abandon the Latina/o tradition of giving children a two-part surname that reflects the lineage of both parents. As one commentator observed, in the United States "cultural supremacy, bureaucratic laziness, racism, and simple ignorance combine to make it exceptionally difficult for the Latino, as a practical matter, to obtain recognition for both last names." Yvonne M. Cherena Pacheco, "Latino Surnames: Formal and Informal Forces in the United States Affecting the Retention and Use of the Maternal Surname," *Marshall Law Review* 18 (1992): 1.

19. Ariz. Const., Art XXVIII (invalidated as discussed in main text). In *Negron v. New York,* 434 F.2d 386 (2d Cir. 1970), the court held the federal constitutional right to confront adverse witnesses entitled the criminal defendant at state expense to the interpretation of witness testimony against him).

20. *Ruiz v. Hull,* 957 P.2d 984 (Ariz. 1998).

21. In early 2001, a district court judge upheld the Utah law against constitutional challenge, interpreting it as merely symbolic. "Official English Law Upheld," *Rocky Mountain News,* March 7, 2001, 7A.

22. *In re Initiative Petition No. 366,* 46 P.3d 123 (Okla. 2002).

23. Mike Allen, "Bush's Mexican Guest Worker Plan to Push English," *Washington Post,* Sept. 1, 2001, A8.

24. Chavez, *Out of the Barrio,* 9.

25. Schmidt, *Language Policy,* 80.

26. *Guadalupe Organization Inc. v. Tempe Elementary School Dist. No. 3,* 587 F.2d 1022 (9th Cir. 1978). The Supreme Court once construed the Civil Rights Act of 1964 to require a school district to establish an educational program for non-English-speaking students, here Chinese students. *Lau v. Nichols,* 414 U.S. 563 (1974). California responded to *Lau* by enacting bilingual education legislation, but the requisites of *Lau* perhaps could be satisfied by offering non-English-speaking children curricula designed to teach English.

27. *Valeria v. Wilson,* 12 F.Supp. 2d 1007 (N.D. Cal. 1998), aff'd; *Valeria v. Davis,* 307 F.3d 1036 (9th Cir. 2002).

28. Kevin R. Johnson and George A. Martínez, "Discrimination by Proxy: The Case of Proposition 227 and the Ban on Bilingual Education," *University of California at Davis Law Review* 33 (2000): 1227, 1268.

29. See Aviva Brandt, "Tavern Owner Sued over English-Only Policy," *Los Angeles Times,* Jan. 21, 1996, A24.

30. Steven W. Bender, "Direct Democracy and Distrust: The Relationship between Language Law Rhetoric and the Language Vigilantism Experience," *Harvard Latino Law Review* 2 (1997): 145 (detailing numerous other examples of private language vigilantism and explaining why the Washington tavern lawsuit was unsuccessful).

31. Ibid., 171–172.

32. "Condo Requires Speaking English," *St. Petersburg Times,* March 4, 1988, B2.

33. Bob Egelkoof, "Court Upholds Landlords' Right to Require Fluent English," *San Francisco Examiner,* Nov. 3, 2000, A5 (jury had found no discrimination in lawsuit in which landlords claimed their policy was to ensure communication in an emergency).

34. *Veles v. Lindow,* 243 F.3d 552 (9th Cir. 2000) (unpublished opinion).

35. See generally Christopher David Ruiz Cameron, "How the Garcia Cousins Lost Their Accents: Understanding the Language of Title VII Decisions Approving English-Only Rules as the Product of Racial Dualism, Latino Invisibility, and Legal Indeterminacy," *California Law Review* 85 (1997): 1347; Juan F. Perea, "English-Only Rules and the Right to Speak One's Primary Language in the Workplace," *University of Michigan Journal of Law Reform* 23 (1990): 265.

36. Bender, "Direct Democracy," 159–160.

37. E.g., Steven W. Bender, "Our Laws Should Encourage, Not Bar, Multilingualism," *Eugene Register Guard*, April 4, 1996, A13.

38. *Hernandez v. Erlenbusch*, 368 F.Supp. 752 (D. Ore. 1973) (finding no evidence that the tavern owners had reason to anticipate the ruckus would be caused by their language policy and refusing to hold them responsible for the battery).

39. Sam Verhovek, "Mother Scolded by Judge for Speaking in Spanish," *New York Times*, Aug. 30, 1995, A9.

40. Ibid.

41. Reyes and Rubie, *Hispanics in Hollywood*, 268 (providing this dialogue).

42. *Matter of Hammermaster*, 985 P.2d 924 (Wash. 1999) (*en banc*) (disciplining judge for singling out Latina/o defendants for inquiries into their citizenship, finding this conduct violated a judicial canon of conduct requiring courteous and dignified treatment of litigants by judges).

43. John Murphy, "Judge Orders Two Men to Learn English," *Philadelphia Inquirer*, Oct. 12, 1996, B2.

44. *Guerrero v. Carleson*, 109 Cal. Rptr. 201 (1973); see also *Carmona v. Sheffield*, 325 F.Supp. 1341 (N.D. Cal. 1971) (concluding that unemployment claimants possess no constitutional right to Spanish-language communications regarding unemployment insurance benefits), aff'd, 475 F.2d 738 (9th Cir. 1973); *Alfonso v. Board of Review*, 444 A.2d 1075 (N.J. 1982) (no right to translation of unemployment appeal rights into Spanish).

45. *Soberal-Perez v. Heckler*, 717 F.2d 36 (2d Cir. 1983).

46. *Frontera v. Sindell*, 522 F.2d 1215 (6th Cir. 1975).

47. *Soberal-Perez*, 717 F.2d at 42.

48. *Alexander v. Sandoval*, 532 U.S. 275 (2001).

49. Schmidt, *Language Policy*, 81.

50. Miss. H.B. 556 (1997).

51. *Alfonso v. Board of Review*, 444 A.2d 1075, 1085 (N.J. 1982) (Wilentz, C.J., dissenting).

52. Bill Ong Hing, *To Be an American: Cultural Pluralism and the Rhetoric of Assimilation* (New York: New York University Press, 1997), 21; Allison M. Dussias, "Waging War with Words: Native Americans' Continuing Struggle against the Suppression of Their Languages," *Ohio State Law Journal* 60 (1999): 901, 912.

53. Gilbert G. Gonzalez, *Chicano Education in the Era of Segregation* (Philadelphia: Balch Institute Press, 1990), 36.

54. Ibid., 43.

55. Ibid., 39, 44.

56. Ibid., 38.

57. Ibid., 45.

58. Margaret E. Montoya, "Law and Language(s): Image, Integration and In-novation," *La Raza Law Journal* 7 (1994): 147, 148.

59. Mel Melendez, "Molera Backs District on Its Spanish Ban," *Arizona Republic,* Aug. 20, 2002, B1.

60. Albert M. Camarillo, "Report Submitted on Behalf of the University of Michigan: The Compelling Need for Diversity in Higher Education," *Michigan Journal of Race and Law* 5 (1999): 339, 347.

61. "In Buchanan's Words," *Washington Post,* Feb. 29, 1992, A2.

62. *Chae Chan Ping v. United States,* 130 U.S. 581, 595 (1889).

63. Bender, "Direct Democracy," 166.

64. Scott Bowles, "Lawmaker Says Capitol Security Aide Used Ethnic Insult," *Washington Post,* April 18, 1996, B1.

65. Kathleen Monje, "Suit Accuses Tavern of Bias against Spanish-Speakers," *The Oregonian,* Oct. 12, 1990, D1 (describing lawsuit against an Oregon tavern with an English-only policy for customers).

66. Aviva Brandt, "English-Only Sign Sparks Furor," *Eugene Register-Guard,* Jan. 14, 1996, B6.

67. Aimee Green, "Yakima Tavern Owner Wins Case but Judge Ruled That English-Only Sign Is Insensitive," *Seattle Times,* Jan. 16, 1997, B3.

68. Charles W. Hall, "Ease Policy on English, Stores Told," *Washington Post,* March 5, 1995, B3.

69. 42 U.S.C. § 2000e-2.

70. Most English-only rule challenges are brought under a disparate impact theory because of the difficulty of establishing discriminatory intent under a disparate treatment theory. Mark Colon, Note, "Line Drawing, Code Switching, and Spanish as Second-Hand Smoke: English-Only Workplace Rules and Bilingual Employees," *Yale Law and Policy Review* 20 (2002): 227, 233–234.

71. Ann Davis, "English-Only Rules Spur Workers to Speak Legalese," *Wall Street Journal,* Jan. 23, 1997, B1; see also EEOC Compliance Manual, Dec. 2, 2002, at http://www.eeoc.gov/docs/national-origin.html#VB1 (last visited April 2003).

72. *Jurado v. Eleven-Fifty Corp.,* 813 F.2d 1406 (9th Cir. 1987) (upholding summary judgment against DJ who failed to produce sufficient evidence that station's English-only policy was racially motivated or that he was discharged on the basis of discriminatory employment criteria).

73. In Title VII disparate impact claims, the plaintiff must establish that the policy in question causes a discriminatory impact; once established, the employer must prove the challenged practice is consistent with a legitimate business necessity. Even if so proven, the plaintiff might still prevail by demonstrating a less discriminatory alternative exists. Most English-only workplace policy challenges run aground at the first stage of the disparate impact analysis. Particularly troubling is that some federal courts have taken the position that bilingual employees are

not affected by English-only rules, as they can simply switch their language as required. *Garcia v. Gloor,* 618 F.2d 264 (5th Cir. 1980). *Gloor* involved a challenge by a bilingual lumber-store employee who was fired for violating the employer's English-only policy when he responded in Spanish to a question in English from another Latino employee about an item a customer had requested. Although the EEOC, by administrative guideline, has determined that English-only rules have a per se discriminatory impact on language minorities, the Ninth Circuit Court of Appeals has refused to apply the guideline, forcing the plaintiff to establish disparate impact in order to compel the employer to come forward with a showing of a legitimate business purpose. *Garcia v. Spun Steak Co.,* 998 F.2d 1480 (9th Cir. 1993); Colon, "Line Drawing," 233–234.

74. Davis, "English-Only Rules."

75. Stuart Silverstein, "Decision Won't Speak to All Firms," *Los Angeles Times,* June 21, 1994, D2 (noting English-language policies are common at hospitals in urban areas with large immigrant populations); "Worker Fired for Speaking Spanish on Job," *Seattle Times,* Aug. 20, 2002, B2 (describing the discharge of a nursing assistant by a Washington nursing home for speaking Spanish).

76. Greg Jaffe, "Rumsfeld Closes Pentagon Office amid Concerns," *Wall Street Journal,* Feb. 27, 2002, A4 (attributing office closure to news reports contending the office was designed to spread disinformation, which Rumsfeld claimed were inaccurate).

77. Terry Frieden, "Justice Kennedy Offers Morals Program," Jan. 26, 2002, at http://www.cnn.com/2002/US/01/27/scotus.morals/index.html (last visited Nov. 2002).

78. Kim Murphy, "Olympic Hospitality an Irony for Utah Latinos," *Los Angeles Times,* Feb. 8, 2002, A1.

79. The Supreme Court has upheld the constitutionality of citizenship requirements for certain public employment positions. See *Cabell v. Chavez-Salido,* 454 U.S. 432 (1982) (upholding California statute requiring peace officers to be citizens against constitutional challenge by noncitizens refused employment as deputy probation officers); *Ambach v. Norwick,* 441 U.S. 68 (1979) (applying rational basis standard to uphold New York law forbidding certification as public schoolteachers of noncitizens who have not manifested an intent to apply for citizenship); *Foley v. Connelie,* 435 U.S. 291 (1978) (upholding New York law requiring citizenship for state police force against equal protection challenge).

80. "Poll Finds Whites Use Stereotypes," *New York Times,* Jan. 10, 1991, B10.

81. Gilbert Paul Carrasco, "Latinos in the United States: Invitation and Exile," in Perea, *Immigrants Out!* 196 (noting the irony that on returning home, Mexican American soldiers from World War II faced discrimination).

82. Reyes and Rubie, *Hispanics in Hollywood,* 20.

83. George Mariscal, ed., *Aztlán and Viet Nam: Chicano and Chicana Experiences of the War* (Berkeley: University of California Press, 1999), 1; see also Juan Ramirez, *A Patriot after All: The Story of a Chicano Vietnam Vet* (Albuquerque: University of New Mexico Press, 1999); Charley Trujillo, ed., *Soldados: Chicanos in Viet Nam* (San Jose, CA: Chusma House, 1990).

84. Richard Delgado and Vicky Palacios, "Mexican Americans as a Legally Cognizable Class under Rule 23 and the Equal Protection Clause," *Notre Dame Lawyer* 50 (1975): 393.

85. Mariscal, *Aztlán and Viet Nam*, 187–203.

86. "Shootings Examined as Possible Backlash," *Fort Worth Star-Telegram*, Sept. 17, 2001, 1.

87. Padilla, "Not a Dirty Mexican," 107.

88. Ed Morales, *Living in Spanglish: The Search for Latino Identity in America* (New York: St. Martin's Press, 2002), 81–82 (reprinting poem).

89. Padilla, "Not a Dirty Mexican," 107.

NOTES TO CHAPTER 7

1. Lothrop Stoddard, *Re-Forging America: The Story of Our Nationhood* (New York: C. Scribner's Sons, 1927), 214.

2. Miller, "Racial Stereotypes Proving Stubborn."

3. Enrique T. Trueba and Lilia I. Bartolomé, "The Education of Latino Students: Is School Reform Enough?" at http://eric-web.tc.columbia.edu/digests/dig123.html (last visited Nov. 2002).

4. See Hadley-Garcia, *Hispanic Hollywood*, 198.

5. Bill Dana, *José Jiménez Greatest Bits* (CD, 2001).

6. "How to Build a Boat," *The Real McCoys*, first aired Nov. 19, 1959.

7. My mother graduated from Garfield High School in the early 1950s, as did my stepfather Luis Acevedo earlier.

8. Acuña, *Anything but Mexican*, 82.

9. Bill Piatt, *Black and Brown in America: The Case for Cooperation* (New York: New York University Press, 1997), 102.

10. Episode 145, "Paris at Last," *I Love Lucy*, first aired Feb. 27, 1956.

11. Susan Ferriss and Ricardo Sandoval, *The Fight in the Fields: Cesar Chavez and the Farmworkers Movement* (New York: Harcourt Brace & Co., 1997), 26.

12. "Candidate Tenders Apology for Remarks about Spanish," *Eugene Register Guard*, June 30, 1996, 4C.

13. Sam Verhovek, "Mother Scolded by Judge for Speaking in Spanish," *New York Times*, Aug. 30, 1995, A9.

14. Gonzalez, *Chicano Education*, 62.

15. Richard J. Herrnstein and Charles A. Murray, *The Bell Curve: Intelligence and Class Structure in American Life* (New York: Free Press, 1994), 275.

16. Ibid., 360.

17. Ibid., 311. For Latinas/os, intelligence testing additionally implicates language barriers.

18. Natalie Angier, "Scientists: DNA Shows Humans Are All One Race," *Denver Post,* Aug. 22, 2000, A2.

19. National Council of La Raza, statement of Raul Yzaguirre on the Hispanic Census Report, Washington, DC, March 6, 2001. Breaking the numbers down further, only about 7 percent of Mexican Americans hold bachelor's degrees, while Cuban Americans exhibit a higher percentage of college education, with 25 percent holding degrees.

20. Ginorio and Huston, *¡Sí, Se Puede!* 1.

21. Dana Canedy, "Troubling Label for Hispanics: 'Girls Most Likely to Drop Out,'" *New York Times,* March 25, 2001, §1, 1.

22. Brian Weber, "Hispanic Dropout Rate Alarming," *Rocky Mountain News,* Feb. 3, 1998, A4.

23. Ibid.

24. Pamela J. Smith, "Looking beyond Traditional Educational Paradigms: When Old Victims Become New Victimizers," *Hamline Law Review* 23 (1999): 102, 151–152.

25. Ferriss and Sandoval, *Fight in the Fields,* 98.

26. Leti Volpp, "Blaming Culture for Bad Behavior," *Yale Journal of Law and the Humanities* 12 (2000): 89, 97.

27. Ginorio and Huston, *¡Sí, Se Puede!* 22.

28. "Survey Finds Hispanics Optimistic about Direction of the Country and Their Futures," April 22, 1998, at http://www.jsri.msu.edu/commconn/latnews/may98b.html#anchor132152 (last visited June 2000).

29. Ibid.

30. Michael A. Olivas, "Professor Graglia, Meet My Father," *Bilingual Review* 23 (May–Aug. 1998): 106–107.

31. Volpp, "Blaming Culture," 97.

32. Ginorio and Huston, *¡Sí, Se Puede!* 22. See also Margaret E. Montoya, "Silence and Silencing: Their Centripetal and Centrifugal Forces in Legal Communication, Pedagogy and Discourse," *Michigan Journal of Race and Law* 5 (2000): 847.

33. See Leslie G. Espinoza, "The LSAT: Narratives and Bias," *American University Journal of Gender and Law* 1 (1993): 121 (arguing that, despite recent efforts to make the Law School Admission Test [LSAT] more inclusive of diverse groups, the test perpetuates bias and disadvantages minority and female applicants to law schools).

34. Pamela J. Smith, "Our Children's Burden: The Many-Headed Hydra of the Educational Disenfranchisement of Black Children," *Howard Law Journal* 42 (1999): 133, 208.

35. An additional factor playing into the backlash against affirmative action is the public perception somehow that affirmative action programs were established for African Americans and women, and that Latinas/os, particularly when viewed as unceasingly arriving in the United States and as abundantly fertile, are crashing the affirmative action party that was never intended for them.

36. *Regents of Univ. of Cal. v. Bakke,* 438 U.S. 265 (1978). Ironically, the opinion of Justice Powell in *Bakke* contended that preference programs may reinforce stereotypes that certain groups are unable to be successful without special protection, a notion that some commentators of color have accepted, and which the Supreme Court revisited in *City of Richmond v. J. A. Croson Co.,* 488 U.S. 469, 493 (1989) (warning that minority government contract program could promote "notions of racial inferiority"). Under this stigmatization theory, employees and college graduates of color are regarded as having suspect credentials. My own view is that affirmative action programs are vital to overcome bias and institutional advantage in the educational system, and any stigma can be addressed by publicizing the existence of more pervasive implicit affirmative action programs that favor Anglos, including legacy admissions in higher education that benefit applicants with family members who attended the same school.

37. Later, the Supreme Court definitively adopted this strict scrutiny standard to review all race-based action by state or local government. *Richmond v. J. A. Croson Co.,* 488 U.S. 469 (1989) (reviewing quota system ensuring 30 percent of municipal contracting work was awarded to minority-owned businesses).

38. The Supreme Court is reviewing the Sixth Circuit's decision in *Grutter v. Bollinger,* 288 F.3d 732 (6th Cir. 2002), which found the admissions policy of the University of Michigan Law School was narrowly tailored to fulfill the compelling interest of diversity. (The Supreme Court also heard arguments in the related case of *Gratz v. Bollinger* challenging the Michigan undergraduate admissions program.) Previously, the Fifth Circuit had rejected Powell's opinion in *Bakke* and refused to treat the goal of a diverse student body as justifying a racial/ethnic classification at the University of Texas School of Law. *Hopwood v. State of Texas,* 78 F.3d 932 (5th Cir. 1996). After the decision in *Hopwood,* Texas adopted a plan awarding admission to its flagship undergraduate campuses to students graduating in the top 10 percent of their high school class, regardless of their SAT scores. See generally Lani Guinier and Gerald Torres, *The Miner's Canary: Enlisting Race, Resisting Power, Transforming Democracy* (Cambridge, MA: Harvard University Press, 2002), 72. The Texas program, similar to policies in California and Florida, as of 2001 had failed to restore the level of Blacks and Latinas/os at the University of Texas before the 1996 *Hopwood* decision. Separate from the diversity rationale, the Supreme Court has recognized the potential to uphold racial classifications as necessary to remedy past discrimination. So far, this justification has not proven decisive in upholding affirmative action programs in higher education.

39. "Elections '96 State Propositions: A Snapshot of Voters," *Los Angeles Times,* Nov. 7, 1996, A29.

40. William C. Kidder, *Affirmative Action in Higher Education: Recent Developments in Litigation, Admissions and Diversity Research,* San Francisco, Jan. 3, 2001 (report prepared for Society of American Law Teachers).

41. *Coalition for Economic Equality v. Wilson,* 122 F.3d 692, 709 (9th Cir. 1997).

42. Kidder, *Affirmative Action,* 19.

43. Ibid.

44. Gonzalez, *Chicano Education,* 256. See also Ediberto Román, "Empire Forgotten: The United States's Colonization of Puerto Rico," *Villanova Law Review* 42 (1997): 1119, 1149 (suggesting one reason for the obsessive interest of the United States in Puerto Rico is its strategic military location).

45. Reginald Horsman, "Anglo-Saxons and Mexicans," in *The Latino/a Condition: A Critical Reader,* ed. Richard Delgado and Jean Stefancic (New York: New York University Press, 1998), 149, 150.

NOTES TO CHAPTER 8

1. Rodolfo Acuña, *Occupied America: A History of Chicanos,* 3d ed. (New York: HarperCollins, 1988), 201 (statement contained in a report prepared for congressional hearings held in 1930 by the House Committee on Immigration and Naturalization on a proposed bill to virtually eliminate immigration from Mexico).

2. Salwen and Soruco, "Hispanic Americans," 161.

3. Mario T. García, "Americanization and the Mexican Immigrant, 1880–1930," in *From Different Shores: Perspectives on Race and Ethnicity in America,* ed. Ronald T. Takaki (New York: Oxford University Press, 1987), 73.

4. De León, *They Called Them Greasers,* 21.

5. Ellis, *Americanization through Homemaking,* 64.

6. Ibid., 14, 47.

7. Christopher Arriola, Comment, "Knocking on the Schoolhouse Door: *Mendez v. Westminster*: Equal Protection, Public Education and Mexican Americans in the 1940s," *La Raza Law Journal* 8 (1995): 166, 177.

8. Gladys Hawkins, Jean Soper, and Jane Henry, *Your Maid from Mexico* (San Antonio: Naylor, 1959), 3; see also Mary Romero, *Maid in the U.S.A.* (New York: Routledge, 1992).

9. Octavio Emilio Nuiry, "Ban the Bandito!" *Hispanic,* July 1996, 26.

10. Report of Political Ecology Group, "Exposing the Greening of Hate, Wooing the Sierra Club: Anti-Immigration Groups Make Unlikely Suitors," available at http://www.igc.apc.org/peg/imm_env/expose.html (last visited Aug. 2001).

11. *Haddad v. Gonzalez,* 576 N.E.2d 658 (Mass. 1991) (landlord who rented

"deplorable" apartment to Latina had suggested that if tenant were cold, he would "come over at night and give her heat" himself; when the tenant asserted counterclaims in the landlord's eviction action, he threatened to report her non-payment of rent to welfare officials in order to cause the termination of her benefits, and he threatened to have her sent back to Puerto Rico).

12. Gonzalez, *Harvest of Empire*, 237.

13. Chideya, *Don't Believe the Hype*, 217.

14. Paul Rogers, "Latinos Take Lead on Environmental Issues," *San Jose Mercury News*, March 11, 2002, A1.

15. Frank Norris, *The Octopus* (New York: Grosset & Dunlap, 1901), 502.

16. Raul Canizares, *Cuban Santeria: Walking with the Night* (Rochester, VT: Destiny Books, 1999), 87.

17. Robert McFadden, "Ritual Slaughter Halted in Bronx by Police Raid," *New York Times*, May 24, 1980, §27, 1.

18. *Church of the Lukumi Babalu Aye, Inc. v. City of Hialeah*, 508 U.S. 520 (1993).

19. Canizares, *Cuban Santeria*, 86.

20. Ray Delgado, "'Bumfights' Makes Gladiators of Homeless," *San Francisco Chronicle*, June 25, 2002, A1.

21. Oklahoma banned cockfighting in 2002.

22. One Latino president of a Florida chapter of the League of Latin American Citizens (LULAC) called for a national boycott of Taco Bell over its use of Dinky.

23. At http://www.publicoffender.com/JOKEMEX.htm (last visited Aug. 2000).

24. Salwen and Soruco, "Hispanic Americans," 161.

25. Nevins, *Operation Gatekeeper*.

26. Andreas, *Border Games*, 89.

27. Nevins, *Operation Gatekeeper*, 4.

28. "SRE Denounces U.S. Border Vigilantes," *The News* (Mexico City), March 22, 2000.

29. Karl Eschbach, Jacqueline Hagan, and Nestor Rodriguez, *Causes and Trends in Migrant Deaths along the U.S.-Mexico Border 1985–1998* (Houston: University of Houston, Center for Immigration Research, 2001).

30. Tom Zeller, "Migrants Take Their Chances on a Harsh Path of Hope," *New York Times*, March 18, 2001, §4, 14.

31. Lisa Richardson and Patrick McDonnell, "Immigration Crackdown Ineffective, Study Finds," *Los Angeles Times*, July 17, 2002, B8.

32. Pauline Arrillaga and Giovanna Dell'orto, "Quest for Better Life Brings Slow Death," *The Oregonian*, May 27, 2001, A13.

33. "Fifteen Migrants Die in Five Days along the Arizona Border," June 12, 2002, available at http://frontera.nmsu.edu (last visited Nov. 2002).

34. Mark Shaffer, "Six from Mexico Drown in Ditch," *Arizona Republic,* Aug. 7, 1997, A1 (reporting at that time six victims had been found; ultimately eight were claimed).

35. Valerie Alvord, "Toxic River Becomes Path to USA," *USA Today,* May 11, 2000, A1.

36. Ben Fox, "Migrants Reach Nameless End," *Chicago Tribune,* May 29, 2001, N8.

37. "Holy Week and the 'Unidentified' Migrants," e-mail from U.S. Mexico Border Program, April 9, 2001 (on file with author).

38. E.g., Ken Ellingwood, "Four Indicted in Deaths of Smuggled Migrants," *Los Angeles Times,* April 15, 1999, A3 (discussing criminal charges brought against the coyotes who were guiding the migrants into California).

39. Ken Ellingwood, "Three Suspected Illegal Immigrants Die," *Los Angeles Times,* March 7, 2000, A3.

40. Ibid.

41. William Booth, "Seven Illegal Migrants Die in Snowstorm," *Washington Post,* April 3, 1999, A3.

42. Steve Shoup, "Four Crash Survivors Queried," *Albuquerque Journal,* Dec. 7, 1999, A1.

43. Tony Perry and Lisa Richardson, "Deaths of Six Reignite Border Debate," *Los Angeles Times,* June 26, 2002, A1.

44. Richard Boudreaux, "Father's Modest Dream Leads to Tragic Journey," *Los Angeles Times,* Oct. 23, 2002, A1.

45. Rubén Martínez, *Crossing Over: A Mexican Family on the Migrant Trail* (New York: Henry Holt and Co., 2001), 4–7.

46. Ibid., 37. One of the mothers of the dead filed a lawsuit against the Border Patrol, claiming negligence in its high-speed chase. The case was settled for $7,000 for each of her dead sons. Ibid., 71, 328.

47. Abigail Goldman, Eric Malnic, and Henry Weinstein, "Taped Beating Stirs Debate: Truck Occupants Share Blame?" *Seattle Times,* April 3, 1996, A1. (Early newspaper accounts reported the victim's name as Leticia Gonzalez.)

48. Ken Hamblin, "Future Illegals Hear Sound of Money as Nightsticks Flail," *Arizona Republic,* April 14, 1996, H5.

49. Nevins, *Operation Gatekeeper,* 128.

50. Zeller, "Migrants Take Their Chances."

51. Geyer, *Americans No More,* 75.

52. Kevin R. Johnson, "Some Thoughts on the Future of Latino Legal Scholarship," *Harvard Latino Law Review* 2 (1997): 101.

53. Nevins, *Operation Gatekeeper,* 88–89.

54. "Evolving Perceptions, Time/CNN Poll," *Time,* June 11, 2001, 46–47.

55. De León, *They Called Them Greasers.*

56. Leonard Pitt, *The Decline of the Californios: A Social History of the*

Spanish-Speaking Californians, 1846–1890 (Berkeley: University of California Press, 1966), 70.

57. Ibid., 71.

58. *Marlar v. State of Arizona,* 666 P.2d 504 (Ariz. Ct. App. 1983).

59. William Claiborne, "'Airport Posse' Takes San Diego Border Control into Its Own Hands," *Washington Post,* May 23, 1996, A3.

60. Tony Perry, "Citizens on the Lookout for Illegal Migrants," *Los Angeles Times,* May 19, 1996, A3; Vincent J. Schodolski, "'Citizens Patrol' Angers Hispanics in San Diego," *Chicago Tribune,* May 26, 1996, C4.

61. E.g., William Branigin, "Violence, Tensions Increasing along the U.S.-Mexican Border," *Washington Post,* June 25, 1990, A16.

62. Tim McGirk Douglas, "Border Clash," *Time,* June 26, 2000, 24.

63. Mirandé, *Gringo Justice,* 137.

64. See generally Rodolfo F. Acuña, "Murder in Arizona . . . It's Only the Third World," at http://www.aztlan.net/acuna4.htm (last visited Nov. 2002).

65. Douglas, "Border Clash."

66. Acuña, "Murder in Arizona."

67. Patrisia Gonzales and Roberto Rodriguez, "$4000: The Price of a Mexican," Aug. 31, 2001, available at http://www.uexpress.com (Column of the Americas, last visited Sept. 2001).

68. "Mexico Blasts Light Sentence for Rancher Who Killed Mexican," *Global News Wire,* Aug. 25, 2001.

69. "Volunteers Plan Armed Border Patrols," *Houston Chronicle,* Nov. 30, 2000, A37. In May 2003, a group of assaulted migrants sued the Ranch Rescue organization and its leader for damages.

70. Gonzalez, *Harvest of Empire,* xii; "Man Charged in Killing of Boy at Border," *San Jose Mercury News,* Dec. 14, 1990, G4.

71. Emi Endo, Valerie Burgher, and Michael Rothfeld, "Lawmaker Apologizes for Remark," *Newsday* (Queens edition), Aug. 31, 2001, A18 (reporting that Suffolk County Republican legislator Michael D'Andre had apologized).

72. E.g., Andrew Smith, "Twenty-five Years for Attack," *Newsday,* Jan. 10, 2002, A3.

73. Lisa Fernandez, "Latino Groups Receive Hate Mail," *San Jose Mercury News,* March 13, 2002, B1.

74. The Sacramento office of the Mexican American Legal Defense and Educational Fund (MALDEF) provided me with a copy of this letter, which is signed by Vashudey Chauhan, an apparent forgery of a signature of someone who is not a suspect.

75. Acuña, *Anything but Mexican,* 124.

76. Carrasco, "Latinos in the United States."

77. Ibid.

78. Gutiérrez, *Walls and Mirrors,* 72.

79. Carrasco, "Latinos in the United States," 194.

80. Andreas, *Border Games,* 109; Nevins, *Operation Gatekeeper,* 128–129.

81. Report from the National INS Raids Task Force of the National Network for Immigrant and Refugee Rights, *Portrait of Injustice: The Impact of Immigration Raids on Families, Workers, and Communities* (Oct. 1998).

82. *Montero v. INS,* 124 F.3d 381 (2d Cir. 1997).

83. *Hoffman Plastic Compounds, Inc. v. NLRB,* 122 S.Ct. 1275 (2002).

84. Bob Egelko, "Court Rules for Firm in Illegal Worker's Firing," *San Francisco Chronicle,* March 28, 2002, A3.

85. *Jurado v. Popejoy Construction Co.,* 853 P.2d 669 (Kan. 1993).

86. *Martinez v. Industrial Commission of Utah,* 720 P.2d 416 (Utah 1986).

87. Eric Schlosser, *Fast Food Nation: The Dark Side of the All-American Meal* (New York: Houghton Mifflin Co., 2001), 169–190.

88. Steven Greenhouse, "Hispanic Workers Die at Higher Rate," *New York Times,* July 16, 2001, A11.

89. Margaret Reeves, Kristin Schafer, Kate Hallward, and Anne Katten, *Fields of Poison: California Farmworkers and Pesticides* (San Francisco: Pesticide Action Network, 1999), 10.

90. Amy Ellis, "Plan Takes Word on Pesticides to Fields in Pasco," *St. Petersburg Times,* Nov. 4, 1999, 6; "Did Pesticides Kill Jose Antonio Casillas?" Washington Newsline, July 1988, available at http://www.afop.org/newsletter/98_07/pesticide.html (last visited Aug. 2001).

91. Reeves et al., *Fields of Poison,* 23.

92. Ellis, "Plan Takes Word on Pesticides."

93. Ibid.

94. Lisa Richardson, "Laughter, Tears in El Centro," *Los Angeles Times,* June 29, 2002, A1.

95. Alicia Bugarin and Elias Lopez, *Farmworkers in California* (Sacramento: California Research Bureau, July 1998), 25.

96. Gonzalez, *Harvest of Empire,* 237–238.

97. *Carmona v. Division of Industrial Safety,* 118 Cal. Rptr. 473 (1975).

98. Ferriss and Sandoval, *Fight in the Fields,* 206–207.

99. Bugarin and Lopez, *Farmworkers in California,* 1.

100. Ibid. Nationally, Latina/o farmers represent less than 2 percent of farm owners. See Guadalupe T. Luna, "'Agricultural Underdogs' and International Agreements: The Legal Context of Agricultural Workers within the Rural Economy," *New Mexico Law Review* 26 (1996): 9.

101. See Luna, "'Agricultural Underdogs,'" 9, 26.

102. Reeves et al., *Fields of Poison,* 11; Andrew Scott Kosegi, Note, "The H-2A Program: How the Weight of Agricultural Employer Subsidies Is Breaking the Backs of Domestic Migrant Farm Workers," *Indiana Law Review* 35 (2001): 269.

103. Ferriss and Sandoval, *Fight in the Fields,* 208.

104. Bugarin and Lopez, *Farmworkers in California,* 23.

105. Ibid., 24.

106. Jorge Casuso, "Migrants Suffer in Fetid Camps," *Chicago Tribune,* Sept. 15, 1991, C3.

107. Ibid.

108. "Sweatshops in the Fields," available at http://www.pcun.org/ (last visited Nov. 2002).

109. Carla Marinucci, "Treated like an Animal for Years," *San Francisco Examiner,* Sept. 26, 1993, B1.

110. Steven Greenhouse, "As Economy Booms, Migrant Workers' Housing Worsens," *New York Times,* May 31, 1998, §1, 1.

111. Daniel Rothenberg, *With These Hands: The Hidden World of Migrant Farmworkers Today* (New York: Harcourt Brace & Co., 1998), 243.

112. Jane E. Larson, "Free Markets Deep in the Heart of Texas," *Georgetown Law Journal* 84 (1995): 179, 191.

113. Ibid., 222.

114. See Mitchel Cohen, "Beware the Violence Initiative Project," April 2000, at http://web.greens.org/s-r/19/19-07.html (last visited Nov. 2002); Haider Rizvi, "An Unscientific Method?" *Village Voice,* April 5, 2000, at http://www.villagevoice.com/issues/0014/rizvi.php (last visited Nov. 2002). The legislation does not appear to have been adopted.

115. Judith A. M. Scully, "Maternal Mortality, Population Control, and the War in Women's Wombs: A Bioethical Analysis of Quinacrine Sterilizations," *Wisconsin International Law Journal* 19 (2001): 103, 114.

116. Churchill, *Little Matter of Genocide,* 249, 376–377.

117. Roberts, *Killing the Black Body,* 90–95.

118. Morales, *Living in Spanglish,* 262.

119. Telarquia refers to premature sexual development, which has been linked to the presence of the chemical substance phthalates.

120. Melanie Feliciano, "A Different Sort of 'Terrorism' on Vieques," *San Francisco Chronicle,* April 8, 2002, B11.

121. Luke W. Cole and Sheila R. Foster, *From the Ground Up: Environmental Racism and the Rise of the Environmental Justice Movement* (New York: New York University Press, 2001), 55.

122. Ibid.

123. Chavez, *Out of the Barrio,* 80.

124. E.g., Evan P. Schultz, "Group Rights, American Jews, and the Failure of Group Libel Laws, 1913–1952," *Brooklyn Law Review* 66 (2000): 71, 90.

125. Rachel F. Moran, "What if Latinos Really Mattered in the Public Policy Debate?" *California Law Review* 85 (1997): 1315, 1322–1323.

126. Menchaca, *Recovering History, Constructing Race,* 287.

127. Ferriss and Sandoval, *Fight in the Fields,* 34.

128. Marco Portales, *Crowding Out Latinos: Mexican Americans in the Public Consciousness* (Philadelphia: Temple University Press, 2000), 11; see also Alonso S. Perales, *Are We Good Neighbors?* (New York: Arno Press, 1974).

129. *Hernandez v. Texas,* 347 U.S. 475, 479–480 (1954).

130. In 1944, a federal court judge in California had enjoined the operators of a public swimming pool and park in San Bernardino from continuing to exclude Mexicans and those of Latin descent from the facilities. *Lopez v. Seccombe,* 71 F.Supp. 769 (S.D. Cal. 1944).

131. Arriola, "Knocking at the Schoolhouse Door," 166, 171.

132. Reyes and Rubie, *Hispanics in Hollywood,* 236.

133. Ferriss and Sandoval, *Fight in the Fields,* 29–30.

134. Ibid., 35.

135. Carrasco, "Latinos in the United States," 196.

136. *Westminster School Dist. of Orange County v. Mendez,* 161 F.2d 774, 782 (9th Cir. 1947) (concurring opinion, J. Denman); *Lopez v. Seccombe,* 71 F.Supp. 769 (S.D. Cal. 1944) (enjoining mayor and others from excluding Latinas/os from swimming pool). Italian Americans are not generally regarded today as Hispanics or Latinas/os.

137. Arriola, "Knocking at the Schoolhouse Door," 174; Jorge C. Rangel and Carlos M. Alcala, "Project Report: De Jure Segregation of Chicanos in Texas Schools," *Harvard Civil Rights–Civil Liberties Law Review* 7 (1972): 307, 360.

138. Gonzalez, *Chicano Education,* 25.

139. Ibid.

140. *Soria v. Oxnard School District Board of Trustees,* 386 F.Supp. 539, 541 (C.D. Cal. 1974).

141. *United States v. Texas Education Agency,* 532 F.2d 380, 387 (5th Cir.), vacated, 429 U.S. 990 (1976), appeal after remand, 564 F.2d 162 (5th Cir. 1977).

142. *United States v. Texas Education Agency,* 564 F.2d 162, 163 (5th Cir. 1977).

143. *Gonzales v. Sheely,* 96 F.Supp. 1004, 1006 (D. Ariz. 1951).

144. Arriola, "Knocking at the Schoolhouse Door," 182; Margaret E. Montoya, "A Brief History of Chicana/o School Segregation: One Rationale for Affirmative Action," *La Raza Law Journal* 12 (2001): 159.

145. *Westminster School Dist. of Orange County v. Mendez,* 161 F.2d 774 (9th Cir. 1947).

146. *Plessy v. Ferguson,* 163 U.S. 537 (1896).

147. *Missouri ex rel. Gaines v. Canada,* 305 U.S. 337 (1938).

148. *Sipuel v. Board of Regents of the University of Oklahoma,* 332 U.S. 631 (1948).

149. Roy L. Brooks, Gilbert Paul Carrasco, and Michael Selmi, *Civil Rights Litigation: Cases and Perspectives,* 2d. ed. (Durham, NC: Carolina Academic Press, 2000), 59–60.

150. *Fisher v. Hurst,* 333 U.S. 147 (1948).

151. Brooks et al., *Civil Rights Litigation,* 60.

152. *Sweatt v. Painter,* 339 U.S. 629 (1950).

153. *Brown v. Board of Education of Topeka,* 347 U.S. 483, 494–495 (1954).

154. Brooks et al., *Civil Rights Litigation,* 30.

155. See Christopher Ramos, "The Educational Legacy of Racially Restrictive Covenants: Their Long Term Impact on Mexican Americans," *St. Mary's Law Review on Minority Issues* 4 (2001): 149.

156. Derrick Bell, *Race, Racism and American Law,* 4th ed. (Gaithersburg, NY: Aspen Law & Business, 2000), 180–181. See also *Milliken v. Bradley,* 418 U.S. 717 (1974) (lower court erred in forcing suburban school districts to participate in desegregation of urban school without a finding that suburban schools participated in segregation).

157. *San Antonio School District v. Rodriguez,* 411 U.S. 1 (1973) (applying the relaxed rational basis standard rather than strict scrutiny because education was not a fundamental right, nor did a distinction based on wealth implicate a suspect class); Bell, *Race, Racism and American Law,* 216–217 (noting that some school finance schemes have been challenged successfully under state constitutional provisions).

158. *Hernandez v. Texas,* 347 U.S. 475 (1954); *Keyes v. School District No. 1, Denver, Colorado,* 413 U.S. 189 (1973).

159. *Diaz v. San Jose Unified School District,* 733 F.2d 660 (9th Cir. 1984).

160. Darryl Fears, "Schools' Racial Isolation Growing," *Washington Post,* July 18, 2001, A3; see Melissa Roderick, "Hispanics and Education," in Cafferty and Engstrom, eds., *Hispanics in the United States,* 123 (detailing harmful consequences of segregated schools for Latinas/os).

161. *Terrell Wells Swimming Pool v. Rodriguez,* 182 S.W.2d 824 (Tex. Ct. Civ. App. 1944).

162. 42 U.S.C. § 2000a.

163. Bender, "Direct Democracy," 151.

164. *Veles v. Lindow,* 243 F.3d 552 (9th Cir. 2000) (unpublished opinion).

165. Bender, "Direct Democracy," 171–172.

166. Sarah J. Mahler, *Salvadorans in Suburbia: Symbiosis and Conflict* (Boston: Allyn and Bacon, 1995), 85.

167. Steven W. Bender, "Consumer Protection for Latinos: Overcoming Language Fraud and English-Only in the Marketplace," *American University Law Review* 45 (1996): 1027.

168. *Gonzales v. Sheely,* 96 F.Supp. 1004, 1007 (D. Ariz. 1951).

169. *Brown v. Board of Education of Topeka*, 347 U.S. 483, 494 (1954).
170. Johnson and Martínez, "Discrimination by Proxy," 1268.
171. *Diaz v. San Jose Unified School District*, 733 F.2d 660 (9th Cir. 1984).
172. *McLaughlin v. State Board of Education*, 89 Cal. Rptr. 2d 295 (Ct. App. 1999).
173. *United States v. Texas*, 498 F.Supp. 1356, 1362 (E.D. Tex. 1980) (from stipulated facts).
174. Ibid.

NOTES TO CHAPTER 9

1. Thanks to my friend and colleague Garrett Epps for this one.
2. Francisco X. Alarcón, Letter to America, in *From the Other Side of Night/ Del otro lado de la noche* (Tucson: University of Arizona Press, 2002), 51.
3. Pedro A. Malavet, "The Accidental Crit II: Culture and the Looking Glass of Exile," *Denver University Law Review* 78 (2001): 753 (footnotes and italics omitted).
4. Yolanda Flores Niemann, Andrea J. Romero, Jorge Arredondo, and Victor Rodriguez, "What Does It Mean to Be 'Mexican'? Social Construction of an Ethnic Identity," *Hispanic Journal of Behavioral Sciences* 21, 1 (Feb. 1999): 47, 52.
5. Ilan Stavans and Lalo Alcaraz, *Latino USA: A Cartoon History* (New York: Basic Books, 2000), 74.
6. Alfredo Véa Jr., *La Maravilla* (New York: Plume, 1993), 35.
7. Julia Alvarez, *How the García Girls Lost Their Accents* (New York: Penguin Group, 1991), 171.
8. Gutiérrez, *Walls and Mirrors*, 73.
9. William Claiborne, "'Airport Posse' Takes San Diego Border Patrol into Its Own Hands," *Washington Post*, May 23, 1996, A3.
10. Yamamoto, "Critical Race Praxis," 851.
11. Piatt, *Black and Brown*, 154.
12. Ozomatli, *Chota* (1998).
13. Oscar Zeta Acosta, *The Revolt of the Cockroach People* (New York: Vintage Book, 1989), 67.
14. Miguel Piñero, *Short Eyes* (New York: Hill and Wang, 1975), 16.
15. Matthiessen, *Sal Si Puedes*, 91.
16. Villarreal, "Culture in Lawmaking," 1214.
17. Mirandé, *Gringo Justice*, 17.
18. Stephanie M. Wildman, with Margalynne Armstrong, Adrienne D. Davis, and Trina Grillo, *Privilege Revealed: How Invisible Preference Undermines America* (New York: New York University Press, 1996).
19. Espinoza, "The LSAT."

NOTES TO CHAPTER 10

1. This sentiment may be found in the observation of some researchers of backlash, or the perception of backlash, against students of color performing well in school, who may be seen negatively by other students of color as "acting White." Lee Jussim and Christopher Fleming, "Self-Fulfilling Prophecies and the Maintenance of Social Stereotypes: The Role of Dyadic Interactions and Social Forces," in Macrae et al., eds., *Stereotypes and Stereotyping*, 161, 186.

2. Internalization of negative media images is addressed in Chapter 1.

3. Padilla, "Not a Dirty Mexican," 104.

4. Kevin R. Johnson, "Immigration and Latino Identity," *Chicano-Latino Law Review* 19 (1998): 197, 203.

5. Ibid.

6. Padilla, "Not a Dirty Mexican," 62–63.

7. Ibid. (remarks of University of Illinois political science professor Louis DeSipio).

8. Johnson, "Immigration and Latino Identity," 204–205.

9. Although she would call the Border Patrol when immigrants ran across her property fronting a border river, Cruz ultimately came to the aid of a young immigrant woman who broke her leg crossing the river. Through flashbacks, it was revealed that Cruz, too, had crossed the river as an immigrant many years before. See generally Elvia R. Arriola, "LatCrit Theory, International Human Rights, Popular Culture, and the Faces of Despair in INS Raids," *University of Miami Inter-American Law Review* 28 (1997): 245; Margaret E. Montoya, "Lines of Demarcation in a Town Called Frontera: A Review of John Sayles' Movie *Lone Star*," *New Mexico Law Review* 27 (1997): 223.

10. Johnson, "Immigration and Latino Identity," 201.

11. Padilla, "Not a Dirty Mexican," 90.

12. Joge and Pérez, *Mainstreaming of Hate*, 29.

13. Roberto Sanchez, "Hispanic Rift—Chicanos vs. Mexican-Born Hatred Splits Groups," *Phoenix Gazette*, Dec. 26, 1994, A1.

14. Cecilia Chan, "Teen's Death Sparks Action Plan," *Los Angeles Daily News*, May 2, 2000, T1.

15. "Guilty Plea Entered in Deaf-Mexicans Case," *San Jose Mercury News*, Dec. 19, 1997, A18.

16. Piatt, *Black and Brown*, 9 (providing statistics of 49 percent of Blacks, 51 percent of Hispanics for the propositions stated).

17. Ibid., 57.

18. Armando Navarro, "The South Central Los Angeles Eruption: A Latino Perspective," in *Los Angeles—Struggles toward Multiethnic Community*, ed. Edward T. Chang and Russell C. Leong (Seattle: University of Washington Press, 1994), 69, 70–71.

19. Sebastian Geraci, Comment, "The Case against Allowing Multiracial Coalitions to File Section 2 Dilution Claims," *University of Chicago Legal Forum* (1995): 389, 404.

20. Piatt, *Black and Brown,* 9.

21. "Death of Cyclist in Miami Triggers Violent Disturbance," *Chicago Tribune,* Jan. 17, 1989, C3.

22. Geraci, "Case against Allowing Coalitions to File."

23. Frank J. Macchiarola and Joseph G. Diaz, "Minority Political Empowerment in New York City: Beyond the Voting Rights Act," *Political Science Quarterly* (1993): 27, 48–51.

24. Hisham Aidi, "Black and Brown in Harlem, USA," available at http://www.africana.com/DailyArticles/index_20000816.htm (last visited July 2002).

25. Twohey, "Role Reversal Jolts Blacks."

26. Athena D. Mutua, "Shifting Bottoms and Rotating Centers: Reflections on LatCrit III and the Black/White Paradigm," *University of Miami Law Review* 53 (1999): 1177, 1186.

27. George A. Martinez, Essay, "African-Americans, Latinos, and the Construction of Race: Toward an Epistemic Coalition," *Chicano-Latino Law Review* 19 (1998): 213, 215.

28. Orlando Patterson, "Race by the Numbers," *New York Times,* May 8, 2001, A27.

29. Rothenberg, *With These Hands,* 194.

30. Twohey, "Role Reversal Jolts Blacks"; Acuña, *Anything but Mexican,* 127–131 (examining sources of Brown-Black tensions).

31. Kevin R. Johnson, "The End of 'Civil Rights' as We Know It? Immigration and Civil Rights in the New Millennium," *UCLA Law Review* 49 (2002): 1481.

32. Richardson, "Laughter, Tears in El Centro."

33. Hing, *To Be an American,* 129.

34. Taunya Lovell Banks, "Both Edges of the Margin: Blacks and Asians in the Mississippi Masala, Barriers to Coalition Building," *Asian Law Journal* 5 (1998): 7, 35.

35. Johnson, "African American and Latina/o Cooperation."

36. Walter C. Farrell Jr. and James H. Johnson Jr., "Minority Political Participation in the New Millennium: The New Demographics and the Voting Rights Act," *North Carolina Law Review* 79 (2001): 1215, 1221.

37. Steven A. Holmes, "Survey Finds Minorities Resent One Another Almost as Much as They Do Whites," *New York Times,* March 3, 1994, B8.

38. Ramon G. McLeod and Maria Alicia Gaura, "Prop. 227 Got Few Latino Votes," *San Francisco Chronicle,* June 5, 1998, A19 (but finding that Asian Americans in highly concentrated, immigrant-rich sectors such as San Francisco generally voted against the measure).

39. Joge and Pérez, *Mainstreaming of Hate,* 5.
40. Sumi K. Cho, "Korean Americans vs. African Americans: Conflict and Construction," in *Reading Rodney King: Reading Urban Uprising,* ed. Robert Gooding-Williams (New York: Routledge, 1993), 196, 199.
41. Kevin R. Johnson, "Racial Hierarchy, Asian Americans and Latinos as 'Foreigners,' and Social Change: Is Law the Way to Go?" *Oregon Law Review* 76 (1997): 347, 356.
42. Elizabeth Wilberg and Chet Barfield, "Racial Brawl Breaks Out at Valley Center School," *San Diego Union-Tribune,* May 12, 2000, B1.
43. See generally Dussias, "Waging War with Words."

NOTES TO CHAPTER 11

1. Román, "Living *La Vida Loca.*"
2. Ibid.
3. Elizabeth M. Iglesias, "Identity, Democracy, Communicative Power, Inter/ National Labor Rights and the Evolution of LatCrit Theory and Community," *University of Miami Law Review* 53 (1999): 575, 647.
4. Keith Aoki, "Is Chan Still Missing? An Essay about the Film *Snow Falling on Cedars* and Representation of Asian Americans in U.S. Films," *UCLA Asian Pacific American Law Journal* 7 (2001): 30, 48.
5. *Prime Time for Latinos: Report II: 2000–2001 Prime Television Season* 8 (Washington, DC: National Hispanic Foundation for the Arts, Sept. 2001).
6. Sherri Burr, "Television and Societal Effects: An Analysis of Media Images of African-Americans in Historical Context," *Journal of Gender, Race and Justice* 4 (2001): 159, 175–176.
7. Reyes and Rubie, *Hispanics in Hollywood,* 25.
8. In this film biography of rocker Ritchie Valens (Valenzuela), Ritchie's brother is a small-time marijuana dealer in the United States.
9. Jessie Seyfer, "Homies a Big Hit with Latinos," *Eugene Register Guard,* May 20, 2000, B6.
10. Yxta Maya Murray, *Locas* (New York: Grove Press, 1997).
11. Luis J. Rodriguez, *Always Running, La Vida Loca: Gang Days in L.A.* (Willimantic, CT: Curbstone Press, 1993).
12. See Monica Brown, *Gang Nation: Delinquent Citizens in Puerto Rican, Chicano, and Chicana Narratives* (Minneapolis: University of Minnesota Press, 2002), 93 (reply of author Murray to criticism by some attacking her stereotypical depiction of Latina villains).
13. A more effective and less offensive approach engages the negative constructions in discarding them. I recall in particular a stand-up comedy routine by Carlos Alazraqui at the twenty-first annual Comedy in the Park event in San Francisco in 2001. He suggested that he had gone to a party with friends where racist

jokes were being told about Mexicans. When he objected, one of the friends explained, "We don't mean you, you don't act Mexican." So, Carlos joked, "I stabbed him. Am I acting Mexican now, *vato loco?*"

14. But see David Alire Garcia, "Calling the Shots Makes Lopez Show a Leader," *Albuquerque Journal,* May 26, 2002, B3 (describing how Lopez refused to use a Latina babysitter in a scene calling for the "bad" babysitter to throw a party with beer).

15. Noreaga, *Mathematics (Esta Loca)* (Penalty 1998) ("Hey, yo, my family is half–Latin King, half–God Body / Half-Blood and half-Ñeta, so nigga, wepa"); lyrics from Sacha Jenkins, Elliott Wilson, Chairman Mao, Gabriel Alvarez, and Brent Rollins, *Ego Trip's Book of Rap Lists* (New York: St. Martin's Press, 1999), 261.

16. "Techno Cumbia" (1995), used by permission.

17. Elijah Wald, *Narcocorrido: A Journey into the Music of Drugs, Guns, and Guerrillas* (New York: HarperCollins, 2001), 122.

18. Ibid., 118.

19. Annie Nakao, "Survey on Black Life Prompts Frank Talk," *San Francisco Chronicle,* Nov. 20, 2001, A1.

20. War and a Lighter Shade of Brown/Hispanic M.C.'s/Proper Dos/Hi-C/Kid Frost, *Rap Declares War* (1992).

21. Jenkins et al, *Book of Rap Lists,* 134.

22. War and a Lighter Shade of Brown/Hispanic M.C.'s/Proper Dos/Hi-C/Kid Frost, *Rap Declares War* (1992).

23. Public Enemy, "By the Time I Get to Arizona" (1991).

24. One of many examples is the Dead Kennedys' album *Bedtime for Democracy* (reissued 2001).

25. Yolanda Broyles-González, *El Teatro Campensino: Theater in the Chicano Movement* (Austin: University of Texas Press, 1994), 190 (citing Broadway critic).

26. At the time of the terrorist attacks, 93 percent of New York's firefighters were White.

27. National Council of La Raza, "Out of the Picture: Hispanics in the Media," in Rodríguez, ed., *Latin Looks,* 21, 28.

28. Hadley-Garcia, *Hispanic Hollywood,* 22.

29. Entman and Rojecki, *Black Image in the White Mind,* 146.

30. Delgado and Stefancic, eds., *Latino/a Condition,* 246 (posing this question as a discussion point for scholars examining treatment of Latinas/os in mass media).

31. Morales, *Living in Spanglish,* 134.

32. Edward Guthmann, "From Stereotypes to a Nuanced View," *San Francisco Chronicle,* Sept. 16, 2001, Datebook 49.

33. Bender, "Will the Wolf Survive?"

34. For an extensive discussion of machismo, see Alfredo Mirandé, *Hombres y Machos: Masculinity and Latino Culture* (Boulder, CO: Westview Press, 1997).

35. Bruce Penniman, "When a School Decides There's No Place for 'West Side Story,'" *Christian Science Monitor,* Dec. 14, 1999, 18.

36. Charles Lyons, *The New Censors: Movies and the Culture Wars* (Philadelphia: Temple University Press, 1997), 107.

37. Ibid., 67.

38. One significant concern with advocating and honing protest as a means of addressing injustice is that among the most successful users of media protest has been the religious right, as evidenced by the impact of protest against the film *The Last Temptation of Christ* (1988). Ibid., 146.

39. Richard Vasquez, "Jose Jimenez [*sic*] 'Dies'—and Pride Lives," *Los Angeles Times,* April 5, 1970, A1.

40. Gina Piccalo, "Protestors Take Aim at 'Toy Story 2' Shoot-Em-Up," *Our Times, Santa Monica,* supplement to *Los Angeles Times,* Dec. 9, 1999, 1.

41. A Latina/o actors' organization, Nosotros, also confronted the Frito Bandito campaign. Actor Ricardo Montalban, president of Nosotros, lamented, "Why couldn't the cartoon have been the Frito Amigo, who gave the chips away instead of the negative image of the bandido who steals?" Reyes and Rubie, *Hispanics in Hollywood,* 30.

42. Noriega, *Shot in America,* 43–50.

43. Margaret Ramirez, "'Seinfeld' Scenes Anger Latinos," *Newsday,* May 9, 1998, A3.

44. Bender, "Will the Wolf Survive?" 750 n.164.

45. *Fall Colors,* 2001–2002 *Prime Time Diversity Report* (Children Now 2002), 26.

46. César G. Soriano, "Latino TV Roles Shrank in 2000, Report Finds," *USA Today,* Sept. 26, 2001, D3.

47. *Fall Colors,* 9. Although the preliminary numbers were up as well for the 2002–2003 season, these gains came from new shows, whose failure would return Latinas/os to their prior standing.

48. "Latinos in Hollywood," *San Francisco Chronicle,* Sept. 16, 2001, Datebook 34.

49. Claudia Kolker, "Latino Groups Urge Boycott of Network TV," *Los Angeles Times,* July 28, 1999, A12. Also in 1999, the NAACP outlined an ambitious agenda confronting network television's exclusion of minority actors and issues. The comprehensive and long-running network scrutiny and protest launched by the NAACP included the potential for legal action against the networks. Greg Braxton, "NAACP Will Fight Network TV Lineups," *Los Angeles Times,* July 12, 1999, A1. The NAACP mentioned pursuing litigation using the theory that invisibility of persons of color violates the 1934 Federal Communications Act. That

act provides that airwaves belong to the public, and the legal action presumably would claim that underrepresentation on network programming violates this mandate. See generally Amber McGovern, "Neutralizing Media Bias through the FCC," *DePaul-LCA Journal of Art and Entertainment Law* 12 (2002): 217, 235; Leonard M. Baynes, "WHITEOUT: The Absence and Stereotyping of People of Color by the Modern Media," *Arizona Law Review* 45 (forthcoming 2003).

50. *Mutual Film Corp. v. Industrial Commission of Ohio,* 236 U.S. 230 (1915) (refusing to accord constitutional protection to moving pictures); overruled in *Burstyn v. Wilson,* 343 U.S. 495, 502 (1952) ("[W]e conclude that expression by means of motion picture is included within the free speech and free press guaranty of the First and Fourteenth Amendments").

51. Douglas Ayer, Roy E. Bates, and Peter J. Herman, "Self-Censorship in the Movie Industry: An Historical Perspective on Law and Social Change," *Wisconsin Law Review* (1970): 791.

52. Gerald Gardner, *The Censorship Papers: Movie Censorship Letters from the Hays Office, 1934–1968* (New York: Dodd, Mead & Company, 1987), 211.

53. Leonard J. Leff and Jerold L. Simmons, *The Dame in the Kimono: Hollywood, Censorship, and the Production Code,* 2d ed. (Lexington: University Press of Kentucky, 2001).

54. July 10, 1934 letter from Joseph I. Breen to J. L. Warner, in *Bordertown* file maintained by the University of Southern California film library.

55. Gardner, *Censorship Papers,* 6.

56. *Burstyn v. Wilson,* 343 U.S. 495, 502 (1952).

57. Chon A. Noriega, "Citizen Chicano: The Trials and Titillations of Ethnicity in the American Cinema, 1935–1962," in Rodríguez, ed., *Latin Looks,* 89 (discussing the PCA's letter to the makers of the film *The Ring*).

58. Ibid. (addressing the film *The Lawless*). Local censors also targeted films perceived as pro-Communist, such as the 1954 film *Salt of the Earth,* which addressed striking Mexican American zinc miners. Lyons, *New Censors,* 29.

59. Anthony York, "George the Good: Will His Vague 'Communities of Character' Initiative Prop Up His Stumbling Presidency?" *Salon,* Aug. 2, 2001, at http://www.salon.com/politics/feature/2001/08/02/bush/ (last visited Nov. 2002).

60. Jonah Goldberg, "President Bush Contracts Potomac Fever," Aug. 9, 2001, at http://www.townhall.com/columnists/jonahgoldberg/printjg20010809.shtml (last visited Nov. 2002).

61. Morales, *Living in Spanglish,* 113 (also noting Piñero appeared in an episode of *Kojak* playing a ruthless killer and in *Miami Vice* playing a "pseudo-pimp denizen of the dark").

62. Lyons, *New Censors,* 122 ("This film is not intended as an indictment of the homosexual world. It is set in one small segment of that world, which is not meant to be representative of the whole").

63. Ibid., 103 ("This film does not intend to demean or to ignore the many positive features of Asian Americans and specifically Chinese American communities. Any similarity between the depiction in this film and any association, organization, individual or Chinatown that exists in real life is accidental").

64. Cortés, "Who Is Maria?" 90–91.

65. Clara E. Rodríguez, "What Can We Do," in Rodríguez, ed., *Latin Looks,* 266. Related to media adopting a self-policing code of ethics against stereotyping, retail outlets, too, should consider such policies. Retailers such as Wal-Mart already censor media that contravene their conception of family values.

66. Michael Pickering, *Stereotyping: The Politics of Representation* (Houndmills, UK: Palgrave, 2001), 12.

NOTES TO CHAPTER 12

1. Román, "Living *La Vida Loca,*" 45.

NOTES TO CHAPTER 13

1. *Rosenblatt v. Baer,* 383 U.S. 75, 86 (1966) (concurring opinion).

2. Brian Lowry, Elizabeth Jensen, and Greg Braxton, "Networks Decide Diversity Doesn't Pay," *Los Angeles Times,* July 20, 1999, A1, 12.

3. Schultz, "Group Rights, American Jews," 121.

4. Mass. Gen. Laws. Ann. chap. 272, §98C.

5. Illinois's constitution still provides for a similarly worded individual-dignity provision:

To promote individual dignity, communications that portray criminality, depravity or lack of virtue in, or that incite violence, hatred, abuse or hostility toward, a person or group of persons by reason of or by reference to religious, racial, ethnic, national or regional affiliation are condemned.

Ill. Const. art. I, §20. In a recent action seeking to declare the *Sopranos* television show as contrary to this provision and offensive to Italian Americans, an Illinois appellate court ruled the state constitution's individual dignity clause was strictly "hortatory" and did not create a cause of action against such communications: "The plain and ordinary meaning of the clause is to condemn such communications, not to make them unlawful." *AIDA v. Time Warner Entertainment Co.,* 772 N.E.2d 953 (Ill. App. Ct. 2002).

6. New Jersey's group libel law prohibited any statement that "incites, counsels, promotes, or advocates hatred, abuse, violence, or hostility against any group or groups of persons residing or being in this state, by reason of race, color, religion or manner of worship." Note the New Jersey statute did not demand falsity, making it more of a proscription of "fighting words" than of libel. In any event, the New Jersey Supreme Court ultimately held the law unconstitutional

under free speech guarantees. *State v. Klapprott,* 22 A.2d 877 (N.J. 1941) (striking down New Jersey's law as void for uncertainty and indefiniteness in proscribing speech advocating "hatred," "abuse," and "hostility").

7. *State v. Beauharnais,* 97 N.E.2d 343, 345 (1951).

8. *Beauharnais v. Illinois,* 343 U.S. 250, 252 (1952).

9. Ibid., 256–257.

10. Ibid., 258.

11. Connecticut (Conn. Gen. Stat. Ann. §53-37) and Massachusetts (Mass. Gen. Laws Ann. chap. 272, §98C) are among the few states that have retained a race-based criminal defamation statute.

12. For example, Minnesota's and Montana's statutes refer to defamation directed at a person or a group or class or association. Minn. Stat. Ann. §609.765; Mont. Code Ann. §45-8-212. Connecticut's statute refers to any person or class of persons, Massachusetts's law to any group, and Nevada's law to any person or community of persons. Conn. Gen. Stat. Ann. §53-37; Mass. Gen. Laws Ann. chap. 272, §98C; Nev. Rev. Stat. Ann. §200.510.

13. *Police Dept. of Chicago v. Mosley,* 408 U.S. 92 (1972).

14. Ibid., 95.

15. *R.A.V. v. St. Paul,* 505 U.S. 377 (1992).

16. *New York Times Co. v. Sullivan,* 376 U.S. 254, 279, 280 (1964).

17. *Garrison v. Louisiana,* 379 U.S. 64, 67 (1964).

18. *Associated Press v. Walker,* 388 U.S. 130 (1967).

19. David F. McGowan and Ragesh K. Tangri, Comment, "A Libertarian Critique of University Restrictions of Offensive Speech," *California Law Review* 79 (1991): 825, 890 n.320.

20. *Gertz v. Robert Welch, Inc.,* 418 U.S. 323, 344–345 (1974).

21. Ibid.

22. *Philadelphia Newspapers, Inc. v. Hepps,* 475 U.S. 767 (1986).

23. *Beauharnais,* 343 U.S. at 265.

24. In *Garrison v. State of Louisiana,* 379 U.S. 64 (1964), the Supreme Court struck down Louisiana's criminal libel law in part because it purported to criminalize true statements made with actual malice. Under the Court's decision in *Sullivan,* one cannot be punished for truthful criticism. *Garrison,* 379 U.S. at 78.

25. In *Beauharnais,* the defendant offered to prove the truth of his hateful statements toward Blacks using crime statistics from Black neighborhoods, testimony that a Black person shot his brother, and a showing that property values declined following Black arrivals in local neighborhoods. The Supreme Court commented that apart from failing to demonstrate the defendant's good motives or justifiable ends, it was doubtful whether this proof would address the truth of the alleged defamatory statements.

26. *Milkovich v. Lorain Journal Co.,* 497 U.S. 1 (1990).

27. *Hustler Magazine, Inc. v. Falwell,* 485 U.S. 46, 50 (1988).

28. "The Simpsons Rubs Rio Officials the Wrong Way," *Newsday,* April 10, 2002, B35; Leah Garchik, "Simpsons in Trouble in Rio," *San Francisco Chronicle,* April 11, 2002, D14.

29. *Old Dominion Branch No. 496, National Association of Letter Carriers, AFL-CIO v. Austin,* 418 U.S. 264 (1974).

30. *Greenbelt Cooperative Publishing Association, Inc. v. Bresler,* 398 U.S. 6 (1970). Finally, at least where media are sued, the Supreme Court requires that a statement on a matter of public concern contain a provably false factual connotation before it can be actionable under state defamation law. The Court gave the following example: "Thus, unlike the statement, 'In my opinion Mayor Jones is a liar,' the statement, 'In my opinion Mayor Jones shows his abysmal ignorance by accepting the teachings of Marx and Lenin,' would not be actionable." *Milkovich v. Lorain Journal Co.,* 497 U.S. 1, 20 (1990).

31. The Court stated:

Libelous utterances not being within the area of constitutionally protected speech, it is unnecessary, either for us or for the State courts, to consider the issues behind the phrase "clear and present danger." Certainly no one would contend that obscene speech, for example, may be punished only upon a showing of such circumstances. Libel, as we have seen, is in the same class.

Beauharnais v. Illinois, 343 U.S. 250, 266 (1952).

32. *Garrison v. Louisiana,* 379 U.S. 64, 70 (1964). See also *Ashton v. Kentucky,* 384 U.S. 195 (1966) (as interpreted by the trial court to proscribe writings calculated to create disturbances of the peace, Kentucky's criminal libel offense was unconstitutionally vague).

33. McGowan and Tangri, "Libertarian Critique," 891. Some courts have raised the same concern. e.g., *Collin v. Smith,* 578 F.2d 1197 (7th Cir. 1978).

34. *Brandenburg v. Ohio,* 395 U.S. 444, 444–445 (1969).

35. Ibid., 447.

36. *Beauharnais v. Illinois,* 343 U.S. 250, 257 (1952).

37. Some have argued that First Amendment protections for speech must be read together with the equal protection guarantee of the Fourteenth Amendment, so that those harming less-powerful groups by perpetuating subordinating ideas cannot find refuge in the First Amendment. See Victor C. Romero, "Restricting Hate Speech against 'Private Figures': Lessons in Power-Based Censorship from Defamation Law," *Columbia Human Rights Law Review* 33 (2001): 1, 12; see also Charles R. Lawrence III, "If He Hollers Let Him Go: Regulating Racist Speech on Campus," *Duke Law Journal* 1990 (1990): 431 (contending that white supremacist speech on campus is forbidden by the equal protection guarantee).

38. *Texas v. Johnson,* 491 U.S. 397, 414 (1989) (refusing conviction of flag burner under state law prohibiting the desecration of a venerated object).

39. *Roth v. United States,* 354 U.S. 476, 487 (1957).

40. *Miller v. California*, 413 U.S. 15 (1973).

41. *Cohen v. California*, 403 U.S. 15 (1971); *American Booksellers Assn., Inc. v. Hudnut*, 771 F.2d 323 (7th Cir. 1985); *Collin v. Smith*, 578 F.2d 1197, 1202 (7th Cir. 1978).

42. *Cohen v. California*, 403 U.S. 15 (1971).

43. *Doe v. University of Michigan*, 721 F.Supp. 852 (E.D. Mich. 1989); *UWM Post, Inc. v. Board of Regents*, 774 F.Supp. 1163 (E.D. Wis. 1991) (striking down University of Wisconsin hate speech rule as overbroad and ambiguous).

44. *Brandenburg v. Ohio*, 395 U.S. 444 (1969).

45. Racist hate speech and negative stereotypes do not fully overlap for defamation purposes. For example, hate speech declaring, "Fuck Mexicans," while likely fueled by negative conceptions of Mexicans and carrying the connotation of Mexicans as subhuman, does not contain a sufficient assertion of fact for defamation purposes. Recall that the Supreme Court has imposed a constitutional requirement on defamation actions that demands an assertion of objective fact. By contrast, a statement such as the one by former professional basketball coach Dan Issel to a heckling fan, "Go drink another beer, you fucking Mexican piece of shit," comes closer to merging hate speech, stereotypes, and a potentially false assertion of fact that those of Mexican ethnicity are more pointedly less than human.

46. Mari J. Matsuda, "Public Response to Racist Speech: Considering the Victim's Story" in Matsuda et al., eds., *Words That Wound*, 17, 35.

47. Ibid., 36.

48. Worthy, "Diversity and Minority Stereotyping."

49. *FCC v. Pacifica Found.*, 438 U.S. 726 (1978) (Carlin's twelve-minute monologue addressed the words *shit, piss, fuck, motherfucker, cocksucker, cunt, and tits*); Heidi Kitrosser, "From Marshall McLuhan to Anthropomorphic Cows: Communicative Manner and the First Amendment," *Northwestern University Law Review* 96 (2002): 1339. See also *Young v. American Mini Theatres, Inc.*, 427 U.S. 50 (1976) (upholding content-based regulation of adult movies under city zoning ordinance requiring dispersal of adult theaters).

50. Worthy, "Diversity and Minority Stereotyping," 565–566.

51. Bok, *Mayhem*, 133–134.

52. Eric Schellhorn, "Peacock Turns Tail on First Amendment," *San Francisco Chronicle*, April 15, 2002, B7. One avenue for permissible content-regulation by government is in its role as a public broadcaster licensee. Thus the operators of public television stations might properly exclude stereotypical content as part of their programming and editorial decisions without running afoul of constitutional free speech guarantees. See Jonathan Goodman, Comment, "The Death of a Princess Cases: Television Programming by State-Owned Public Broadcasters and Viewers' First Amendment Rights," *University of Miami Law Review* 36 (1982): 779.

53. See Worthy, "Diversity and Minority Stereotyping," 544; *Red Lion Broadcasting v. FCC,* 395 U.S. 367 (1969).

54. Virginia Escalante, "The Politics of Chicano Representation in the Media," in *Chicano Renaissance: Contemporary Cultural Trends,* ed. David R. Maciel, Isidro D. Ortiz, and María Herrera-Sobek (Tucson: University of Arizona Press, 2000), 131, 157. Freed from First Amendment constraints applicable when confronting broadcasters, activists targeting non-speech-based discrimination have contested licensing and other regulatory (e.g., merger) approvals sought by banks, based on their community record of lending to minority groups.

55. *Central Hudson Gas & Electric Corp. v. Public Service Commission,* 447 U.S. 557 (1980).

56. Deseriee A. Kennedy, "Marketing Goods, Marketing Images: The Impact of Advertising on Race," *Arizona State Law Journal* 32 (2000): 615, 689–690.

57. Matsuda, "Public Response to Racist Speech." See also Richard Delgado and David H. Yun, "Pressure Valves and Bloodied Chickens: An Analysis of Paternalistic Objections to Hate Speech Regulation," *California Law Review* 82 (1994): 871 (responding to this argument).

58. Aryeh Neier, *Defending My Enemy: American Nazis, the Skokie Case, and the Risks of Freedom* (New York: Dutton, 1979).

59. See Bell, *Race, Racism and American Law,* 131–154 (providing a critical race critique of color-blind constitutionalism).

60. *Red Lion Broadcasting Co. v. FCC,* 395 U.S. 367 (1969).

61. *Banzhaf v. FCC,* 405 F.2d 1082 (D.C. Cir. 1968); Noriega, *Shot in America,* 44.

62. Noriega, *Shot in America,* 46 (explaining that the complaint with the FCC was never filed and other legal and political pressures were applied).

63. *Syracuse Peace Council,* 2 F.C.C.R. 5043 (1987), aff'd, 867 F.2d 654 (D.C. Cir. 1989).

64. Kitrosser, "From Marshall McLuhan," 1384.

65. Schultz, "Group Rights, American Jews."

66. Another commentator in 1942 articulated a democracy-based justification for criminal libel laws:

> In the political as in the economic struggle, modern democracy operates through the interplay of group activities, and it is through participation in groups that persons contribute to the social welfare and develop their individual capacities. Hence, defamatory attacks on groups are attacks both on the pluralistic forces which make up a democratic society and derivatively on the individual members whose own status derives from their group affiliations.

David Riesman, "Democracy and Defamation: Control of Group Libel," *Columbia Law Review* 42 (1942): 727, 731 (but noting the competing policy concern that each group be subject to scrutiny and criticism of opposing groups and its own membership).

67. *Beauharnais v. Illinois,* 343 U.S. 250, 263 (1952).

68. Schultz, "Group Rights, American Jews" (also describing the early 1900s campaign by a Jewish antidefamation organization against negative stereotypes in such media as newspapers, films, and theater).

69. Kenneth Lasson, "Group Libel versus Free Speech: When Big Brother Should Butt In," *Duquesne Law Review* 23 (1984): 77, 122–124.

70. Hartman, "Revitalizing Group Defamation," 881–882.

71. *Beauharnais,* 343 U.S. at 256–257.

72. *Gertz v. Robert Welch, Inc.,* 418 U.S. 323, 340 (1974).

73. Gilbert Paul Carrasco, "Hate Speech and the First Amendment: On a Collision Course?" *Villanova Law Review* 37 (1992): 723, 739–741. See also Steven H. Shiffrin, *Dissent, Injustice, and the Meanings of America* (Princeton, NJ: Princeton University Press, 1999). Shiffrin points out that the allowance of defamation actions recognizes that to some extent reputational interest outweighs the societal interest in free expression. He also argues that the harm caused by hate speech outweighs its minimal marketplace value, yet Shiffrin advocates remedying only targeted hate speech—that directed at a specific victim—as opposed to diffuse racist speech directed at a racial group. Ibid., 83–86.

74. Richard Delgado and David Yun, "The Neoconservative Case against Hate-Speech Regulation—Lively, D'Souza, Gates, Carter, and the Toughlove Crowd," *Vanderbilt Law Review* 47 (1994): 1807, 1816; Delgado and Yun, "Pressure Valves."

75. See Richard Delgado and David Yun, "'The Speech We Hate': First Amendment Totalism, the ACLU, and the Principle of Dialogic Politics," *Arizona State Law Journal* 27 (1995): 1281, 1298–1299 (viewing hate speech as a subordinating weapon used by the empowered to maintain their position against subjugated groups seeking change).

76. See Robert M. O'Neil, *The First Amendment and Civil Liability* (Bloomington: Indiana University Press, 2001), 24 (noting that most courts came to treat broadcast defamation as libel rather than slander).

77. *Gertz,* 418 U.S. at 349-350.

78. Under the rigorous constitutional standards demanded by the Supreme Court, MEChA could recover only for its actual injury, rather than being awarded presumed or punitive damages, unless it established the statement was made with knowledge of falsity or reckless disregard for the truth.

79. *Michigan United Conservation Clubs v. CBS News,* 665 F.2d 110, 112 (6th Cir. 1981) ("Because M.U.C.C. was not mentioned in the films, the District Court correctly decided as a matter of law that the films were not 'of and concerning' the organization").

80. *Mikolinski v. Burt Reynolds Prod. Co.*, 409 N.E.2d 1324 (Mass. App. Ct. 1980).

81. *Puerto Rican Legal Defense Fund v. Grace*, 9 Media L. Rptr. 1514 (N.Y. Sup Ct. 1983).

82. Restatement (Second) of Torts §564A.

83. Ibid., comment a.

84. *Massbaum v. RCA*, No. CV-86-0225, 1986 WL 14629 (E.D.N.Y. Oct. 23, 1986).

85. *Michigan United Conservation Clubs v. CBS News*, 665 F.2d 110 (6th Cir. 1981). Although most courts rigidly deny defamation actions by individuals based on statements targeting large groups, a few courts have adopted more flexible standards that do not necessarily deny standing to challenge group defamation. For example, the Oklahoma Supreme Court allowed a college football player to sue a magazine publisher that suggested unidentified members of the Oklahoma football team were using amphetamines. Here, the football player was well known and the group, though sizable, would not compare in size to racial or ethnic groups or subgroups. See *Fawcett Publications, Inc. v. Morris*, 377 P.2d 42 (Okla. 1962); Jeffrey S. Bromme, Note, "Group Defamation: Five Guiding Factors," *Texas Law Review* 64 (1985): 591.

86. *Mikolinski v. Burt Reynolds Prod. Co.*, 409 N.E.2d 1324 (Mass. App. Ct. 1980).

87. *Anyanwu v. Columbia Broadcasting System, Inc.*, 887 F.Supp. 690 (S.D.N.Y. 1995).

88. Joseph H. King Jr., "Reference to the Plaintiff Requirement in Defamatory Statements Directed at Groups," *Wake Forest Law Review* 35 (2000): 343, 359.

89. *Khalid Abdullah Tariq Al Mansour Faissal Fahd Al Talal v. Fanning*, 506 F.Supp. 186 (N.D. Cal. 1980).

90. *Puerto Rican Legal Defense Fund v. Grace*, 9 Media L. Rptr. 1514 (N.Y. Sup. Ct. 1983).

91. King, "Reference to the Plaintiff Requirement," 359.

92. W. E. Shipley, Annot., "Injunction as Remedy Against Defamation of Person," *American Law Reports 2d* 47 (1956): 715. The defamation action on behalf of all Nigerians doing business with American citizens sought injunctive relief as well as damages and a public apology from CBS and other defendants. The court dismissed the claim because the defamation did not refer to the plaintiffs, failing to address specifically whether the outcome should be different since injunctive relief was sought. *Anyanwu v. Columbia Broadcasting System, Inc.*, 887 F.Supp. 690 (S.D.N.Y. 1995).

93. *Kuhn v. Warner Bros. Pictures, Inc.*, 29 F.Supp. 800 (S.D.N.Y. 1939).

94. Ellyn Tracy Marcus, Comment, "Group Defamation and Individual Actions: A New Look at an Old Rule," *California Law Review* 71 (1983): 1532, 1549.

95. *Ramos v. Sameric Corp.,* 5 Phila. Co. Rptr. 301, 1981 WL 207364 (Pa. Ct. Common Pleas, March 3, 1981). Apparently, a separate and ultimately unsuccessful action for damages was filed against Time-Life Films on a group libel theory by the Inter-Racial Committee against Fort Apache. Lyons, *New Censors,* 87.

96. King, "Reference to the Plaintiff Requirement," 359–360.

97. Romero, "Restricting Hate Speech," 8–9.

98. *Brandenburg v. Ohio,* 395 U.S. 444 (1969).

99. Ausness, "Application of Product Liability Principles," 603, 656.

100. *Zamora v. Columbia Broadcasting System,* 480 F.Supp. 199 (S.D. Fla. 1979).

101. *Yakubowicz v. Paramount Pictures Corp.,* 536 N.E.2d 1067 (Mass. 1989). See also *Byers v. Edmondson,* 826 So.2d 551 (La. Ct. App. 2002) (action by shooting victim against makers of film *Natural Born Killers* properly dismissed because film did not incite shooting and was thus protected under First Amendment; court also declined to extend the obscenity exception to encompass violence).

102. *Bill v. Vargas,* 187 Cal. Rptr. 625 (Ct. App. 1982); see generally O'Neil, *First Amendment,* 137–162.

103. Claudia Kolker, "Latino Groups Urge Boycott of Network TV," *Los Angeles Times,* July 28, 1999, A12.

104. These SEC rules also govern companies with more than $10 million in assets that have an equity class of stock held by five hundred or more shareholders.

105. S.E.C. Rule 14a-8.

106. Ibid.

107. SEC no-action letter to Kellogg Company, Feb. 3, 1989, at 1989 WL 245747. When the SEC issues no-action letters to companies seeking to omit resolutions, almost no chance exists that the SEC will pursue any enforcement action when the company excludes the proposal. Although the proponent could challenge the company's exclusion in federal court and seek a judicial interpretation and application of these SEC rules, the rules appear to hold scant potential for a favorable result where the resolution addresses stereotypes.

108. SEC no-action letter to Tootsie Roll Industries, Inc., Jan. 31, 2002, at 2002 WL 188377.

109. SEC no-action letter to the Quaker Oats Company, March 16, 1999, at 1999 WL 152450; see also 1987 WL 107894 (proposal targeting marketing in Southeast Asia of "Darkie Black and White Toothpaste" with Al Jolson–like blackface image, withdrawn by proponent).

110. SEC no-action letter to General Electric Company, Jan. 21, 1998, at 1998 WL 23987.

111. Ibid.

112. Ibid.

113. SEC no-action letter to Kmart Corporation, March 13, 1992, at 1992 WL 52787.

114. SEC letter to CBS Inc., March 7, 1991, at 1991 WL 178540; SEC letter to General Electric Co., Jan. 25, 1991, at 1991 WL 176574.

115. Bender, "Silencing Culture."

116. Ibid.

117. Amicus Brief of FLA-187 Committee, *Arizonans for Official English v. Arizona*, 65 U.S.L.W. 4169 (1997).

118. Vargas, "Judicial Review of Initiatives," 517–527.

119. Margaret L. Paris, "Why It Matters," *St. Louis University Law Journal* 45 (2001): 495.

120. Carlin, "What Becomes of the Resurrected?" One juvenile court judge in California once suggested a Latino youth ought to commit suicide: "That's what I think of people of this kind. You are lower than animals. . . . Maybe Hitler was right." Marjorie S. Zatz and Coramae Richey Mann, "The Power of Images," in *Images of Color, Images of Crime,* ed. Marjorie S. Zatz and Coramae Richey Mann (Los Angeles: Roxbury Publishing Co., 1998), 1, 3.

121. See Jody Armour, "Stereotypes and Prejudice: Helping Legal Decision-makers Break the Prejudice Habit," *California Law Review* 83 (1995): 733 (contending that nonprejudiced persons can suppress ingrained stereotypes and touting instructions in court that challenge such otherwise nonprejudiced jurors to recognize and resist their automatic discriminatory tendencies as enhancing fairness); Lee, "Race and Self-Defense" (advocating antistereotype instructions in self-defense cases).

122. Colo. Const. art. II, § 30a.

123. Fla. Const. art. II, § 9.

124. Bender, "Direct Democracy," 167.

NOTES TO CHAPTER 14

1. Kevin R. Johnson, "Lawyering for Social Change: What's a Lawyer to Do?" *Michigan Journal of Race and Law* 5 (1999): 201.

2. Ibid., 206.

3. Here I mean a Black president who would represent the Black community, which is overwhelmingly Democratic.

4. bell hooks, *Black Looks: Race and Representation* (Boston: South End Press, 1992), 33.

5. National Council of La Raza Census Information Center, "Hispanic Poverty Fact Sheet," Washington, DC, Nov. 2000.

6. Bugarin and Lopez, *Farmworkers in California,* 1.

7. Roberts, *Killing the Black Body,* 118.

8. John Johnson, "Crowded Living in California's Open Spaces," *Los Angeles Times,* Feb. 4, 2002, A1.

9. Frank Rudy Cooper, "The Un-Balanced Fourth Amendment: A Cultural Study of the Drug War, Racial Profiling and Arvizu," *Villanova Law Review* 47 (2002): 851.

10. This letter is excerpted in Chapter 8.

11. Johnson, "Puerto Rico," 116.

12. Until television and other media adequately portray Latinas/os in number and substance, parents might "kill" their television and offer children alternative channels of information on race and ethnicity. Latina/o groups should facilitate this educational development by producing such educational materials.

13. Berg, *Latino Images,* 23 (positing that the antidote to stereotyping is information about the Other).

14. Denise Gellene, "Advertising in Their Own Images," *Los Angeles Times,* April 2, 1998, D4.

15. Johnson, "End of 'Civil Rights.'"

16. Albert Smyth ed., *The Writings of Benjamin Franklin* 3 (New York: Macmillan, 1905), 73.

17. Johnson, "End of 'Civil Rights.'"

18. Bender, "Consumer Protection for Latinos," 1046.

19. Johnson, "End of 'Civil Rights,'" 1486–1487.

20. See also Richard Delgado, "Two Ways to Think about Race: Reflections on the Id, the Ego, and Other Reformist Theories of Equal Protection," *Georgetown Law Journal* 89 (2001): 2279, 2285 (suggesting that Irish and Italian immigrants were regarded as nonwhite until they joined forces in oppressing Blacks).

21. The Chicana/o manifesto, "El Plan Espiritual de Aztlán," calls for restitution for "past economic slavery, political exploitation, ethnic and cultural psychological destruction and denial of civil and human rights." Recently, a federal court in California dismissed a class action against the U.S. government and other defendants seeking wages withheld during and after World War II in the bracero program. *Cruz v. U.S.A.,* 219 F.Supp. 2d 1027 (N.D. Cal. 2002).

22. Susan M. Akram and Kevin Johnson, "Race, Civil Rights, and Immigration Law after September 11, 2001: The Targeting of Arabs and Muslims," *New York University Annual Survey of American Law* 58 (2002): 295.

23. Keith Aoki, "A Tale of Three Cities: Thoughts on Asian American Electoral and Political Power after 2000," *UCLA Asian Pacific American Law Journal* 8 (2001): 1.

24. Keith L. Alexander, "NAACP Campaign Changed More than TV," *USA Today,* Feb. 15, 2000, B3. The coalition has not been without tension; other groups once bristled over their perceived exclusion from the agreement reached by the NAACP with NBC and, lately, the NAACP has issued reports of network

television diversity performance separate from those reports issued by the Multi-Ethnic Media Coalition on behalf of Asians, Natives, and Latinas/os.

25. See National Hispanic Media Coalition, at http://www.nhmc.org/activities .html (last visited Sept. 2002).

26. See Delgado, "Two Ways to Think about Race," 2294 (questioning the benefit of interethnic coalitions aimed at persuading Anglos to view people of color more positively and suggesting that with such a focus it would be easy for such coalitions to miss an opportunity to confront embedded institutional structures of inequality).

27. Karen Brodkin, *How Jews Became White Folks and What That Says about Race in America* (New Brunswick, NJ: Rutgers University Press, 1998). Latinas/os should also pursue class-based coalition with working-class Anglos to confront labor conditions and government economic policies.

28. National Council of La Raza Census Information Center, "Hispanic Poverty Fact Sheet," Nov. 2000.

29. Ginorio and Huston, *¡Sí, Se Puede!* vii.

30. Lizette Alvarez, "Hispanic Voters Hard to Profile, Poll Finds," *New York Times*, Oct. 4, 2002, A20.

Index

About the Author

Steven Bender is a law professor at the University of Oregon who studies and teaches subjects ranging from property and commercial law to race relations. He was born and raised in East Los Angeles in his Mexican American mother's household. For many years he has been active in national and local academic and community Latina/o organizations.